Essential Mathematics

Book 8i

David Rayner

Elmwood Press

© David Rayner

First published 2001 by
Elmwood Press
80 Attimore Road
Welwyn Garden City
Herts. AL8 6LP
Tel. 01707 333232

All rights reserved. No part of this publication may be reproduced, stored in a retrieval system, or transmitted, in any form or by any means, electronic, mechanical, photocopying, recording or otherwise, without permission in writing from the publisher or under licence from the Copyright Licensing Agency Ltd. Further details for such licenses may be obtained from the A.L.C.S., 74 New Oxford Street, London WC1A 1EF

British Library Cataloguing in Publication Data

Rayner, David

© David Rayner
The moral rights of the author have been asserted.
Database right Elmwood Press (maker)

ISBN 1 902 214 102

Reprinted 2006

Numerical answers are published in a separate book

Artwork by Stephen Hill

Typeset and illustrated by Tech-Set, Gateshead, Tyne and Wear
Printed and bound by Bookwell

PREFACE

Essential Mathematics Books *7i*, *8i* and *9i* are written for pupils of 'average' ability in years *7*, *8* and *9*. Most classrooms contain children with a range of abilities in mathematics. These books are written to cater for this situation.

The author is an enthusiastic supporter of the National Numeracy Strategy. The books have been prepared with the cooperation of teachers and pupils in NNS pilot schools. It is encouraging that most teachers are confident that this more structured approach will help to raise standards of understanding and attainment. There is a comprehensive NNS guide at start of the book with references to all topics.

There is no set path through the books but topics appear in the order suggested in the NNS planning charts. Broadly speaking, parts 1 and 2 can be studied in the Autumn Term, parts 3 and 4 in the Spring Term and parts 5 and 6 in the Summer Term.

The author believes that children learn mathematics most effectively by *doing* mathematics. Many youngsters who find mathematics difficult derive much more pleasure and enjoyment from the subject when they are doing questions which help them build up their confidence. Pupils feel a greater sense of satisfaction when they work in a systematic way and when they can appreciate the purpose and the power of the mathematics they are studying.

No text book will have the 'right' amount of material for every class and the author believes that it is better to have too much material rather than too little. Consequently teachers should judge for themselves which sections or exercises can be studied later. On a practical note, the author recommends the use of exercise books consisting of 7 mm squares.

Opportunities for work towards the 'Using and Applying Mathematics' strand appears throughout the book. Many activities, investigations, games and puzzles are included to provide a healthy variety of learning experiences. The author is aware of the difficulties of teaching on 'Friday afternoons' or on the last few days of term, when both pupils and teachers are tired, and suitable activities are included.

The author is indebted to his co-authors David Allman and Laurence Campbell whose work from the first edition of Essential Mathematics has been included where appropriate. The author would also like to thank his colleagues at school, in particular Christine Godfrey who has written material for this book.

David Rayner

CONTENTS

Page

Part 1

1.1	Sequences	1
1.2	Fractions	8
1.3	Indices	15
1.4	Area	20
1.5	Negative numbers	26
1.6	Properties of numbers	33

Part 2

2.1	Estimating and checking answers	37
2.2	Rules of algebra	44
2.3	Geometrical reasoning	50
2.4	Construction and locus	56
2.5	Measures	61
2.6	Solving problems 1	65

Part 3

3.1	Written calculations	72
3.2	Averages and range	79
3.3	Mental calculations	84
3.4	Order of operations	94
3.5	Using a calculator	95
3.6	Reflection	101
3.7	Formulas and expressions	107
3.8	Mid book review	113

Part 4

4.1	Rotation and combined transformations	121
4.2	Real-life graphs	126
4.3	Brackets and equations	132
4.4	Handling data	141
4.5	Fractions, decimals, percentages	153
4.6	Solving problems 2	158

Page

Part 5

5.1	Ratio and proportion	164
5.2	Enlargement	170
5.3	Sequences, the nth term	175
5.4	Drawing graphs	182
5.5	Congruent shapes, tessellation	193
5.6	Mathematical reasoning	196
5.7	Using a spreadsheet on a computer	202

Part 6

6.1	Probability	204
6.2	Percentages	213
6.3	Statistical problems	216
6.4	3-D Objects	219
6.5	Bearings and scale drawing	223
6.6	Volume	228
6.7	Mathematical games	233

Part 7

7.1	Check up	239
7.2	Review exercises	242

Teaching programme: Year 8

Using and applying mathematics and solve problems

Applying mathematics and solving problems

2.6 • Solve more demanding problems and investigate in a range of contexts: number, algebra, shape, space and measures, and handling data; compare and evaluate solutions.

4.6 • **Identify the necessary information to solve a problem; represent problems and interpret solutions in algebraic, geometric or graphical form,** using correct notation and appropriate diagrams.

2.6 • Solve more complex problems by breaking them into smaller steps or tasks, choosing and using efficient techniques for calculation, algebraic manipulation and graphical representation, and resources, including ICT.

5.6 • **Use logical argument to establish the truth of a statement;** give solutions to an appropriate degree of accuracy in the context of the problem.

5.6 • Suggest extensions to problems, conjecture and generalise; identify exceptional cases or counter-examples.

Numbers and the number system

Place value, ordering and rounding

3.1 • Read and write positive integer powers of 10; multiply and divide integers and decimals by 0.1, 0.01.

3.1 • Order decimals.

2.1 • Round positive numbers to any given power of 10; round decimals to the nearest whole number or to one or two decimal places.

Integers, powers and roots

3.1 • Add, subtract, multiply and divide integers.

1.6 • Recognise and use multiples, factors (divisors), common factor, highest common factor, lowest common multiple and primes; find the prime factor decomposition of a number (e.g. $8000 = 2^6 \times 5^3$).

1.3 • Use squares, positive and negative square roots, cubes and cube roots, and index notation for small positive integer powers.

Fractions, decimals, percentages, ratio and proportion

4.5 • Know that a recurring decimal is a fraction; use division to convert a fraction to a decimal; order fractions by writing them with a common denominator or by converting them to decimals.

1.2 • Add and subtract fractions by writing them with a common denominator; calculate fractions of quantities (fraction answers); multiply and divide an integer by a fraction.

6.2 • Interpret percentage as the operator 'so many
4.5 hundredths of' and express one given number as a percentage of another; **use the equivalence of fractions, decimals and percentages to compare proportions; calculate percentages and find the outcome of a given percentage increase or decrease.**

5.1 Consolidate understanding of the relationship between ratio and proportion; reduce a ratio to its simplest form, including a ratio expressed in different units, recognising links with fraction notation; **divide a quantity into two or more parts in a given ratio; use the unitary method to solve simple word problems involving ratio and direct proportion.**

Calculations

Number operations and the relationships between them

3.1 • Understand addition and subtraction of fractions and integers, and multiplication and division of integers; use the laws of arithmetic and inverse operations.

3.4 • Use the order of operations, including brackets, with more complex calculations.

Mental methods and rapid recall of number facts

3.3 • Recall known facts, including fraction to decimal conversions; use known facts to derive unknown facts, including products involving numbers such as 0.7 and 6, and 0.03 and 8.

3.3 • Consolidate and extend mental methods of calculation, working with decimals, fractions and percentages, squares and square roots, cubes and cube roots; solve word problems mentally.

2.1 • Make and justify estimates and approximations of calculations.

Written methods

3.1 • Consolidate standard column procedures for addition and subtraction of integers and decimals with up to two places.

3.1 • **Use standard column procedures for multiplication and division of integers and decimals, including by decimals such as 0.6 or 0.06; understand where to position the decimal point by considering equivalent calculations.**
For calculations with fractions and percentages, see above.

Calculator methods

3.5 • Carry out more difficult calculations effectively and efficiently using the function keys for sign change, powers, roots and fractions; use brackets and the memory.

3.5 • Enter numbers and interpret the display in different contexts (negative numbers, fractions, decimals, percentages, money, metric measures, time).

Checking results
2.1 • Check a result by considering whether it is of the right order of magnitude and by working the problem backwards.

Algebra

Equations, formulae and identities
2.2 • Begin to distinguish the different roles played by letter symbols in equations, formulae and functions; know the meanings of the words *formula* and *function*.

2.2 • Know that algebraic operations follow the same conventions and order as arithmetic operations; use index notation for small positive integer powers.

4.3 • **Simplify or transform linear expressions by collecting like terms; multiply a single term over a bracket.**

4.3 • Construct and solve linear equations with integer coefficients (unknown on either or both sides, without and with brackets) using appropriate methods (e.g. inverse operations, transforming both sides in same way).

5.4 • Begin to use graphs and set up equations to solve simple problems involving direct proportion.

3.7 • Use formulae from mathematics and other subjects; **substitute integers into simple formulae**, including examples that lead to an equation to solve, and positive integers into expressions involving small powers (e.g. $3x^2 + 4$ or $2x^3$); derive simple formulae.

Sequences, functions and graphs
1.1 • Generate and describe integer sequences.

1.1 • Generate terms of a linear sequence using term-to-term and position-to-term definitions of the sequence, on paper and using a spreadsheet or graphical calculator.

5.3 • Begin to use linear expressions to describe the nth term of an arithmetic sequence, justifying its form by referring to the activity or practical context from which it was generated.

5.4 • Express simple functions in symbols; represent mappings expressed algebraically.

5.4 • Generate points in all four quadrants and **plot the graphs of linear functions, where y is given explicitly in terms of x**, on paper and using ICT; **recognise that equations of the form $y = mx + c$ correspond to straight-line graphs.**

4.2 • Construct linear functions arising from real-life problems and plot their corresponding graphs; discuss and interpret graphs arising from real situations.

Shape, space and measures

Geometrical reasoning: lines, angles and shapes
2.3 • **Identify alternate angles and corresponding angles;** understand a proof that:
 – the sum of the angles of a triangle is 180° and of a quadrilateral is 360°;
 – the exterior angle of a triangle is equal to the sum of the two interior opposite angles.

2.3 • Solve geometrical problems using side and angle properties of equilateral, isosceles and right-angled triangles and special quadrilaterals, explaining reasoning with diagrams and text; classify quadrilaterals by their geometric properties.

5.5 • Know that if two 2-D shapes are congruent, corresponding sides and angles are equal.

6.4 • Know and use geometric properties of cuboids and shapes made from cuboids; begin to use plans and elevations.

Transformations
4.1 • Transform 2-D shapes by simple combinations of rotations, reflections and translations, on paper and using ICT; identify all the symmetries of 2-D shapes.

 • Recognise and visualise the transformation and symmetry of a 2-D shape:

5.2 • Understand and use the language and notation associated with enlargement; **enlarge 2-D shapes, given a centre of enlargement and a positive whole-number scale factor;** explore enlargement using ICT.

6.5 • Make simple scale drawings.

Coordinates
5.4 • Given the coordinates of points A and B, find the mid-point of the line segment AB.

Construction
2.4 • **Use straight edge and compasses to construct:**
 – **the mid-point and perpendicular bisector of a line segment;**
 – the perpendicular from a point to a line;
 – **the perpendicular from a point on a line;**
 construct a triangle, given three sides (SSS); use ICT to explore these constructions.

2.4 • Find simple loci, both by reasoning and by using ICT, to produce shapes and paths, e.g. an equilateral triangle.

Measures and mensuration
2.5 • Use units of measurement to estimate, calculate and solve problems in everyday contexts involving length, area, volume, capacity, mass, time, angle and bearings; know rough metric equivalents of imperial measures in daily use (feet, miles, pounds, pints, gallons).

6.5 • Use bearings to specify direction.
1.4 • **Deduce and use formulae for the area of a triangle, parallelogram** and trapezium; calculate areas of compound shapes made from rectangles and triangles.
6.6 • **Know and use the formula for the volume of a cuboid; calculate volumes and surface areas of cuboids** and shapes made from cuboids.

Handling data

Specifying a problem, planning and collecting data

6.3 • Discuss a problem that can be addressed by statistical methods and identify related questions to explore.
6.3 • Decide which data to collect to answer a question, and the degree of accuracy needed; identify possible sources.
6.3 • Plan how to collect the data, including sample size; construct frequency tables with given equal class intervals for sets of continuous data; design and use two-way tables for discrete data.
6.3 • Collect data using a suitable method, such as observation, controlled experiment, including data logging using ICT, or questionnaire.

Processing and representing data, using ICT as appropriate

3.2 • Calculate statistics, including with a calculator; recognise when it is appropriate to use the range, mean, median and mode and, for grouped data, the modal class; calculate a mean using an assumed mean; construct and use stem-and-leaf diagrams.
4.4 • **Construct, on paper and using ICT:**
  – **pie charts for categorical data;**
  – **bar charts and frequency diagrams for discrete and continuous data;**
  – **simple line graphs for time series;**
  – **simple scatter graphs;**
  identify which are most useful in the context of the problem.

Interpreting and discussing results

4.4 • Interpret tables, graphs and diagrams for both discrete and continuous data, and draw inferences that relate to the problem being discussed; relate summarised data to the questions being explored.
3.2 • Compare two distributions using the range and one or more of the mode, median and mean.
6.3 • Communicate orally and on paper the results of a statistical enquiry and the methods used, using ICT as appropriate; justify the choice of what is presented.

Probability

6.1 • Use the vocabulary of probability when interpreting the results of an experiment; appreciate that random processes are unpredictable.
6.1 • Know that if the probability of an event occurring is p, then the probability of it not occurring is $1 - p$; **find and record all possible mutually exclusive outcomes for single events and two successive events in a systematic way**, using diagrams and tables.
6.1 • Estimate probabilities from experimental data; understand that:
  – if an experiment is repeated there may be, and usually will be, different outcomes;
  – increasing the number of times an experiment is repeated generally leads to better estimates of probability.
6.1 • Compare experimental and theoretical probabilities in different contexts.

Part 1

1.1 Sequences

Sequences are very important in mathematics. Scientists carrying out research will often try to find patterns or rules to describe the results they obtain from experiments.

- A number sequence is a set of numbers in a given order
- Each number in a sequence is called a *term*.
- Here are three sequences. Try to find the next term.

  a 5, 8, 12, 17, ?
  b $\frac{1}{2}$, 1, 2, 4, ?
  c 15, 14, 16, 13, 17, ?

Exercise 1

1. The numbers in boxes make a sequence. Find the next term.

   (a) | 9 | 7 | 5 | 3 | □ |

   (b) | 4 | 9 | 14 | 19 | □ |

   (c) | 2 | 9 | 16 | 23 | □ |

   (d) | 2 | 3 | 5 | 8 | 12 | □ |

In Questions **2** to **17** write down the sequence and find the next term.

2. 21, 17, 13, 9,
3. 60, 54, 48, 42,
4. 1, 2, 4, 8, 16,
5. $\frac{1}{2}$, 1, $1\frac{1}{2}$, 2,
6. 3, $4\frac{1}{2}$, 6, $7\frac{1}{2}$
7. 60, 59, 57, 54, 50,
8. 5, 7, 10, 14,
9. 3, 30, 300, 3000,
10. 1·7, 1·9, 2·1, 2·3,
11. 1, 3, 9, 27,
12. 8, 4, 0, −4, −8,
13. 7, 5, 3, 1, −1,
14. 1, 2, 4, 7, 11
15. −2, −1, 0, 1,
16. 200, 100, 50, 25,
17. 11, 10, 8, 5, 1,

18. Write down the sequence and find the missing number.

(a) 3, 6, 12, 24, 48

(b) 4, ☐, 10, 13, 16

(c) 32, 16, 8, 4, ☐

(d) ☐, 6, 3, 0, −3

Exercise 2

1. Here is the start of a sequence of rectangles

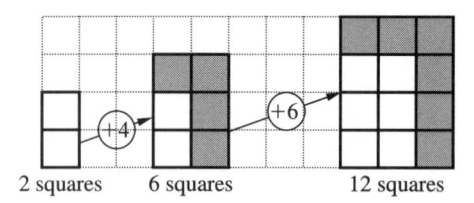

2 squares   6 squares   12 squares

(a) Draw the next rectangle in the sequence and count the squares.
(b) The number of squares in the rectangles makes a number pattern. Copy and complete the boxes and circles below.

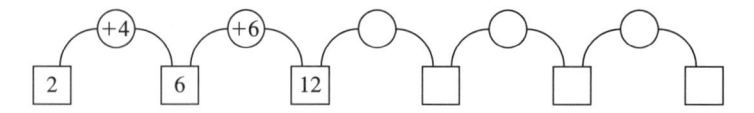

2, (+4), 6, (+6), 12, ◯, ☐, ◯, ☐, ◯, ☐

2. In the sequence of squares the number of matches is shown.

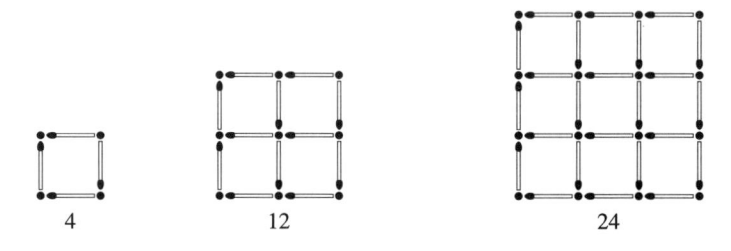

4   12   24

(a) Draw the next square in the sequence and write down the number of matches in the square.
(b) Copy and complete the number pattern below.

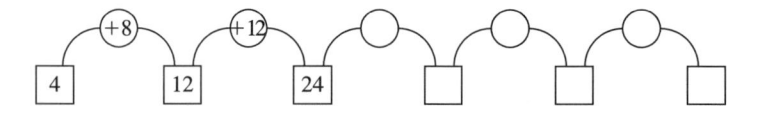

4, (+8), 12, (+12), 24, ◯, ☐, ◯, ☐, ◯, ☐

3. Copy this pattern and write down the next three lines. Do not use a calculator!

$1 \times 999 = 999$
$2 \times 999 = 1998$
$3 \times 999 = 2997$
$4 \times 999 = 3996$

4. (a) Copy this pattern and write down the next two lines

$3 \times 5 = 15$
$33 \times 5 = 165$
$333 \times 5 = 1665$
$3333 \times 5 = 16\,665$

(b) Copy and complete $333\,333\,333 \times 5 =$

5. (a) Look at the pattern below and then continue it for a further three rows.

$2^2 + 2 + 3 = 9$
$3^2 + 3 + 4 = 16$
$4^2 + 4 + 5 = 25$
$\vdots \quad \vdots \quad \vdots \quad \vdots$

(b) Write down the line which starts
$12^2 + \ldots$

6. Copy each sequence and find the missing numbers.

(a) ☐, $-3, -1, 1, 3,$ ☐
(b) $1 \times 2^2, 2 \times 3^2, 3 \times 4^2,$ ☐
(c) $10, 9, 7, 4,$ ☐, ☐
(d) $1, 2, 6, 24, 120,$ ☐
(e) $\frac{1}{3}, \frac{2}{5}, \frac{3}{7}, \frac{4}{9},$ ☐

7. (a) Copy this pattern and write down the next line.

$1 \times 9 = 9$
$21 \times 9 = 189$
$321 \times 9 = 2889$
$4321 \times 9 = 38\,889$
$54\,321 \times 9 = 488\,889$

(b) Complete this line $87\,654\,321 \times 9 =$

8. (a) Copy this pattern and write down the next line.

$1 + 9 \times 0 = 1$
$2 + 9 \times 1 = 11$
$3 + 9 \times 12 = 111$
$4 + 9 \times 123 = 1111$

(b) Find the missing numbers

$\boxed{} + 9 \times \boxed{} = 1111111$

9. (a) Copy this pattern and write down the next line

$3 \times 4 = 3 + 3 \times 3$
$4 \times 5 = 4 + 4 \times 4$
$5 \times 6 = 5 + 5 \times 5$

(b) Copy and complete

$10 \times 11 =$
$11 \times 12 =$

10.* The odd numbers can be added in groups to give an interesting sequence

$1 \qquad\qquad\qquad = 1 = 1^3 \quad (1 \times 1 \times 1)$
$\quad 3 + 5 \qquad\qquad = 8 = 2^3 \quad (2 \times 2 \times 2)$
$\qquad 7 + 9 + 11 \ = 27 = 3^3 \quad (3 \times 3 \times 3)$

The numbers 1, 8, 27 are called *cube* numbers. Another cube number is 5^3 (we say '5 cubed')

$5^3 = 5 \times 5 \times 5 = 125$

Write down the next three rows of the sequence to see if the sum of each row always gives a cube number.

11.* A famous sequence in mathematics is Pascal's triangle.

(a) Look carefully at how the triangle is made.
Write down the next row. It starts: 1 7 ...
(b) Look at the diagonal marked A.
Predict the next three numbers in the sequence
1, 3, 6, 10, 15, ...
(c) Work out the *sum* of the numbers in each row of Pascal's triangle. What do you notice?
(d) Without writing down all the numbers, work out the sum of the numbers in the 10th row of the triangle.

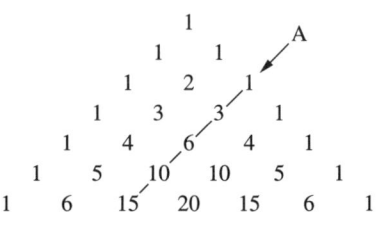

Sequence rules

For the sequence 3, 7, 11, 15, 19, ... the first term is 3 and the term-to-term rule is 'add 4'.

For the sequence 30, 27, 24, 21, ... the term-to-term rule is 'subtract 3'.

For the sequence 2, 5, 11, 23, ... the term-to-term rule is 'double and add 1'.

Exercise 3

1. Here is a sequence 7, 12, 17, 22, 27, ... Write down
   (a) The first term
   (b) The term-to-term rule.

2. Copy and complete the table

Sequence	First-term	Rule
(a) 5, 7, 9, 11, 13 ...		
(b) 80, 77, 74, 71, ...		
(c) 3, 6, 12, 24, ...		

3. The first term of a sequence is 4 and the term-to-term rule is 'add 7'. Write down the first five terms of the sequence.

4. You are given the first term and the rule of several sequences. Write down the first five terms of each sequence.

	First term	Rule
(a)	6	add 3
(b)	32	subtract 2
(c)	5	double
(d)	6000	divide by 10

5. The rule for the number sequences below is

   'double and add 1'

   Find the missing numbers
   (a) 3 → 7 → 15 → 31 → ☐
   (b) ☐ → 9 → 19 → 39
   (c) ☐ → 7 → ☐ → ☐

6. The rule for the sequences below is

    'multiply by 3 and take away 1'

    Find the missing numbers.
    (a) $1 \rightarrow 2 \rightarrow 5 \rightarrow \square$
    (b) $\square \rightarrow 8 \rightarrow 23 \rightarrow \square$
    (c) $4 \rightarrow \square \rightarrow \square \rightarrow \square$

7. Write down the rule for each of these sequences
    (a) $2\frac{1}{4}, 2\frac{1}{2}, 2\frac{3}{4}, 3, \ldots$
    (b) $7, 14, 28, 56, \ldots$
    (c) $2, 1\cdot9, 1\cdot8, 1\cdot7, \ldots$
    (d) $180, 90, 45, 22\frac{1}{2}, \ldots$

8. Find the rule for each sequence and then find the missing numbers.
    (a) $1 \rightarrow \square \rightarrow 4 \rightarrow 8 \rightarrow 16$
    (b) $\square \rightarrow 11 \rightarrow 19 \rightarrow 27 \rightarrow 35$
    (c) $0.5 \rightarrow 5 \rightarrow \square \rightarrow 500$
    (d) $\square \rightarrow 2\cdot2 \rightarrow 2\cdot1 \rightarrow 2 \rightarrow \square$

9. Look at this sequence
$$3^2 = 9$$
$$33^2 = 1089$$
$$333^2 = 110\,889$$
$$3333^2 = 11\,108\,889$$

    Write down the value of $33\,333^2$ and the value of $33\,333\,333^2$.

10. Copy and complete the following sequence.

    $2 \times 99 = 198$
    $3 \times 99 = 297$
    $4 \times 99 = 396$
    $5 \times 99 = \square$
    $\square \times 99 = \square$

11.* (a) What is the next term in the sequence $1, 2, 3, \ldots$?
    There is more than one possible answer.
    The sequence may continue $1, 2, 3, 4, 5, \ldots$ (add 1)
    or it may continue $1, 2, 3, 5, 8, 13, \ldots$ (add the last 2 terms)

    (b) Look at the sequence which starts $2, 4, 8, \ldots$
    Write down the next three terms in *two different* ways so that a consistent rule applies.

Flow diagrams

Exercise 4

Copy each flow diagram and put each of the numbers 1, 2, 3, 4, 5, 6, 7 in the box marked N. Work out what number would be printed in each case.

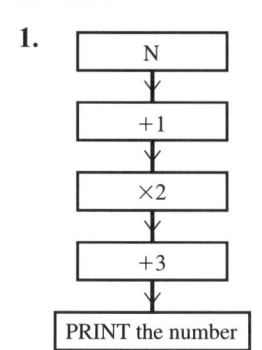

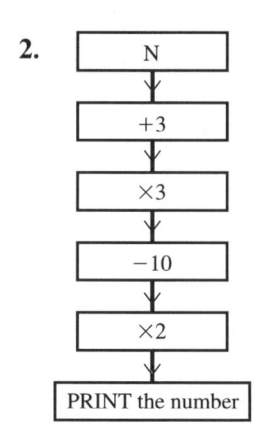

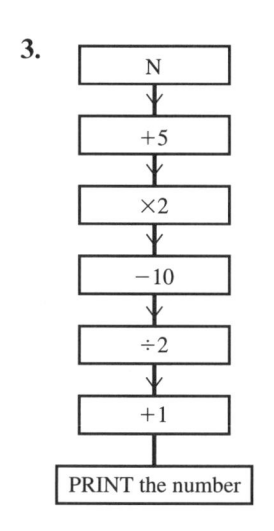

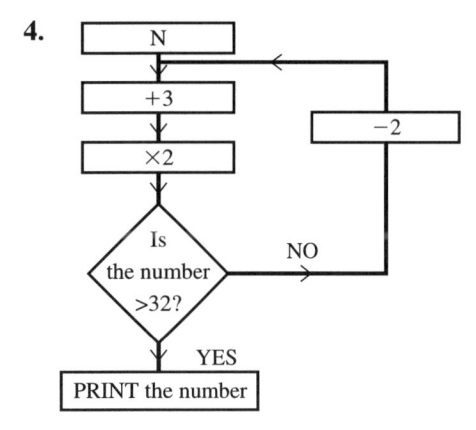

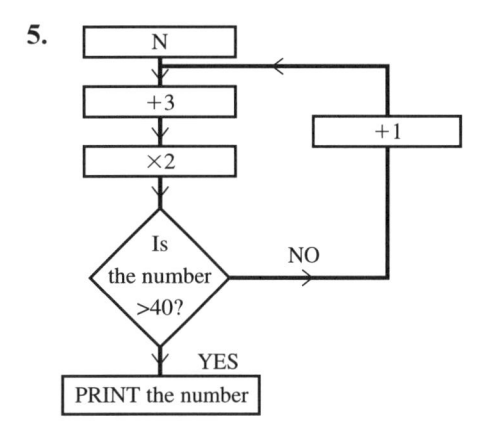

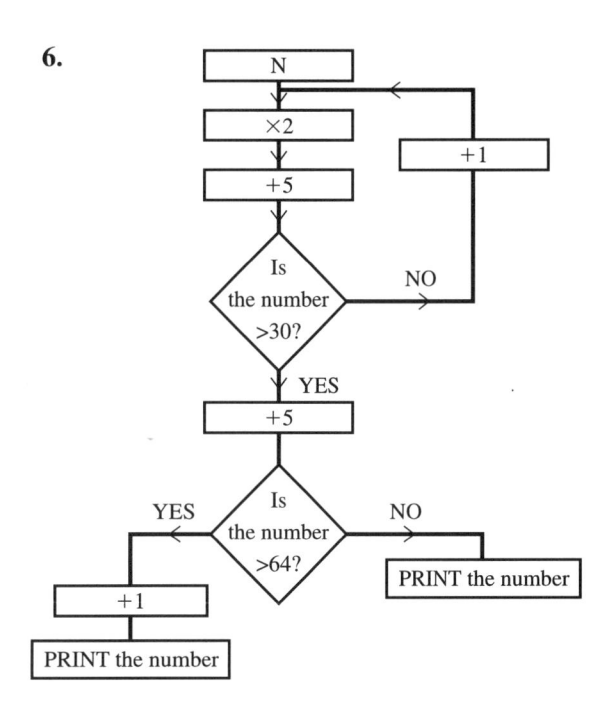

1.
N → +1 → ×2 → +3 → PRINT the number

2.
N → +3 → ×3 → −10 → ×2 → PRINT the number

3.
N → +5 → ×2 → −10 → ÷2 → +1 → PRINT the number

4.
N → +3 → ×2 → Is the number >32?
- NO → −2 → (back to +3)
- YES → PRINT the number

5.
N → +3 → ×2 → Is the number >40?
- NO → +1 → (back to +3)
- YES → PRINT the number

6.
N → ×2 → +5 → Is the number >30?
- NO → +1 → (back to ×2)
- YES → +5 → Is the number >64?
  - YES → +1 → PRINT the number
  - NO → PRINT the number

1.2 Fractions

Equivalent fractions

- In the diagram, $\frac{3}{6}$ of the shape is shaded. If you look at it a different way you can see that $\frac{1}{2}$ of the shape is shaded. 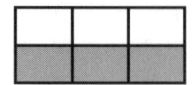
  The two fractions $\frac{3}{6}$ and $\frac{1}{2}$ are the same.
  We say they are equivalent.
  We normally use the simpler fraction which in this case is $\frac{1}{2}$.

- In this diagram, $\frac{4}{12}$ of the shape is shaded.
  A simpler fraction, which is the same as $\frac{4}{12}$, is $\frac{1}{3}$.
  You can *cancel* $\frac{4}{12}$ by dividing 4 and 12 by 4. 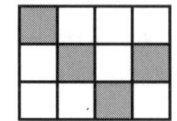
  So $\dfrac{\cancel{4}^{\,1}}{\cancel{12}_{\,3}} = \dfrac{1}{3}$.

Exercise 1

In Questions **1** to **9** write down the fraction shaded. If possible write the fraction in a simpler form.

1. 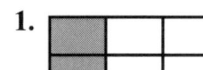
2. 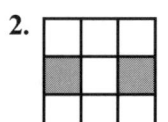
3. 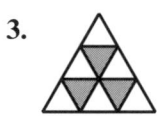
4. 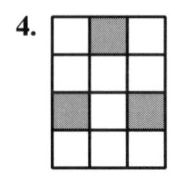
5. 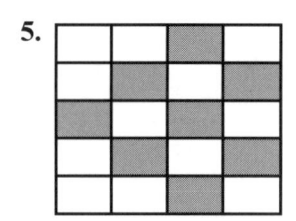
6.

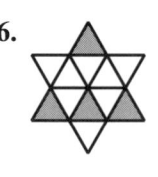

In Questions **7** to **22** fill in the missing numbers

7. $\dfrac{4}{8} = \dfrac{\square}{2}$

8. $\dfrac{6}{8} = \dfrac{\square}{4}$

9. $\dfrac{8}{12} = \dfrac{\square}{3}$

10. $\dfrac{2}{10} = \dfrac{\square}{5}$

11. $\dfrac{9}{12} = \dfrac{3}{\square}$

12. $\dfrac{15}{30} = \dfrac{1}{\square}$

13. $\dfrac{3}{9} = \dfrac{1}{\square}$

14. $\dfrac{9}{15} = \dfrac{\square}{5}$

15. $\dfrac{3}{7} = \dfrac{\square}{14}$

16. $\dfrac{3}{5} = \dfrac{\square}{10}$

17. $\dfrac{1}{4} = \dfrac{\square}{8}$

18. $\dfrac{3}{10} = \dfrac{\square}{30}$

19. $\dfrac{9}{24} = \dfrac{\square}{8}$

20. $\dfrac{5}{7} = \dfrac{25}{\square}$

21. $\dfrac{16}{24} = \dfrac{2}{\square}$

22. $\dfrac{\square}{7} = \dfrac{15}{35}$

Find the odd one out.

23. $\frac{2}{3}, \frac{4}{9}, \frac{4}{6}$ **24.** $\frac{1}{5}, \frac{3}{15}, \frac{3}{10}$ **25.** $\frac{3}{4}, \frac{8}{12}, \frac{6}{9}$

26. $\frac{2}{5}, \frac{6}{15}, \frac{4}{10}$ **27.** $\frac{5}{8}, \frac{6}{10}, \frac{12}{20}$ **28.** $\frac{3}{8}, \frac{5}{12}, \frac{6}{16}$

Adding and taking away

- Fractions can be added when they have the same denominator (bottom number).
- Here are some easy ones.
$\frac{1}{5} + \frac{2}{5} = \frac{3}{5}, \quad \frac{2}{7} + \frac{3}{7} = \frac{5}{7}, \quad \frac{1}{10} + \frac{5}{10} = \frac{6}{10}$
- In these questions one of the fractions has to be changed to an equivalent fraction

(a) $\frac{1}{2} + \frac{1}{4}$ (b) $\frac{1}{6} + \frac{1}{3}$ (c) $\frac{5}{8} - \frac{1}{4}$

$= \frac{2}{4} + \frac{1}{4}$ $= \frac{1}{6} + \frac{2}{6}$ $= \frac{5}{8} - \frac{2}{8}$

$= \frac{3}{4}$ $= \frac{3}{6}$ $= \frac{3}{8}$

Exercise 2

Work out

1. $\frac{1}{7} + \frac{2}{7}$ **2.** $\frac{1}{6} + \frac{4}{6}$ **3.** $\frac{5}{8} + \frac{1}{8}$

4. $\frac{2}{9} + \frac{3}{9}$ **5.** $\frac{3}{10} + \frac{4}{10}$ **6.** $\frac{3}{11} + \frac{2}{11}$

Draw fraction charts, using squared paper, and use them with the remaining questions

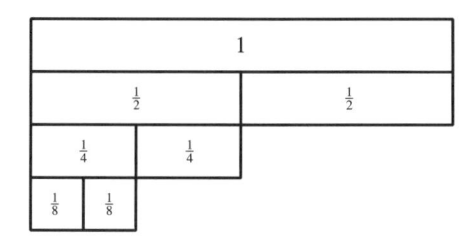

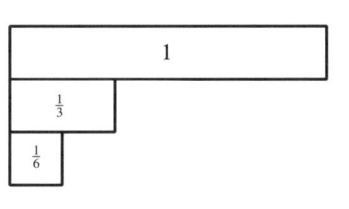

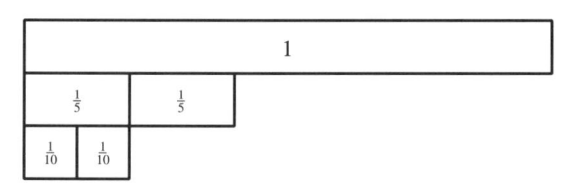

In Questions **7 to 15** fill in the missing numbers.

7. $\frac{1}{2} = \frac{\ }{8}$ **8.** $\frac{2}{3} = \frac{\ }{6}$ **9.** $\frac{3}{5} = \frac{\ }{10}$

10. $\frac{3}{4} = \frac{\ }{8}$ **11.** $\frac{4}{5} = \frac{\ }{10}$ **12.** $\frac{1}{3} = \frac{\ }{6}$

13. $\frac{1}{2} = \frac{\ }{10}$ **14.** $\frac{1}{4} = \frac{2}{\ }$ **15.** $\frac{8}{10} = \frac{\ }{5}$

Work out

16. $\frac{1}{4} + \frac{1}{2}$
17. $\frac{1}{6} + \frac{2}{3}$
18. $\frac{3}{8} + \frac{1}{2}$
19. $\frac{3}{8} + \frac{1}{4}$
20. $\frac{4}{5} + \frac{1}{10}$
21. $\frac{2}{5} + \frac{3}{10}$
22. $\frac{7}{8} - \frac{1}{2}$
23. $\frac{2}{3} - \frac{1}{6}$
24. $\frac{1}{2} - \frac{1}{8}$
25. $\frac{3}{5} - \frac{1}{10}$
26. $\frac{3}{4} - \frac{3}{8}$
27. $\frac{5}{6} - \frac{1}{3}$
28. $\frac{1}{5} + \frac{1}{10}$
29. $\frac{1}{8} + \frac{1}{16}$
30. $\frac{1}{10} + \frac{1}{20}$

31. Joe gave $\frac{1}{8}$ of his sweets to his brother and $\frac{1}{4}$ of his sweets to his sister. What fraction did he give away altogether?

32. Kate gave $\frac{1}{10}$ of her toys to a friend and $\frac{1}{5}$ of her toys to her sister. What fraction of her toys does she still have?

33. In her will a woman leaves $\frac{1}{2}$ of her money to her son, $\frac{1}{4}$ to her daughter, $\frac{1}{8}$ to her dog and the rest to her goldfish.
What fraction does the goldfish receive?

34. In an election, everyone voted for either A, B or C. If A got $\frac{1}{4}$ of the votes and B got $\frac{3}{8}$ of the votes, what fraction of the votes did C get?

Harder questions

- To work out $\frac{1}{2} + \frac{1}{5}$ we have to change *both* fractions so that they have the same denominator (bottom number).
  So $\frac{1}{2} + \frac{1}{5}$
  $= \frac{5}{10} + \frac{2}{10}$ (Think: 'What number do 2 and 5 go into?')
  $= \frac{7}{10}$

- To work out $\frac{3}{4} - \frac{1}{6}$ we have to change *both* fractions
  So $\frac{3}{4} - \frac{1}{6}$
  $= \frac{9}{12} - \frac{2}{12}$ (Think: 'What number do 4 and 6 go into?')
  $= \frac{7}{12}$

Exercise 3

1. Copy and complete these calculations

   (a) $\frac{1}{2} + \frac{2}{5}$
   $= \frac{5}{10} + \frac{4}{10}$
   $=$

   (b) $\frac{3}{5} - \frac{1}{2}$
   $= \frac{\Box}{10} - \frac{\Box}{10}$
   $=$

   (c) $\frac{1}{2} - \frac{1}{5}$
   $= \frac{\Box}{10} - \frac{\Box}{10}$
   $=$

2. Copy and complete these calculations

(a) $\dfrac{1}{3} + \dfrac{2}{5}$

$= \dfrac{\square}{15} + \dfrac{6}{15}$

$=$

(b) $\dfrac{1}{2} + \dfrac{1}{7}$

$= \dfrac{\square}{14} + \dfrac{\square}{14}$

$=$

(c) $\dfrac{2}{5} + \dfrac{1}{4}$

$= \dfrac{8}{20} + \dfrac{\square}{20}$

$=$

3. Work out

(a) $\tfrac{1}{3} + \tfrac{1}{7}$

Think: What do 3 and 7 go into?

(b) $\tfrac{1}{5} + \tfrac{1}{6}$

Think: What do 5 and 6 go into?

4. These diagrams illustrate the addition $\tfrac{1}{4} + \tfrac{1}{3}$.

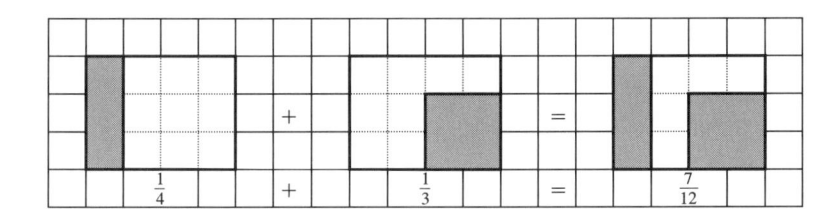

$\tfrac{1}{4} \quad + \quad \tfrac{1}{3} \quad = \quad \tfrac{7}{12}$

Copy the diagrams below, one for each part.

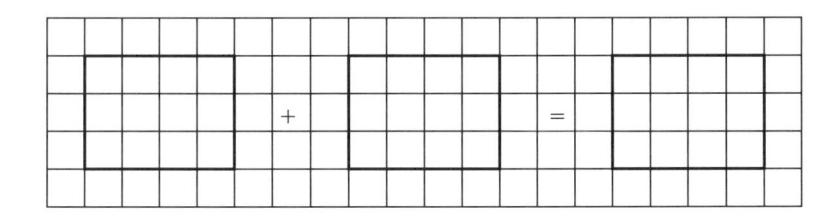

Shade in the diagrams to show the additions

(a) $\tfrac{1}{12} + \tfrac{1}{4}$
(b) $\tfrac{1}{6} + \tfrac{2}{3}$
(c) $\tfrac{1}{3} + \tfrac{1}{12}$

5. Work out

(a) $\tfrac{1}{2} + \tfrac{1}{3}$
(b) $\tfrac{2}{3} - \tfrac{1}{2}$
(c) $\tfrac{2}{3} + \tfrac{1}{4}$
(d) $\tfrac{1}{6} + \tfrac{1}{4}$
(e) $\tfrac{1}{3} + \tfrac{1}{4}$
(f) $\tfrac{3}{4} - \tfrac{1}{3}$

6. Work out

(a) $\tfrac{1}{3} + \tfrac{1}{5}$
(b) $\tfrac{2}{5} + \tfrac{2}{3}$
(c) $\tfrac{1}{4} + \tfrac{1}{5}$
(d) $\tfrac{4}{5} - \tfrac{1}{2}$
(e) $\tfrac{2}{3} - \tfrac{1}{4}$
(f) $\tfrac{2}{3} - \tfrac{1}{5}$

Fraction of a number

- The dungeon of a castle contained 135 prisoners of whom $\frac{4}{5}$ were innocent of any crime.
  How many innocent prisoners were there?
- We need to work out $\frac{4}{5}$ of 135.
  $\frac{1}{5}$ of $135 = 135 \div 5$
  $\phantom{\frac{1}{5} \text{ of } 135} = 27$
  So $\frac{4}{5}$ of $135 = 27 \times 4$
  $\phantom{\text{So } \frac{4}{5} \text{ of } 135} = 108$

There were 108 innocent prisoners in the dungeon.

Exercise 4

Work out

1. $\frac{2}{5}$ of 100
2. $\frac{3}{4}$ of 40
3. $\frac{2}{3}$ of 15
4. $\frac{5}{6}$ of 24
5. $\frac{3}{5}$ of 260
6. $\frac{3}{4}$ of 92
7. $\frac{5}{8}$ of £496
8. $\frac{2}{7}$ of £3500
9. $\frac{4}{5}$ of 80 kg

10. The petrol tank of a car holds 60 litres. How much petrol is in the tank when it is $\frac{4}{5}$ full?

11. In six years Michael Owen scored 198 goals and $\frac{2}{9}$ of these were headers. How many headers did he score?

12. Susie's new jeans are 96 cm long when she buys them. After washing they shrink to $\frac{7}{8}$ of their previous length. What is the new length of the jeans?

13. In a spelling test full marks were 48. How many marks did Belize get if he got $\frac{5}{6}$ of full marks?

14. What fraction of £1 is 27 p?
    What fraction of 1 m is 97 cm?
    What fraction of 1 kg is 250 g?
    What fraction of 1 km is 1 m?
    What fraction of one year is one day?
    What fraction of one year is December?

15. On each bounce a ball rises to $\frac{3}{4}$ of its previous height. How high will a ball bounce if it is dropped from a height of 2 metres?

16. In a sale, spiders, which normally cost £12, were sold at '$\frac{2}{5}$ off'. How much did the spiders cost in the sale?

Work out

17. $\frac{5}{7}$ of £175
18. $\frac{2}{9}$ of $378
19. $\frac{5}{6}$ of 204 kg
20. $\frac{1}{8}$ of 12 hours
21. $\frac{3}{8}$ of 12 hours
22. $\frac{3}{4}$ of £4·20
23. $\frac{1}{10}$ of £55
24. $\frac{2}{3}$ of 1275 m
25. $\frac{5}{8}$ of £4976

Cancelling

Sometimes it is easier work out multiplication by cancelling.
Examples:

(a) $\dfrac{5}{\cancel{9}_{3}} \times \cancel{12}^{4} = \dfrac{20}{3} = 6\frac{2}{3}$

(b) $\dfrac{3}{\cancel{8}_{2}} \times \cancel{12}^{3} = \dfrac{9}{2} = 4\frac{1}{2}$

(c) $\dfrac{5}{\cancel{12}_{4}} \times \cancel{15}^{5} = \dfrac{25}{4} = 6\frac{1}{4}$

Exercise 5

1. $\dfrac{5}{\cancel{8}_{2}} \times \cancel{12}^{3} = \dfrac{\square}{\square} = \square$
2. $\dfrac{3}{\cancel{7}_{1}} \times \cancel{14}^{2} = \dfrac{\square}{\square} = \square$
3. $\dfrac{5}{\cancel{12}_{3}} \times \dfrac{\cancel{16}^{4}}{1} = \dfrac{\square}{\square} = \square$
4. $\dfrac{2}{\cancel{9}_{3}} \times \dfrac{\cancel{15}^{5}}{1} = \dfrac{\square}{\square} = \square$

Work out, using cancelling.

5. $\dfrac{7}{8} \times 12$
6. $\dfrac{5}{8} \times 10$
7. $\dfrac{7}{10} \times 5$
8. $\dfrac{7}{12} \times 16$
9. $\dfrac{2}{3} \times 6$
10. $\dfrac{3}{4} \times 10$
11. $\dfrac{2}{5} \times 20$
12. $\dfrac{5}{6} \times 4$
13. $\dfrac{3}{4} \times 6$
14. $\dfrac{1}{8} \times 10$
15. $\dfrac{1}{20} \times 15$
16. $\dfrac{2}{15} \times 20$
17. $\dfrac{5}{6}$ of 9
18. $\dfrac{5}{21}$ of 14
19. $\dfrac{11}{36}$ of 9
20. $\dfrac{1}{32}$ of 24

Work out. [Remember that $\frac{2}{3} \times 8$ is the same as $8 \times \frac{2}{3}$.]

21. $3 \times \dfrac{1}{6}$
22. $12 \times \dfrac{1}{8}$
23. $8 \times \dfrac{3}{10}$
24. $9 \times \dfrac{1}{15}$
25. $4 \times \dfrac{5}{8}$
26. $16 \times \dfrac{1}{24}$
27. $11 \times \dfrac{7}{33}$
28. $24 \times \dfrac{7}{60}$

Dividing an integer by a fraction

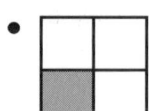

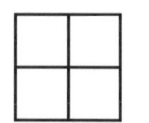

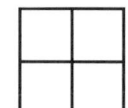

- How many quarters are there in 3?
  Answer: 12

- $2 \div \frac{1}{3}$ 'How many thirds are there in 2?' Answer: 6
- $5 \div \frac{1}{2}$ 'How many halves are there in 5?' Answer 10

Exercise 6

1. (a) How many thirds are there in 1?
   (b) How many thirds are there in 2?
   (c) How many thirds are there in 4?

2. (a) How many quarters are there in 1?
   (b) How many quarters are there in 3?
   (c) How many quarters are there in 6?

3. (a) How many tenths are there in 2?
   (b) How many fifths are there in 3?
   (c) How many sevenths are there in 2?

How many thirds are there in 33?

4. Work out
   (a) $1 \div \frac{1}{5}$
   (b) $3 \div \frac{1}{2}$
   (c) $1 \div \frac{1}{10}$
   (d) $2 \div \frac{1}{2}$
   (e) $9 \div \frac{1}{3}$
   (f) $12 \div \frac{1}{3}$

5. (a) Look at the pattern.
   $60 \times \frac{1}{5} = 12$ $12 \div \frac{1}{5} = 60$
   $30 \times \frac{2}{5} = 12$ $12 \div \frac{2}{5} = 30$
   $20 \times \frac{3}{5} = 12$ $12 \div \frac{3}{5} = 20$
   $15 \times \frac{4}{5} = 12$ $12 \div \frac{4}{5} = 15$

   (b) Copy and complete this pattern
   $60 \times \frac{1}{6} = 10$ $10 \div \frac{1}{6} = 60$
   $30 \times \frac{2}{6} = 10$ $10 \div \frac{2}{6} = \square$
   $20 \times \frac{3}{6} = 10$ $10 \div \frac{3}{6} = \square$
   $15 \times \frac{4}{6} = \square$ $10 \div \frac{4}{6} = \square$
   $12 \times \frac{5}{6} = \square$ $10 \div \frac{5}{6} = \square$

6. Copy and complete
   (a) $10 = \square \times \frac{1}{2}$
   (b) $\square \times \frac{1}{3} = 8$
   (c) $\square \times \frac{1}{4} = 5$
   (d) $\square \times \frac{1}{3} = 2$
   (e) $11 = \square \times \frac{1}{2}$
   (f) $\square \times \frac{1}{5} = 5$

1.3 Indices

Square numbers

We use indices, which are sometimes known as 'powers', to shorten what would otherwise be long expressions

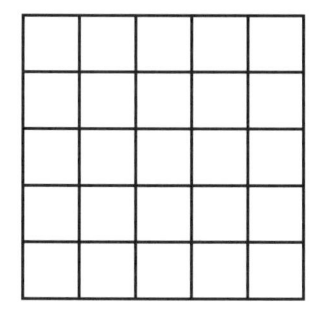

This diagram shows 25 unit squares arranged to form one larger square. Each side is 5 units long.

- We say '5 squared = 25'
  We write this as $5^2 = 25$
  We work it out like this: 5^2
  $= 5 \times 5$
  $= 25$

  *the small 2 means 'multiply by itself,' **not** 'multiply by 2'*

Exercise 1

1. Copy and complete this table.

We say	We write	We work out	Answer
4 squared	4^2	4×4	
3 squared		3×3	
	6^2		36
7 squared			
		8×8	
	12^2		

2. (a) Write down all the square numbers from 1 to 144.
   (b) Look at the last digits of the square numbers. What numbers do not appear as last digits?
   (c) Could 523 be a square number?
   Could 947 be a square number?

Cube numbers

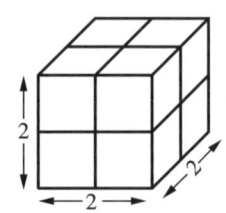

The diagram opposite shows 8 unit cubes arranged to form one larger cube.
Each side of the cube is 2 units long.

- We say '2 cubed = 8'
  We write this as $2^3 = 8$
  We work it out like this: 2^3
  $= 2 \times 2 \times 2$
  $= 4 \times 2$
  $= 8$

  the small 3 means 'multiply 3 lots of 2 together,' Not $3 \times 2 = 6$

Exercise 2

1. Copy and complete this table. You may need a calculator to help you.

We say	We write	We work out	Answer
4 cubed	4^3	$4 \times 4 \times 4$	
3 cubed		$3 \times 3 \times 3$	
	6^3		216
5 cubed			
		$9 \times 9 \times 9$	
	10^3		
			1

Higher powers

- Beyond squares and cubes we say 'to the power of'
- For 2^6 we say '2 to the power of 6'
  We write this as $2^6 = 2 \times 2 \times 2 \times 2 \times 2 \times 2$
- On a calculator we press $\boxed{2}\ \boxed{x^y}\ \boxed{6}\ \boxed{=}$
- Either with or without a calculator, we work out $2^6 = 64$.

Exercise 3

1. Copy and complete this table, using a calculator to help you obtain the answers.

We say	We write	We work out	Answer
2 to the power of 4	2^4	$2 \times 2 \times 2 \times 2$	
3 to the power of 4		$3 \times 3 \times 3 \times 3$	
	4^4		256
5 to the power of 2			
	6^5		7776
		$8 \times 8 \times 8 \times 8 \times 8$	
		$9 \times 9 \times 9$	
	3^9		
10 to the power of 2			
2 to the power of 10			

2. The numbers 10, 100, 1000 ... form the basis of the number system.
Write each of the numbers 10, 100, 1000, 100 000 and 1 million as powers of 10.

Square roots

- The square shown has an area of 225 cm².
  How long is a side of the square?
  In other words, what number *multiplied* by *itself* makes 225?
  The answer is the *square root* of 225.
  On a calculator press $\boxed{225}$ $\boxed{\sqrt{}}$.
  The side of the square is 15 cm.   (Check $15 \times 15 = 225$).

- Most numbers do *not* have an exact square root.
  Here is a square of area 226 cm².
  To find the length of a side of the square, work out $\sqrt{226}$.
  On a calculator press $\boxed{226}$ $\boxed{\sqrt{}}$.

The calculator shows 15·033296.
To two decimal places, the side of the square is 15·03 cm.
Teachers note: Rounding off to 2 decimal places is covered in section 2.4.

Exercise 4

1. Work out without a calculator:
   (a) $\sqrt{16}$ (b) $\sqrt{25}$ (c) $\sqrt{64}$ (d) $\sqrt{100}$ (e) $\sqrt{49}$

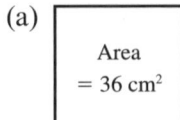

2. Find the sides of these squares:
   (a) Area = 36 cm²
   (b) Area = 9 cm²
   (c) Area = 144 cm²

3. Use a calculator to find the following, correct to one decimal place.
   (a) $\sqrt{51}$ (b) $\sqrt{84}$ (c) $\sqrt{79}$ (d) $\sqrt{109}$ (e) $\sqrt{89}$
   (f) $\sqrt{13}$ (g) $\sqrt{7}$ (h) $\sqrt{200}$ (i) $\sqrt{741}$ (j) $\sqrt{5000}$

4. We can find an estimate for the square root of 11 as follows:

   We know that $\sqrt{9} < \sqrt{11} < \sqrt{16}$.

   So $3 < \sqrt{11} < 4$

   Use this method to find estimates for the following:
   (a) $\sqrt{6}$ (b) $\sqrt{55}$ (c) $\sqrt{110}$ (d) $\sqrt{32}$

Consecutive sums: an investigation

- Consecutive numbers are whole numbers which appear next to each other on the number line: 4, 5, 6 are consecutive.

  7, 10 are not consecutive

- Using only sets of consecutive numbers it is possible to form all the numbers from 1 to 40 except for the powers of two (1, 2, 4, 8, 16, 32).

- Copy and complete the table opposite to find the consecutive sums for every number from 1 to 40 except powers of 2.
  Some target numbers can be formed in more than one way.

Target	Consecutive sum
1	Impossible
2	Impossible
3	1 + 2
4	Impossible
5	2 + 3
6	1 + 2 + 3
⋮	
40	6 + 7 + 8 + 9 + 10

- Continue the pattern to 100. You should look at your results and use any patterns you can see to help you.

Power sums: an investigation

A Here is a list of the first six powers of 2.

$2^0 = 1$
$2^1 = 2$
$2^2 = 4$
$2^3 = 8$
$2^4 = 16$
$2^5 = 32$

(Yes! 2^0 really is 1. Check it on a calculator. We will discuss the power zero in a later book.)

- Using only the numbers 1, 2, 4, 8, 16 and 32 it is possible to form all the whole numbers from 1 to 32 inclusive, by adding and subtracting.

(We call them 'power *sums*' even though we sometimes subtract.)

Target	Power sum
1	1
2	2
3	4 − 1
4	4
5	4 + 1
6	2 + 4
7	1 + 2 + 4
⋮	⋮
32	32

- You may use each of 1, 2, 4, 8, 16, 32 only once.

  E.g. $5 = 2 + 2 + 1$ is not allowed.

  $5 = 4 + 1$ is allowed.

- Copy and complete the table above to find power sums for every number from 1 to 32.

- Can you continue the pattern to 63? 127? ...

B

$3^0 = 1$
$3^1 = 3$
$3^2 = 9$
$3^3 = 27$

Here are the first four powers of 3. Using only these numbers it is possible to form all the whole numbers between 1 and 40. Copy and complete the table, again using each number only *once*.

Target	Power sum
1	1
2	3 − 1
3	3
4	1 + 3
5	9 − 3 − 1
⋮	⋮
40	?

1.4 Area

Triangle

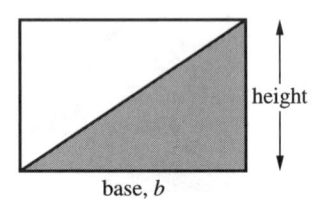

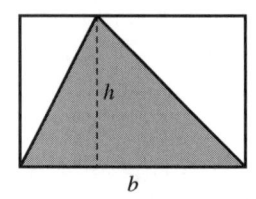

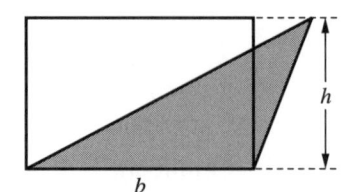

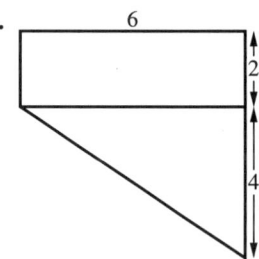

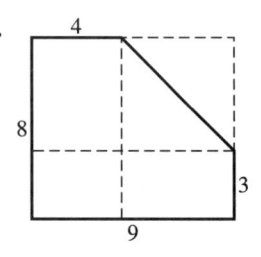

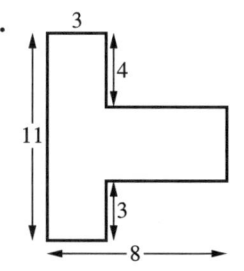

For each shaded triangle, area of triangle $= \frac{1}{2} b \times h$

Exercise 1

Calculate the area of each shape. The lengths are in cm.

1. Rectangle, 4 by 2
2. Square, 5 by 5
3. Triangle, base 6, height 3 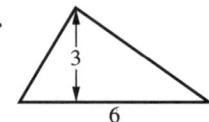
4. Right-angled triangle, legs 5 and 8
5. Shape with rectangle 6 by 2 on top and triangle below, height 4
6. Shape: rectangle 8 by 3 on top, triangle below; total height 7
7. L-shape: top part 3 wide, 5 tall; bottom extension 4 wide, 2 tall
8. Square 8 by 8 with triangle cut; width 4 on top, 3 on right, base 9
9. T-shape: top 10 by 2, stem 3 by 5
10. Shape: outer 8 wide, 4+2=? tall; notch 5 by 2 at top, 2 at top
11. Cross-like shape: width 8, height 11, with 3 top, 4, 3 bottom notches
12. Z/C-shape: total height 8, width 5, with 3-wide arms and 1-tall bars

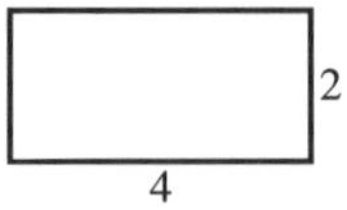

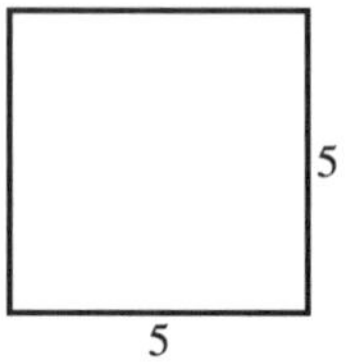

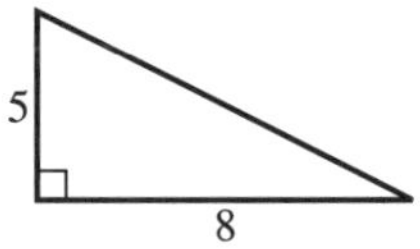

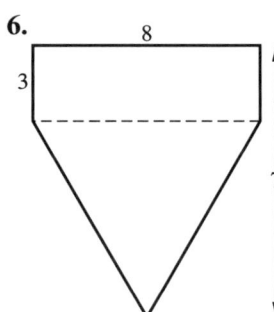

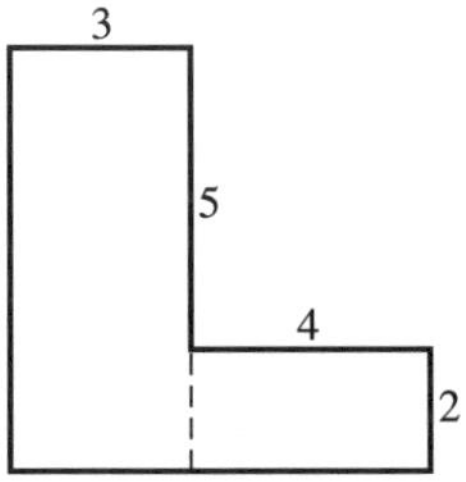

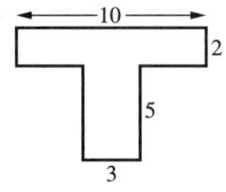

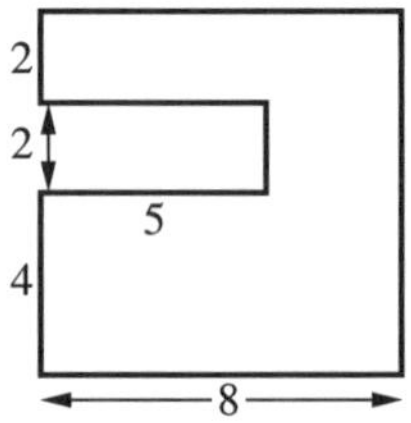

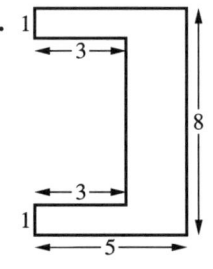

In Questions **13** to **20** the area is written inside the shape. Calculate the length of the side marked *x*.

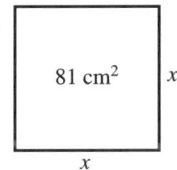

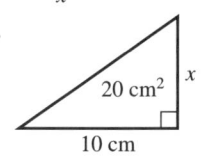

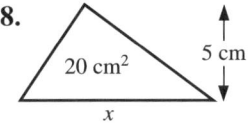

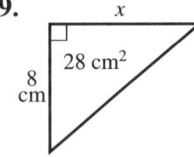

13. 24 cm², 8 cm, x
14. 40 cm², 8 cm, x
15. 81 cm², x
16. 28 cm², 14 cm, x
17. 20 cm², 10 cm, x
18. 20 cm², 5 cm, x
19. 28 cm², 8 cm, x
20. 32 cm², x

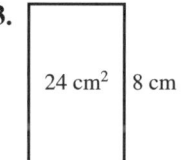

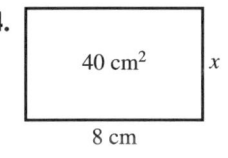

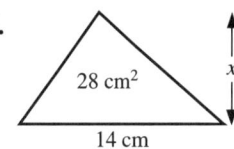

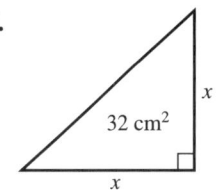

Irregular shapes

It is not easy to find the exact area of the triangle shown because we do not know either the length of the base or the height.

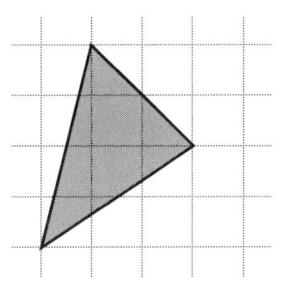

We could measure both lengths but this would introduce a small error due to the inevitable inaccuracy of the measuring.

- A good method is to start by drawing a rectangle around the triangle. The corners of the triangle lie either on the sides of the rectangle or at a corner of the rectangle.

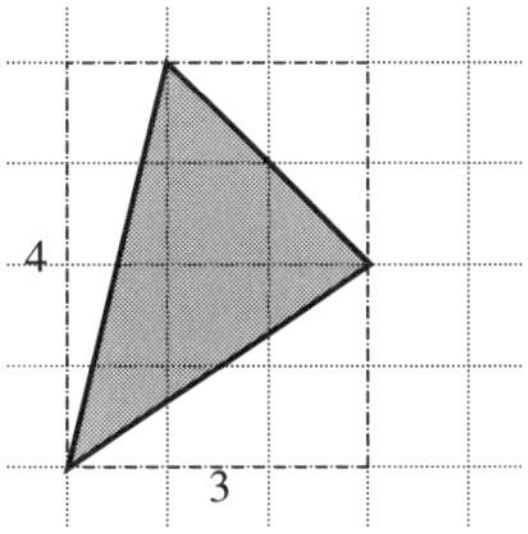

  Calculate the area of the rectangle.
  In this example: Area of rectangle $= 3 \times 4$
  $= 12$ square units.

- Now find the areas of the three triangles marked A, B and C. This is easy because the triangles each have a right angle.
  Use the symbol '△A' to mean 'triangle A'

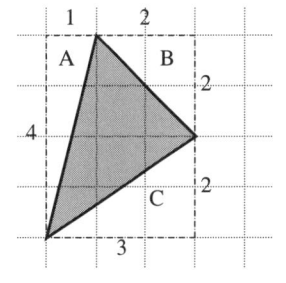

  Area of $\triangle A = \dfrac{4 \times 1}{2} = 2$ square units

  Area of $\triangle B = \dfrac{2 \times 2}{2} = 2$ square units

  Area of $\triangle C = \dfrac{3 \times 2}{2} = 3$ square units

  Now we can find the area of the required triangle by subtracting the areas of △A, △B and △C from the area of the rectangle.

  Area of shaded triangle $= 12 - (2 + 2 + 3) = 5$ square units.

Exercise 2

1. (a) Copy the diagram shown.
   (b) Work out the areas, in square units, of triangles A, B and C.
   (c) Work out the area of the square enclosed by the dotted lines.
   (d) Hence work out the area of the shaded triangle.

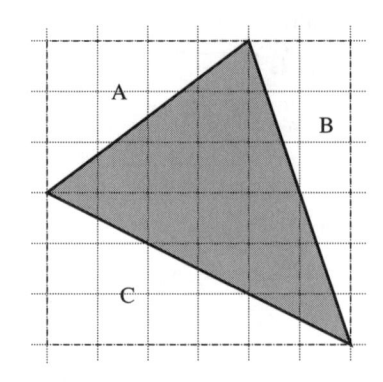

In the following questions use the method of Question **1** to find the area of each shape.

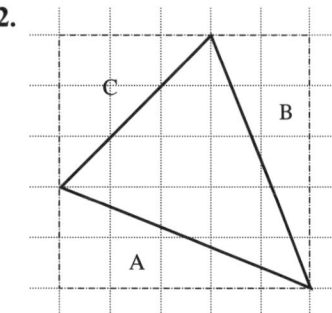

2.

3.

4.

5.

6.

7.

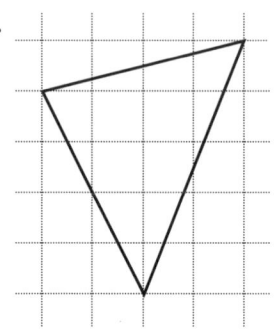

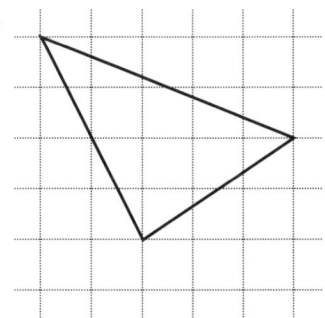

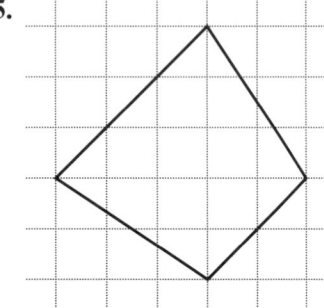

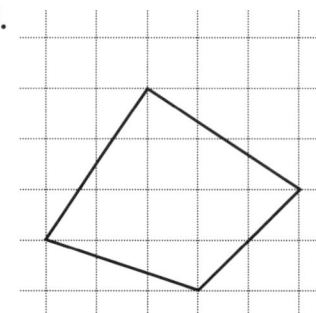

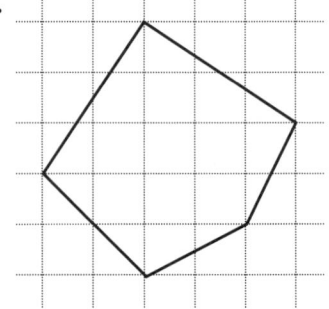

For Questions **8** to **14** draw axes with x and y from 0 to 10.
Plot the points given, join them up in order, and find the area of each shape.

8. (1, 7), (3, 2), (7, 6).

9. (4, 2), (6, 8), (1, 3).

10. (1, 2), (3, 6), (7, 5), (5, 3).

11. (3, 1), (8, 3), (5, 6), (1, 4)

12. (2, 0), (7, 1), (8, 4), (5, 5), (1, 3)

13. (3, 1), (6, 0), (9, 2), (7, 5), (3, 6), (1, 4)

14. (2, 3), (5, 1), (11, 5), (9, 7), (5, 8), (2, 8), (0, 6), (2, 3).

Parallelogram and trapezium

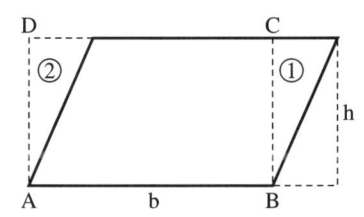

Area of parallelogram
= area of rectangle ABCD + area of △1 − area of △2.
But area of △1 = area of △2

∴ area of parallelogram = b × h

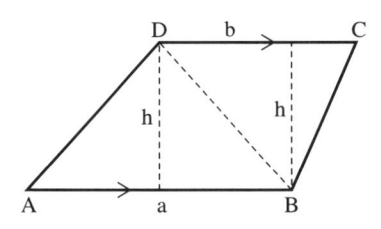

Area of trapezium = area of △ABD + area of △DCB
$= \frac{1}{2}ah + \frac{1}{2}bh$
$= \frac{1}{2}(a+b)h$

area of trapezium = $\frac{1}{2}$ (sum of parallel sides) × height

Exercise 3

Calculate the area of each shape. The lengths are in cm.

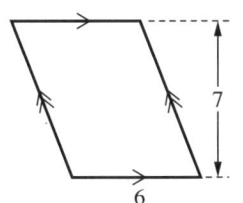

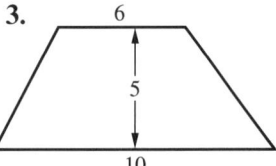

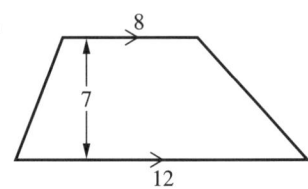

1. [parallelogram, base 8, height 5]
2. [parallelogram, base 6, height 7]
3. [trapezium, parallel sides 6 and 10, height 5]
4. [trapezium, parallel sides 8 and 12, height 7]
5. [parallelogram, base 5, height 5] 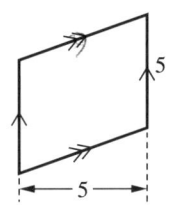
6. Find the shaded area [rectangle 9 × 4 with triangle of top 3]

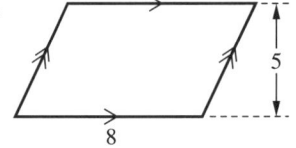

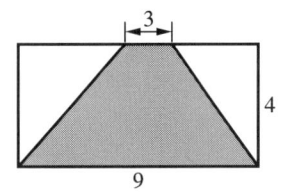

7. Sketch a trapezium with parallel sides of length 5 cm and 7 cm. The distance between the parallel sides is 4 cm. Calculate the area of the trapezium.

8. A parallelogram has a base of length 10 cm and an area of 60 cm². Calculate the height of the parallelogram.

9. The area of the trapezium shown is 12 cm². Find a possible set of values for a, b and h.

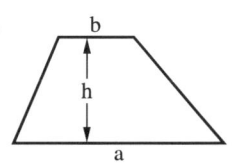

Area problems

Exercise 4

1. The diagram shows a picture 10 cm by 6 cm surrounded by a border 4 cm wide. What is the area of the border?

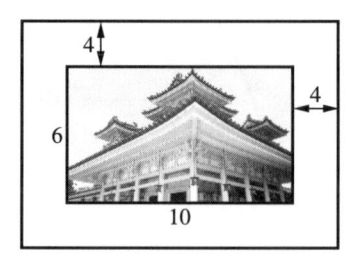

2. A floor measuring 4 m by 5 m is to be covered by square tiles measuring 50 cm by 50 cm. How many tiles are needed?

3. How many panes of glass 30 cm by 20 cm can be cut from a sheet which is 1 metre square?

4. Find the shaded area. All the lengths are in cm.

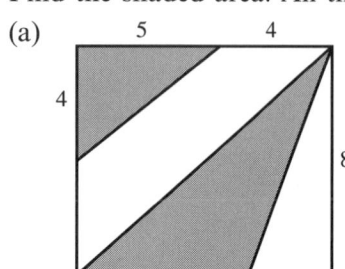

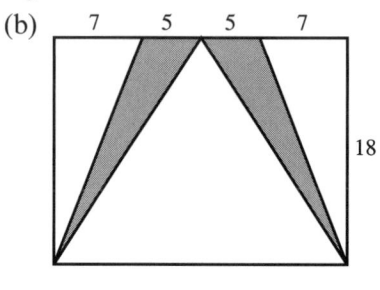

   (a)

   (b)

5. A rectangular field measures 500 m by 1 km. Find the area of the field in hectares. $(1 \text{ hectare} = 10\,000 \text{ m}^2)$

6. A rectangular field 300 m long has an area of 6 hectares. Calculate the width of the field.

7. Farmland is sold at £2500 per hectare. How much would you pay for a rectangular piece of farmland measuring 300 m by 400 m?

8. A line starts at A and goes along the dotted lines to B. It divides the area of the rectangle into two halves.
   (a) Draw a rectangle like the one here and draw a line from C to D which divides the area of the rectangle into two halves.
   (b) Draw a second rectangle and draw a line from C to D which divides the area of the rectangle into two parts so that one part has *twice* the area of the other part.

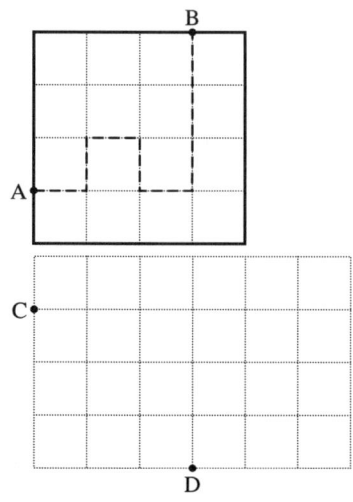

9. Here are some shapes made with centimetre squares.

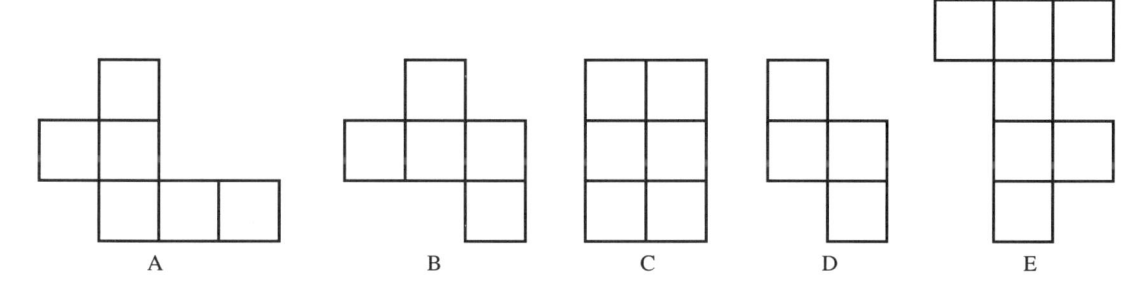

   (a) Which shape has an area of 4 cm²?
   (b) Which shape has a perimeter of 12 cm?
   (c) Which two shapes have the same perimeter?

10. Look at these shapes made with equilateral triangles.

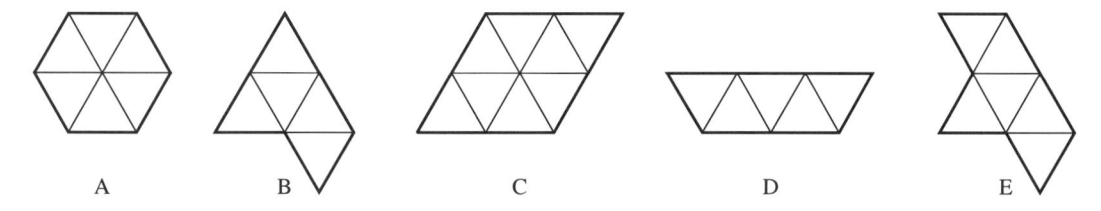

    (a) Which shape has the largest area?
    (b) Which shape has the same area as shape A?
    (c) Which shape has the same perimeter as shape C?

11. Here are two shapes *both* with a perimeter of 32 cm.
    Calculate the *area* of each shape.

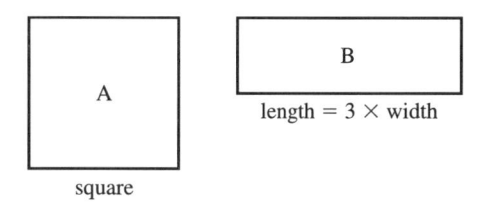

    A square

    B length = 3 × width

12.* A gardener is spreading fertilizer on his lawn (but not the pond in the middle!). The instructions only say that 2 measures of the fertilizer will treat 10 m² of lawn. Each measure of fertilizer costs 60 p.
    Find the cost of the fertilizer required.

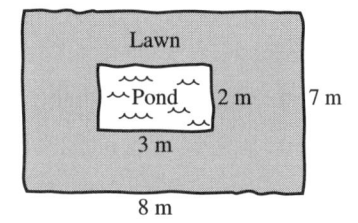

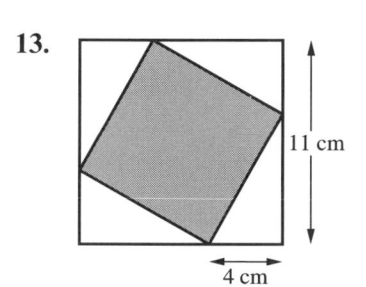

13. The diagram shows a shaded square inside a larger square. Calculate the area of the shaded square.

1.5 Negative numbers

- If the weather is very cold and the temperature is 3 degrees below zero, it is written −3°.
- If a golfer is 5 under par for his round, the scoreboard will show −5.
- On a bank statement if someone is £55 overdrawn [or 'in the red'] it would appear as −£55.

  These above are examples of the use of negative numbers.

- An easy way to begin calculations with negative numbers is to think about changes in temperature:
  (a) Suppose the temperature is −2° and it rises by 7°.
      The new temperature is 5°.
      We can write −2 + 7 = 5.
  (b) Suppose the temperature is −3° and it falls by 6°.
      The new temperature is −9°.
      We can write −3 − 6 = −9.

Exercise 1

In Questions **1** to **12** move up or down the thermometer to find the new temperature.

1. The temperature is +8° and it falls by 3°.
2. The temperature is +4° and it falls by 5°.
3. The temperature is +2° and it falls by 6°.
4. The temperature is −1° and it falls by 6°.
5. The temperature is −5° and it rises by 1°.
6. The temperature is −8° and it rises by 4°.
7. The temperature is −3° and it rises by 7°.
8. The temperature is +4° and it rises by 8°.
9. The temperature is +9° and it falls by 14°.
10. The temperature is −13° and it rises by 13°.
11. The temperature is −6° and it falls by 5°.
12. The temperature is −25° and it rises by 10°.

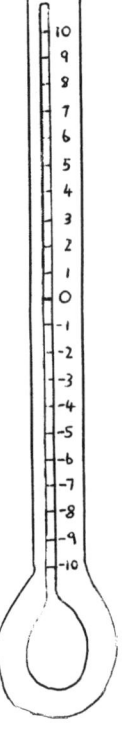

Adding and subtracting

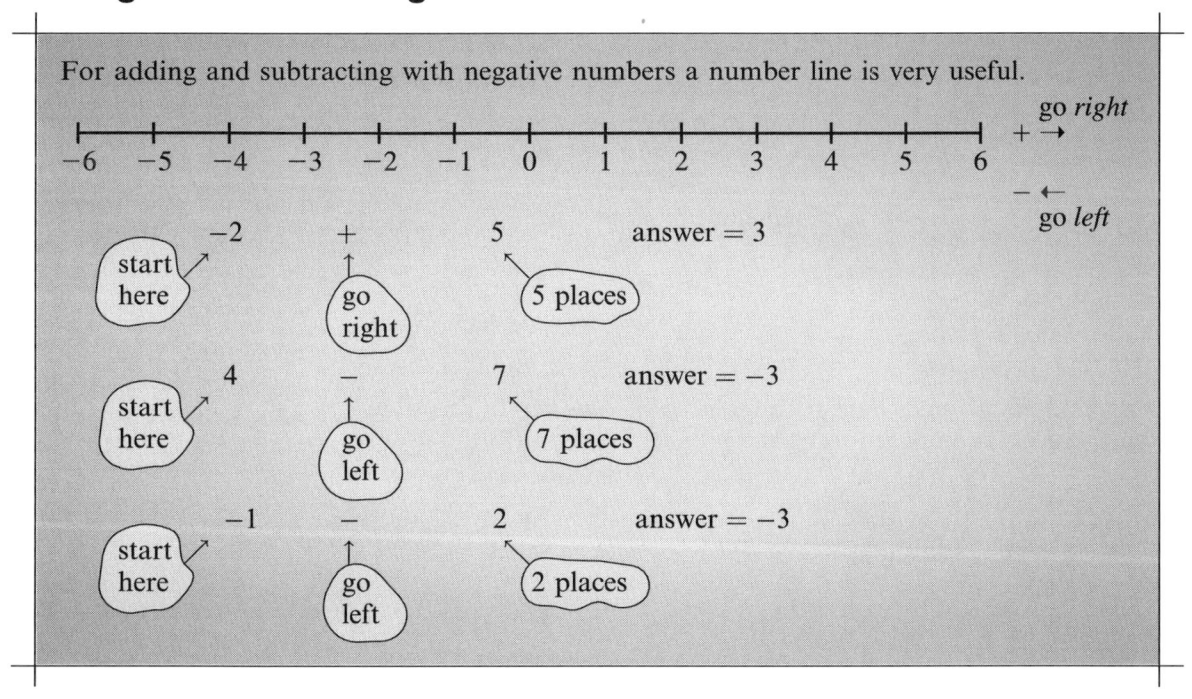

For adding and subtracting with negative numbers a number line is very useful.

```
-6  -5  -4  -3  -2  -1  0  1  2  3  4  5  6       + →  go right
                                                   - ←  go left
```

start here → $-2 + 5$ (go right, 5 places) answer = 3

start here → $4 - 7$ (go left, 7 places) answer = -3

start here → $-1 - 2$ (go left, 2 places) answer = -3

Exercise 2

1. Use a number line to work out
   (a) $4 - 5$ (b) $-2 + 4$ (c) $-3 + 6$ (d) $-2 - 1$
   (e) $3 - 7$ (f) $-2 + 5$ (g) $4 - 9$ (h) $-3 + 2$
   (i) $-5 - 1$ (j) $7 - 8$ (k) $4 - 7$ (l) $-3 + 8$

2. Work out
   (a) $6 - 11$ (b) $-3 - 3$ (c) $-5 + 4$ (d) $-3 + 3$
   (e) $8 - 12$ (f) $11 - 13$ (g) $-4 - 4$ (h) $10 - 20$
   (i) $-5 - 15$ (j) $-3 - 13$ (k) $8 - 5$ (l) $-6 + 20$

3. Copy each sentence and fill in the missing numbers.
   (a) 9, 6, 3, ☐, ☐
   (b) ☐, -1, 3, 7, 11
   (c) ☐, ☐, -10, -5, 0

4. Copy and complete the addition squares

   (a)
+	7	-1		
		0		-1
-3			1	
2	9			
			3	

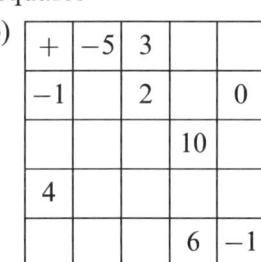

   (b)
+	-5	3		
-1		2		0
			10	
4				
			6	-1

Two signs together

The calculation 8 − (+3) can be read as '8 take away positive 3'.

Similarly 6 − (−4) can be read as '6 take away negative 4'.

It is possible to replace *two* signs next to each other by *one* sign as follows:

```
+ + = +
− − = +
− + = −
+ − = −
```

Remember: 'same signs: +'
'different signs: −'

When two adjacent signs have been replaced by one sign in this way, the calculation is completed using the number line as before.

Work out the following

(a)   −7 + (−4)
     = −7 − 4
     = −11

(b)   8 + (−14)
     = 8 − 14
     = −6

(c)   5 − (+9)
     = 5 − 9
     = −4

(d)   6 − (−2)
     = 6 + 2
     = 8

Exercise 3

1. Work out
   (a) 5 + (−2)
   (b) 4 + (−5)
   (c) 6 + (−6)
   (d) 4 + (−8)
   (e) 8 − (+2)
   (f) 7 − (+8)
   (g) 3 − (−1)
   (h) 4 − (−2)
   (i) 6 − (−3)
   (j) 4 − (−4)
   (k) 9 − (+1)
   (l) 10 − (+5)

2. Work out
   (a) 4 − (−2)
   (b) 6 − (−6)
   (c) 8 + (−10)
   (d) 3 + (−2)
   (e) 8 + (+2)
   (f) 7 − (+4)
   (g) 6 − (−5)
   (h) 4 − (−2)
   (i) 10 + (−20)
   (j) 15 + (−16)
   (k) 9 + (−12)
   (l) −3 − (−4)

3. Copy and complete the tables

a	9	3	8	3	2	5	4	7		
b	5	5	3	7	−2	−2			4	2
a−b	4	−2					−2	−3	−3	−1

a	−3	4	3	5	7	4	6			
b			−3	−1				5	−1	2
a−b	−3	−5			8	10	6	2	3	−2

Multiplying and dividing

- In the sequence of multiplications shown, the numbers in column A go down by one each time.
The numbers in column B go down by five each time

$$\begin{array}{c} \quad\ \text{A} \quad\ \text{B} \\ \quad\ \downarrow \quad\ \downarrow \\ 5 \times \ \ 3 = \ \ 15 \\ 5 \times \ \ 2 = \ \ 10 \\ 5 \times \ \ 1 = \ \ \ 5 \\ 5 \times \ \ 0 = \ \ \ 0 \end{array}$$

Continuing the sequence:
We see that:

$$\begin{array}{l} 5 \times -1 = \ -5 \\ 5 \times -2 = -10 \\ 5 \times -3 = -15 \end{array}$$

'When a positive number is multiplied by a negative number the answer is negative'.

- In this sequence the numbers in column C go down by one each time.
The numbers in column D *increase* by 3 each time.

$$\begin{array}{c} \quad\ \text{C} \quad\ \text{D} \\ \quad\ \downarrow \quad\ \downarrow \\ -3 \times \ \ 3 = -9 \\ -3 \times \ \ 2 = -6 \\ -3 \times \ \ 1 = -3 \\ -3 \times \ \ 0 = \ \ 0 \end{array}$$

Continuing the sequence:

$$\begin{array}{l} -3 \times -1 = \ 3 \\ -3 \times -2 = \ 6 \\ -3 \times -3 = \ 9 \end{array}$$

We see that:

'When two negative numbers are multiplied together the answer is positive.'

Summary of rules.
(a) When two numbers with the *same sign are multiplied together, the answer is positive.*
(b) When two numbers with *different signs are multiplied together, the answer is negative.*
(c) For division the rules are the same as for multiplication.

Examples: $\quad -3 \times (-7) = 21 \quad\quad 5 \times (-3) = -15 \quad\quad -12 \div 3 = -4$
$\quad\quad\quad\quad\ \ 20 \div (-2) = -10 \quad\quad -10 \div (-20) = \frac{1}{2} \quad\quad -1 \times (-2) \times (-3) = -6$

29

Exercise 4

Copy and complete the multiplication square below. Some numbers inside the square are shown as an explanation.

Exercise 5

Work out

1. $5 \times (-2)$
2. -2×4
3. $7 \times (-2)$
4. $-3 \times (-2)$
5. $-3 \times (-1)$
6. $-4 \times (-1)$
7. -5×2
8. $5 \times (-1)$
9. -4×2
10. $-3 \times (-3)$
11. $6 \times (-3)$
12. $-8 \times (-1)$
13. $12 \div (-2)$
14. $-8 \div (-1)$
15. $6 \div (-2)$
16. $-10 \div (-2)$
17. $-20 \div (-1)$
18. $12 \div (-3)$
19. $-3 \div (-1)$
20. $9 \div (-3)$

21. Work out
    (a) $-7 \times (-2)$
    (b) -3×6
    (c) $8 \div (-8)$
    (d) $10 \times (-3)$
    (e) $-2 \times (-2)$
    (f) $-12 \div 3$
    (g) $-5 \times (-4)$
    (h) -1×23
    (i) $-2 \times (-2)^2$
    (j) $0 \times (-7)$
    (k) $(-3)^2$
    (l) $-3 \times (-2) \times (-3)$

22. Find the missing numbers
    (a) $-4 \times \square = 12$
    (b) $3 \times \square = -12$
    (c) $-8 \div -4 = \square$
    (d) $5 \times \square = -5$
    (e) $\square \times (-3) = 9$
    (f) $12 \div \square = -6$
    (g) $\square \div (-3) = 2$
    (h) $\square \div 5 = -4$
    (i) $-2 \times \square = 20$
    (j) $-3 \times \square = 6$
    (k) $-2 \times \square = 4$
    (l) $(-1)^2 = \square$

Review exercise

This exercise has questions involving addition, subtraction, multiplication and division.

1. Work out
   (a) $-7 + 13$
   (b) $-5 - (-4)$
   (c) -7×4
   (d) $-12 \div (-12)$
   (e) $-6 + (-3)$
   (f) $-10 + 10$
   (g) $-8 - 5$
   (h) $12 - 60$
   (i) $3 \times (-3)$
   (j) $(-2)^2$
   (k) $5 - (-5)$
   (l) $6 \div (-6)$

2. Find the missing numbers
   (a) $5 \times \Box = -50$
   (b) $-2 \div \Box = 1$
   (c) $\Box - 3 = 12$
   (d) $\Box + (-7) = -9$
   (e) $10 - \Box = -3$
   (f) $\Box \div (-3) = -1$
   (g) $-7 - 7 = \Box$
   (h) $\Box \times (-7) = 14$
   (i) $1 - \Box = -9$
   (j) $-3 \times \Box = 0$
   (k) $8 - \Box = -8$
   (l) $(-1)^3 = \Box$

3. Work out
   (a) $-3 + (-2)$
   (b) $-8 \div 8$
   (c) $5 + (-7)$
   (d) $-2 \times \left(-\frac{1}{2}\right)$
   (e) $8 \div (-8)$
   (f) $-7 - (-2)$
   (g) $-12 \div (-2)$
   (h) $(-3)^3$
   (i) $6 + (-6 \cdot 5)$
   (j) $(-8 + 2)^2$
   (k) $(-2)^2 \times (-3)$
   (l) $(-3 - (-2))^2$

4. Copy and complete the addition square shown. The numbers inside the square are found by adding together the numbers across the top and down the side.

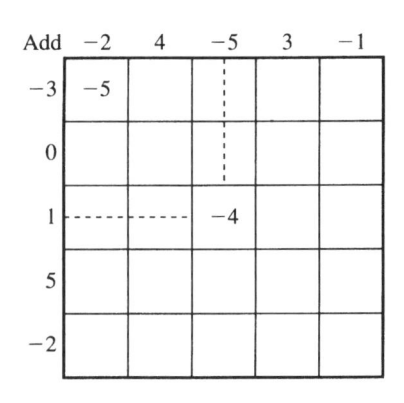

Add	−2	4	−5	3	−1
−3	−5				
0					
1			−4		
5					
−2					

5. Copy and complete the *multiplication* square shown.

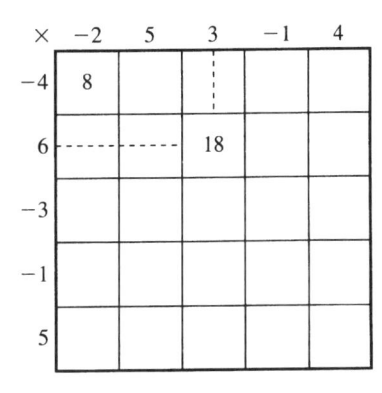

×	−2	5	3	−1	4
−4	8				
6			18		
−3					
−1					
5					

6. The sum of the numbers -3 and 4 is 1 and their product is -12. ('product' means multiplied together)
   (a) Find two numbers whose sum is 3 and whose product is -10.
   (b) Find two numbers whose sum is -1 and whose product is -12.
   (c) Find two numbers whose sum is 4 and whose product is -12.

7. Copy and complete the table.

	Sum	Product	Two numbers
(a)	−7	10	
(b)	−13	30	
(c)	−5	6	
(d)	5	−6	
(e)	−8	12	
(f)	−2	−15	
(g)	−13	42	

Practice tests

Questions on negative numbers are more difficult when the different sorts are mixed together. Do one of these tests every two weeks or so.

Test 1
1. $-8 - 8$
2. $-8 \times (-8)$
3. -5×3
4. $-5 + 3$
5. $8 - (-7)$
6. $20 - 2$
7. $-18 \div (-6)$
8. $4 + (-10)$
9. $-2 + 13$
10. $+8 \times (-6)$
11. $-9 + (+2)$
12. $-2 - (-11)$
13. $-6 \times (-1)$
14. $2 - 20$
15. $-14 - (-4)$
16. $-40 \div (-5)$
17. $5 - 11$
18. -3×10
19. $9 + (-5)$
20. $7 \div (-7)$

Test 2
1. $-10 \times (-10)$
2. $-10 - 10$
3. $-8 \times (+1)$
4. $-8 + 1$
5. $5 + (-9)$
6. $15 - 5$
7. $-72 \div (-8)$
8. $-12 - (-2)$
9. $-1 + 8$
10. $-5 \times (-7)$
11. $-10 + (-10)$
12. $-6 \times (+4)$
13. $6 - 16$
14. $-42 \div (+6)$
15. $-13 + (-6)$
16. $-8 - (-7)$
17. $5 \times (-1)$
18. $2 - 15$
19. $21 + (-21)$
20. $-16 \div (-2)$

Test 3
1. $-2 \times (+8)$
2. $-2 + 8$
3. $-7 - 6$
4. $-7 \times (-6)$
5. $+36 \div (-9)$
6. $-8 - (-4)$
7. $-14 + 2$
8. $5 \times (-4)$
9. $11 + (-5)$
10. $11 - 11$
11. $-9 \times (-4)$
12. $-6 + (-4)$
13. $3 - 10$
14. $-20 \div (-2)$
15. $16 + (-10)$
16. $-4 - (+14)$
17. $-45 \div 5$
18. $18 - 3$
19. $-1 \times (-1)$
20. $-3 - (-3)$

Test 4
1. $-4 + 4$
2. $-4 \times (+4)$
3. $-2 - 12$
4. $-2 \times (-12)$
5. $3 + (-4)$
6. $4 - (-10)$
7. $-22 \div 11$
8. $-9 + 7$
9. $-6 - (-13)$
10. $-3 \times (-11)$
11. $4 - 5$
12. $-20 - (+10)$
13. $4 \times (-7)$
14. $7 - (-12)$
15. $9 - 18$
16. $56 \div (-7)$
17. $7 - 6$
18. $-11 + (+2)$
19. $-2 \times (+8)$
20. $-8 \div (-2)$

1.6 Properties of numbers

Prime numbers, factors, multiples
- A *prime* number is divisible by just two different numbers: by itself and by one. Notice that 1 is *not* a prime number.

  Here are some prime numbers: $\boxed{7}$ $\boxed{23}$ $\boxed{11}$
- The *factors* of 15 divide into 15 exactly.

  $\boxed{1 \times 15}$ $\boxed{3 \times 5}$ The factors of 15 are 1, 3, 5 and 15.
- The first four *multiples* of $\boxed{6}$ are $\boxed{6, 12, 18, 24}$

  The first four multiples of $\boxed{11}$ are $\boxed{11, 22, 33, 44}$

Exercise 1

1. Find all the factors of
   (a) 12   (b) 30   (c) 17   (d) 50

2. 7 is a factor of which numbers between 20 and 30?

3. (a) List the factors of 24.
   (b) List the factors of 40.
   (c) List the common factors of 24 and 40. [i.e. the numbers which are in list (a) and list (b).]

4. (a) List the factors of 28.
   (b) List the factors of 36.
   (c) List the common factors of 28 and 36.
   (d) Write down the highest common factor of 28 and 36.

5. Find the highest common factor of
   (a) 24 and 42   (b) 35 and 49

6. Factors occur in pairs. For example $48 = 1 \times 48, 2 \times 24, 3 \times 16, 4 \times 12, 6 \times 8$
   Write down all the factor pairs for
   (a) 28   (b) 30

7. The number in the square is the product of the two numbers on either side of it. Copy and complete:

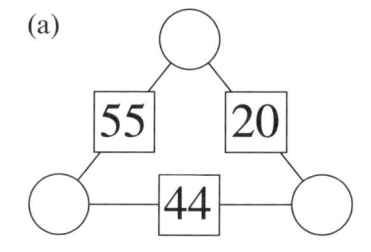

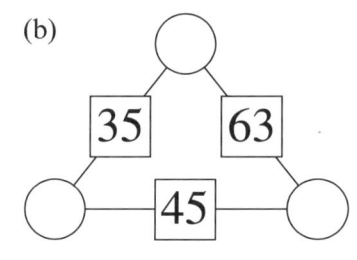

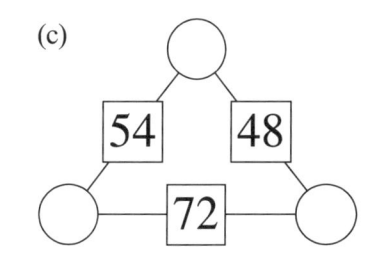

   (a) 55, 20, 44   (b) 35, 63, 45   (c) 54, 48, 72

8. Write down the first four multiples of
   (a) 3   (b) 7   (c) 10   (d) 15

9. Here are the first six multiples of 12 and 15

   | 12 : | 12 | 24 | 36 | 48 | 60 | 72 |
   | 15 : | 15 | 30 | 45 | 60 | 75 | 90 |

   Write down the lowest common multiple of 12 and 15. [i.e. the lowest number which is in both lists.]

10. Copy and complete the first five multiples of 6 and 8.

    6 : 6, 12, ☐, ☐, ☐
    8 : 8, ☐, ☐, ☐, ☐

    Write down the L.C.M. of 6 and 8

11. The number $\boxed{n}$ is a multiple of 7 between 30 and 40.

    The number $\boxed{m}$ is a multiple of 9 between 40 and 50.
    Work out $n + m$.

12. True or false:
    (a) 'All multiples of 9 are multiples of 3.'
    (b) 'All factors of 12 are factors of 6.'
    (c) 'All numbers have an even number of different factors.'

13. Which of these are prime numbers: $\boxed{13, 21, 27, 31, 49, 51, 63, 65, 67}$

14. Add together all the prime numbers less than 16.

15. 60 is mid-way between 2 prime numbers. What are they?

16. (a) How many even prime numbers are there?
    (b) How many prime numbers have 5 as their last digit?

17. The number 13 is prime. When the digits are reversed we get 31, and 31 is also prime.
    Find two more numbers with this property.

18. Here are the first three triangle numbers.

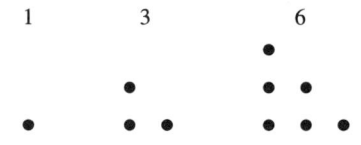

    ```
              1        3           6
                                   •
                       •          • •
              •       • •        • • •
    ```

    Draw similar diagrams to show
    the next two triangle numbers.
    Show that consecutive pairs of triangle numbers add up to make square numbers.

Prime factor decomposition

Factors of a number which are also prime numbers are called prime factors. We can find these prime factors using a 'factor tree'. Here are two examples.

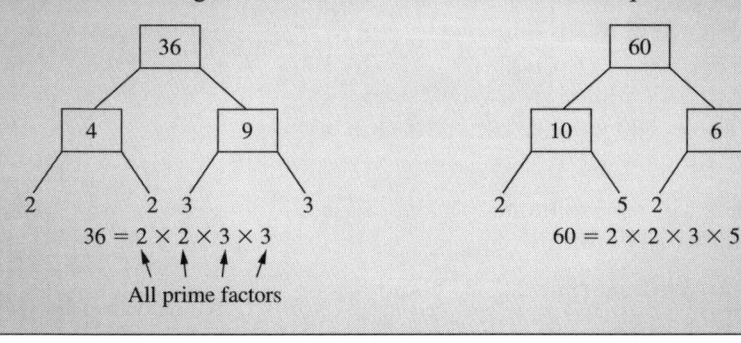

$36 = 2 \times 2 \times 3 \times 3$
↑ ↑ ↑ ↑
All prime factors

$60 = 2 \times 2 \times 3 \times 5$

Exercise 2

1. Draw a factor tree for 108 and for 300. Remember that you only stop when you get to prime numbers.

2. Draw factor trees for the following numbers.
   (a) 24   (b) 81   (c) 84   (d) 200
   (e) 294 (f) 630 (g) 392 (h) 3960

3. $154 = 2 \times 7 \times 11$ and $1365 = 3 \times 5 \times 7 \times 13$. Find the highest common factor of 154 and 1365. [i.e. the highest number that goes into 154 and 1365.]

4. $105 = 3 \times 5 \times 7$ and $330 = 2 \times 3 \times 5 \times 11$. Find the highest common factor of 105 and 330. [i.e. the highest number that goes into 105 and 330.]

5. $975 = 3 \times 5 \times 5 \times 13$ and $550 = 2 \times 5 \times 5 \times 11$.
   Find the highest common factor (H.C.F.) of 975 and 550.

6. Use your answers to Question **1** to find the H.C.F. of 108 and 300.

7. Which prime number is closest to 80?

8. Some prime numbers can be written as the sum of 2 square numbers e.g. $1^2 + 2^2 = 5$.
   Find 5 two-digit prime numbers that can be written as the sum of two square numbers. [Hint: start by listing the square numbers.]

9. Is 689 a prime number? Test by dividing 689 by the prime numbers 2, 3, 5, 7, 11, 13, 17, 19, ... If 689 is divisible by any of these numbers, it is *not* prime.

10. Use your calculator to find which of the following are prime numbers.
    (a) 293 (b) 407 (c) 799 (d) 335
    (e) 709 (f) 1261 (g) 923 (h) 1009

11. The prime numbers up to 100 or 200 can be found as follows:
    - Write the numbers in 8 columns (leave space underneath to go up to 200 later).
    - Cross out 1 and draw circles around 2, 3, 5 and 7.
    - Draw 4 vertical lines to cross out the even numbers (apart from 2).
    - Draw 6 diagonal lines to cross out the multiples of 3.
    - Draw 2 diagonal lines to cross out the multiples of 7.
    - Cross out any numbers ending in 5.
    - Draw circles around all the numbers which have not been crossed out. These are the prime numbers. Check that you have 25 prime numbers up to 100.

1	2	3	4	5	6	7	8
9	10	11	12	13	14	15	16
17	18	19	20	21	22	23	24
25	26	27	28	29	30	31	32
33	34	35	36	37	38	39	40
41	42	43	44	45	46	47	48
49	50	51	52	53	54	55	56
57	58	59	60	61	62	63	64
65	66	67	68	69	70	71	72
73	74	75	76	77	78	79	80
81	82	83	84	85	86	87	88
89	90	91	92	93	94	95	96
97	98	99	100	101	102	103	104

A   B

12. Selmin looked at her circled prime numbers and she thought she noticed a pattern. She thought that all the prime numbers in columns A and B could be written as the sum of two square numbers.
    For example $17 = 1^2 + 4^2$
    $41 = 4^2 + 5^2$

    Was Selmin right? Can *all* the prime numbers in columns A and B be written like this?

13. Extend the table up to 200 and draw in more lines to cross out multiples of 2, 3 and 7. You will also have to cross out any multiples of 11 and 13 which would otherwise be missed. (Can you see why?)
    Does the pattern which Selmin noticed still work?

Part 2

2.1 Estimating and checking answers

Rounding off

- Using a calculator, $\sqrt{11} = 3\cdot3166248$
  We can *round off* this number to either 1 or 2 decimal places.
- Rounding to one decimal place.
  If the figure in the 2nd decimal place is *5 or more*, round up. Otherwise do not
- Rounding to two decimal places.
  If the figure in the 3rd decimal place is *5 or more*, round up. Otherwise do not.

  $2\cdot761 = 2\cdot8$ to 1 d.p.
  $13\cdot45 = 13\cdot5$ to 1 d.p.
  $0\cdot337 = 0\cdot3$ to 1 d.p.

  $1\cdot4281 = 1\cdot43$ to 2 d.p.
  $0\cdot0742 = 0\cdot07$ to 2 d.p.
  $8\cdot555 = 8\cdot56$ to 2 d.p.

Exercise 1

1. Round off these numbers correct to one decimal place.
   (a) 8·24 (b) 7·166 (c) 0·762 (d) 11·27
   (e) 0·352 (f) 8·741 (g) 11·518 (h) 0·648

2. Round off these numbers correct to two decimal places.
   (a) 1·246 (b) 8·043 (c) 11·222 (d) 3·084
   (e) 0·1355 (f) 22·456 (g) 0·8592 (h) 6·097

3. Work out these answers on a calculator and then round off the answers correct to two decimal places.
   (a) $11\cdot21 \div 7$ (b) $0\cdot54 \times 8\cdot1$ (c) $4216 \div 214$ (d) $12\cdot6 \times 0\cdot071$
   (e) $\sqrt{13}$ (f) $\sqrt{8\cdot5}$ (g) $1\cdot36^2$ (h) $0\cdot97^2$
   (i) $0\cdot77 \times 0\cdot78$ (j) $11\cdot82 \div 13$ (k) $2\cdot4 \times 0\cdot716$ (l) $\sqrt{(4\cdot2 \times 3\cdot5)}$

4. Round off these numbers to the nearest hundred..
   (a) 1741 (b) 22 483 (c) 807·1 (d) 15 255
   (e) 562·8 (f) 2222   (g) 3552 (h) 1027

Estimating lengths

Exercise 2

1. Estimate the lengths shown. Use the ruler as a guide

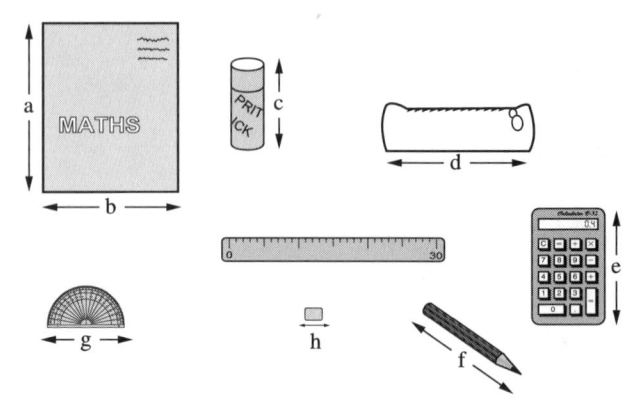

2. Look at the picture. The person is about 2 metres tall.

   Estimate the height of:

   (a) The top of the roof of the house
   (b) The ladder
   (c) The tree
   (d) The telegraph pole
   (e) The nest box on the tree.

3. Estimate the reading on each thermometer.

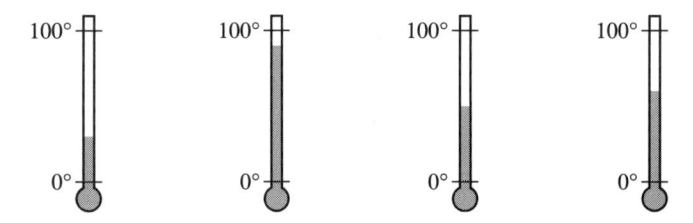

Calculating with estimates

- Harry worked out $506 \cdot 3 \div 9 \cdot 5$ and wrote down $5 \cdot 3295$.
  He can check his answer by working with estimates.
  Instead of $506 \cdot 3$ use 500, instead of $9 \cdot 5$ use 10.
   So $500 \div 10 = 50$.
  Clearly Harry's answer is wrong. He put the decimal point in the wrong place.

- Here are three more calculations with estimates.

    (a) $31 \cdot 2 \times 9 \cdot 2$ (b) $28 \cdot 4 \div 0 \cdot 971$ (c) 11% of £78·99
    $\approx 30 \times 10$ $\approx 30 \div 1$ $\approx \frac{1}{10}$ of £80
    ≈ 300 ≈ 30 $\approx$ £8

Exercise 3

Do not use a calculator. Decide, by estimating, which of the three answers is closest to the exact answer. Write the calculation and the approximate answer for each question (use $\approx$).

	Calculation	A	B	C
1.	$97 \cdot 9 \times 11 \cdot 3$	90	500	1000
2.	$6 \cdot 73 \times 9 \cdot 65$	30	70	300
3.	$1 \cdot 03 \times 60 \cdot 6$	6	60	200
4.	$2 \cdot 3 \times 96$	200	90	20
5.	$18 \cdot 9 \times 21 \cdot 4$	200	400	4000
6.	$5 \cdot 14 \times 5 \cdot 99$	15	10	30
7.	$811 \times 11 \cdot 72$	8000	4000	800
8.	99×98	1 million	100 000	10 000
9.	$1 \cdot 09 \times 29 \cdot 6$	20	30	60
10.	$81\,413 \times 10 \cdot 96$	8 million	1 million	800 000
11.	$601 \div 3 \cdot 92$	50	100	150
12.	$402 \div 4 \cdot 97$	8	0·8	80
13.	$58 \cdot 4 \div 0 \cdot 98$	60	300	600
14.	$0 \cdot 2 \times 111 \cdot 3$	10	20	180
15.	$217 \div 201 \cdot 4$	0·2	1	10
16.	$88 \cdot 4 + 95 + 141$	300	100	3000
17.	$0 \cdot 32 + 0 \cdot 294$	0·06	0·1	0·6
18.	$10 \cdot 1^3 \times 8 \cdot 4$	800	4000	8000
19.	24% of £16 100	£40	£400	£4000
20.	11% of £198·20	£10	£20	£200

Exercise 4

Do not use a calculator for these questions.

1. A do-it-yourself table and chairs kit cost £38·49. Estimate the total cost of 11 kits.

2. Daily disposable contact lenses cost 96p per pair. Find the approximate cost of 2 years supply of lenses.

3. A cut-price video was sold at £6.95 per copy. Estimate the total cost of 42 copies.

4. The rent for a flat is £95 per week. Estimate the total spent on rent in one year.

5. 2105 people share the cost of hiring a cruise boat. Roughly how much does each person pay, if the total cost was half a million pounds?

6. A boxer earned a fee of $5 million for a fight which lasted 1 minute 35 seconds. Estimate the money he earned per second of the fight.

In Questions **7** and **8** there are six calculations and six answers. Write down each calculation and insert the correct answer from the list given. Use estimation.

7. (a) 5·9 × 6·1   (b) 19·8 ÷ 5   (c) 32 × 9·9
   (d) 0·89 + 14·7   (e) 4·5 × 44   (f) 4141 ÷ 40

Answers:	198, 35·99, 103·5, 15·59, 316·8, 3·96

8. (a) 102·8 ÷ 5   (b) 11·2 ÷ 98·6   (c) 3 × 0·41
   (d) 34 × 2·9   (e) 51 × 3·9   (f) 238·6 ÷ 4·7

Answers:	50·76, 20·56, 1·23, 198·9, 98·6, 0·114

9. Write the decimal point in the correct place.
   (a) length of a football pitch   9572 m
   (b) weight of an 'average' new born baby   3124 kg
   (c) width of this book   1831 mm
   (d) area of the classroom floor   560 m^2
   (e) weight of a packet of sugar   100 kg
   (f) diameter of a football   3140 cm

10. At a fun fair, customers pay 95p for a ride on a giant spinning wheel. The operator sells 2483 tickets during the weekend and his costs for electricity and rent were £114. Estimate his profit over the weekend.

11. A quick way of adding lots of figures on a shopping bill is to round every number to the nearest pound.
So £2·43 becomes £2, £0·91 becomes £1, £0·24 becomes £0 and so on.

(a) Use this method to estimate the totals below:

(i) WSKAS COCKTAIL *	0.85	(ii) PLN BAGUETTE		0.49
H/EATING MINCE	3.95	FOIL	*	0.65
HAWAIIAN CRN	1.85	LETTUCE ROUND		0.24
PAIN AU CHOC	0.54	JW TUNA MAYO		0.75
PAIN AU CHOC	0.54	SOYA MILK		0.47
PAIN AU CHOC	0.54	SOYA MILK		0.47
BUTTER	0.89	ORNGE MRMLDE		0.74
BUTTER	0.89	YOGHURT		0.99
EGGS	0.78	SPGHTI/HOOPS		0.26
PORK/CHICK/PIE	2.03	CHEESE		1.34
MED.MAT.CHDR.	1.21	WHISKAS	*	0.45
HOT PIES	1.47	WHISKAS	*	0.45
POT. WAFFLES	1.39	VINEGAR		0.68
WHOLE BRIE	1.01	KING EDWARDS.		0.99
MUFFINS	0.49	UHT H/FAT MILK	*	0.26
BACON RASHERS	0.65	APPLES		1.89
BEETROOT	0.99	WHISKAS	*	0.45
LOOSE CHEESE	0.99	PEACHES		0.24
		FROM. FRAIS		0.72

(b) Use a calculator to work out the exact total for part (i). Compare the answer with your estimate above.

12. Estimate:

(a) the number of times your heart beats in one day (24 h),

(b) the thickness of one page in this book.

13. (a) In 1989 thousands of people formed a human chain right across the U.S.A., a distance of about 4300 km.
Estimate the number of people in the chain.

(b) Estimate the number of people needed to form a chain right around the equator. (Assume you have enough people volunteering to float for a while in the sea.) The distance right around the equator is about 40 000 km.

14. Give an estimate for each of the following calculations

(a) $\dfrac{62 \cdot 4 \times 19 \cdot 3}{10 \cdot 7}$

(b) $\dfrac{3198 - 207}{93 \cdot 7}$

(c) 52% of £987·50

(d) $30 \cdot 23^2 - 112$

(e) $\frac{2}{3}$ of 589 m

(f) $\dfrac{407 \cdot 5 + 2 \cdot 794}{15 \cdot 6 + 24 \cdot 7}$

Checking answers

Here are five calculations followed by appropriate checks, using inverse operations.
(a) $22.5 \div 5 = 4.5$ check $4.5 \times 5 = 22.5$
(b) $29.5 - 1.47 = 28.03$ check $28.03 + 1.47$
(c) $78.5 \times 20 = 1570$ check $1570 \div 20$
(d) $\sqrt{11} = 3.31662$ check 3.31662^2
(e) $14.7 + 28.1 + 17.4 + 9.9$ check $9.9 + 17.4 + 28.1 + 14.7$
[add in reverse order]

Exercise 5

1. Work out the following and check using inverse operations
   (a) $83.5 \times 20 = \square$ check $\square \div 20$
   (b) $104 - 13.2 = \square$ check $\square + 13.2$
   (c) $228.2 \div 7 = \square$ check $\square \times 7$
   (d) $\sqrt{28} = \square$ check $\square^2$
   (e) $11.5 + 2.7 + 9.8 + 20.7$ check $20.7 + 9.8 + 2.7 + 11.5$

2. (a) Will the answer to 64×0.8 be larger or smaller than 64?
   (b) Will the answer to $210 \div 0.7$ be larger or smaller than 210?
   (c) Will the answer to 17.4×0.9 be larger or smaller than 17.4?

3. Here are the answers obtained by six children. Some are correct but some are clearly impossible or highly unlikely.
   Decide which answers are 'OK' and which are 'impossible' or 'highly unlikely'.

   (a) Top speed of winning snail = 10 m/sec
   (b) Time taken to walk 1 mile to school = 21 minutes
   (c) The height of Mrs Brown's washing machine = 315 cm
   (d) Number of bricks needed to build a 2 bedroom house = 1 million
   (e) The mean value of the numbers 32, 35, 31, 36, 32 = 37.8
   (f) One per cent of the UK population = 60 000 people.

Estimating game

- This is a game for two players. On squared paper draw an answer grid with the numbers shown.

Answer grid

198	1089	99	100	360	18
180	450	22	440	155	1980
1240	200	45	62	100	550
40	620	495	279	800	55
2000	80	220	10	891	250
4950	1550	1000	3960	3069	341

- The players now take turns to choose two numbers from the question grid below and multiply them on a calculator.

Question grid

2	5	9
11	20	31
40	50	99

The number obtained is crossed out on the answer grid using the player's own colour.

- The game continues until all the numbers in the answer grid have been crossed out. The object is to get four answers in a line (horizontally, vertically or diagonally). The winner is the player with most lines of four.

- A line of *five* counts as *two* lines of four.
  A line of *six* counts as *three* lines of four.

2.2 Rules of algebra

- A algebraic *expression* is formed from letter symbols and numbers. For example $3n$, $4n+5$ and $1-2x$ are all expressions. Notice that there is no equals sign in an expression.

- In an *equation*, like $2n-1=15$, n is one particular unknown number.

- In the *formula* $A = LB$, A, L and B are variable quantities, related by the formula.
  If we know the values of L and B we can calculate the value of A.

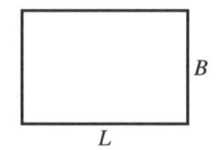

- In the *function* $y = 2x + 7$, the value of y can be found for any chosen value of x.

Basic algebra

- $3 \times n = 3n$
  $m \times n = mn$
  $n \times (a+b) = n(a+b)$
  $(c+d) \div x = \dfrac{c+d}{x}$

- Like terms can be added:
  $3a + b + 2a + 5b = 5a + 6b$
  $n^2 + 3n^2 = 4n^2$
  $4n + 5 - 2n - 8 = 2n - 3$

- Cancelling fractions:
  $\dfrac{\cancel{4} \times 3}{\cancel{4}} = 3 \qquad \dfrac{2 \times \cancel{d}}{\cancel{d}} = 2$

  $\dfrac{\cancel{n} \times n \times n}{\cancel{n}} = n^2 \qquad \dfrac{6x}{2} = 3x$

- A flow diagram can be used to show the correct order of operations.
  For the expression $3(4n-1)$ we have:

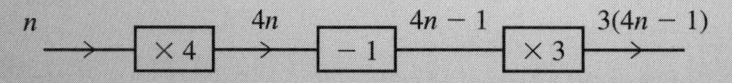

  $n \longrightarrow \boxed{\times 4} \xrightarrow{4n} \boxed{-1} \xrightarrow{4n-1} \boxed{\times 3} \xrightarrow{3(4n-1)}$

- Sometimes you are not sure that two expressions are the same.
  Check by putting in numbers.

  (a) Is $2n^2$ equal to $(2n)^2$?
  Try $n = 1$: $2n^2 = 2 \times 1^2$
  $\qquad\qquad\qquad\; = 2$
  $\qquad\quad (2n)^2 = (2 \times 1)^2$
  $\qquad\qquad\qquad\; = 4$
  So $2n^2 \neq (2n)^2$

  (b) Is $\dfrac{6n}{3}$ equal to $2n$?

  Try $n = 1$: $\dfrac{6n}{3} = \dfrac{6 \times 1}{3} = 2$

  $\qquad\qquad\quad 2n = 2 \times 1 = 2$

  So $\dfrac{6n}{3} = 2n$

Exercise 1

In questions **1** to **15** answer 'true' or 'false'.

1. $5 \times n = 5 + n$
2. $a \times a = a^2$
3. $a + b = b + a$
4. $t \times t \times t = 3t$
5. $h \times 3 = 3h$
6. $p - q = q - p$
7. $a + A = 2a$
8. $a + a^2 = a^3$
9. $n \times n \times n = n^3$
10. $4n - n = 4$
11. $a \div 5 = \dfrac{a}{5}$
12. $(a + b) \div n = \dfrac{a+b}{n}$
13. $m \div 4 = 4 \div m$
14. $\dfrac{n+n}{n} = 2$
15. $a \times b \times a = a^2 b$

16. Here are some cards. $\boxed{3n}$ $\boxed{n+2}$ $\boxed{n+n}$ $\boxed{n}$ $\boxed{n^2}$ $\boxed{2n \div 2}$ $\boxed{n^3}$ $\boxed{n-2}$ $\boxed{3n-n}$ $\boxed{2 \div n}$ $\boxed{n \times n}$

    (a) Which cards will always be the same as $\boxed{2n}$?

    (b) Which card will always be the same as $\boxed{n \times n \times n}$?

    (c) Which card will always be the same as $\boxed{\dfrac{2}{n}}$?

    (d) Draw a new card which will always be the same as $\boxed{2n + 2n}$.

17. In the expression $3(2n + 4)$, three operations are performed in the following order:

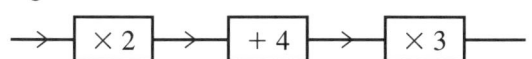

    $\rightarrow \boxed{\times 2} \rightarrow \boxed{+ 4} \rightarrow \boxed{\times 3} \rightarrow$

    Draw similar diagrams to show the correct order of operations for the following expressions.

    (a) $4n - 3$
    (b) $7(6n + 3)$
    (c) $\dfrac{5n - 2}{3}$
    (d) $x^2 + 5$
    (e) $(x + 2)^2$
    (f) $\dfrac{(3x^2 - 2)}{5}$

In Questions **18** to **32** simplify the expressions.

18. $\dfrac{n}{n}$
19. $\dfrac{5a}{a}$
20. $\dfrac{n^2}{n}$
21. $2n^2 - n^2$
22. $a + b + c + a$
23. $m - 3 + 3m$
24. $pq + pq$
25. $\dfrac{n \times n \times n}{n}$
26. $\dfrac{a + a + a}{a}$
27. $\dfrac{4x}{2}$
28. $\dfrac{a^2}{a^3}$
29. $\dfrac{n}{2} + \dfrac{n}{2}$
30. $3p - 1 - 3p + 2$
31. $8n \div 8$
32. $a^2 \times a$

Using letters for numbers

> Find the expressions you are left with.
>
> (a) Start with n, multiply by 5 and then add 8. $\quad n \longrightarrow 5n \longrightarrow 5n+8$
>
> (b) Start with a, subtract b and then add 10. $\quad a \longrightarrow a-b \longrightarrow a-b+10$
>
> (c) Start with p, add 3 then multiply the result by 4. $\quad p \longrightarrow p+3 \longrightarrow 4(p+3)$
>
> (d) Start with m, subtract t and then square the result. $\quad m \longrightarrow m-t \longrightarrow (m-t)^2$
>
> Notice that *brackets* are needed in parts (c) and (d).

Exercise 2

Write down the expression you get. If any of your answers contain brackets, do not remove them.

1. Start with n, multiply by 5 then add x.
2. Start with n, add x and then multiply the result by 5.
3. Start with h, multiply by 6 and then subtract t.
4. Start with h, subtract t and then multiply the result by 6.
5. Start with b, add x and then multiply the result by 5.
6. Start with b, multiply by a and then add x.
7. Start with y, square it and then multiply the result by 3.
8. Start with n, multiply by d and then subtract 3.
9. Start with a, double it and then add A.
10. Start with h, subtract H and then multiply the result by 5.
11. Start with x, subtract 8 and then multiply the result by 5.
12. Start with x, square it and then add 2.
13. Start with y, double it and then subtract 3.
14. Start with a, add 10 and then square the result.
15. Here is a flow diagram for the expression $2(3n+7)$

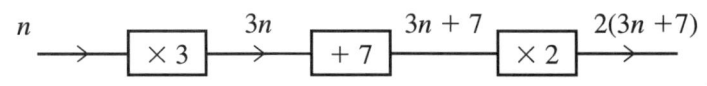

    $n \longrightarrow \boxed{\times 3} \xrightarrow{3n} \boxed{+7} \xrightarrow{3n+7} \boxed{\times 2} \xrightarrow{2(3n+7)}$

    Find the expression for each of the following flow charts:

    (a) $n \to \boxed{\times 2} \to \boxed{-4} \to \boxed{\times 5} \to$
    (b) $n \to \boxed{\times 5} \to \boxed{+7} \to \boxed{\times 3} \to$
    (c) $n \to \boxed{+2} \to \boxed{\times 5} \to \boxed{-3} \to$
    (d) $n \to \boxed{\div 2} \to \boxed{+6} \to \boxed{\times 4} \to$
    (e) $n \to \boxed{\text{square}} \to \boxed{+7} \to \boxed{\times 8} \to$
    (f) $n \to \boxed{+3} \to \boxed{\text{square}} \to \boxed{\times 6} \to$

16. Draw the flow diagram for the following expressions.

    (a) $2n+7$
    (b) $3(5n-3)$
    (c) $\dfrac{6n+1}{5}$
    (d) n^2-3
    (e) $(n+5)^2$
    (f) $3(n^2-1)$

Write down the expression you get.

17. Start with y, cube it, add 6, and then treble the result.
18. Start with x, multiply by 4 and then take the result *away from* 15.
19. Start with y, double it and then take the result away from 10.
20. Start with x, take it away from 3 and then multiply the result by 6.
21. Start with a, multiply by 7, take the result away from 12 and then multiply the result by 4.
22. A girl has 82 pence. If she spends c pence, how much is she left with?
23. Terry has 30 pence. His father then gives him another t pence and then he spends h pence. How much money does he have now?
24. A machine makes x chocolates every minute. It runs for 5 minutes, after which 7 of the chocolates are rejected. How many good chocolates did the machine make in the 5 minutes?
25. A small bag of peanuts contains y nuts, and a large bag contains 5 times as many. If a boy buys a large bag and then eats 9 nuts, how many are left in his bag?
26. Bill used to earn £d per week. He then had a rise of £6 per week. How much will he now earn in 7 weeks?
27. A tile weighs t kg. How much do n tiles weigh?

Exercise 3

1. Draw your own addition square like the one shown here.

	1	2	3	4	5	6	7	8	9
1	2	3	4	5	6	7	8	9	10
2	3	4	5	6	7	8	9	10	11
3	4	5	6	7	8	9	10	11	12
4	5	6	7	8	9	10	11	12	13
5	6	7	8	9	10	11	12	13	14
6	7	8	9	10	11	12	13	14	15
7	8	9	10	11	12	13	14	15	16
8	9	10	11	12	13	14	15	16	17
9	10	11	12	13	14	15	16	17	18

2. Here are some 2 by 2 squares taken from the main square.

4	5
5	6

9	10
10	11

14	15
15	16

Add up the four numbers in each square. What do you notice?

3. In this 2 by 2 square the smallest number is 8. Draw the square and fill in the missing numbers.

8	?
?	?

4. In another 2 by 2 square the *largest* number is 8. Draw the square and fill in the missing numbers.

5. In a 2 by 2 square the four numbers add up to 44. Draw the square and fill in the numbers.

6. Here is a 3 by 3 square taken from the main square. Add up the nine numbers in the square. What do you notice?

4	5	6
5	6	7
6	7	8

7. Add up the four *corner* numbers in a 3 by 3 square. Copy and complete this sentence: 'In a 3 by 3 square the sum of the four corner numbers is _____ times the middle number.'

8. (a) Here is a 2 by 2 square. The top left number is x. The other three main numbers are shown.

x	$x+1$
$x+1$	$x+2$

(b) Draw the three squares shown and use x's to write down the other 3 numbers in each square.

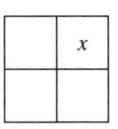

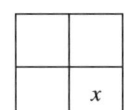

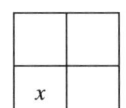

9. This is harder. Draw the square shown and use x's to fill in the other 8 numbers.

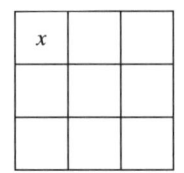

10. Draw this square and then use x's to write down the other 3 *corner* numbers.

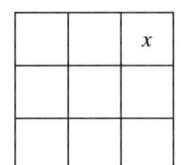

11. We do not always use x. What are the 4 corner numbers in this square?

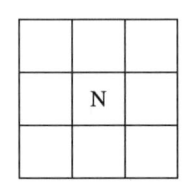

12. A large 'T' can be drawn inside the number square so that all 5 numbers in the T are inside the square.

1	2	3	4	5	6	7	8
9	10	11	12	13	14	15	16
17	18	19	20	21	22	23	24
25	26	27	28	29	30	31	32
33	34	35	36	37	38	39	40
41	42	43	44	45	46	47	48
49	50	51	52	53	54	55	56
57	58	59	60	61	62	63	64

The T can be moved around but it must stay upright.
The 'T-number' is the number in the middle of the top row. So this is T18.

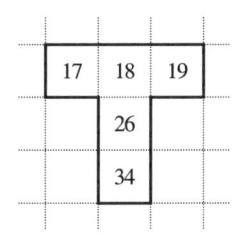

17	18	19
	26	
	34	

(a) What is the smallest possible T-number?

(b) Work out the total of the numbers in T21

(c) Work out, as *quickly* as you can
(Total of numbers in T37) − (Total of numbers in T36)

(d) Fill in the numbers for T75

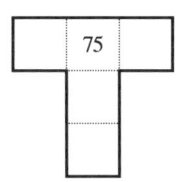

(e) Use x's to write the numbers for Tx

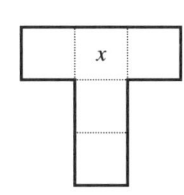

2.3 Geometrical reasoning

Angle facts reminder

- The angles in a triangle add up to 180°.

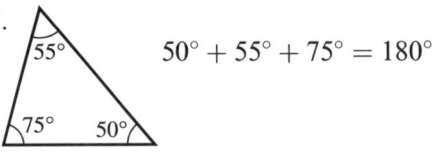

$50° + 55° + 75° = 180°$

An *isosceles* triangle has two equal angles and two equal sides. Isosceles triangles have line symmetry.

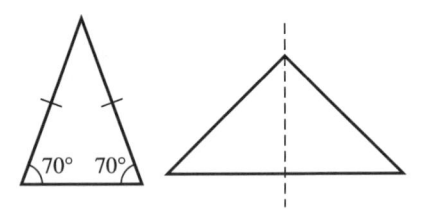

- The angles on a straight line add up to 180°.

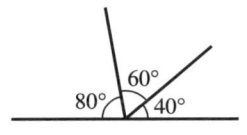

- The angles at a point add up to 360°.

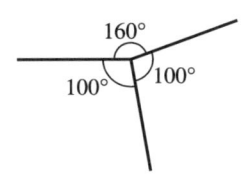

Angles in quadrilaterals

Draw a quadrilateral of any shape on a piece of paper or card and cut it out. Mark the four angles *a*, *b*, *c* and *d* and tear them off.

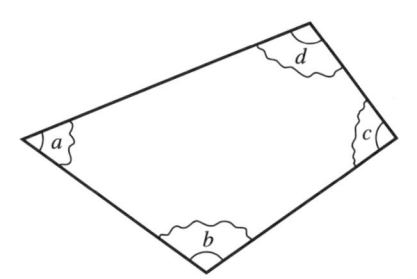

Arrange the four angles about a point

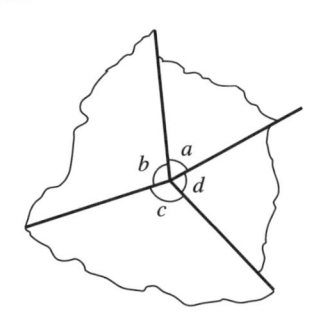

The angles in a quadrilateral add up to 360°

Exercise 1

Find the angles marked with letters.

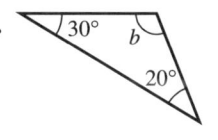

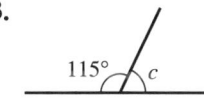

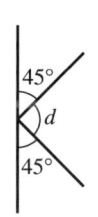

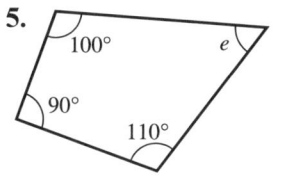

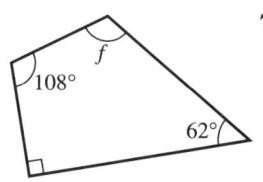

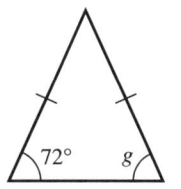

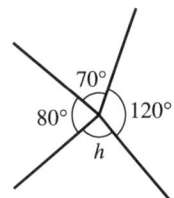

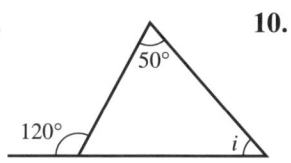

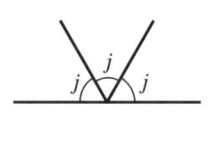

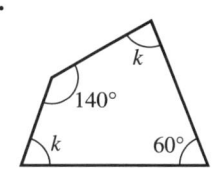

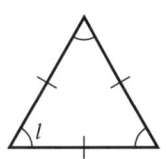

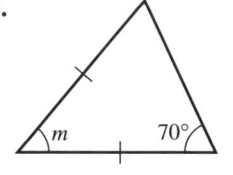

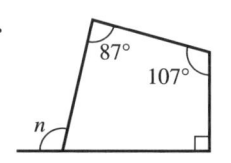

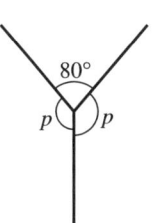

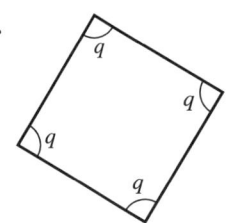

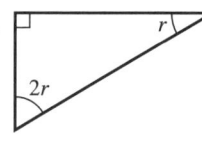

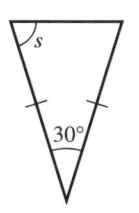

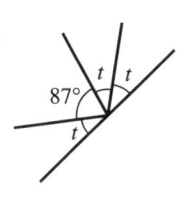

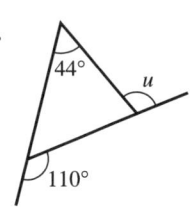

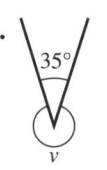

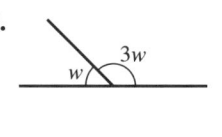

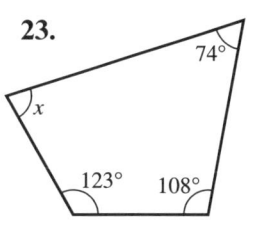

1. Triangle with angles 70°, 40°, and a.

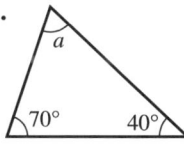

2. Triangle with angles 30°, 20°, and b.

3. Angles on a straight line: 115° and c.

4. Angles around a point on a line: 45°, 45°, and d.

5. Pentagon with angles 100°, 90°, 110°, e, and one more.

6. Quadrilateral with angles 108°, 62°, 90° (right angle), and f.

7. Isosceles triangle with base angles 72° and g.

8. Angles around a point: 70°, 120°, 80°, and h.

9. Triangle with exterior angle 120°, interior 50°, and i.

10. Three equal angles j, j, j on a straight line.

11. Quadrilateral with angles 140°, 60°, k, k.

12. Equilateral triangle, angle l.

13. Isosceles triangle with 70° and m.

14. Quadrilateral with 87°, 107°, 90°, and n.

15. Angles around a point: 80°, p, p.

16. Quadrilateral with four angles q.

17. Right triangle with angles 90°, r, $2r$.

18. Isosceles triangle with apex 30° and s.

19. Three angles t, t, t with 87°.

20. Triangle with 44°, 110°, and u.

21. Angle 35° with reflex angle v.

22. Angles on a line: w and $3w$.

23. Quadrilateral with 74°, 108°, 123°, and x.

24. Isosceles triangle with line of symmetry, 20° at apex and base angle y.

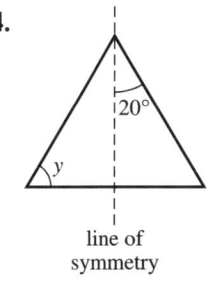

Angles and parallel lines

Two straight lines are *parallel* if they never meet.
They are always the same distance apart.
In the diagram, lines AB and CD are parallel.
Lines which are parallel are marked with arrows.
The line XY cuts AB and CD.

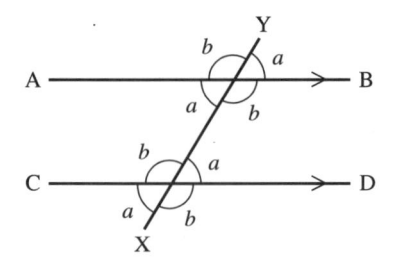

All the angles marked *a* are equal.
All the angles marked *b* are equal.
Remember:

'All the acute angles are equal and all the obtuse angles are equal.'

Many people prefer to think about 'Z' angles, (alternate angles) and 'F' angles (corresponding angles)

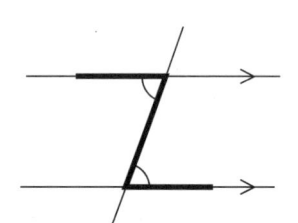

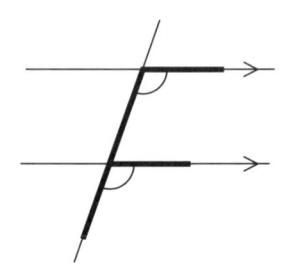

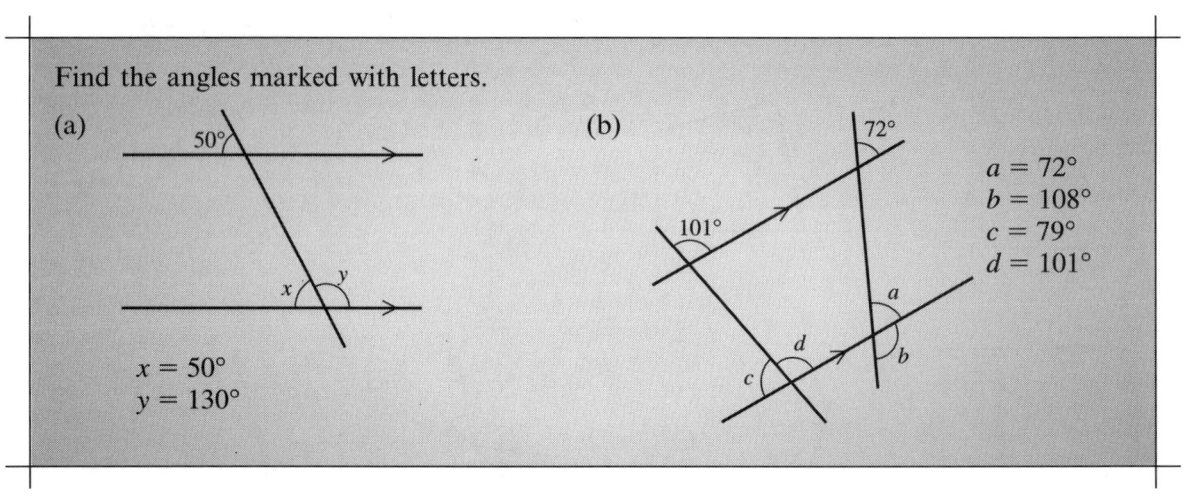

Find the angles marked with letters.

(a) $x = 50°$
$y = 130°$

(b) $a = 72°$
$b = 108°$
$c = 79°$
$d = 101°$

Exercise 2

Find the angles marked with letters.

1. 70°, a, b, c

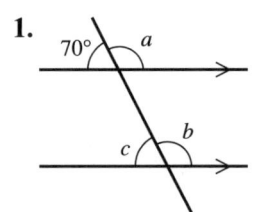

2. 65°, d, e, f

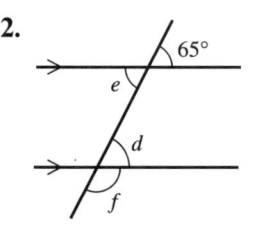

3. 104°, g, h, i

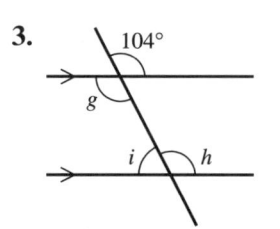

4. m, 68°, k, l

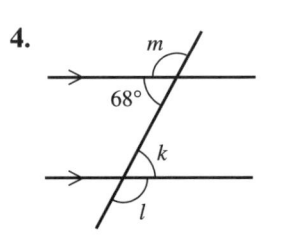

5. [diagram with angles 69°, o, n]
6. [diagram with angles 60°, b, 65°, a, c]
7. [diagram with angles 130°, e, f, d, 55°]
8. [diagram with angles 73°, p, q, s, r, 97°]
9. [diagram with angles 40°, 80°, t, s, u]
10. [diagram with angles v, 49°, w]
11. [diagram with angles 50°, 64°, c, b, a]
12. [diagram with angles 30°, 85°, d, e, f]

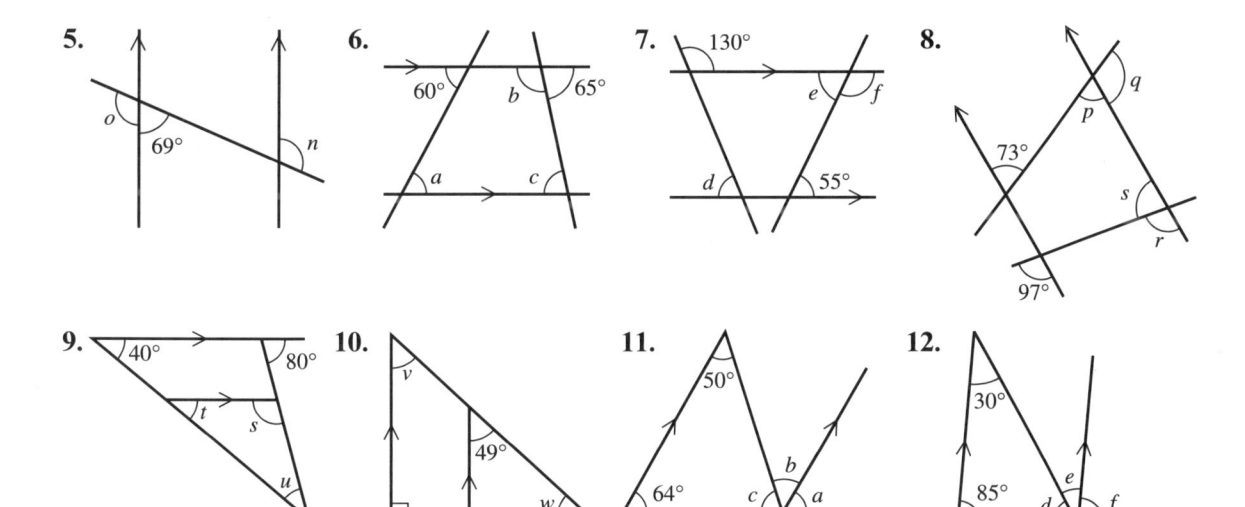

Mixed questions

Exercise 3

This exercise contains a mixture of questions which require a knowledge of all parts of this section.

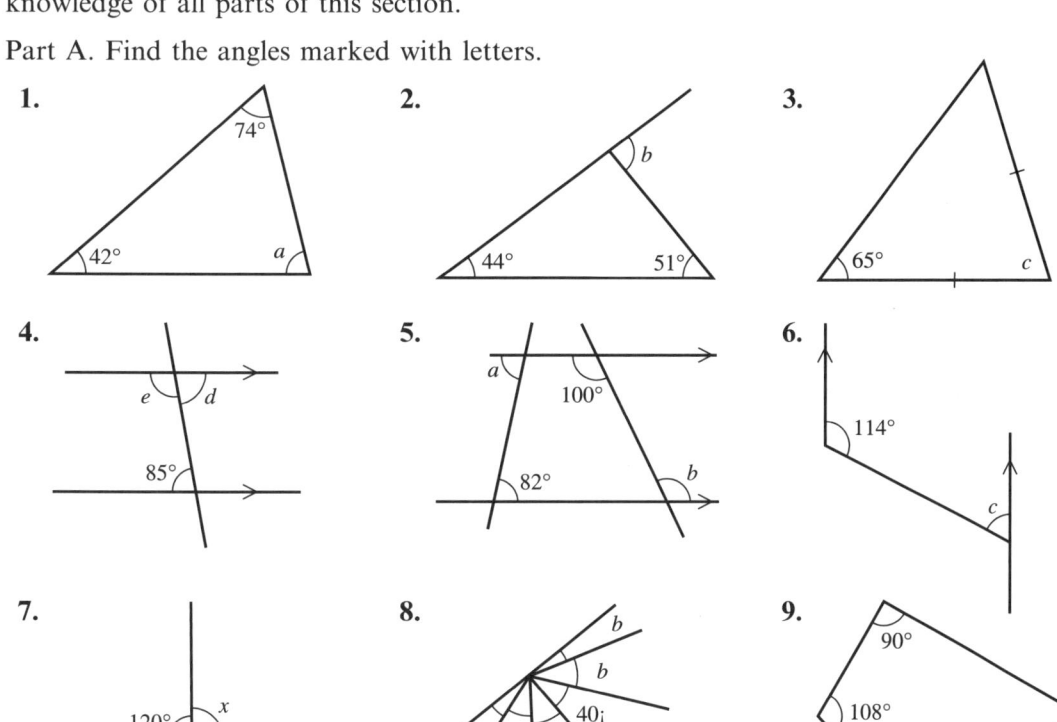

Part A. Find the angles marked with letters.

1. [triangle with angles 74°, 42°, a]
2. [triangle with angles b, 44°, 51°]
3. [triangle with angles 65°, c, and two equal sides marked]
4. [parallel lines with angles e, d, 85°]
5. [diagram with angles a, 100°, 82°, b]
6. [diagram with angles 114°, c]
7. [intersecting lines with 120°, x, x, x]
8. [diagram with angles b, b, 40°, b, b, b]
9. [quadrilateral with angles 90°, 108°, 94°, y]

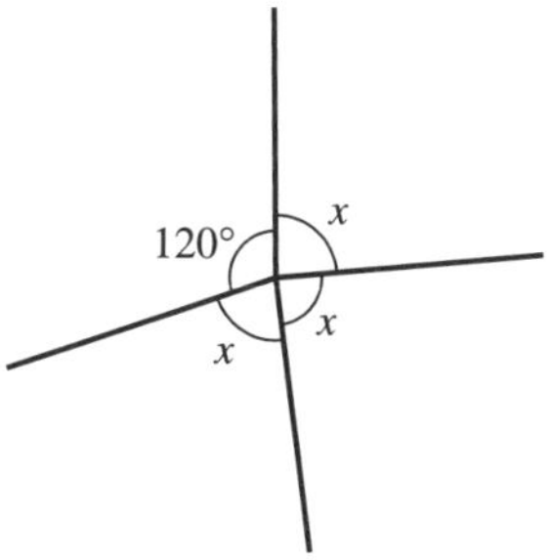

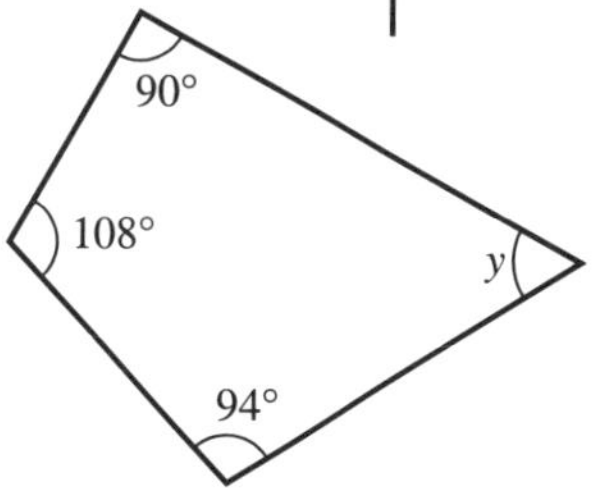

10. (quadrilateral with angles 95°, 77°, 83°, x)

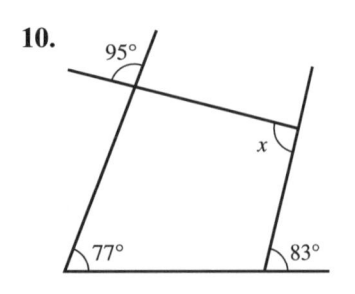

11. (triangle with angles 2c, 3c, c)

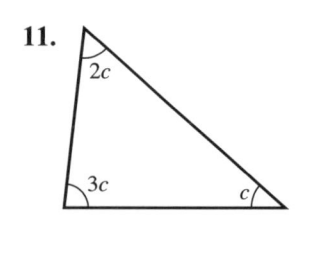

12. (triangle with 70° at top, 115° exterior on left, d exterior on right)

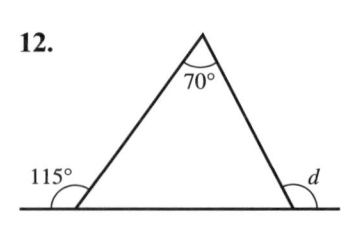

Part B
Find the angles marked with letters. Draw each diagram and show your working.

13. (isosceles triangle with exterior angle b)

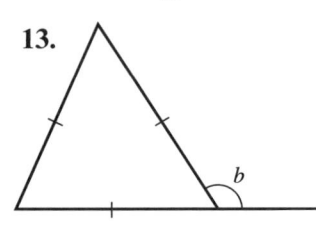

14. (isosceles triangle with apex c, base exterior 110°)

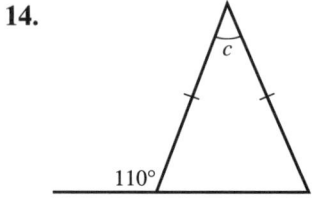

15. (trapezium with parallel sides, angles x, 100°, 75°, y)

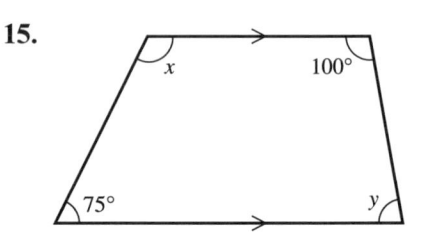

16. (triangle with 50° at top, marks indicating isosceles, f at bottom left)

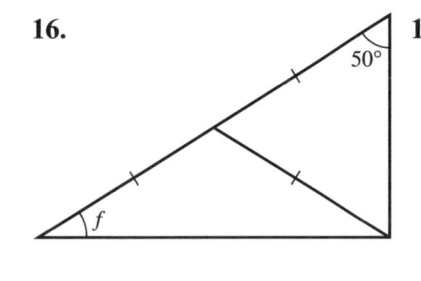

17. (triangle with 55°, 25°, d)

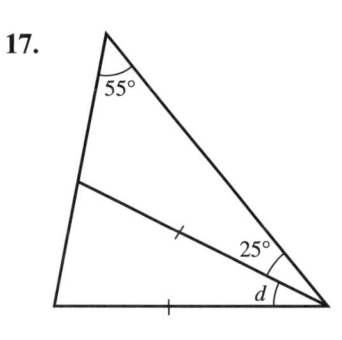

18. (isosceles triangle with 66°, and e between triangle and a parallel line)

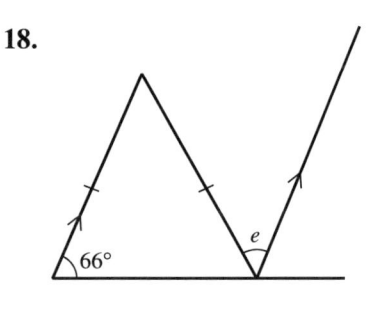

Proving results

- So far we have *demonstrated* that the sum of the angles in a quadrilateral is 360°, by cutting out the angles and rearranging them. A demonstration like this might not work for every conceivable quadrilateral. When we *prove* results it means that the result is true for every possible shape. We often prove one simple result and then use that result to prove further results (and so on).

- Example
  When straight lines intersect, opposite angles are equal.
  By definition, the angle on one whole turn is 360°.
  So $a + b + a + b = 360°$
  $\therefore$ $a + b = 180°$
  This proves that the sum of the angles on a straight line is 180°.

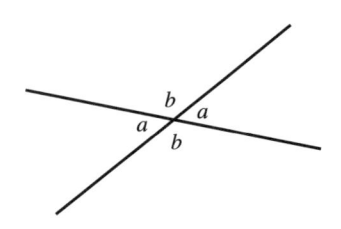

Exercise 4

1. Copy and complete this proof for the sum of the angles in a triangle.

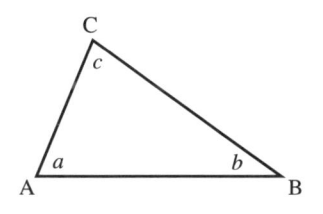

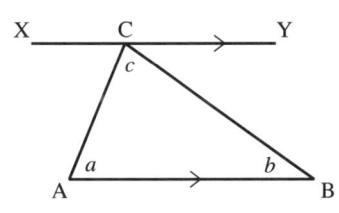

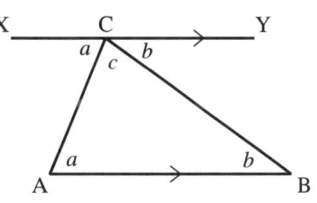

Here is △ABC.   Draw line XCY parallel to AB.

$A\widehat{B}C = Y\widehat{C}B$ alternate angles)
$B\widehat{A}C = \boxed{}$ (alternate angles)
$a + b + c = \boxed{}$ (angles on a straight line)
angles in a triangle: $a + b + c = 180°$

2. Copy and complete this proof for the sum of the angles in a quadrilateral.

Draw any quadrilateral ABCD with diagonal BD.

Now $a + b + c = \boxed{}$ (angles in a △)

and $d + e + f = \boxed{}$ (angles in a △)

∴ $a + b + c + d + e + f = \boxed{}$

This proves the result.

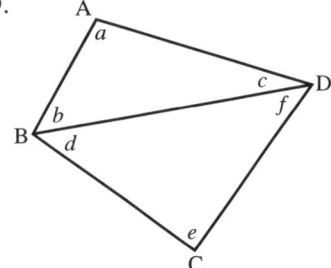

3. To prove that the exterior angle of a triangle is equal to the sum of the two interior opposite angles.

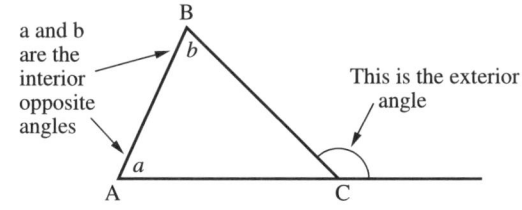

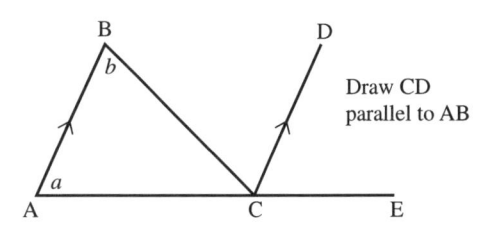

a and b are the interior opposite angles

This is the exterior angle

Draw CD parallel to AB

Copy and complete the proof:

$B\widehat{A}C = D\widehat{C}E$ (corresponding angles) ('F' angles)

$A\widehat{B}C = \boxed{}$ (alternate angles) ('Z' angles)

∴ $\boxed{} = \boxed{} + \boxed{}$

4. Explain why opposite angles of a parallelogram are equal.

[Use alternate and corresponding angles.]

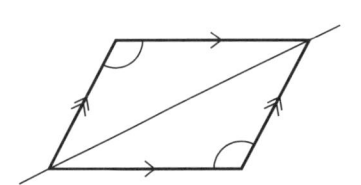

2.4 Construction and locus

Constructing a triangle given three sides

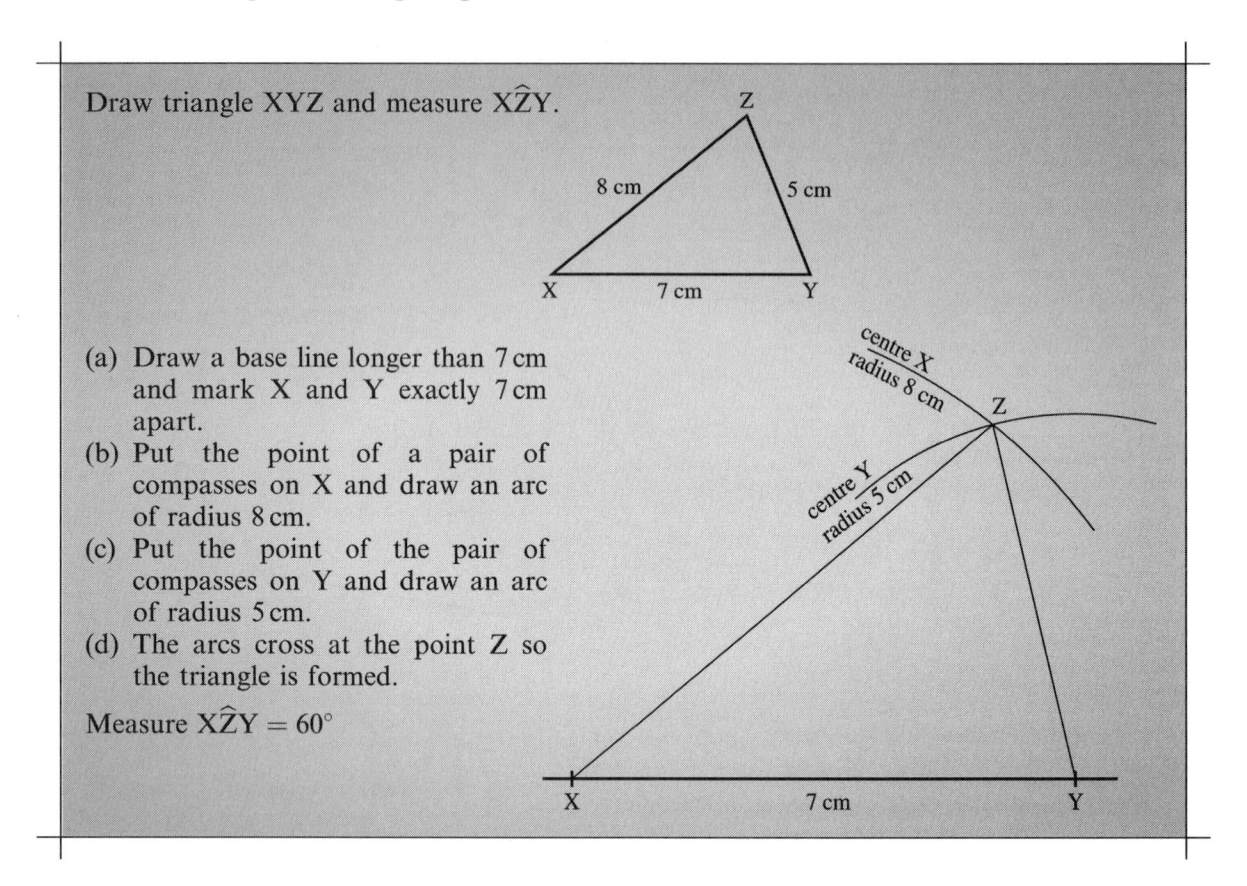

Draw triangle XYZ and measure $X\hat{Z}Y$.

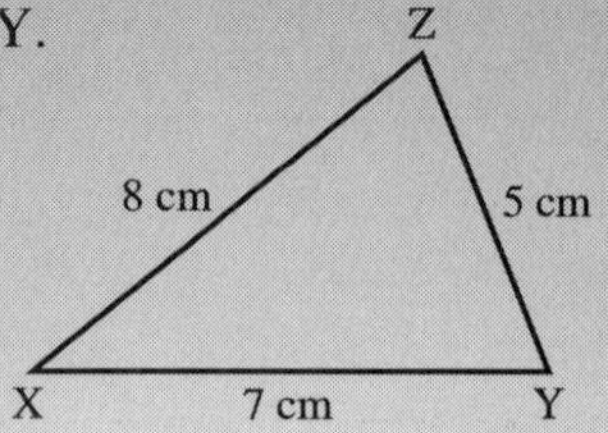
Z
8 cm
5 cm
X
7 cm
Y

(a) Draw a base line longer than 7 cm and mark X and Y exactly 7 cm apart.

(b) Put the point of a pair of compasses on X and draw an arc of radius 8 cm.

(c) Put the point of the pair of compasses on Y and draw an arc of radius 5 cm.

(d) The arcs cross at the point Z so the triangle is formed.

Measure $X\hat{Z}Y = 60°$

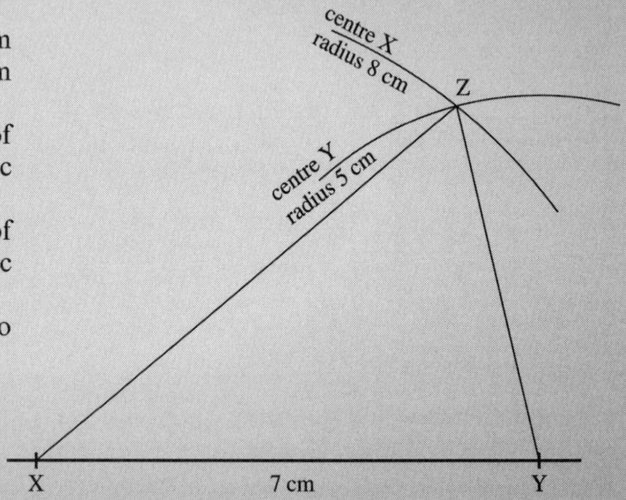
centre X
radius 8 cm
Z
centre Y
radius 5 cm
X
7 cm
Y

Exercise 1

In Questions **1** to **6** construct each triangle and measure the angle x.

1.

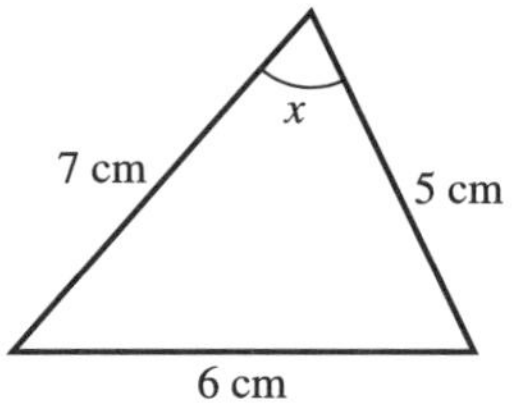
x
7 cm
5 cm
6 cm

2.

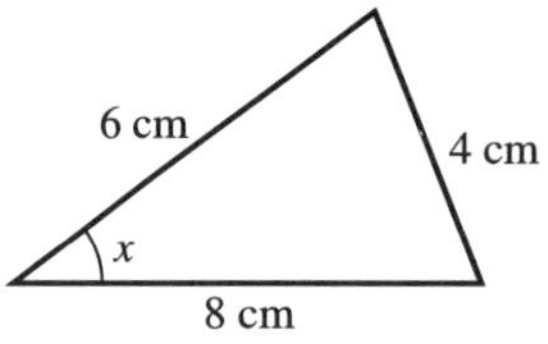
6 cm
4 cm
x
8 cm

3.

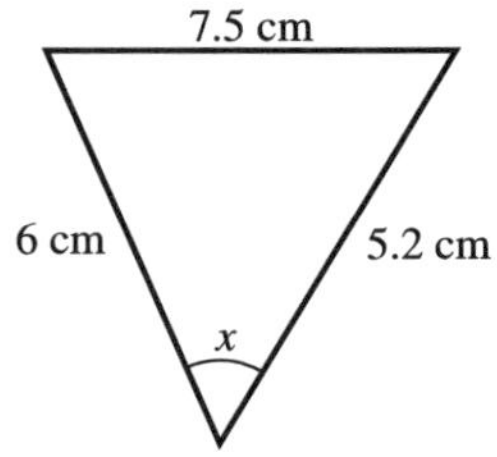
7.5 cm
6 cm
5.2 cm
x

4.

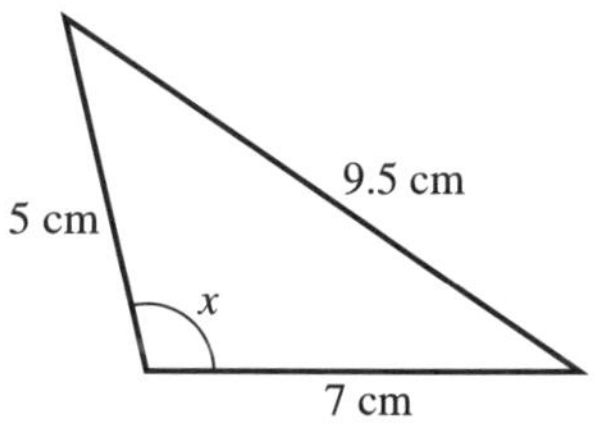

5 cm, 9.5 cm, 7 cm, angle x

5.

5.5 cm, 8 cm, 8.2 cm, angle x

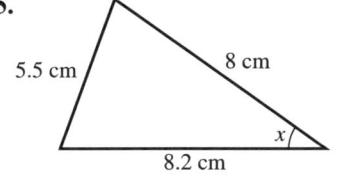

6.

9.5 cm, 6.2 cm, 6 cm, angle x

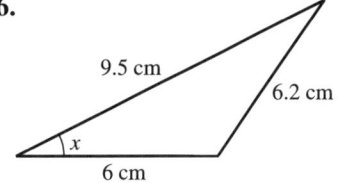

Questions **7**, **8**, and **9** are more difficult.

7.

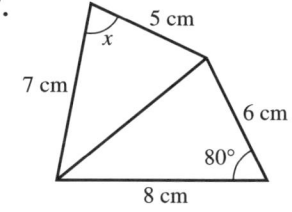

5 cm, 7 cm, 6 cm, 8 cm, 80°, angle x

8.

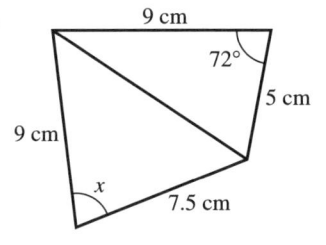

9 cm, 72°, 5 cm, 9 cm, 7.5 cm, angle x

9.

8.2 cm, 8 cm, 7.1 cm, 4 cm, 83°, angle x

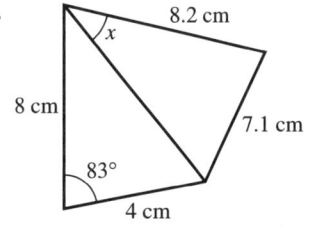

10. A disused airfield is to be sold at a price of £5500 per hectare.
(1 hectare = 10 000 m²).
The outline of the airfield is a quadrilateral but it is not a rectangle. The area can be found by splitting it into two triangles and then finding the area of each part.
Find the selling price of the airfield.
[Use a scale of 1 cm to 100 m]

> You need to use the formula 'area = $\frac{1}{2}$ base × height' to find the area of a triangle.

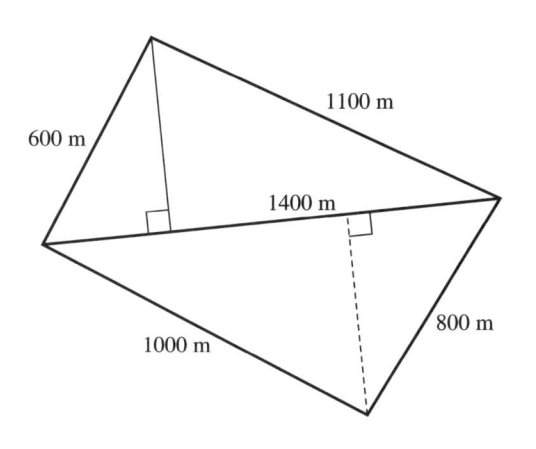

600 m, 1100 m, 1400 m, 1000 m, 800 m

Locus

The *locus* of a point is the path traced out by the point as it moves.

(a) An athlete runs around a track. The locus looks like this

(b) Alan throws a ball to Ben.

the locus is the curve

Exercise 2

1. Mark two points A and B, 5 cm apart. Draw crosses at six points which are an equal distance from A and B. The crosses form the locus of points which are an equal distance [equidistant] from A and B.

    A•

    B•

2. Mark a point C with a dot. Draw crosses at ten points which are all 5 cm from C. The crosses form the locus of points which are 5 cm from C. Describe the locus.

3. With a dot, mark the bottom right corner of the page you are on. Draw crosses at six points which are the same distance from the two edges of the page.
   Describe the locus of the crosses you have drawn.

4. Imagine a clock. Describe the locus of the tip of the minute hand as the time goes from 9 o'clock to 10 o'clock.

5. Describe the locus of the tip of the *hour* hand as the time goes from 3 o'clock to 9 o'clock.

6. We trace a locus when we use LOGO. Draw the locus with the following instructions.

    (a) FD 10, RT 90, FD 10, RT 90, FD 10, RT 90, FD 10
    (b) FD 20, RT 120, FD 20, RT 120, FD 20
    (c) REPEAT 6 [FD 10, RT 60]

7. Use LOGO to draw shapes of your own choice. For example: a regular octagon, a rectangle, (more difficult) a spiral

8. A car moves forward in a straight line.
   Sketch the locus of the valve on one of the wheels.

Standard constructions (using compasses)

Exercise 3 [use plain unlined paper]

You are given examples of standard constructions marked A, B, C, D. You are then asked to draw your own constructions using *only* a pencil, a straight edge and a pair of compasses.

A Perpendicular bisector of a line segment AB.

With centres A and B draw two arcs.
The perpendicular bisector is shown as a broken line.

---

1. Draw a horizontal line AB of the length 6 cm. Construct the perpendicular bisector of AB.

2. Draw a vertical line CD of length 8 cm. Construct the perpendicular bisector of CD.

3. (a) Using a set square,
    Draw a right-angled triangle ABC as shown.
    For greater accuracy draw lines slightly
    longer than 8 cm and 6 cm and *then* mark
    the points A, B and C.
   (b) *Construct* the perpendicular bisector of AB.
   (c) Construct the perpendicular bisector of AC
   (d) If done accurately, your two lines from (b)
    and (c) should cross exactly on the line BC.

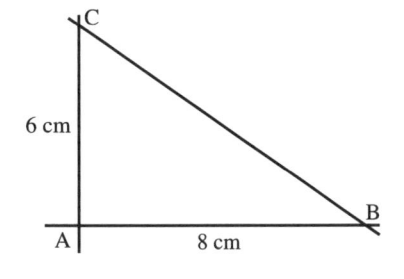

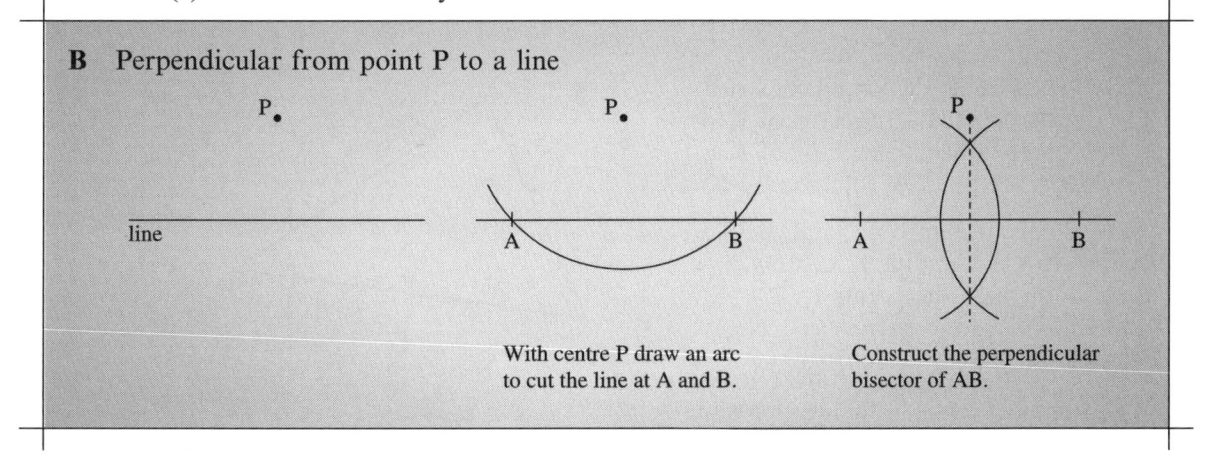

B Perpendicular from point P to a line

With centre P draw an arc to cut the line at A and B.

Construct the perpendicular bisector of AB.

4. Draw a line and a point P about 4 cm from the line. Construct the line which passes through P which is perpendicular to the line.

> **C Perpendicular from a point P on a line.**
>
> With centre P draw arcs to cut the line at A and B. Now bisect AB as above in (**A**).

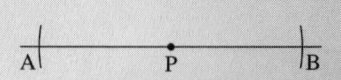

5. Draw a line and a point Q on the line. Construct the perpendicular from the point Q.

> **D Bisector of an angle**
>
> With centre A draw arc PQ.
> With centres at P and Q draw two more arcs.
> The angle bisector is then drawn.

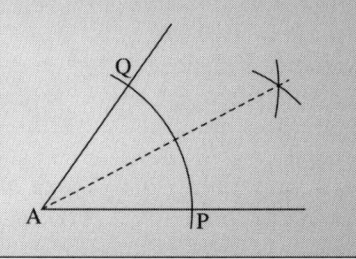

6. Draw an angle of about 70°. Construct the bisector of the angle.

7. Draw an angle of about 120°. Construct the bisector of the angle.

8. Draw any triangle ABC and construct the bisectors of angles B and C to meet at point Y.

    With centre at Y draw a circle which just touches the sides of the triangle.
    This is the *inscribed* circle of the triangle.

9. Draw *any* triangle KLM and construct
    (a) the perpendicular bisector of KM
    (b) the perpendicular bisector of KL.
        Mark the point of intersection X.

    Take a pair of compasses and, with centre at X and radius KX, draw a circle through the points K, L and M. This is the *circumcircle* of triangle KLM.

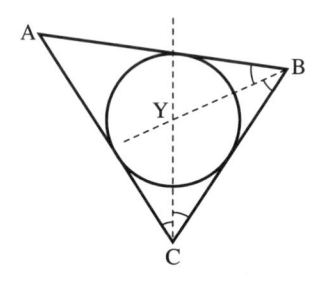

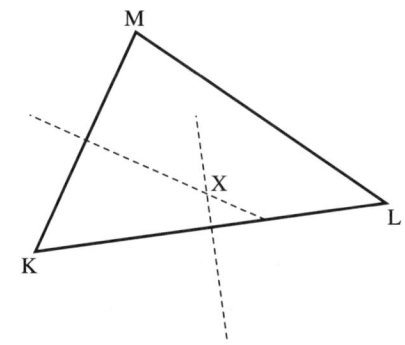

    Repeat the construction for another triangle of different shape.

2.5 Measures

Metric units

Here is a summary of the most important units

Length
10 mm = 1 cm
100 cm = 1 m
1000 m = 1 km

Mass
1000 g = 1 kg
1000 kg = 1 tonne

Volume
1000 ml = 1 litre or 1 l
1 ml = 1 cm^3

Exercise 1

What unit would you use to measure the following:

1. The mass of this book.
2. The length of a pencil.
3. The distance from London to Paris.
4. The length of an ant.
5. The mass of a heavy goods vehicle.
6. The amount of water in a swimming pool.
7. Your height.
8. Your mass.
9. The capacity of a car's petrol tank.
10. The amount of liquid in a cup of tea.

Copy and complete the following:

11. 1·25 m = _____ cm
12. 0·35 m = _____ cm
13. 3 m = _____ cm
14. 17 cm = _____ m
15. 250 cm = _____ m
16. 5 cm = _____ m
17. 40 mm = _____ cm
18. 300 mm = _____ cm
19. 5 mm = _____ cm
20. 1500 m = _____ km
21. 750 m = _____ km
22. 10 000 m = _____ km
23. 2 kg = _____ g
24. 8·52 kg = _____ g
25. 0·625 kg = _____ g
26. 325 g = _____ kg
27. 1627 g = _____ kg
28. 2 tonnes = _____ kg
29. 440 ml = _____ l
30. 1976 ml = _____ l
31. 2500 ml = _____ l
32. 2·5 litres = _____ ml
33. 75 l = _____ ml
34. 1·76 l = _____ ml

35. Copy and complete each sentence.

(a) The width of the classroom is about ☐ m.

(b) The height of the door is about ☐ cm.

(c) A can of coke has a capacity of about ☐ ml.

(d) The width of thumbnail is about ☐ mm.

Changing units

Many people still 'think' using the old imperial units. here are the approximate conversions, which you should *learn*.

> 1 m ≈ 3 feet
> 8 km ≈ 5 miles
> 1 kg ≈ 2·2 pounds
> 1 litre is just less than 2 pints
> 1 gallon ≈ 4·5 litres

Exercise 2

Copy and complete the following.

1. 5 m ≈ ☐ feet
2. 10 kg ≈ ☐ pounds
3. 2 litres ≈ ☐ pints
4. 5 miles ≈ ☐ km
5. 2 gallons ≈ ☐ litres
6. 6 feet ≈ ☐ m
7. 10 gallons ≈ ☐ litres
8. 16 km ≈ ☐ miles
9. 3 kg ≈ ☐ pounds
10. 100 m ≈ ☐ feet
11. 500 g ≈ ☐ pounds
12. 50 miles ≈ ☐ km

13. Here are scales for changing:
    A kilograms and pounds,
    B litres and gallons.
    In this question give your answers to the *nearest whole number*.
    (a) About how many kilograms are there in 4½ pounds?
    (b) About how many litres are there in 1·5 gallons?
    (c) About how many pounds are there in 2·7 kilograms?

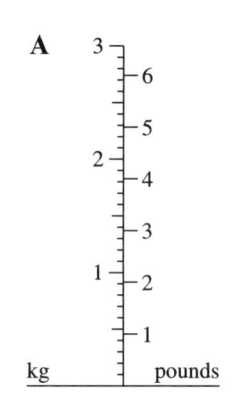

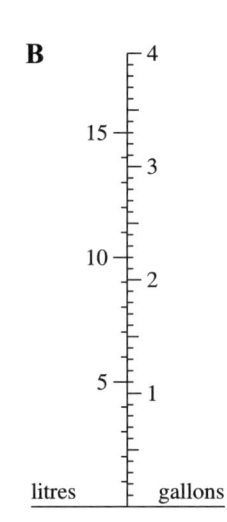

14. An ant walks 2 metres in 30 seconds. About how many feet will it walk in 60 seconds?

15. A car travels at a speed of 80 km/h for one hour.
    (a) How far does the car travel in km?
    (b) How far does the car travel in miles?

16. A litre of petrol costs 90p. About how much will 1 gallon cost?

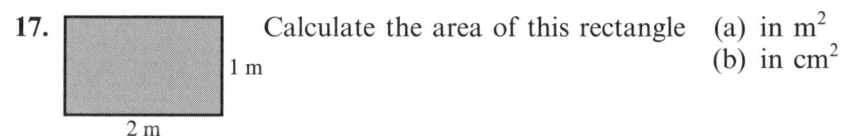

17. Calculate the area of this rectangle   (a) in m²
(b) in cm²

(rectangle 2 m by 1 m)

18. A large rectangular plastic sheet measures 200 cm by 10 m.
(a) Find the area of the sheet in m².
(b) A hectare is an area of 10 000 m². How many sheets are needed to cover 1 hectare?

19. A square field has a perimeter of 800 m.
(a) How long is each side of the field?
(b) Calculate the area of the field in m².
(c) Convert this area into hectares.

20. Mr Smith lives in a very rough area of Orpington. Ordinary cars tend to be hijacked so he converted his Citroen into a tank. He drives 10 miles to work and petrol costs £4 per gallon. The tank goes $\frac{1}{4}$ mile on 1 gallon of petrol.
How much does it cost to drive to work?

21. At noon on April 1 a giant egg-timer was started.
It was due to stop 1020 seconds later.
At what time did it stop?

22. A film starts at 8.00 p.m. and lasts 100 minutes.
When does it end?

23. A giant conveyor belt moves 100 kg of coal every minute.
How many tonnes of coal will be moved in 1 hour?

24. Which is longer: 2000 seconds or half an hour? Show your working.

25. A newspaper reported that Bill Gates, the chairman of Microsoft, earned $30 every second of every day.
How much did he earn in one day?

26. At a charity cake sale all the proceeds were collected in 10p coins and then the coins were arranged in a long straight line for a newspaper photo.
If the diameter of a 10p coin is just under one inch and the line of coins was 50 metres long, roughly how much money was raised?

Exercise 3

Some, though not all of the measurements below are reasonable. Use your common sense to help you complete this table. Where the measurement given is obviously wrong write a more sensible number.

Object	Measurement	Object	Measurement
Pound coin		Football	
Tennis ball		Family car	
This book		Newborn baby	
Chair height		Bag of sugar	
Tennis court		Biro	
Car speed		Labrador	
Pile of pound coins		Badminton net	
12 year old boy		50 seater coach	

A bag of sugar weighs about 2 pounds

A one pound coin weighs about 200 g

A tennis ball has a diameter of about 3 inches

A tennis court is about 20 yards long.

A 50-seater coach is about 15 metres long

IF A FULL SIZE PLASTIC FOOTBALL WAS FILLED WITH WATER IT WOULD CONTAIN ABOUT 3 LITRES

A normal family car weighs about 160 kg.

A fully grown labrador weighs about 4 kg

An 'average' new-born baby weighs about six ounces.

At a speed of 75 m.p.h. a car travels about one kilometre in a minute.

A pile of 100 one pound coins would be about 2 metres high

A badminton net is about 3 feet high

This book is about 4 mm thick.

An ordinary biro is about $2\frac{1}{2}$ inches long

The height of the seat of a normal chair is about 18 inches.

An average 12 year old boy weighs about six stones

2.6 Solving problems 1

Exercise 1

1. Find the missing digits
   (a) ☐☐☐ ÷ 3 = 50
   (b) ☐☐ × 6 = 312
   (c) ☐☐ − 35 = 99
   (d) ☐☐☐ ÷ 9 = 54

2. Write down *two* possible answers for the missing digits. Ask a friend to check your solutions.

   3 0 × ☐☐ ÷ ☐ = 60

3. A roll of wallpaper is cut into five strips. A room requires 40 strips of wallpaper. How much will it cost if one roll of wallpaper costs £9?

4. Angela buys five 18 p stamps and twenty 25 p stamps. How much change will she receive from a £10 note?

5. One day a quarter of the class is absent and 21 children are present. How many children are there in the class when no one is away?

6. Here is a row of numbers
   1 2 3 4 5 6 7 8 9 10 11 12 13 14 15 16 17
   (a) Find *two* numbers next to each other which add up to 17
   (b) Find *three* numbers next to each other which add up to 30.
   (c) Find *four* numbers next to each other which add up to 30.

7. Every day he plays, a snooker player uses 20 g of chalk on his cue. He plays 300 days a year. How much chalk will he use if he plays for 20 years? Give the answer in kg.

8. Work out, without a calculator.
   (a) 5·6 − 3·34
   (b) 3·2 ÷ 5
   (c) 0·21 × 1000
   (d) 2548 ÷ 7
   (e) 352 × 8
   (f) 12 + 8·8

9. In a supermarket five boxes of chocolates can be bought for £16·25. How many boxes can be bought for £26?

10. I think of a number. If I double the number and then take away ten the answer is 210. What number was I thinking of?

Exercise 2

1. Write down the next number in each sequence
   (a) 3, 9, 15, 21, ☐
   (b) 1, 2, 4, 7, ☐
   (c) 80, 40, 20, 10, ☐

2. The sides of a rectangle are in the ratio 2:1. Its perimeter is 120 cm. Find the dimensions of the rectangle.

3. Work out
   (a) $-8 + 3$
   (b) $-6 \times (-2)$
   (c) $-8 - 5$
   (d) $3 \times (-3)$
   (e) $-8 \div 2$
   (f) $-3 \times (-4)$

4. Find the shaded area.

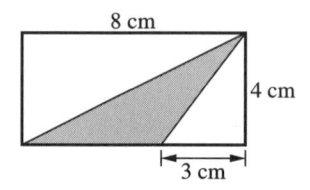

5. What number, when divided by 6 and then multiplied by 5, gives an answer of 40?

6. A 20 p coin is 2 mm thick. Graham has a pile of 20 p coins which is 18 cm tall. What is the value of the money in Graham's pile of coins?

7. The test results of 100 students are shown below.

Result	5	6	7	8	9	10
Number of pupils	7	14	22	18	24	15

The pass mark in the test was 7. What percentage of the students failed?

8. In a 'magic' square the sum of the numbers in any row, column or main diagonal is the same. Copy and complete these magic squares.

(a)
6		2
	5	
8		

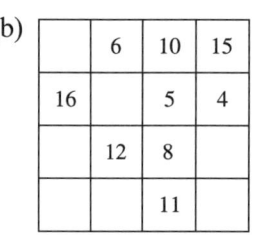

(b)
	6	10	15
16		5	4
	12	8	
		11	

9. This table shows the approximate weights of coins

1 p	2 p	5 p	10 p	20 p
3·6 g	7·2 g	3·2 g	6·5 g	5·0 g

(a) What is the weight of two coins with a value of 15 p?
(b) What is the lightest weight with a value of 65 p made from these coins?

10. Write down the most appropriate *metric* unit for measuring:
    (a) the capacity of a car's fuel tank,
    (b) the height of the Eiffel Tower,
    (c) the mass of a Jumbo Jet,
    (d) the area of a small farm.

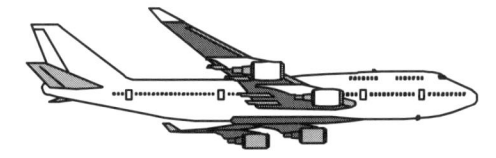

Exercise 3

1. Find the number indicated by the arrow on the scales below.

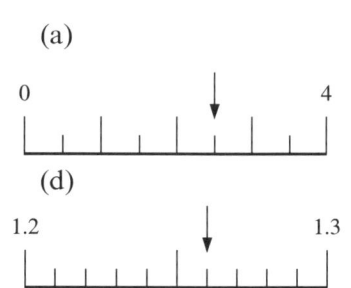

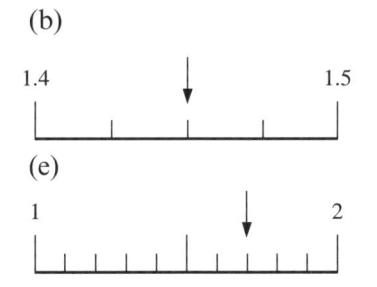

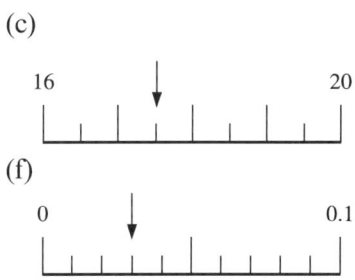

   (a) 0 to 4
   (b) 1.4 to 1.5
   (c) 16 to 20
   (d) 1.2 to 1.3
   (e) 1 to 2
   (f) 0 to 0.1

2. (a) A corn field is a rectangle measuring 300 m by 600 m. Find the area of the field in hectares (1 hectare = 10 000 m²).
   (b) Each hectare produces 3 tonnes of corn. How much corn is produced in this field?

3. The numbers 1 to 12 are arranged on the star so that the sum of the numbers along each line is the same.

   Copy and complete the star.

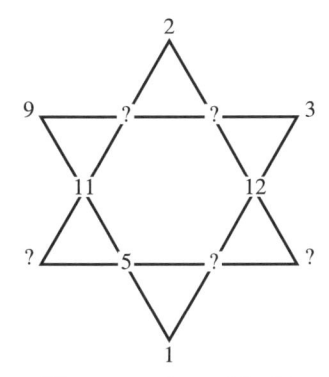

4. A jar with 8 chocolates in it weighs 160 g. The same jar with 20 chocolates in it weighs 304 g. How much does the jar weigh on its own?

5. Here is a subtraction using the digits
   2, 3, 4, 5, 6.
   Which subtraction using all the digits
   2, 3, 4, 5, 6 has the smallest positive answer?

   $$465 - 23$$

6. The pupils in a school were given a general knowledge quiz. A mark of 30 or more was a 'pass'.
   Some of the results are given in the table.
   Copy and complete the table with the missing entries.

	Passed	Failed	Total
Boys		267	452
Girls		174	
Total		441	821

7. George Washington's father planted a tree when his son was born. George Washington died in 1799 aged 67. How old was the tree in 1998?

8. Work out, without a calculator.
   (a) $1404 \div 6$ (b) 217×5 (c) $915 - 262$
   (d) 5.3×1000 (e) $26.5 \div 10$ (f) $0.94 + 3.2$

9. Copy and complete the additions.

   (a)
   ```
         3 2 □
         2 □ 1
      + □ 2 4
      ─────────
      □ 1 8 9
   ```

   (b)
   ```
         3 2 □
         4 □ 2
      + □ 2 4
      ─────────
      □ 4 3 3
   ```

10. Use the clues to find the mystery number
    • the sum of the digits is 8
    • the number reads the same forwards as backwards
    • the number is less than 2000
    • the number has four digits

Exercise 4

1. Write down the number that is ten more than
   (a) 374 (b) 2485 (c) 263·1 (d) 2195

2. (a) Write down the largest 2 figure *even* number you can think of.
   (b) Write down the smallest possible *odd* number using the digits 1, 5, 8.

3. 504 people were invited to a banquet. How many tables were needed if eight people sat at each table?

4. Six touching circles of radius 5 cm are shown. Calculate the area of the triangle shaded.

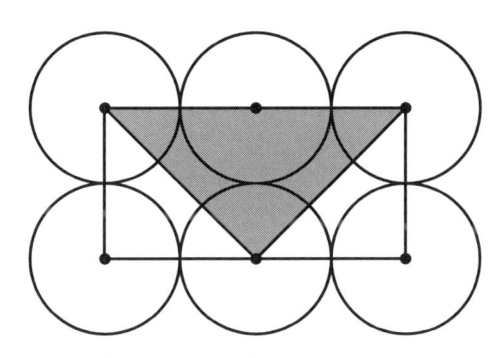

5. Work out
   (a) $-17 + 4$
   (b) $-7 - 5$
   (c) $-3 \times (-2)$
   (d) $8 - (-3)$
   (e) $-12 \div (3)$
   (f) $-8 + (-4)$

6. A film starts at 7.30 p.m. and lasts 75 minutes. When does it finish?

7. A man gives a total of £7 to his two children so that his daughter receives 60p more than his son. How much does his daughter receive?

8. A chef uses 200 ml of oil in 4 days. How many days will a 10 litre drum of oil last?

9. The square ACDE is cut into seven pieces. Find the area, in square units, of
   (a) triangle EDI
   (b) square BJIG
   (c) parallelogram FGHE.

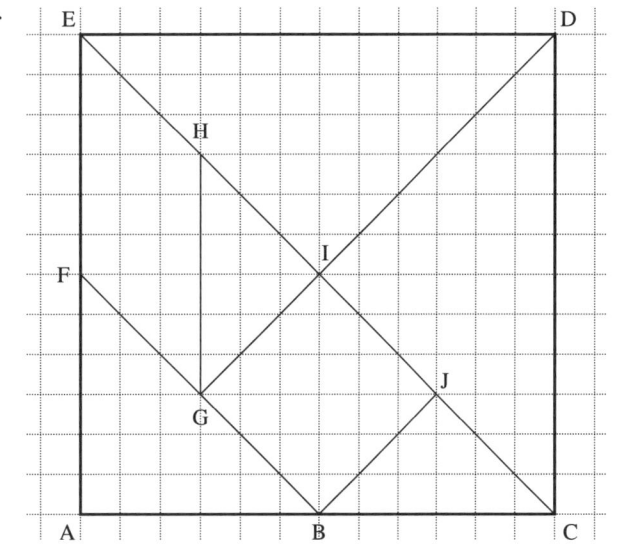

10. Every year the Government spends about £8·8 billion paying teachers (who deserve every penny they get). A wad of a hundred £10 notes is about 1 cm thick. As a publicity stunt, the Minister of Education decides to make a single pile of £10 notes of total value £8·8 billion. How high would the pile be? (1 billion = 1000 million)

Exercise 5

Calculators may be used

1. Here is some information about how much 'fast food' is eaten in five European countries.
   (a) How many McDonald's restaurants were there altogether?
   (b) How many fast food outlets were there altogether in France?
   (c) A hamburger is cheaper in the U.K. than in Germany. What *percentage* of the German price does a customer in the U.K. pay?
   (d) Use the figures in the first table to work out an estimate for the total population of Italy.

   WHAT WE SPEND ON FAST FOOD

	Total spent	Cost per head
UK	£2.42billion	£41
France	£1.70billion	£29
Germany	£1.68billion	£20
Spain	£427million	£11
Italy	£176million	£3

   NUMBER OF OUTLETS PER COUNTRY

	UK	France	Germany	Italy	Spain
McDonald's	732	553	735	142	119
Burger King	420	40	141	–	120
Pizza Hut	347	121	111	–	131
KFC	365	7	32	–	33

   THE McDONALD'S INDEX

	UK	Italy	France	Spain	Germany
Hamburger	59p	90p	92p	86p	£1

2. A map has a scale of 1 to 100 000. Calculate the actual length of a lake which is 8 cm long on the map.

3. A saleswoman is paid a basic salary of £4200 per year, plus commission of 4% on all her sales. Calculate her total salary if her sales totalled
   (a) £10 000   (b) £30 000   (c) £100 000

4. Copy and complete this multiplication square.

×	9	3		
		15		35
		24		
2				
			32	56

5. One litre of petrol costs 89·2 p and one litre of oil costs 82 p.
   (a) Find the cost of 100 litres of petrol
   (b) Find the cost of 10 litres of oil
   (c) Find the total cost of 1000 litres of petrol and 100 litres of oil.

6. Find two consecutive numbers with a product of 552
   Find four consecutive numbers with a total of 130
   Find *any* two numbers with a product of 837
   Find a pair of numbers with a sum of 19 and a product of 48.

7. Here are some number machines. Find the missing numbers.

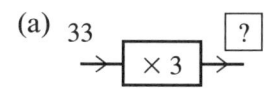

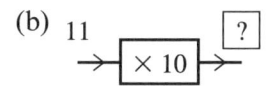

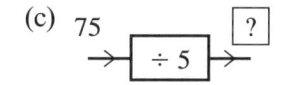

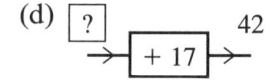

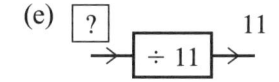

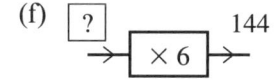

(a) 33 → ×3 → ?

(b) 11 → ×10 → ?

(c) 75 → ÷5 → ?

(d) ? → +17 → 42

(e) ? → ÷11 → 11

(f) ? → ×6 → 144

8. Find the operations for these mystery machines

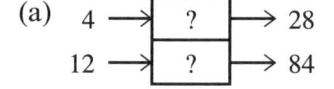

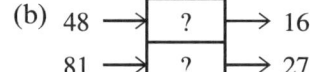

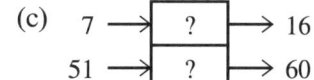

(a) 4 → ? → 28
    12 → ? → 84

(b) 48 → ? → 16
    81 → ? → 27

(c) 7 → ? → 16
    51 → ? → 60

(d) 11 → ? → 33
    15 → ? → 45

(e) 59 → ? → 48
    16 → ? → 5

(f) 21 → ? → 40
    37 → ? → 56

9. Figaro, the cat, is so clean that his picture is now on stamps. He requires 800 ml of water for his daily wash. How many litres of water will he use in one year?

10. (a) Use a calculator to work out
    (i) 350 ÷ 99
    (ii) 350 ÷ 999
    (iii) 350 ÷ 9999
    (b) Use your answers to *predict* the answer to 350 ÷ 99 999, correct to 9 decimal places.
    (c) Predict the answer to 350 ÷ 999 999, correct to 11 decimal places.

11. A school orders the box of books shown below and is charged £85, of which £1·60 is postage. What is the cost of each book?

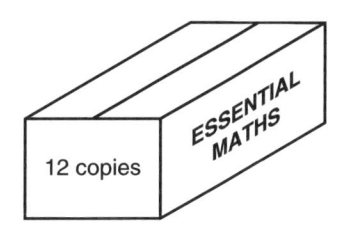

12 copies
ESSENTIAL MATHS

Part 3

3.1 Written calculations

(a) $56 + 711 + 8$

$$\begin{array}{r} 56 \\ 711 \\ +8 \\ \hline 775 \\ 1 \end{array}$$

(b) $383 - 57$

$$\begin{array}{r} 3\,{}^{7}\!\!\!/8\,{}^{1}\!\!\!/3 \\ -57 \\ \hline 326 \end{array}$$

(c) 214×7

$$\begin{array}{r} 214 \\ \times 7 \\ \hline 1498 \\ 2 \end{array}$$

(d) $5 \cdot 6 + 12 \cdot 32$

$$\begin{array}{r} 5 \cdot 60 \leftarrow \text{add zero} \\ +12 \cdot 32 \\ \hline 17 \cdot 92 \end{array}$$

[Line up the decimal points]

(e) $5 \cdot 26 \times 10$
$= 52 \cdot 6$

Move the digits one place to the left

(f) $28 \cdot 1 \div 100$
$= 0 \cdot 281$

Move the digits two places to the right.

(g) 34×200
$= 34 \times 2 \times 100$
$= 6800$

(h) $79 \cdot 2 \div 6$

$$6 \overline{)7\,{}^{1}\!9 \cdot {}^{1}\!2} = 13 \cdot 2$$

(i) $17 - 5 \cdot 4$

$$\begin{array}{r} 1\,{}^{6}\!\!\!/7 \cdot {}^{1}\!0 \\ -5 \cdot 4 \\ \hline 11 \cdot 6 \end{array}$$

Exercise 1

Work out, without a calculator

1. $847 + 325$
2. $7140 + 396$
3. $294 - 157$
4. $6293 - 1734$
5. 35×4
6. 73×6
7. 214×8
8. 315×7
9. 23×100
10. 315×10
11. 17×1000
12. $5 \cdot 62 \times 10$
13. $59 \div 10$
14. $647 \div 100$
15. $8 \cdot 3 \div 10$
16. $219 \div 1000$
17. 43×20
18. 26×300
19. 124×200
20. $5184 + 2787$
21. $5615 - 3916$
22. $284 + 19 + 564$
23. 316×5
24. $56\,000 \div 20$
25. $19 \cdot 2 - 5 \cdot 8$
26. $11 + 5 \cdot 2$
27. 173×8
28. $868 \div 7$
29. $98 \cdot 7 \div 7$
30. $0 \cdot 38 - 0 \cdot 252$
31. $73 \cdot 2 \div 100$
32. $5 \cdot 1 \times 100$

33. $42 + 0.72 + 5.3$ **34.** $5.48 \div 4$ **35.** $2900 - 1573$ **36.** 0.95×9
37. $14490 \div 6$ **38.** $4000 - 264$ **39.** 5.24×0.5 **40.** $8.52 \div 4$
41. 52×400 **42.** $234 + 23.4$ **43.** $0.612 \div 6$ **44.** 5.2×2000
45. $0.0924 \div 4$ **46.** $0.72 - 0.065$ **47.** 73×30 **48.** $5.7 \div 100$

Place value

Exercise 2

1. Arrange in order of size, smallest first.
   (a) 0·73, 0·718, 0·7
   (b) 0·405, 0·5, 0·41
   (c) 0·3, 0·035, 0·029
   (d) 0·06, 0·058, 0·0511

2. Write the number half way between:
   (a) 0·2 and 0·8
   (b) 0·4 and 0·5
   (c) 0·02 and 0·08
   (d) 0·1 and 0·2
   (e) 0·06 and 0·07

3. Write each statement with either $>$, $<$ or $=$ in the space.
   (a) 0·032 ☐ 0·004
   (b) 0·728 ☐ 0·73
   (c) 0·3 cm ☐ 3 mm
   (d) 0·005 ☐ 0·0006
   (e) 0·6 m ☐ 55 cm
   (f) 0·09 ☐ 0·1

4. (a) What is 0·01 more than 3·29?
   (b) What is 0·001 more than 0·628?
   (c) What is 0·01 less than 6·4?
   (d) What is 0·001 less than 0·426?

5. Copy each sequence and fill in the spaces.
   (a) 2·67, 2·68, 2·69, ☐, ☐
   (b) 1·52, 1·51, 1·5, ☐, ☐
   (c) 3·6, 3·8, 4, ☐, ☐
   (d) ☐, 5, 5·01, 5·02, ☐

6. What has to be added or subtracted to change:
   (a) 3·24 to 3·26
   (b) 0·714 to 0·712
   (c) 0·142 to 0·152
   (d) 0·599 to 0·6

7. **What's in the boot, then?**

   A MOTORIST who was stopped for a routine police check in Colchester, Essex, was found to be wearing Wellington boots filled with baked beans in tomato sauce.
   Officers warned him to choose more suitable footwear. A spokesman said: "We have no idea why he was doing it but it is an offence not to be in proper control of a car. Wearing boots full of baked beans could cause the driver to be distracted and have an accident."

   (a) Estimate the number of tins required to fill a pair of wellington boots
   (b) Explain why this question is in the section on 'place value'.

Multiplying by 0·1 and 0·01

- Multiplying by 0·1 is the same as multiplying by $\frac{1}{10}$ or dividing by 10.

  Examples:
  $$5 \times 0\cdot1 = 5 \times \tfrac{1}{10} = 5 \div 10$$
  $$= 0\cdot5$$
  $$0\cdot2 \times 0\cdot1 = 0\cdot2 \times \tfrac{1}{10} = 0\cdot2 \div 10$$
  $$= 0\cdot02$$

  $$7 \times 0\cdot1 = 7 \times \tfrac{1}{10} = 7 \div 10$$
  $$= 0\cdot7$$
  $$0\cdot35 \times 0\cdot1 = 0\cdot35 \times \tfrac{1}{10} = 0\cdot35 \div 10$$
  $$= 0\cdot035$$

- Multiplying by 0·01 is the same multiplying by $\frac{1}{100}$ or dividing by 100.

  Examples:
  $$4 \times 0\cdot01 = 4 \times \tfrac{1}{100} = 4 \div 100$$
  $$= 0\cdot04$$

  $$17 \times 0\cdot01 = 17 \times \tfrac{1}{100} = 17 \div 100$$
  $$= 0\cdot17$$

Exercise 3

Work out
1. $8 \times 0\cdot1$
2. $3 \times 0\cdot1$
3. $12 \times 0\cdot1$
4. $26 \times 0\cdot1$
5. $0\cdot4 \times 0\cdot1$
6. $0\cdot7 \times 0\cdot1$
7. $0\cdot9 \times 0\cdot1$
8. $0\cdot24 \times 0\cdot1$
9. $8 \times 0\cdot01$
10. $6 \times 0\cdot01$
11. $15 \times 0\cdot01$
12. $7 \times 0\cdot01$
13. $52 \times 0\cdot01$
14. $63 \times 0\cdot01$
15. $0\cdot6 \times 0\cdot001$
16. $5\cdot2 \times 0\cdot01$
17. $11 \times 0\cdot1$
18. $9 \times 0\cdot1$
19. $23 \times 0\cdot01$
20. $0\cdot5 \times 0\cdot1$

Multiplying decimal numbers

- $5 \times 0\cdot3$ is the same as $5 \times \tfrac{3}{10}$. Work out $(5 \times 3) \div 10 = 15 \div 10 = 1\cdot5$

  $4\cdot2 \times 0\cdot2$ is the same as $4\cdot2 \times \tfrac{2}{10}$. Work out $(4\cdot2 \times 2) \div 10 = 8\cdot4 \div 10 = 0\cdot84$

  $21\cdot4 \times 0\cdot05$ is the same as $21\cdot4 \times \tfrac{5}{100}$. Work out $(21\cdot4 \times 5) \div 100 = 107 \div 100 = 1\cdot07$

  Here is a final check:
  When we multiply two decimal numbers together, the answer has the same number of figures to the right of the decimal point as the total number of figures to the right of the decimal point in the question.

  Examples:
  (a) $0\cdot3 \times 0\cdot4$
  $(3 \times 4 = 12)$
  So $0\cdot3 \times 0\cdot4 = 0\cdot12$

  (b) $0\cdot7 \times 0\cdot05$
  $(7 \times 5 = 35)$
  So $0\cdot7 \times 0\cdot05 = 0\cdot035$

Exercise 4

1. 7×0.2
2. 8×0.3
3. 12×0.2
4. 5×0.03
5. 0.7×3
6. 23×0.02
7. 0.9×0.5
8. 6×0.06
9. 12×0.05
10. 0.7×0.7
11. 8×0.1
12. 14×0.3
13. 15×0.03
14. 0.4×0.04
15. 0.001×0.6
16. 33×0.02
17. 1.2×0.3
18. 3.2×0.2
19. 1.4×0.4
20. 2.1×0.5
21. 3.61×0.3
22. 2.1×0.6
23. 0.31×0.7
24. 0.42×0.02
25. 0.33×0.02
26. 3.24×0.01
27. 8.11×0.07
28. 16.2×0.8
29. 5.06×0.05
30. 30.9×0.3
31. 0.2^2
32. 0.4^2

- 12.2×27 is approximately $10 \times 30 = 300$

$$12.2 \times 27 = (12.2 \times 10 \times 27) \div 10$$
$$= (122 \times 27) \div 10$$

$$\begin{array}{r} 277 \\ \times\ 27 \\ \hline \end{array}$$

$122 \times 20 \quad 2440$
$122 \times 7 \quad\ \ 854$
$\qquad\qquad\ \ \overline{3294}$

Answer: $3294 \div 10 = 329.4$

- 18.4×3.2 is approximately $20 \times 3 = 60$

$$18.4 \times 3.2 = (18.4 \times 10 \times 3.2 \times 10) \div 100$$
$$= (184 \times 32) \div 100$$

$$\begin{array}{r} 184 \\ \times\ 32 \\ \hline \end{array}$$

$184 \times 30 \quad 5520$
$184 \times 2 \quad\ \ 368$
$\qquad\qquad\ \overline{5888}$

Answer: $5888 \div 100 = 58.88$

Exercise 5

Work out, after finding an approximate answer first.

1. 6.2×2.1
2. 5.3×32
3. 4.7×15
4. 3.8×17
5. 11.4×15
6. 21.4×21
7. 15.2×13
8. 23.6×25
9. 2.3×1.2
10. 3.5×1.5
11. 4.3×2.3
12. 2.4×1.8
13. 6.5×3.2
14. 8.4×4.1
15. 0.22×1.4
16. 0.33×1.7
17. 13.2×1.4
18. 14.5×3.3
19. 21.2×2.4
20. 31.5×1.5
21. 35.6×1.9
22. 42.3×2.7
23. 8.64×4.7
24. 0.332×42
25. 0.32×5.6
26. 1.52×1.7
27. 0.35×0.13
28. 0.51×0.24

Dividing by 0·1 and 0·01

- $1 \div 0 \cdot 1 = 1 \div \frac{1}{10} \ldots$ How many $\frac{1}{10}$s are there in 1? Answer: 10

  $7 \div 0 \cdot 1 = 7 \div \frac{1}{10} \ldots$ How many $\frac{1}{10}$s are there in 7? Answer: 70

  $5 \cdot 2 \div 0 \cdot 1 = 5 \cdot 2 \div \frac{1}{10} \ldots$ How many $\frac{1}{10}$s are there in 5·2? Answer: 52

  $1 \div 0 \cdot 01 = 1 \div \frac{1}{100} \ldots$ How many $\frac{1}{100}$s are there in 1? Answer: 100

  $13 \div 0 \cdot 01 = 13 \div \frac{1}{100} \ldots$ How many $\frac{1}{100}$s are there in 13? Answer: 1300

- We see that: dividing by 0·1 is the same as multiplying by 10,

  dividing by 0·01 is the same as multiplying by 100.

$3 \div 0 \cdot 1 = 3 \times 10$ $14 \div 0 \cdot 1 = 14 \times 10$ $0 \cdot 4 \div 0 \cdot 1 = 0 \cdot 4 \times 10$
$= 30$ $= 140$ $= 4$

$7 \div 0 \cdot 01 = 7 \times 100$ $52 \div 0 \cdot 01 = 52 \times 100$ $0 \cdot 7 \div 0 \cdot 01 = 0 \cdot 7 \times 100$
$= 700$ $= 5200$ $= 70$

Exercise 6

1. $5 \div 0 \cdot 1$
2. $9 \div 0 \cdot 1$
3. $11 \div 0 \cdot 1$
4. $6 \div 0 \cdot 1$
5. $32 \div 0 \cdot 1$
6. $0 \cdot 7 \div 0 \cdot 1$
7. $0 \cdot 9 \div 0 \cdot 1$
8. $1 \cdot 3 \div 0 \cdot 1$
9. $3 \div 0 \cdot 01$
10. $11 \div 0 \cdot 01$
11. $4 \div 0 \cdot 01$
12. $0 \cdot 3 \div 0 \cdot 01$
13. $0 \cdot 8 \div 0 \cdot 01$
14. $57 \div 0 \cdot 01$
15. $1 \cdot 9 \div 0 \cdot 01$
16. $0 \cdot 42 \div 0 \cdot 01$

17. Find the missing numbers

    (a) $12 \div 0 \cdot 1 = \square$ (b) $7 \div \square = 70$ (c) $3 \div \square = 300$

    (d) $\square \div 0 \cdot 1 = 20$ (e) $1 \cdot 2 \div 0 \cdot 01 = \square$ (f) $1 \cdot 7 \div \square = 17$

Dividing by any decimal number

To divide by any decimal number we transform the calculation into a division by a *whole number*.

Examples $3 \cdot 6 \div 0 \cdot 2 = 36 \div 2 = 18$ [Multiply 3·6 and 0·2 by 10.]

$1 \cdot 5 \div 0 \cdot 03 = 150 \div 3 = 50$ [Multiply 1·5 and 0·03 by 100.]

Since both numbers are multiplied by 10 or 100 the answer is not changed.

Exercise 7

Work out, without a calculator

1. $1.46 \div 0.2$
2. $2.52 \div 0.4$
3. $0.942 \div 0.3$
4. $0.712 \div 0.2$
5. $0.375 \div 0.5$
6. $0.522 \div 0.6$
7. $6.54 \div 0.2$
8. $1.944 \div 0.6$
9. $0.1368 \div 0.04$
10. $0.228 \div 0.04$
11. $0.498 \div 0.06$
12. $5.04 \div 0.7$
13. $3.744 \div 0.09$
14. $0.1685 \div 0.005$
15. $0.2846 \div 0.2$
16. $0.0585 \div 0.09$
17. $0.0257 \div 0.005$
18. $1.872 \div 0.08$
19. $0.268 \div 0.4$
20. $0.39 \div 0.006$
21. $0.42 \div 0.03$
22. $7.041 \div 0.01$
23. $0.1638 \div 0.001$
24. $15.33 \div 0.07$
25. $0.993 \div 0.3$
26. $1.05 \div 0.6$
27. $8.4 \div 0.02$
28. $7.52 \div 0.4$
29. $4.006 \div 0.002$
30. $17.4 \div 0.2$
31. $54 \div 0.3$
32. $32 \div 0.4$

Hidden words

(a) Start in the top left box.

(b) Work out the answer to the calculation in the box.

(c) Find the answer in the top corner of another box.

(d) Write down the letter in that box.

(e) Repeat steps (b), (c) and (d) until you arrive back at the top left box. What is the message.

1.

6.4 L 5×15	66 N $2^3 + 33$	274 E 20% of 50	985 S 15×100	12 S $756 \div 9$
422 N 10^3	75 S $150 - 67$	1.68 R 8×22	10 C $8.7 \div 10$	2.4 I $37 + 385$
3.85 U 0.16×10	176 E $421 - 147$	0.87 H $5 + 1.4$	1000 F $8.4 \div 5$	83 O $385 \div 7$
55 L $1000 - 15$	1500 I $\frac{2}{3}$ of 99	1.6 N 0.4×6	35 I 25% of 48	84 S $5.32 - 1.47$

2.

612	0·8	0·77	0·2	0·62
T	T	W	V	T
1·8 + 8·2	5% of 400	$2^3 \times 6$	5 × 69	20% of 65
32	10	13	18	250
C	B	R	E	U
50 000 ÷ 200	$\frac{2}{5}$ of 450	0·6 × 2·6	80% of 80	$0·9^2 - 0·1^2$
1·56	0·6	180	0·15	64
E	R	E	S	S
$\frac{3}{8}$ of 48	$\frac{1}{2}$ of 0·3	$(0·2)^2$	6·4 ÷ 0·2	806 − 194
0·04	0·27	20	48	345
A	O	D	N	E
10% of 2	770 ÷ 1000	0·3 − 0·03	3·1 × 0·2	4·2 ÷ 7

3.

45	4	371	21	0·51
H	H	C	A	S
$\frac{1}{2} + \frac{1}{4}$	2^4	10 ÷ 1000	5 ÷ 8	21 − 5 × 4
896	0·06	0·05	0·01	34
M	E	L	E	Y
$1^2 + 2^2 + 3^3$	51 ÷ 100	1% of 250	$5 \times (5 - 2)^2$	5·1 × 100
0·625	1	$\frac{3}{4}$	$\frac{3}{8}$	32
T	O	M	S	I
$\frac{2}{3} \times \frac{1}{5}$	6000 ÷ 20	4 + 5 × 6	0·3 × 0·2	53 × 7
510	16	2·5	300	$\frac{2}{15}$
C	A	Y	N	C
$\frac{3}{5}$ of 35	$\frac{1}{2} - \frac{1}{8}$	8 + 888	$\frac{1}{4} - 0·2$	20 ÷ (12 − 7)

3.2 Averages and range

☐ **The mean**
All the data is added and the total is divided by the number of items. In everyday language the word 'average' usually stands for the mean.

☐ **The median**
When the data is arranged in order of size, the median is the one in the middle. If there are two 'middle' numbers, the median is in the middle of these two numbers [i.e. the mean of the two numbers].

☐ **The mode**
The mode is the number or quality (like a colour) which occurs most often. Sometimes a set of data will have no mode, two modes or even more and this is a problem which we cannot avoid.

☐ **Range**
The range is not an average but is the difference between the largest value and the smallest value in a set of data. It is useful in comparing sets of data when the *spread* of the data is important.

Exercise 1

1. (a) Find the mean of the numbers 4, 13, 5, 7, 9, 6, 5
   (b) Find the median of the numbers 6, 20, 1, 16, 2, 12, 6, 3, 8, 6, 8
   (c) Find the mode of the numbers 13, 2, 11, 2, 10, 4, 5, 10, 8, 10

2. In several different garages the cost of one litre of petrol is
   55p, 52·8p, 56·4p, 53·1p, 59p, 53·8p, 57p.
   What is the median cost of one litre of petrol?

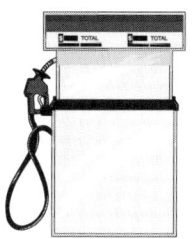

3. Six girls have heights of 1·48 m, 1·51 m, 1·47m, 1·55 m, 1·40 m and 1·59 m.
   (a) Find the mean height of the six girls.
   (b) Find the mean height of the remaining five girls when the tallest girl leaves.

4. Mrs Green gave birth to five babies (two girls and three boys) which weighed 1·3 kg, 1·2 kg, 1·45 kg, 1·35 kg and 1·3 kg. What was the median weight of the babies?

5. Sally throws a dice eight times and wins 20p if the median score is more than 3. The dice shows 6, 1, 2, 6, 4, 1, 3, 6. Find the median score. Does she win 20p?

6. The temperature was recorded at 0400 in seven towns across the U.K. The readings were 08, 18, −48, 18, −28, −58, −48. What was the median temperature?

7. The test results for a class of 30 pupils were as follows:

Mark	3	4	5	6	7	8
Frequency	2	5	4	7	6	6

What was the modal mark?

8. Find the range of the following sets of numbers:
   (a) 4, 11, 3, 8, 22, 5, 7, 30, 18
   (b) 9, 18, 100, 64, 11, 26
   (c) 4, −2, 6, 4, 5, 10, 3.

9. The range for nine numbers on a card is 60. One number is covered by a piece of blu-tac. What could that number be? [There are two possible answers.]

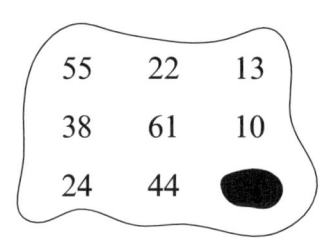

   55 22 13
   38 61 10
   24 44 ●

10. There were seven people sleeping in a tent. The mean age of the people was 20 and the range of their ages was 7. Write each statement below and then write next to it whether it is *True, Possible* or *False*.
    (a) The oldest person in the tent was 9 years older than the youngest.
    (b) The youngest person in the tent was 18 years old.
    (c) Every person in the tent was 20 years old.

11. There were ten children on a coach journey. The mean age of the children was 11 and the range of their ages was 4. Write each statement below and then write next to it whether it is *True, Possible* or *False*.
    (a) The youngest child was 9 years old
    (b) Every child was 11 years old.
    (c) All the children were at least 10 years old

12. Lauren has five cards. The five cards have a mean of 7 and a range of 4. What are the missing numbers?

| 7 | 7 | 7 | | |

13. For the set of numbers below, find the mean and the median.

$$1, 3, 3, 3, 4, 6, 99.$$

Which average best describes the set of numbers?

14. In a history test, Andrew got 62%. For the whole class, the mean mark was 64% and the median mark was 59%. Which 'average' tells him whether he is in the 'top' half or the 'bottom' half of the class?

15. Write down five numbers so that:
the mean is 7
the median is 6
the mode is 4.

Frequency tables

When a set of data consists of many numbers it is convenient to record the information in a frequency table. It is possible to find the mean, median and mode directly from the table as shown in the example below.

The frequency table shows the number of goals scored in 15 football matches.

number of goals	0	1	2	3	4	5 or more
frequency	2	5	4	3	1	0

(a) We *could find the mean as follows:*

$$\text{mean} = \frac{(0+0+1+1+1+1+1+2+2+2+2+3+3+3+4)}{15}$$

A better method is to multiply the number of goals by the respective frequencies.

$$\text{mean} = \frac{(0 \times 2) + (1 \times 5) + (2 \times 4) + (3 \times 3) + (4 \times 1)}{15}$$

mean = 1·73 goals (correct to 2 d.p.)

(b) The median is the 8th number in the list, when the numbers are arranged in order. The median is, therefore, 2 goals.

(c) The modal number of goals is 1, since more games had 1 goal than any other number.

Exercise 2

1. The frequency table shows the weights of 30 eggs laid by the hens on a free range farm.

weight	44 g	48 g	52 g	56 g	60 g
frequency	5	6	7	9	3

Find the mean weight of the eggs.

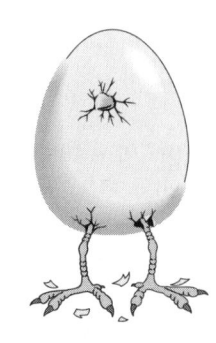

2. The frequency table shows the weights of the 40 pears sold in a shop.

weight	70 g	80 g	90 g	100 g	110 g	120 g
frequency	2	7	9	11	8	3

Calculate the mean weight of the pears.

3. The frequency table shows the price of a Mars bar in 30 different shops.

price	49p	50p	51p	52p	53p	54p
frequency	2	3	5	10	6	4

Calculate the mean price of a Mars bar.

4. The marks, out of 10, achieved by 25 teachers in a spelling test were as follows:

mark	5	6	7	8	9	10
frequency	8	7	4	2	3	1

Find (a) the mean mark
 (b) the median mark
 (c) the modal mark.

5. A golfer played the same hole 30 times with the following results.

score	3	4	5	6	7	8
frequency	2	11	5	5	3	4

(a) Find his mean score, median score and modal score on the hole.
(b) Which average best represents the data? Explain why.

Stem and leaf diagrams

Data can be displayed in groups in a stem and leaf diagram.
Here are the marks of 20 girls in a science test.

| 47 | 53 | 71 | 55 | 28 | 40 | 45 | 62 | 57 | 64 |
| 33 | 48 | 59 | 61 | 73 | 37 | 75 | 26 | 68 | 39 |

We will put the marks into groups 20–29, 30–39.:... 70–79.
We will choose the tens digit as the 'stem' and the units as the 'leaf'.

The first four marks are shown [47, 53, 71, 55]

Stem (tens)	Leaf (units)
2	
3	
4	7
5	3 5
6	
7	1

The complete diagram is below ...... and then with the leaves in numerical order:

Stem	Leaf
2	8 6
3	3 7 9
4	7 0 5 8
5	3 5 7 9
6	2 4 1 8
7	1 3 5

Stem	Leaf
2	6 8
3	3 7 9
4	0 5 7 8
5	3 5 7 9
6	1 2 4 8
7	1 3 5

The diagram shows the shape of the distribution. It is also easy to find the mode, the median and the range.

Exercise 3

1. The marks of 24 children in a test are shown

41	23	35	15	40	39	47	29
52	54	45	27	28	36	48	51
59	65	42	32	46	53	66	38

Stem	Leaf
1	
2	3
3	5
4	1
5	
6	

Draw a stem and leaf diagram. The first three entries are shown.

2. Draw a stem and leaf diagram for each set of data below

(a)
| 24 | 52 | 31 | 55 | 40 | 37 | 58 | 61 | 25 | 46 |
| 44 | 67 | 68 | 75 | 73 | 28 | 20 | 59 | 65 | 39 |

(b)
| 30 | 41 | 53 | 22 | 72 | 54 | 35 | 47 |
| 44 | 67 | 46 | 38 | 59 | 29 | 47 | 28 |

Stem	Leaf
2	
3	
4	
5	
6	
7	

3. Here is the stem and leaf diagram showing the masses, in kg, of some people on a bus.
   (a) Write down the range of the masses
   (b) How many people were on the bus?
   (c) What is the median mass?

Stem (tens)	Leaf (units)
3	3 7
4	1 2 7 7 8
5	1 6 8 9
6	0 3 7
7	4 5
8	2

4. In this question the stem shows the units digit and the leaf shows the first digit after the decimal point.
   Draw the stem and leaf diagram using the following data:

   2·4 3·1 5·2 4·7 1·4 6·2 4·5 3·3
   4·0 6·3 3·7 6·7 4·6 4·9 5·1 5·5
   1·8 3·8 4·5 2·4 5·8 3·3 4·6 2·8

   key
   3|7 means 3·7

Stem	Leaf
1	
2	
3	
4	
5	
6	

   (a) What is the median?
   (b) Write down the range.

3.3 Mental calculations

Mental calculation strategies

In Book 7i we discussed three strategies for mental calculation. Here is a reminder of each technique.

A 'Easy-to-add' numbers
   $16 + 57 + 24 = 16 + 24 + 57 = 40 + 57 = 97$
   $23 + 68 + 7 = 23 + 7 + 68 = 30 + 68 = 98$
   $45 + 108 + 35 = 45 + 35 + 108 = 80 + 108 = 188$

B Splitting numbers
   $33 + 48$: $30 + 40 = 70$ and $3 + 8 = 11$
             So $33 + 48 = 70 + 11 = 81$
   $264 + 38$: $260 + 30 = 290$ and $4 + 8 = 12$
             So $264 + 38 = 290 + 12 = 302$

C Add/subtract 9, 19, 29 … 11, 21, 31 …, adjusting by one
   $57 + 19 = 57 + 20 - 1 = 77 - 1 = 76$
   $109 + 39 = 109 + 40 - 1 = 149 - 1 = 148$
   $65 - 29 = 65 - 30 + 1 = 35 + 1 = 36$
   $111 - 59 = 111 - 60 + 1 = 51 + 1 = 52$

Practice questions

A
1. $7 + 13 + 49$
2. $18 + 57 + 12$
3. $25 + 37 + 25$
4. $31 + 55 + 29$
5. $28 + 2 + 67$
6. $55 + 99 + 25$
7. $17 + 13 + 68$
8. $64 + 16 + 27$
9. $42 + 56 + 8$
10. $23 + 25 + 17$
11. $16 + 9 + 44$
12. $91 + 54 + 9$

B
1. $23 + 35$
2. $51 + 37$
3. $44 + 37$
4. $32 + 69$
5. $57 + 59$
6. $67 + 27$
7. $108 + 58$
8. $124 + 33$
9. $63 + 74$
10. $125 + 62$
11. $45 + 68$
12. $53 + 84$

C
1. $55 + 19$
2. $64 + 39$
3. $87 + 9$
4. $55 + 31$
5. $27 + 41$
6. $74 + 29$
7. $25 + 61$
8. $84 - 19$
9. $74 - 59$
10. $93 - 61$
11. $87 - 29$
12. $113 - 81$

New strategies

D Doubling large numbers: work from the left

- double 63 = double 60 + double 3 = $120 + 6 = 126$
- double 79 = double 70 + double 9 = $140 + 18 = 158$
- double 127 = double 100 + double 20 + double 7 = $200 + 40 + 14 = 254$
- double 264 = double 200 + double 60 + double 4 = $400 + 120 + 8 = 528$

E (a) Multiplying by doubling and then halving:

- 23×5 $23 \times 10 = 230$ $230 \div 2 = 115$
- 7×45 $7 \times 90 = 630$ $630 \div 2 = 315$
- 11×15 $11 \times 30 = 330$ $330 \div 2 = 165$

(b) To multiply by 50, multiply by 100, then halve the re

- 23×50 $23 \times 100 = 2300$ $2300 \div 2 = 1150$
- 38×50 $38 \times 100 = 3800$ $3800 \div 2 = 1900$

(c) To multiply by 25, multiply by 100, then divide by 4

- 44×25 $44 \times 100 = 4400$ $4400 \div 4 = 1100$
- 56×25 $56 \times 100 = 5600$ $5600 \div 4 = 1400$

36×25
$36 \times 100 = 3600$
$3600 \div 4 = 900$

F Multiplying by 19 or 21 ... or by 49 or 51 ... or by 99 or 101

- $15 \times 21 = (15 \times 20) + 15$
  $= 300 + 15$
  $= 315$
- $14 \times 51 = (14 \times 50) + 14$
  $= 700 + 14$
  $= 714$
- $23 \times 101 = (23 \times 100) + 23$
  $= 2300 + 23$
  $= 2323$
- $17 \times 19 = (17 \times 20) - 17$
  $= 340 - 17$
  $= 323$
- $16 \times 49 = (16 \times 50) - 16$
  $= 800 - 16$
  $= 784$
- $19 \times 99 = (19 \times 100) - 19$
  $= 1900 - 19$
  $= 1881$

Practice questions

D 1. double 54   2. double 38   3. double 67   4. double 73
     5. double 28   6. double 79   7. double 115   8. double 126
     9. double 87   10. double 66   11. double 237   12. double 342

E 1. 22×50 2. 32×50 3. 24×25 4. 16×25
     5. 8×35 6. 8×15 7. 7×45 8. 9×35
     9. 14×50 10. 13×20 11. 18×50 12. 12×25

F 1. 7×21 2. 9×51 3. 11×41 4. 23×31
     5. 9×19 6. 6×29 7. 7×99 8. 15×99
     9. 12×101 10. 55×101 11. 23×1001 12. 15×999

Mental arithmetic tests

There are several sets of mental arithmetic questions in this section. It is intended that a teacher will read out each question twice, with all pupils' books closed. The answers are written down without any written working. Only a pencil or pen may be used.

Test 1

1. Add together five, four and nineteen.
2. Write the number that is eight less than three hundred.
3. What is five hundred and forty six to the nearest hundred?
4. What is nine multiplied by six?
5. Write the number eight thousand and six in figures.
6. Write nought point seven as a fraction.
7. Change seven and a half metres into centimetres.
8. What is four point six multiplied by one thousand?
9. How many thirds are there in two whole ones?
10. Twenty six per cent of the people in a survey did not like cheese. What percentage liked cheese?
11. The side of a square is five centimetres. What is the area of the square?
12. A bus journey starts at six fifty. It lasts for thirty five minutes. At what time does it finish?
13. At mid-day the temperature is seven degrees celsius. By midnight it has fallen twelve degrees. What is the temperature at midnight?
14. How many groups of 5 can be made from 100?
15. Write down a factor of twenty seven, which is greater than one.
16. What is six thousand divided by ten?
17. What number is eight squared?
18. How many seventeens are there in three hundred and forty?
19. What is the difference between 3·3 and 5·5?
20. How much does each person receive when a prize of £200 is shared between 5 people?
21. How many more than 27 is 40?
22. Twenty per cent of a number is twelve. What is the number?
23. Find the change from a £10 note if you spend £3·20.
24. How many altogether are 7, 6 and 5?
25. What is the remainder when 40 is divided by 7?

Test 2

1. What are two eighteens?
2. Add together 7, 8 and 9.
3. Divide 8 into 48.
4. Multiply 15 by 4.
5. Write $\frac{3}{4}$ as a percentage.
6. Work out 13 divided by 10 as a decimal.
7. What number is 40 less than 75?
8. Share a cost of £56 between 7 people.
9. What four coins make 67p?
10. What is the product of 60 and 3?
11. I have 2 dogs and 5 cats. What fraction of my pets are cats?
12. What is the cost of 2 C.D.s at £6·99 each?
13. Subtract the sum of 7 and 8 from 40.
14. One quarter of a number is 3·5. What is the number?
15. I have one 10p, three 5p and one 50p coin. How much money do I have?
16. Lemons cost 12p each. What is the cost of 7 lemons?
17. Apples cost 75p for five. What is the cost of one apple?
18. A bunch of grapes costs 64p. What is the change from £1?
19. How many 20p coins do I need for £2·80?
20. A shirt costs £15·95 new. I get a discount of £4. How much do I pay?
21. I share 60 sweets equally among 5 people. How many sweets does each receive?
22. The area of a square is 36 cm². How long is each side?
23. What must I spend from £20 to leave £14·50?
24. How many millimetres are there in 10 metres?
25. Write 5.30 a.m. in 24 hour clock time.

Test 3

1. What is the perimeter of a square with sides 8 cm?
2. Write one fifth as a percentage.
3. What number is half way between 4·2 and 4·8?
4. I have six 20p, one 5p and one 2p coin. How much do I have?
5. A poster costs three pounds. Andrew saves sixty pence per week. How many weeks will it be before he can buy it?
6. Screws cost 8 pence each. What is the cost of 25 screws?
7. Hooks cost 70 pence for five. What is the cost of 1 hook?
8. A pair of earrings costs £1·23. What is the change from £2?
9. How many 5p coins do I need for 85p?
10. A drill costs £34 new. I get a discount of £8·50. How much do I pay?
11. A T.V. programme starts at 9.50 and ends at 10.40. How long is the programme?
12. I travel at 60 m.p.h. for 4 hours. How far do I travel?
13. Work out ten per cent of £65.
14. Susie has 3 red pens and 4 black pens. What fraction of her pens are black?
15. Jacqui make a phone call from 18.40 until 19.21. How long is the call in minutes?
16. What five coins make 62p?
17. Write the number fifty thousand and six in figures.
18. The product of two numbers is thirty nine. One of the numbers is three. What is the other?
19. Change four and a half metres into centimetres.
20. Subtract 18 from 150.
21. Write three fifths as a decimal.

22. Increase forty pounds by 25 percent.
23. I buy three magazines at 99p each. What change do I get from £10?
24. How many lengths of 8 cm can be cut from 50 cm?
25. How many minutes are there in $2\frac{3}{4}$ hours?

Test 4

1. What are 37 twos?
2. What is the smaller angle between the hands of a clock at 8 o'clock?
3. Two angles of a triangle are 55° and 30°. What is the third angle?
4. What is 50% of £44?
5. How many 5p coins are needed to make £10?
6. A car costing £8500 is reduced by £120. What is the new price?
7. What number is twice as big as sixty-nine?
8. On a tray fourteen out of fifty peaches are rotten. What percentage is that?
9. Add together 11, 18 and 9.
10. A C.D. cost £13·55. Find the change from a £20 note.
11. What five coins make 51p?
12. What is $\frac{2}{3}$ of £186?
13. Write one twentieth as a decimal.
14. How many minutes are there between 8.15 p.m. and 10.20 p.m.?
15. A pools prize of six million pounds is shared equally between one hundred people. How much does each person receive?
16. If June 14th is a Tuesday what day of the week is June 23rd?
17. True or false: 1 kg is about 2 pounds?
18. How many millimetres are there in 3·5 metres?
19. A daily newspaper costs 25p from Monday to Saturday and 45p on Sunday. What is the total cost for the seven days?
20. Write $\frac{3}{4}$ as a decimal.
21. A clock ticks once every second. How many times does it tick between six o'clock and seven o'clock?
22. Add eleven to nine times eight
23. A rectangular piece of wood measures 15 cm by 10 cm. What is its area?
24. An egg box holds six eggs. How many boxes are needed for 100 eggs?
25. How many 19p stamps can I buy for a pound?

Test 5

1. By how much is three kilos more than 800 grams?
2. How many 20p coins do I need to make £400?
3. How many square centimetres are there in one square metre?
4. How much more than £108 is £300?
5. Two angles of a triangle are 44° and 54°. What is the third angle?
6. Work out 10% of £5000.
7. My watch reads ten past eight. It is 15 minutes fast. What is the correct time?
8. A 50p coin is 2 mm thick. What is the value of a pile of 50p coins 2 cm high?
9. Add together £2·35 and £4·15.
10. A ship was due at noon on Friday but arrived at 8.00 a.m. on Saturday. How many hours late was the ship?
11. By how much is half a metre longer than 1 millimetre? (answer in mm).
12. What number is thirty-five more than eighty?
13. How many minutes are there in two and a half hours?

14. From nine times seven take away five.
15. A T.V. show lasting 45 minutes starts at 10 minutes to eight. When does it finish?
16. A train travels at an average speed of 48 mph. How far does it travel in 2 hours?
17. What is the perimeter of a square of side 14 cm?
18. A string of length 390 cm is cut in half. How long is each piece?
19. A half is a quarter of a certain number. What is the number?
20. A man died in 1993 aged 58. In what year was he born?
21. *Roughly* how many millimetres are there in one foot?
22. Write down ten thousand pence in pounds.
23. What is a quarter of two hundred and ten?
24. Find two ways of making 66p using five coins.
25. John weighs 8 stones and Jim weighs 80 kg. Who is heavier?

Test 6

1. What number is 10 less than nine thousand?
2. I want to buy 4 records, each costing £4·49. To the nearest pound, how much will my bill be?
3. How many magazines costing 95p can I buy with £10?
4. What is the total of 57 and 963?
5. What is a half of a half of 10?
6. True or false: 3 feet is slightly longer than 1 metre.
7. A triangle has a base 4 cm and a height of 10 cm. What is its area?
8. What number is exactly mid-way between 3·7 and 3·8?
9. Work out two squared plus three squared.
10. The pupils in Darren's class are given lockers numbered from 32 to 54. How many pupils are there in Darren's class?
11. Write 7 divided by 100 as a decimal.
12. Jane is 35 cm taller than William, who is 1·34 metres tall. How tall is Jane?
13. A toy train travels 6 metres in seconds. How far will it go in one minute?
14. Which is larger: 2 cubed or 3 squared?
15. What number is next in the series 1, 2, 4, 8, ...?
16. Write the number '$2\frac{1}{2}$ million' in figures.
17. Joe borrowed £4·68 from his father. He paid him back with a £10 note. How much change did he receive?
18. What is a tenth of 2·4?
19. I think of a number and subtract 6. The result is equal to 7 times 3. What is the number?
20. Write down the next prime number after 32.
21. How much longer is 7·5 metres than 725 centimetres?
22. How many lines of symmetry does a square have?
23. What is a quarter of a half?
24. Work out 200 times 300.
25. How many edges does a cube have?

KS3 tests

The next 2 tests are written in the form of the Key Stage 3 mental arithmetic tests.

Each question will be repeated once. You have 5 seconds to answer questions 1 to 6, 10 seconds to answer questions 7 to 20 and 15 seconds to answer the remaining questions. You will be told to put down your pen after the correct time interval for each question.

Work out the answer to each question in your head and write down only the answer. Sometimes other useful information, such as the numbers used in the question, has been written down to help you. Look at the sheets on page 93.

Test 1

- Time: 5 seconds
  1. Look at the numbers on your answer sheet. What is half their total?
  2. Change one hundred and forty millimetres into centimetres.
  3. What is sixty-three divided by nine?
  4. Look at the equation. Write down the value for n.
  5. Your answer sheet shows a fraction. Write the fraction in its simplest form.
  6. Write four fifths as a decimal number.

- Time: 10 seconds
  7. Look at the expression. What is its value when x equals six?
  8. A TV film starts at five minutes to seven. It lasts forty-five minutes. At what time does the film finish?
  9. What is one hundred and forty minus eighty?
  10. On a coach there are fifty pupils. Thirty of the pupils are girls. A pupil is chosen at random. What is the probability that a girl is chosen?
  11. Look at your answer sheet. Work at the answer.
  12. Ten per cent of a number is eight. What is the number?
  13. A pond is fifteen feet long. About how many metres is that?
  14. Write the number two and a half million in figures.
  15. Look at the equation. Use it to work out the value of $2x$.
  16. Estimate the size of this angle in degrees.
  17. Estimate the value of fifty-two per cent of sixteen pounds ninety pence.
  18. How many halves are there altogether in four and a half?
  19. What is five hundred minus forty-five?
  20 n stands for a number. Write an expression for the following: 'add six to n, then multiply the result by three'.

- Time: 15 seconds
21. Pete and Bob share some money in the ratio of one to two. Pete's share is fifteen pounds. How much money is Bob's share?
22. What is one quarter of two hundred thousand?
23. Write two consecutive numbers that add up to thirty-five.
24. Use the calculation on your answer sheet to help you to work out how many seventeens there are in two thousand two hundred and ten.
25. Divide twenty-two pounds between four people. How much money does each person get?
26. Write an approximate answer to the calculation on your answer sheet.
27. Find n, if two times n minus one equals eleven.
28. Your answer sheet shows the marks by four pupils in a test. What is the mean mark?
29. Work out three plus four plus five all squared.
30. A man's heart beats 80 times in 1 minute. How many times does it beat in one hour?

Test 2

- Time: 5 seconds
1. Write the number five hundred and sixty-seven to the nearest hundred.
2. What is five point two multiplied by one thousand?
3. Work out five per cent of four hundred.
4. Simplify the expression on your answer sheet.
5. What is the sum of the numbers on your answer sheet?
6. What is one tenth of half a million?

- Time: 10 seconds
7. Look at the expression. What is its value when x equals four?
8. Tim's height is one point seven metres. Greg's height is one hundredth of a metre more than Tim's height. What is Greg's height?
9. Twenty per cent of a number is eleven. What is the number?
10. Two angles in a triangle are each sixty-five degrees. What is the size of the third angle?
11. In a group of sixty-three children, twenty-eight are girls. How many are boys?
12. What is the area of this triangle?
13. The value of four x plus y is sixteen.
Write the value of eight x plus two y.

14. Divide two by nought point one.
15. Michelle got thirty out of fifty on a test. What percentage did she get?
16. Work out one plus two plus three all squared.
17. Look at the inequalities on your answer sheet. Write down one possible value for x.
18. How many eighths are there in one half?
19. Multiply six point nought two by one thousand.
20. On the answer sheet find the missing number.

- Time: 15 seconds:

21. What is the cost of two items at two pounds ninety-nine pence each?
22. Look at these numbers. Put a ring around the smallest number.
23. Write an approximate answer to the calculation on your answer sheet.
24. Each side of a square is thirty-two centimetres. What is the perimeter of the square?
25. Look at these pairs of numbers. Between which pair of numbers does the square root of thirty-three lie? Put a ring around the correct pair.
26. Look at the calculation on your answer sheet.
    What is sixteen multiplied by nineteen?
27. A map has a scale of one to one thousand.
    What is the actual length of a path which is 8 cm long on the map?
28. Look at the expression on your answer sheet. Write down the value of the expression when x equals nought.
29. Which has the longer perimeter: a square of side 10 cm or an equilateral triangle of side 15 cm?
30. A film started at eight fifty p.m. and ended two and a quarter hours later. When did it finish?

Test 1 Answer sheet

Time: 5 seconds

Question	Answer	
1		18 22
2	cm	
3		
4		$3n = 12$
5		$\frac{14}{21}$
6		

Time: 10 seconds

7		$5x$
8		
9		
10		50 pupils, 30 girls
11		$32 - (12 + 7)$
12		
13	m	
14		
15		$x - 3 = 30$
16		⟨
17		52% £16.90
18		
19		
20		

Time: 15 seconds

21		1:2 £15
22		
23		
24		$17 \times 260 = 4420$, 2210
25		£22 4
26		41.22×9.87
27		
28		1, 3, 4, 4
29		$(3 + 4 + 5)^2$
30		

Test 2 Answer sheet

Time: 5 seconds

Question	Answer	
1		567
2		5.2
3		
4		$a \times a \times a$
5		2.3 2.7 2.3 2.7
6		

Time: 10 seconds

7		$2(x + 1)$
8		$1.7\,\text{m}$ $\frac{1}{100}\,\text{m}$
9		
10		
11		
12	cm²	(triangle: 8 cm base, 7 cm height)
13		$4x + y$ $8x + 2y$
14		2 0.1
15	%	
16		$(1 + 2 + 3)^2$
17		$-4 < x < 0$
18		
19		6.02
20		$3 \times \square - 1 = 11$

Time: 15 seconds

21	£	
22		0.3 0.18 0.35 0.332 0.2
23		$497.3 \div 1.97$
24		
25		3, 4 4, 5 5, 6 6, 7 7, 8
26		$32 \times 19 = 608$
27		1 : 1000 8 cm
28		$(x - 3)(x + 2)$
29		
30		8.50 pm $2\frac{1}{4}$

3.4 Order of operations

- The table below shows the order in which mathematical operations are performed.

B rackets	( )	do first
I indices	x^y	do next
D ivision	÷	do this pair next
M ultiplication	×	
A ddition	+	do this pair next
S ubtraction	−	

Examples

(a) $9 + 3 \times 4$
  $= 9 + 12$
  $= 21$

(b) $20 - 8 \div 2$
  $= 20 - 4$
  $= 16$

(c) $15 \div (7 - 2)$
  $= 15 \div 5$
  $= 3$

(d) $7 + 3^2$
  $= 7 + 9$
  $= 16$

Remember the word 'B I D M A S'.

Exercise 1

Work out the following. Show every step in your working.

1. $7 + 2 \times 4$
2. $9 - 2 \times 3$
3. $(10 - 3) \times 4$
4. $12 \div 3 - 1$
5. $15 + 9 \div 3$
6. $9 + 26 \div 13$
7. $10 + 3 \times 10$
8. $44 - 11 \times 2$
9. $36 \div (20 - 8)$
10. $(15 + 4) \times 2$
11. $10 + 10 \times 10$
12. $27 - 7 - 10$
13. $7 + 2 \times 2 - 6$
14. $12 - (6 \times 1) + 2$
15. $1 + 12 \div (15 - 9)$
16. $(4 \times 5) - (6 \div 2)$
17. $100 - (66 \div 3)$
18. $(100 \times 2) \div (101 - 99)$
19. $6 + 28 \div 7 - 3$
20. $20 \div 5 - 18 \div 6$
21. $2 \times (3 \times 2 - 1)$
22. $\dfrac{18 + 2}{2}$
23. $\dfrac{60}{9 + 6}$
24. $\dfrac{35 + 25}{9 - 7}$

25. Work at 5×3^2 [Remember: work out 3^2 and then multiply by 5.]

26. Work out
    (a) $7 + 3^2$
    (b) $10 - 2^3$
    (c) $4^2 - 6$
    (d) $1^4 + 5^2$
    (e) $(1 + 1)^2$
    (f) $2 \times (3^2 - 1)$
    (g) $(20 - 15)^2 \div 5$
    (h) $(3^2 + 4^2) \div 25$
    (i) $64 \div 8 - 2^3$
    (j) $\dfrac{3^2 - 1}{4}$
    (k) $\dfrac{5^2}{2 + 3}$
    (l) $\dfrac{(1 + 2)^2 + 1}{10}$

Exercise 2

Copy each question and write brackets so that each calculation gives the correct answer.

1. $3 + 2 \times 5 = 25$
2. $8 + 3 \times 4 = 44$
3. $3 \times 4 + 2 = 18$
4. $7 + 5 \times 6 = 37$
5. $4 \times 9 - 4 = 20$
6. $7 \times 18 - 7 = 77$
7. $30 - 15 \times 3 = 45$
8. $56 - 7 \div 7 = 7$
9. $36 \div 4 + 5 = 4$
10. $16 - 10 \div 18 \div 6 = 2$
11. $6 + 14 \div 2 = 10$
12. $9 + 15 \div 8 = 3$
13. $8 + 2 \times 6 - 5 = 10$
14. $51 \div 3 + 5 = 22$
15. $11 + 6 \times 4 = 68$
16. $10 - 2 + 2^2 = 4$
17. $1 + 9 + 10 \div 4 = 5$
18. $3 + 5 \times 9 - 8 = 8$
19. $8 - 2^3 + 1 = 1$
20. $8 + 15 \div 3 \times 0 = 0$

3.5 Using a calculator

Exercise 1

Use a calculator and give the answer correct to two decimal places.

1. 3.4×1.23
2. $20.4 - 5.7412$
3. 0.341^2
4. $0.17 + 2.89 - 1.514$
5. $3.2^2 - 2.8$
6. $4.6 \times 1.9 + 8.05$
7. $0.54 \times 0.87 - 0.1$
8. $8.7 \div 2.73$
9. $12.5 - 0.516 + 1.2$
10. $\dfrac{8.9}{7.4}$
11. $\dfrac{20.2}{5.6} + 8.2$
12. $\dfrac{8.65}{6} - 0.12$

In Questions 13 to 30 remember 'BIDMAS'.

13. $2.6 + 2.7 \times 1.9$
14. $8.01 + 0.8 \times 3.2$
15. $7.93 + 5 \div 12$
16. $8.6 \div 0.7 - 5.55$
17. $8 \div 0.55 + 2.33$
18. $8.06 + 1.4 \times 1.5$
19. $3.5 + \dfrac{8.5}{1.34}$
20. $1.53^2 + 2.53$
21. $6.4 + \dfrac{1.7}{0.85}$
22. $8.65 + 30 \div 8.2$
23. $5.44 + 1.37^2$
24. $6.4^2 \div 19$
25. $0.751 - 0.14 \times 0.9$
26. 2.3^3
27. $10 + 10 \times 10$
28. $8.9 + \dfrac{19.6}{15}$
29. $\dfrac{2.7 + 5.65}{3.3}$
30. $\dfrac{11.2 - 5.67}{1.9}$

Using brackets

Most calculators have brackets buttons like these $[(\_\_\_]$, $[\_\_\_)]$.

When you press the left hand bracket button $[(\_\_\_]$ you may see

$[\ C01 \quad\quad 0. \ ]$ ignore this.

When the right hand bracket button is pressed you will see that the calculation inside the brackets has been performed. Try it.

Don't forget to press the $[=]$ button at the end to give the final answer.

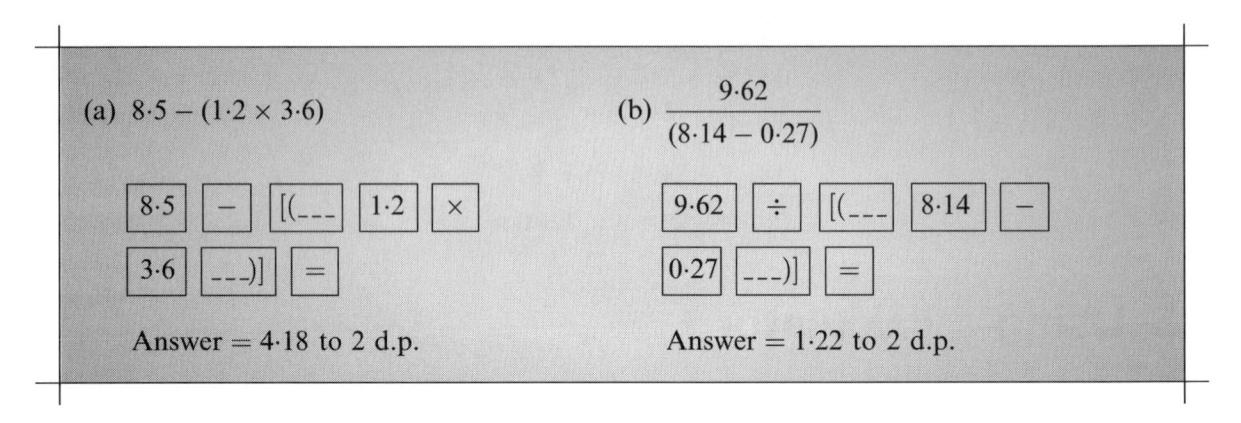

(a) $8 \cdot 5 - (1 \cdot 2 \times 3 \cdot 6)$

$\boxed{8 \cdot 5}$ $\boxed{-}$ $\boxed{[(\_\_\_}$ $\boxed{1 \cdot 2}$ $\boxed{\times}$
$\boxed{3 \cdot 6}$ $\boxed{\_\_\_)]}$ $\boxed{=}$

Answer = 4·18 to 2 d.p.

(b) $\dfrac{9 \cdot 62}{(8 \cdot 14 - 0 \cdot 27)}$

$\boxed{9 \cdot 62}$ $\boxed{\div}$ $\boxed{[(\_\_\_}$ $\boxed{8 \cdot 14}$ $\boxed{-}$
$\boxed{0 \cdot 27}$ $\boxed{\_\_\_)]}$ $\boxed{=}$

Answer = 1·22 to 2 d.p.

Exercise 2

Work out and give the answer correct to 2 decimal places.

1. $11 \cdot 52 - (3 \cdot 14 \times 2 \cdot 6)$
2. $12 \cdot 5 + (3 \cdot 8 \div 6)$
3. $(5 \cdot 27 + 8 \cdot 2) \div 2 \cdot 7$
4. $9 \cdot 6 + (8 \cdot 7 \div 11)$
5. $(9 \cdot 5 \div 7) - 0 \cdot 44$
6. $13 \cdot 7 - (8 \cdot 2 \times 1 \cdot 31)$
7. $6 \cdot 31 - \left(\dfrac{8 \cdot 2}{1 \cdot 9}\right)$
8. $\left(\dfrac{7 \cdot 65}{1 \cdot 5}\right) - 3 \cdot 06$
9. $\dfrac{3 \cdot 63}{3 \cdot 9 + 0 \cdot 121}$
10. $(2 \cdot 26 + 3 \cdot 15 + 8 \cdot 99) \div 1 \cdot 45$
11. $5 \cdot 89 \times (1 \cdot 8 - 0 \cdot 633)$
12. $17 \cdot 8 \div (5 \cdot 8 - 4 \cdot 95)$
13. $(11 \cdot 2 \div 7) \times 2 \cdot 43$
14. $(3 \cdot 65 + 1 \cdot 4 - 2 \cdot 34) \times 2 \cdot 6$
15. $35 - (8 \cdot 7 \times 2 \cdot 65)$
16. $\dfrac{(9 \cdot 37 + 8 \cdot 222)}{2 \cdot 47}$
17. $\dfrac{11 \cdot 23}{(9 \cdot 7 - 6 \cdot 66)}$
18. $\dfrac{(114 - 95 \cdot 6)}{14}$

19. $2.7^2 - 1.56$ **20.** $0.73^2 \times 5.2$ **21.** $6.6 + 4.1^2$
22. $(1.5 + 2.61)^2$ **23.** $(8.2 - 6.93)^2$ **24.** $(2.4 \times 0.15)^2$
25. $8.9 - (1.35)^2$ **26.** $(2.7^2 - 3.3) \div 5$ **27.** $2.1^2 + 3.11^2$
28. $\left(\dfrac{4.5}{8}\right) + \left(\dfrac{4.7}{7}\right)$ **29.** $3.2^2 - \left(\dfrac{4.2}{3.7}\right)$ **30.** $\dfrac{2.6^2}{(1.4 + 1.91)}$

Hint: Use the $\boxed{x^2}$ key

Fractions

- The $\boxed{a\,^b\!/_c}$ key is used for fractions.

  To enter $\frac{3}{4}$, press $\boxed{3}$ $\boxed{a\,^b\!/_c}$ $\boxed{4}$. You see $\boxed{3\lrcorner 4}$

  To enter $5\frac{1}{3}$, press $\boxed{5}$ $\boxed{a\,^b\!/_c}$ $\boxed{1}$ $\boxed{a\,^b\!/_c}$ $\boxed{3}$. You see $\boxed{5\lrcorner 1\lrcorner 3}$

Exercise 3

Work out

1. $\frac{2}{3} + \frac{1}{4}$ **2.** $\frac{5}{6} + \frac{1}{3}$ **3.** $\frac{8}{9} + \frac{1}{3}$ **4.** $\frac{4}{15} + \frac{1}{2}$
5. $\frac{3}{5} - \frac{1}{2}$ **6.** $\frac{7}{8} - \frac{1}{16}$ **7.** $\frac{5}{7} - \frac{1}{2}$ **8.** $\frac{5}{6} - \frac{1}{5}$
9. $\frac{9}{10} + \frac{1}{20}$ **10.** $\frac{11}{12} - \frac{3}{4}$ **11.** $\frac{4}{9} \times \frac{1}{2}$ **12.** $\frac{3}{11} \times \frac{1}{4}$
13. $2\frac{1}{4} + \frac{2}{3}$ **14.** $3\frac{2}{3} - 1\frac{1}{2}$ **15.** $4\frac{1}{2} + \frac{5}{8}$ **16.** $\frac{1}{6} + 3\frac{3}{4}$
17. $3\frac{1}{5} \times 1\frac{1}{2}$ **18.** $4\frac{1}{2} \div \frac{3}{4}$ **19.** $3\frac{1}{2} \div \frac{2}{5}$ **20.** $21 \div 5\frac{1}{4}$

21. Copy and complete.

(a) $1\frac{1}{4} + 2\frac{1}{5} = \square$ (b) $\square + 3\frac{1}{3} = 4\frac{1}{2}$ (c) $\square + \frac{5}{6} = 1\frac{3}{4}$
(d) $\square - \frac{3}{7} = \frac{3}{4}$ (e) $\square \div \frac{2}{3} = 2$ (f) $\square \times 1\frac{2}{5} = \frac{1}{2}$

22. Copy and complete.

(a)
+		$\frac{3}{5}$		$1\frac{3}{4}$
	$\frac{5}{8}$		$\frac{5}{6}$	
$\frac{1}{4}$				
$2\frac{1}{2}$	$2\frac{5}{8}$			
			$\frac{11}{15}$	

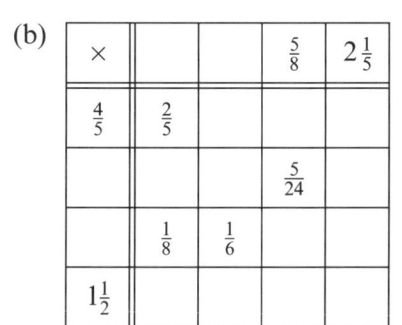

(b)
×			$\frac{5}{8}$	$2\frac{1}{5}$
$\frac{4}{5}$	$\frac{2}{5}$			
			$\frac{5}{24}$	
	$\frac{1}{8}$	$\frac{1}{6}$		
$1\frac{1}{2}$				

Negative numbers

- On a calculator the $\boxed{+/-}$ key changes the sign of a number from (+) to (−) or from (−) to (+).
- On most calculators we press $\boxed{+/-}$ *after* the number.

On graphics calculators we press it before the number, though this varies according to the model.

On a calculator work out:
(a) $-5 \cdot 2 + 7 \cdot 81$
Press the keys
$\boxed{5 \cdot 2}\ \boxed{+/-}\ \boxed{+}\ \boxed{7 \cdot 81}\ \boxed{=}$
Answer = 2·61

(b) $7 \cdot 5 \div (-0 \cdot 04)$

$\boxed{7 \cdot 5}\ \boxed{\div}\ \boxed{0 \cdot 04}\ \boxed{+/-}\ \boxed{=}$
Answer = −187·5
Notice that we do not *need* the brackets buttons. You may use them if you prefer.

Exercise 4

Work out the following. Give the answer correct to one decimal place where appropriate.

1. -7×3
2. $-5 \times (-2)$
3. $8 \div (-4)$
4. $10 \times (-4)$
5. $-2 \times (-2)$
6. $-12 \div 3$
7. $-5 \times (-4)$
8. $-8 - 11$
9. $-7 + 2$
10. $-9 + 30$
11. $-20 \div 4$
12. $-16 - 15$
13. $-3 \cdot 4 \times (-2 \cdot 5)$
14. $-0 \cdot 5 \times 6 \cdot 8$
15. $12 \cdot 5 - (-2 \cdot 5)$
16. $-1 \cdot 1 \times (-1 \cdot 1)$
17. $-8 \div (-0 \cdot 25)$
18. $-6 \cdot 8 \div 0 \cdot 1$
19. $\dfrac{-8 \times (-3)}{4}$
20. $\dfrac{12}{(3 \times (-2))}$
21. $\dfrac{20}{(-2)} + 8$
22. $-11 \cdot 4 + 1 \cdot 71$
23. $-9 \cdot 2 - 7 \cdot 4 + 15 \cdot 2$
24. $-4 \cdot 74 - (-13 \cdot 08)$
25. $\dfrac{(-8 \cdot 23) \times (-1 \cdot 24)}{3 \cdot 6}$
26. $\dfrac{5 \cdot 1 \times (-1 \cdot 42)}{(-1 \cdot 7)}$
27. $\dfrac{(-2 \cdot 3) \times (-2 \cdot 8)}{(-3 \cdot 5)}$
28. $(-3 \cdot 6)^2 + 2 \cdot 7$
29. $(-3 \cdot 91)^2 - 7$
30. $17 \cdot 4 - (-7 \cdot 2)^2$
31. $-6 \cdot 2 + (-8 \cdot 4)$
32. $-91 + (-8 \cdot 1)^2$
33. $-2 \cdot 5 \times (-1 \cdot 7)$
34. $-7 \cdot 2 + \left(\dfrac{4 \cdot 3}{1 \cdot 5}\right)$
35. $-8 \cdot 7 \times \left(\dfrac{7 \cdot 2}{11}\right)$
36. $(-7 \cdot 2 + 4)^2$

Calculator words

- When you hold a calculator display upside down some numbers appear to form words: `4508` spells "Gosh"

  `0.70` spells "Old"

  (ignoring the decimal point)

Exercise 5

Translate this passage using a calculator and the clues below:

"①!" shouted Olag out of the window of his ②. "I need some ③ / ④ for my dinner. Do you ⑤ them?"
"⑥ did" ⑦ / ⑧ "I even took off the ⑨ for free. ⑩ / ⑪ / ⑫ they were. The problem is that all the ⑬ were eaten in the ⑭, mostly by ⑮. ⑯ / ⑰ such a ⑱ / ⑲ lately. ⑳ and ㉑ are always ㉒ because of the amount of ㉓ they drink every night"

"㉔ well, he is the ㉕ I suppose" Olag grumbled "Roast ㉖ again tonight then ..."

Clues to passage

①: $2(9-4)$
②: $(3 \div 40) + 0.0011$
③: $\frac{3}{8} - (39.2 \div 10^4)$
④: $5 \times 12 \times 100 - 7$
⑤: $(90 \times 80) + (107 \times 5)$
⑥: $\sqrt{0.01} \times 10$
⑦: $(68 + 1.23) \div 200$
⑧: $101^2 - (5 \times 13) - 2$
⑨: $750^2 + (296\,900 \div 20)$
⑩: $2^3 \times 5^2 \times 3 + 16.3 + 1.7$
⑪: $(70\,000 \div 2) + (3 \times 2)$
⑫: $11\,986 \div 2$
⑬: $(600^2 - 6640) \div 10$
⑭: $200^2 - 685$
⑮: $(0.5^2 \times 0.6)$
⑯: $\sqrt{289} \times 2$
⑰: $836.4 \div 17 + 1.8$
⑱: $30^2 + 18$
⑲: $5^3 \times 64.6$
⑳: $(63\,508 \times 5) - 3$
㉑: $\sqrt{(1160 - 4)}$
㉒: 1.3803×0.25
㉓: $(32 \times 10^3) + 8$
㉔: $2^3 \times 5$
㉕: $(5^3 \times 2^2 \times 11) + 8$
㉖: $7 \times 10^7 - 9\,563\,966$

Crossword

Copy this crossword puzzle and complete it using the clues below. [The answers are calculator words.]

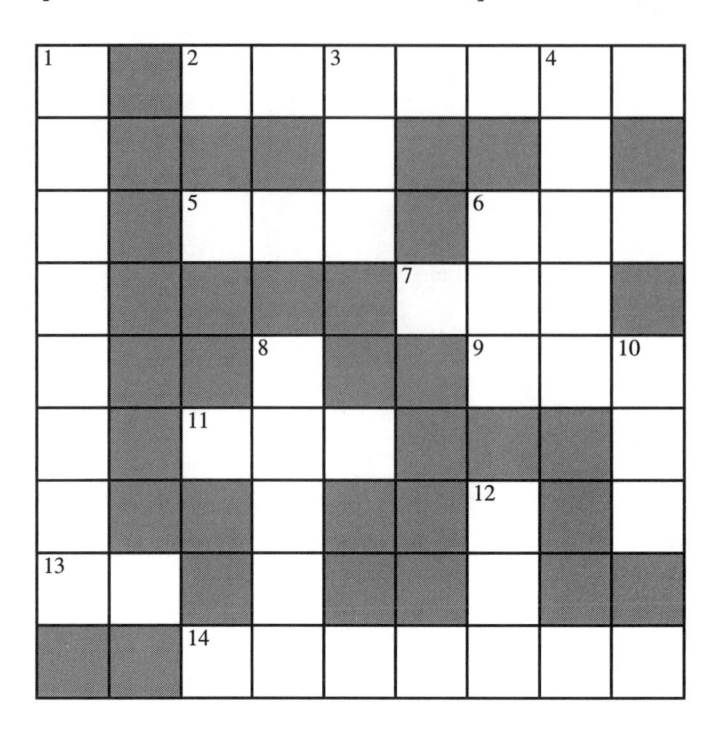

Across

$2 : 4 \times 10^6 - 218\,363$	can be read
$5 : (2 \times 5 \times 7 \times 10) + 10$	fuel
$6 : 9^2 \times 10 - 1$	slang for mouth
$7 : 1000 - (7^2 \times 10 - 4)$	not hers
$9 : \frac{1}{2} - \frac{3}{25}$	it's time for …
$11 : (8^2 \times 10) - (8 \times 4)$	no good for farming
$13 : \frac{3}{5} + \frac{3}{10}$	don't stop
$14 : (6000^2 \div 10) + (500 \times 700) - 18\,462$	imprison

Down

$1 : (2 \times 10^4 \times 3 \times 10^3) + (75 \times 76 \times 77) - 2866$	fond of slugs
$3 : \frac{3}{4}(1000) - 11$	hair treatment
$4 : 50 \times 700 + 2^3 - 1$	might fall off
$6 : (2 \times 3^4 \times 5) + 3^2$	part of a boat
$8 : (2^5 \times 10^3) + (0.8 \div 0.1)$	it's bad for you
$10 : (65 \times 10) - (2 \times 5 \times 2 \times 2)$	… you might find treasure
$12 : (5000 - 1550) \div 10$	rhymes with 'knee'

3.6 Reflection

Reflections are quite common in everyday life. Think of examples of reflections:
- in the classroom
- at home
- anywhere

- The shape on the right has line symmetry. This can be checked by either paper folding, using tracing paper or by using a mirror.
  In a mathematical reflection we imagine a line of symmetry which acts like a double-sided mirror.

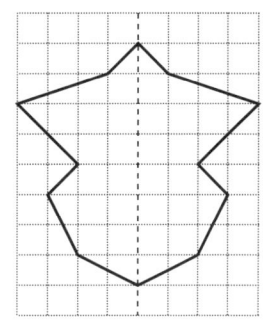

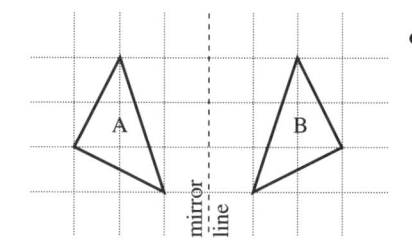

- Triangle B is the image of triangle A under reflection in the mirror line. Similarly triangle A is the image of triangle B under reflection in the same line.

- In the reflection on the right, the image of the shape ABCD is the shape A'B'C'D'.
  Notice that the perpendicular distance from A to the mirror line is the same as the perpendicular distance from A' to the mirror line. Similarly B, C and D are the same perpendicular distances from the line as B', C' and D' respectively.

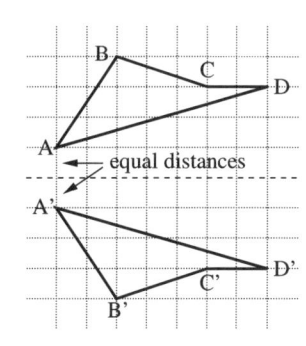

- Extra care is required when the mirror line lies along a diagonal.
  Notice that the line PP′ is perpendicular to the mirror line.

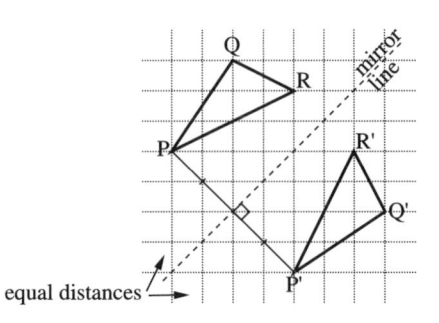

- The mirror line can pass through the shape which is being reflected, as shown here.

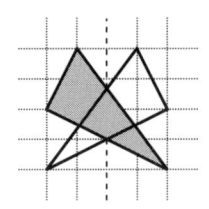

Exercise 1

Copy each shape on squared paper and draw the image after reflection in the broken line.

1. 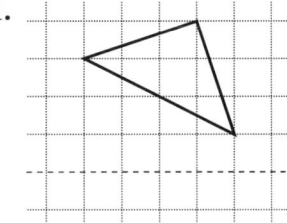
2. 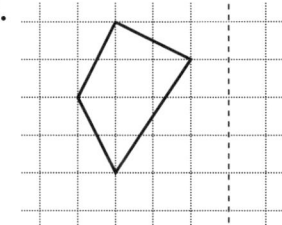
3. 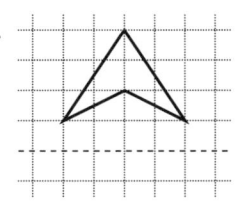
4. 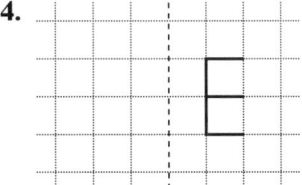
5. 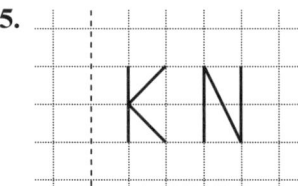
6. 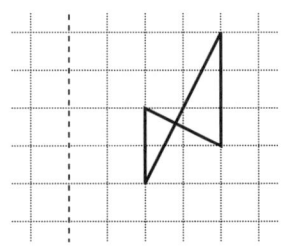
7. 
8. 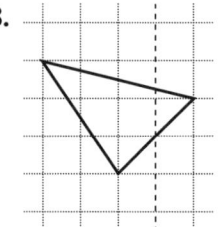
9.

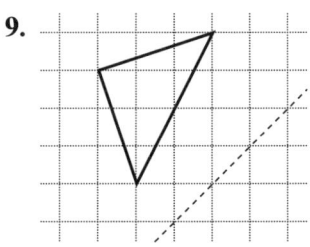

10.

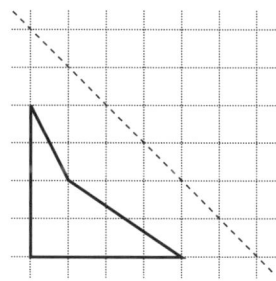

11.

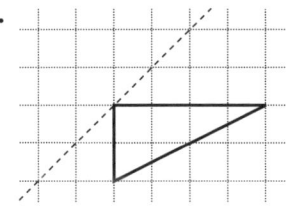

12.

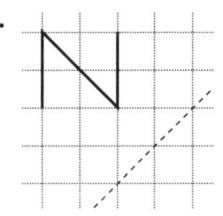

13. Write your own name in capital letters and then reflect the letters in a horizontal line.

14. Draw any shape of your own design (not too complicated!) and then reflect it in either a horizontal, vertical or diagonal line.

In Questions **15** to **17** first reflect the shape in line 1 and then reflect the image in line 2.

15.

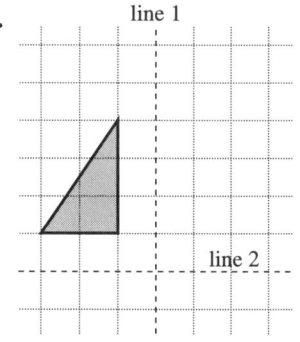

16.

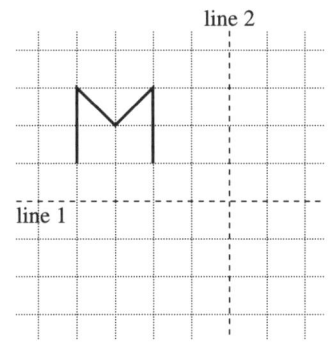

17.

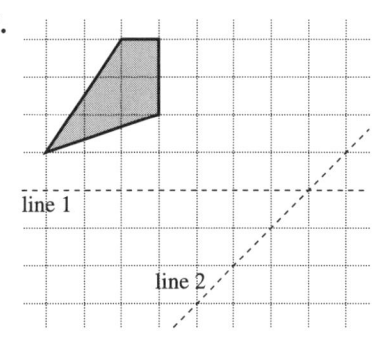

Questions **18** to **20** are more difficult reflections. Copy each shape and draw the image after reflection in the broken line.

18.

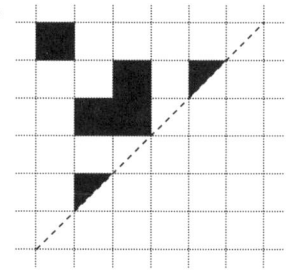

19.

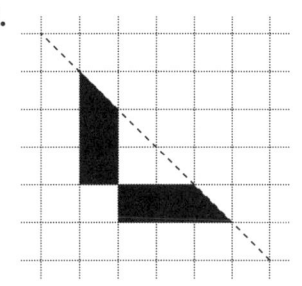

20.

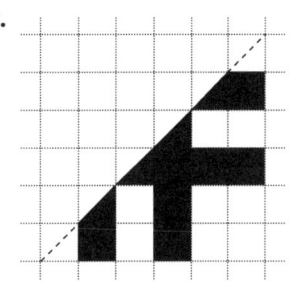

Using coordinates

(a) Triangle 2 is the image of triangle 1 under reflection in the x axis.

We will use the shorthand '△' for 'triangle'.

(b) △3 is the image of △2 under reflection in the line $x = -1$.

(c) △4 is the image of △1 under reflection in the line $y = x$.

Teacher's note. There is work on equations of lines in section 5.1, 'Graphs of straight lines'.

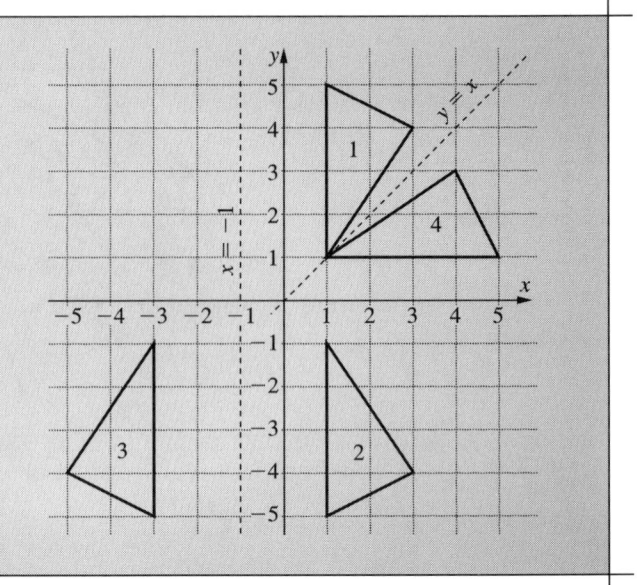

Exercise 2

1. Copy the diagram.
   (a) Reflect the shape in the x axis. Label the image A.
   (b) Reflect the shape in the y axis. Label the image B.

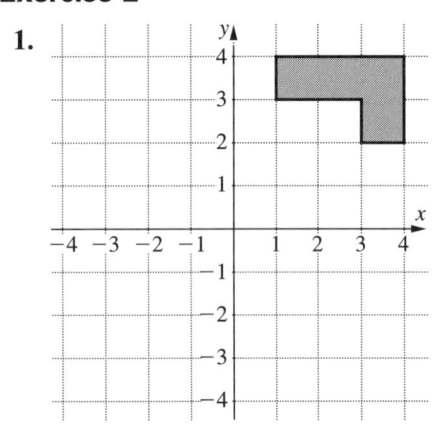

2. Copy the diagram onto squared paper.
   (a) Reflect the shaded triangle in $y = 2$. Label the image A.
   (b) Reflect the shaded triangle in $x = 1$. Label the image B.
   (c) Reflect the shaded triangle in the x axis. Label the image C.

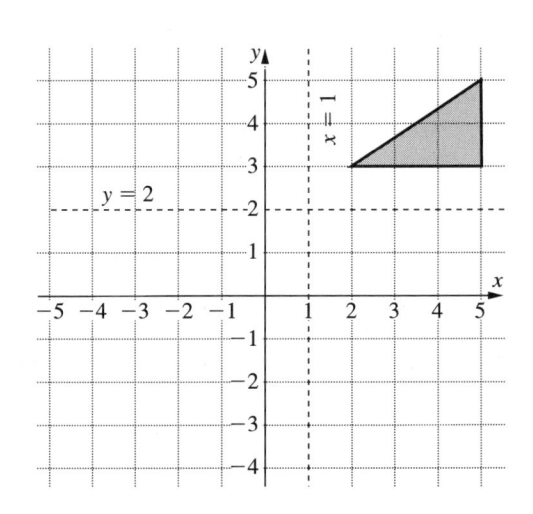

3. Copy the diagram onto squared paper.
Draw the image of the shaded triangle under reflection in:
(a) $y = 1$, label it $\triangle$A
(b) $x = -1$, label it $\triangle$B
(c) $y = x$, label it $\triangle$C

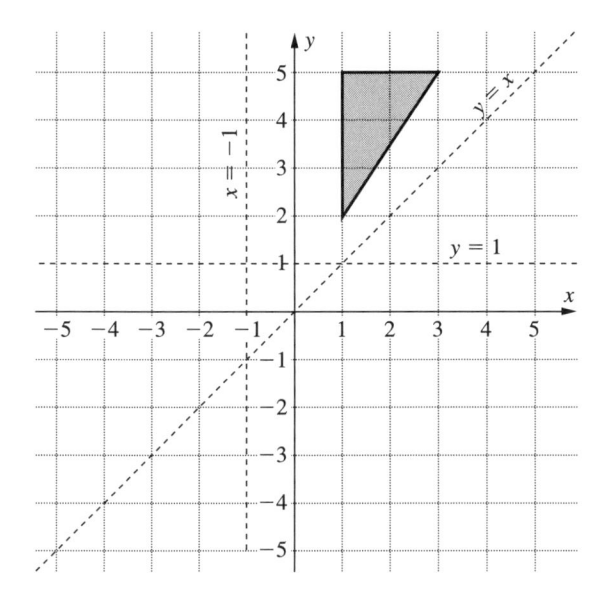

4. (a) Draw x and y axes with values from -6 to $+6$ and draw shape A which has vertices at (3, 1), (5, 3), (5, 1), (4, 0)
(b) Reflect shape A in the x axis onto shape B.
(c) Reflect shape A in the y axis onto shape C.
(d) Reflect shape A in the line $y = x$ onto shape D.

5. (a) Draw x and y axes with values from -6 to $+6$ and draw shape A which has vertices at (1, -2), (3, -3), (3, -4), (1, -6)
(b) Reflect shape A in the y axis onto shape B.
(c) Reflect shape B (not shape A!) in the line $y = x$ onto shape C.
(d) Reflect shape C in the line $y = 1\frac{1}{2}$ onto shape D.
(e) Write down the coordinates of the vertices of shape D.

6. (a) Draw x and y axes with values from -6 to $+6$ and draw shape P which has vertices at (-4, 2), (-4, 3), (-3, 5), (-3, 2).
(b) Reflect shape P in the line $y = 2$ onto shape Q.
(c) Reflect shape Q in the y axis onto shape R.
(d) Reflect shape R in the line $y = x$ onto shape S.
(e) Write down the coordinate of the vertices of shape S.

7. Write down the equation of the mirror line for the following reflections:
   (a) △A → △C
   (b) △A → △B
   (c) △D → △G
   (d) △F → △E
   (e) △F → △D

   Remember:
   The x axis is also the line $y = 0$,
   The y axis is also the line $x = 0$.

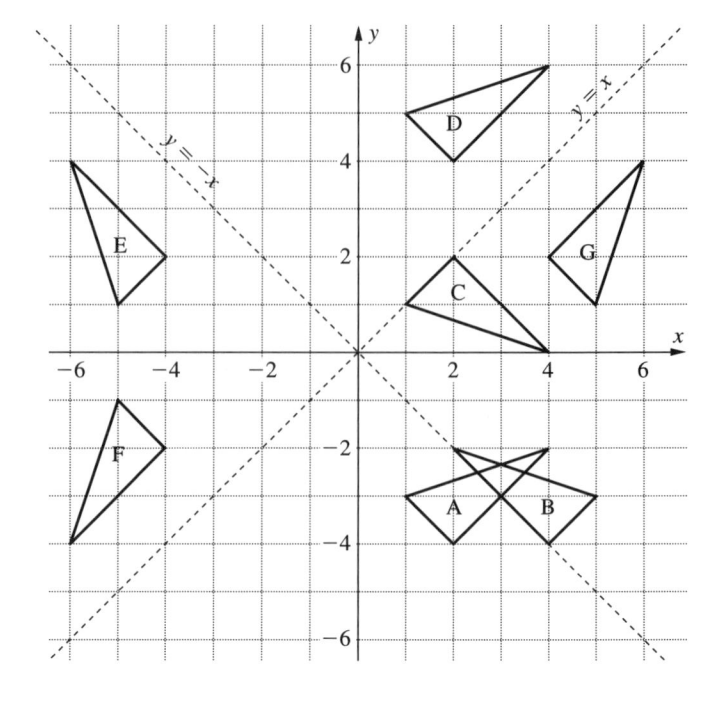

8. (a) Draw x and y axes with values from -6 to $+6$ and draw △1 with vertices at (3, 1), (6, 1), (6, 3).
   (b) Reflect △1 in the line $y = x$ onto △2.
   (c) Reflect △1 in the y axis onto △3.
   (d) Reflect △2 in the y axis onto △4.
   (e) Find the equation for the reflection △3 onto △4.

9. (a) Draw △1 with vertices at $(-4, 4)$, $(-4, 6)$, $(-1, 6)$.
   (b) Reflect △1 in the line $x = -\frac{1}{2}$ onto △2.
   (c) Reflect △2 in the line $y = x$ onto △3.
   (d) Reflect △1 in the line $y = x$ onto △4.
   (e) Find the equation for the reflection △3 onto △4.

10. The word 'AMBULANCE' is to be printed on the front of an ambulance so that a person in front of the ambulance will see the word written the right way round, when viewed in the driver's mirror. How should the word be printed on the front of the ambulance?

11. (a) In what country did 'Napoleon' live? Write your answer in "mirror writing."
    (b) Whose statue is on top of a column in Trafalgar Square?
    (c) Which famous mathematician made a discovery after an apple fell on his head?

3.7 Formulas and expressions

Substituting into a formula
(a) In the formula $s = ut$, s, u and t are variable quantities.
s is for distance,
u is for speed,
t is for time taken.
When $u = 3$ and $t = 10$, $s = ut$
$$s = 3 \times 10 = 30$$
(b) When the wind velocity is v, the cost of damage, £C, is given by the formula

$C = 500\,v + 20\,000$

When $v = 100$, $C = 500 \times 100 + 20\,000$

$C = 70\,000$

The cost of damage = £70 000

Exercise 1

In Questions **1** to **12** you are given a formula. Find the value of the letter required in each case.

1. $x = 3y + 2$
   Find x when $y = 4$

2. $a = 4b + 1$
   Find a when $b = 5$

3. $c = \dfrac{d}{5} + 3$
   Find c when $d = 15$

4. $e = \dfrac{f}{2} - 4$
   Find e when $f = 8$

5. $g = 8h + 7$
   Find g when $h = 6$

6. $i = 5j - 3$
   Find i if $j = 7$

7. $k = \dfrac{l}{3} + 4$
   Find k when $l = 21$

8. $m = \dfrac{n}{4} - 2$
   Find m when $n = 32$

9. $p = 6q + 5$
   Find p when $q = 13$

10. $r = \dfrac{s}{6} - 8$
    Find r when $s = 66$

11. $t = \dfrac{4u + 3}{5}$
    Find t when $u = 3$

12. $v = 3(5w - 6)$
    Find v when $w = 2$

13. x and y are connected by the formula $x = 3(y - 4)$
    Find x when $y = 8$

14. a and b are connected by the formula $a = 100 - 5b$
    Find a when $b = 20$.

Exercise 2

1. Here are some polygons.

Number of sides:	3	4	5
Sum of angles:	180°	360°	540°

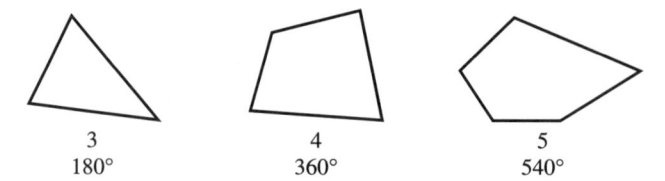

   The sum of the angles in a polygon with n sides is given by the formula, $\text{sum of angles} = (n-2) \times 180°$

   (a) Find the sum of the angles in a hexagon (6 sides).
   (b) Find the sum of the angles in a polygon with 102 sides.
   (c) Show that the formula gives the correct answer for the sum of the angles in a pentagon (5 sides).

2. Here is a formula $h = 5t - 4$.
   Find the value of h when
   (a) $t = 2$ (b) $t = 10$ (c) $t = 6$

3. Using the formula $p = 100 + 2x$, find the value of p when
   (a) $x = 3$ (b) $x = 100$ (c) $x = \frac{1}{2}$

4. Suppose you add the numbers from 1 to 50: $1 + 2 + 3 + \ldots + 49 + 50$.
   The answer is $\frac{50 \times 51}{2} = 1275$.

   If you add the numbers from 1 to any number n the answer is given by the formula $\text{sum} = \frac{n(n+1)}{2}$.

   (a) Use the formula to find the sum of the numbers from 1 to 10. (i.e. $1 + 2 + 3 + \ldots + 9 + 10$).
   (b) Check your answer by adding the numbers in the normal way.
   (c) Use the formula to find the sum of the numbers from 1 to 99.

5. Below are several different formulas for z in terms of x.
   Find the value of z in each case.
   (a) $z = 10x - 6$, $x = 5 \cdot 5$
   (b) $z = \frac{5x + 3}{2}$, $x = 3$
   (c) $z = 3(2x + 5)$, $x = 2$

6. In the formulas below t is given in terms of n and a. Find the value of t in each case.
   (a) $t = 5a + 2n$; $a = 3$, $n = 4$
   (b) $t = 6a + 3n - 10$; $a = 2$, $n = 1$
   (c) $t = an + 7$; $a = 5$, $n = 2$

7. Here is a sequence of shapes made from sticks

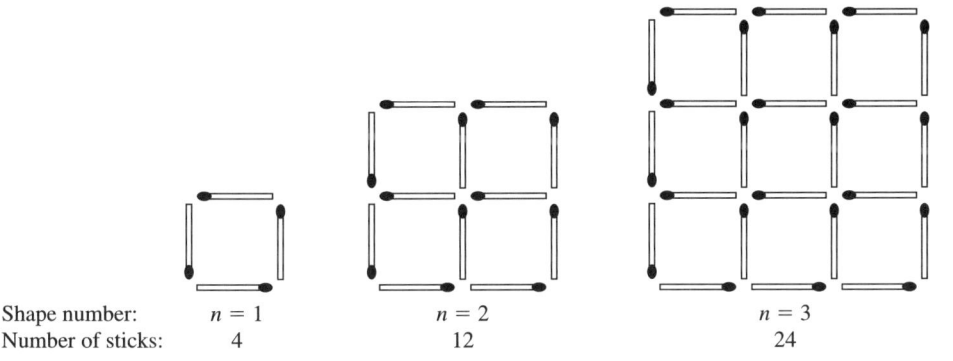

Shape number:	$n = 1$	$n = 2$	$n = 3$
Number of sticks:	4	12	24

The formula for the number of sticks in shape number n is

$\boxed{\text{number of sticks} = 2n^2 + 2n}$. (Note: $2n^2 = 2(n^2)$)

(a) Check that the formula gives the correct answer for $n = 1$ and for $n = 2$.
(b) Use the formula to find the number of sticks in shape number 10.

8. An estimate for the volume of a cylinder of radius r and height h is given by the formula $V = 3r^2h$.
(a) Find the value of V when $r = 10$ and $h = 2$.
(b) Find the value of V when $r = 5$ and $h = 4$.

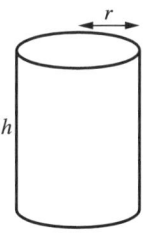

9. Find the value of c using the formulas and values given.
(a) $c = mx + 7$; $m = 5$, $x = -1$
(b) $c = 2t + t^2$; $t = 3$
(c) $c = 2pq + p^2$; $p = 3$, $q = 2$
(d) $c = (a + b^2)$; $a = 5$, $b = -2$

10. If $T = a^2 + 3a - 5$, find the values of T when
(a) $a = 3$ (b) $a = 10$ (c) $a = 1$

11. The total surface area A of the solid cuboid shown is given by the formula
$A = 2bc + 2ab + 2ac$
Find the value of A when $a = 2$, $b = 3$, $c = 4$.

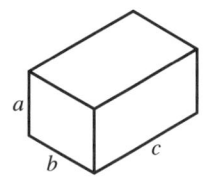

12. The diagram shows a rectangle with a diagonal drawn. The area of the shaded triangle is A.
Find a formula for A using b and h.

13. In the polygons below, diagonals are drawn from one vertex.

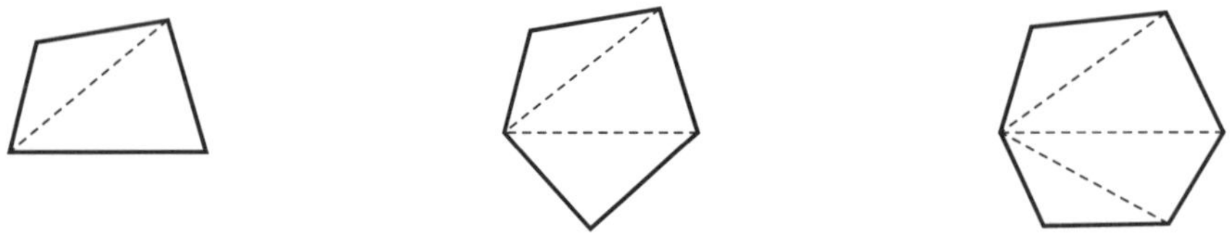

$n = 4$ sides
$d = 1$ diagonal

$n = 5$ sides
$d = 2$ diagonals

$n = 6$ sides
$d = 3$ diagonals

Find a formula connecting the number of diagonals and the number of sides. Write '$d = \ldots\ldots$'.

14. In this sequence black squares are surrounded by white squares.

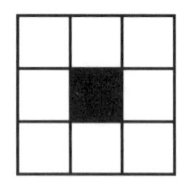

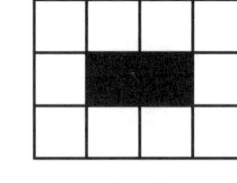

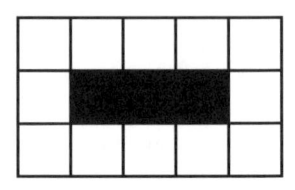

Black squares: $b = 1$ $b = 2$ $b = 3$
White squares: $w = 8$ $w = 10$ $w = 12$

(a) Draw the next diagram in the sequence and make a table.

black squares, b	1	2	3	4
white squares, w	8	10	12	

(b) Work out the number of white squares in the diagram which has 20 black squares.

(c) Write the formula, without words, for the number of white squares. Use b for the number of black squares and w for the number of white squares. Write '$w =$ '.

Expressions

An expression does *not* have an equals sign. For example: $3x - 7$; $2a + b$; $5y - 10$. These are all expressions.

Below are three expressions involving a, b, c and d. Find the value of each expression given that $a = 3$, $b = 2$ $c = 5$, $d = -1$

(i) $5a + 7$
      $= 5 \times 3 + 7$
      $= 15 + 7$
      $= 22$

(ii) $2b + d$
       $= 2 \times 2 + (-1)$
       $= 4 - 1$
       $= 3$

(iii) $ab + 5c$
        $= (3 \times 2) + (5 \times 5)$
        $= 6 + 25$
        $= 31$

Notice that the working goes *down* the page, not across. This helps to avoid errors.

Exercise 3

In Questions **1** to **10** find the value of each expression

1. $2x + 1$ if $x = 4$
2. $3x - 1$ if $x = 2$
3. $5x - 2$ if $x = 3$
4. $4x + 3$ if $x = 3$
5. $10 + a$ if $a = 5$
6. $7 - a$ if $a = 4$
7. $12 - b$ if $b = 6$
8. $16 + b$ if $b = 3$
9. $4 + 3c$ if $c = 6$
10. $20 - 2c$ if $c = 7$

11. Find the value of these expressions when $n = 3$.
    (a) $n^2 - 1$ (b) $2n^2$ (c) n^3

12. Find the value of these expressions when $a = 1\cdot5$.
    (a) $2a + 5$ (b) $6 - a$ (c) $3(a - 1)$

13. Find the value of these expressions when $x = 2$.
    (a) $\dfrac{x+2}{x}$ (b) $\dfrac{x+4}{x-1}$ (c) $\dfrac{1}{x} + 4$

14. Find the value of these expressions when $n = -2$.
    (a) $n + 5$ (b) $3n$ (c) $n - 1$
    (d) $5n$ (e) $n + 10$ (f) n^2

Exercise 4

In Questions **1** to **10** find the value of the expressions given that $n = 3$
$p = -1$

1. $p + 1$
2. $2(n + 1)$
3. $3(n - 1)$
4. p^2
5. $n + p$
6. $3p$
7. $n^2 - 1$
8. $2(3n - 1)$
9. $\dfrac{n+5}{n-1}$
10. $\dfrac{p+1}{p}$

In Questions **11** to **34** find the value of the expressions given that $a = 5$
$b = 4$
$c = 1$
$d = -2$

11. $5a - c$
12. $2b + a$
13. $a + d$
14. $3c - b$
15. $4b + c$
16. $2d - a$
17. $5b + 10$
18. $a + b + c$
19. $b - c$
20. $7 - 2a$
21. $25 + 5b$
22. $3a - 4d$
23. $a^2 + b^2$
24. $ac + b$
25. $6 - 2c$
26. $d^2 + 4$
27. $ab + c$
28. $5d - 2c$
29. $b^2 + cd$
30. $5a + b + d$
31. $bd + c^2$
32. $2(a - c)$
33. $3(a + d)$
34. $a(c + b)$

Race game

START

Top row (left to right): $w-3$ | $1-3x$ | x | $2(3-x)$ | $4-p$ | $a+2$ | $c+1$ | $4-x$ | $2y$

Left column (top to bottom): $2(a-3)$ | $1-y$ | $3n-9$ | $a-2$ | $\dfrac{3x}{x}$

Right column (top to bottom): $5-p$ | $b+5$ | $3z$ | $11-3t$ | $2(a+1)$

Bottom row (left to right): $5-t$ | $p+3$ | $3(2-x)$ | $(4-x)^2$ | $t+1$ | $2x-7$ | $6-m$ | $\dfrac{2n}{n}$ | $-8+c$

Players take turns to roll a dice.
The number rolled gives the value of the letter in the expression on each square
The value of the expression determines how many squares the player moves (forward for a positive number, backwards for a negative number).
For example, if you are on the square '$x-3$' and you throw a 5 you move forward 2 places.

The winner is the first player to move around the circuit. [You can also play 'first player to make 3 circuits' or any other number.]

Teachers note: The diagram may be photocopied and enlarged to fill an A4 sheet. This makes the game easier to play.

3.8 Mid book review

Review exercise 1 contains questions on Part 1 topics.
Review exercise 2 contains questions on Part 2 topics.
Review exercise 3 contains questions on Part 3 topics.
The Cross number puzzles contain questions on a wide range of topics.

Review exercise 1

1. Find the next number in each sequence.
   (a) 2, 20, 200,
   (b) 3, 6, 12, 24,
   (c) 50, 49, 47, 44,
   (d) 3·3, 3·2, 3·1, 3
   (e) 500, 50, 5,
   (f) 5, 7, 11, 17, 25

2. The rule for the sequences below is '*double and add 3*'
   Find the missing numbers.
   (a) $1 \longrightarrow 5 \longrightarrow 13 \longrightarrow \Box$
   (b) $2 \longrightarrow \Box \longrightarrow \Box$
   (c) $\Box \longrightarrow 9 \longrightarrow \Box$

3. Write down the rule for each sequence.
   (a) $1\frac{1}{2}$, 2, $2\frac{1}{2}$, 3,
   (b) $3\frac{1}{2}$, 7, 14, 28,
   (c) 3, 2·8, 2·6, 2·4

In Question **4** to **9** state what fraction of each strip is shaded.

4. 5. 6. 7. 8. 9.

10. What percentage could be used in each sentence?
    (a) Three quarters of the pupils at a school could not spell 'parallel'.
    (b) Three out of five workers voted for longer holidays.
    (c) One in three cats prefer 'Whiskas'.
    (d) Half of the teachers at a school thought they were paid too much.
    (e) One in four mothers think their children do too much homework.

11. Work out
(a) $\frac{1}{4} + \frac{1}{8}$
(b) $\frac{1}{8} + \frac{3}{4}$
(c) $\frac{1}{10} + \frac{1}{5}$
(d) $\frac{2}{3} - \frac{1}{6}$
(e) $\frac{2}{3}$ of 60
(f) $\frac{3}{5}$ of 40
(g) $\frac{4}{7}$ of 350
(h) $\frac{1}{4} + \frac{2}{3}$

12. Work out
(a) $1 \div \frac{1}{5}$ (how many fifths are there in 1?)
(b) $2 \div \frac{1}{10}$
(c) $1 \div \frac{1}{8}$
(d) $3 \div \frac{1}{3}$

13. Find the area of each shape. All lengths are in cm.
(a) triangle with height 4 and base 6
(b) parallelogram with base 8 and height 5
(c) trapezium with parallel sides 3 and 7, height 4

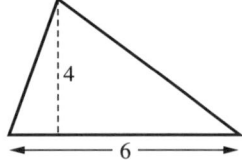

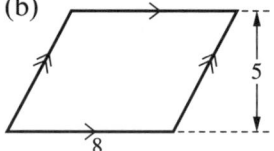

14. The perimeter of a rectangle is 24 cm. The sides of the rectangle are in the ratio 2:1. Calculate the area of the rectangle.

15. Calculate the shaded area

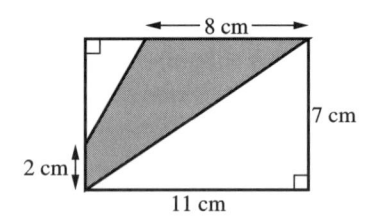

(diagram: rectangle 11 cm by 7 cm with shaded triangle, 8 cm top, 2 cm left)

16. Work out, without a calculator:
(a) 4^2
(b) 2^3
(c) 1^5
(d) 10^3

17. Use a calculator to find the square roots, correct to 1 decimal place.
(a) $\sqrt{15}$
(b) $\sqrt{7}$
(c) $\sqrt{135}$
(d) $\sqrt{8 \cdot 21}$

18. Work out
(a) $-2 - 3$
(b) $6 - 9$
(c) -2×4
(d) $-3 \times (-2)$
(e) $-4 + 10$
(f) $6 \times (-2)$
(g) $-7 + 7$
(h) $2 - 20$

19. Copy and complete the magic squares

(a)
6		2
	5	
8		

(b)
−4	3	−5
	−7	0

Review exercise 2

1. A CD is sold at £10·95 each. Estimate the total cost of 485 CDs.

2. Here are six calculations and six answers. Write down each calculation and insert the correct answer from the list below. Use estimation.
   (a) $79·6 \div 4$
   (b) $145 \div 150$
   (c) $288·2 \div 6$
   (d) $52·2 + 47·6$
   (e) $10·4 \div 97$
   (f) $416 \div 1·97$

   Answers: 0·97, 99·8, 19·9, 0·11, 211·2, 48·0

3. Answer 'true' or 'false'
   (a) $3 \times n = 3 + n$
   (b) $a \times 5 = 5a$
   (c) $a + b + a = 2a + b$
   (d) $n + 2n = 3n$
   (e) $n \div 3 = \dfrac{n}{3}$
   (f) $n \times n = n^2$

4. (a) Write an expression for the cost of n packets at 20 p each.
   (b) Write an expression for the cost of n stamps at 10 p each.

5. (a) Find the change from 100 p for six stamps at 10 p each.
   (b) Write an expression for the change from 100 p for n stamps at 10 p each.

6. Look at the sequence of square numbers.
   (a) Write a similar expression for 6^2.
   (b) Write a similar expression for 20^2.

   $2^2 = 1^2 + 2 \times 1 + 1$
   $3^2 = 2^2 + 2 \times 2 + 1$
   $4^2 = 3^2 + 2 \times 3 + 1$
   $5^2 = 4^2 + 2 \times 4 + 1$

7. Find the angles marked with letters
   (a)
   (b)
   (c)

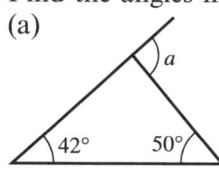

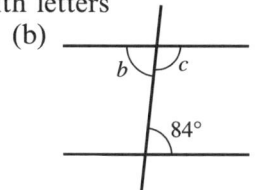

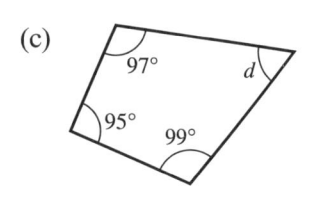

8. Choose a *metric* unit to measure:
   (a) the distance from Paris to Berlin
   (b) the thickness of a 5p coin
   (c) the weight of a calculator
   (d) the amount of petrol in a car's tank
   (e) the amount of honey in a teaspoon

9. Draw an accurate copy of each triangle and find the length x and the angle y.

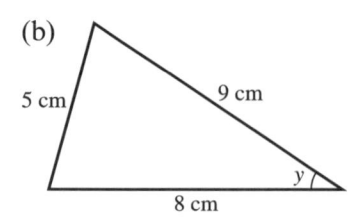

   (a) [Triangle with base 8.6 cm, base angles 44° and 34°, side x opposite the 34° angle]

   (b) [Triangle with sides 5 cm and 9 cm, base 8 cm, with angle y]

10. (a) *Construct* the perpendicular bisector of AB.

    [Line segment AB of length 8 cm]

    (b) *Construct* the bisector of the angle A.

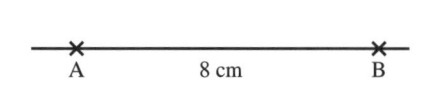

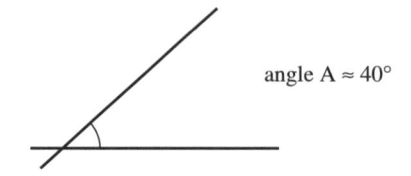

    [Angle A ≈ 40°]

11. A spoon contains 20 ml of cough mixture. How many spoons can be filled from a one litre bottle of cough mixture?

12. Which is more:
    (a) 5 metres of rope or 5 feet of rope?
    (b) 6 pounds of apples or 6 kg of apples?
    (c) A road 10 km long or a road 10 miles long?

13. Paul's car averages 30 miles to 1 gallon of petrol. Petrol costs £4 a gallon. If Paul drives 27 600 miles in one year, how much does his petrol cost?

14. The time is 6.08. What was the time half an hour ago?

15. Gill and Ashni each have 15 sweets.
    (a) Gill eats $\frac{2}{5}$ of her sweets. How many does she eat?
    (b) Ashni eats 5 of her sweets. What *fraction* of her sweets does she eat?

16. There were 4 candidates in a class election. Mary got $\frac{1}{3}$ of the votes, George got $\frac{1}{3}$ of the votes, Henry got $\frac{1}{6}$.
    What fraction did Sheena, the 4th candidate get?

17. Work out $1 + [87654321 + 12345678]$.

18. I am a 3 digit number. The product of my digits is 2.
    I am an odd number, greater than 200. What number am I?

Review exercise 3

1. (a) Write in order, smallest first: £1·25, 65p, £0·8
   (b) What number is mid-way between 3·4 and 3·5?
   (c) True or false   (i) $0·1 > 0·01$
   (ii) $6 \times 0·1 > 6$

2. Work out, without a calculator
   (a) $7 \times 0·1$
   (b) $16 \times 0·01$
   (c) $1·2 \times 10$
   (d) $6 \div 0·1$
   (e) $4 \div 0·01$
   (f) $1·2 \div 0·1$

3. Work out, without a calculator
   (a) $7·56 + 4$
   (b) $15 \times 0·3$
   (c) $1·2 \times 0·7$
   (d) $8 \div 5$
   (e) $8·64 \div 0·4$
   (f) $562·7 \div 100$

4. The stem and leaf diagram shows the marks obtained in a test.
   (a) What is the median mark?
   (b) What is the range?

   ```
   3 | 1 3
   4 | 4 4 5 7 8
   5 | 2 2 3 4 6 9
   6 | 3 4 7 8
   7 | 5 6
   ```

5. The total mass of five greyhounds is 76 kg. Calculate the mean mass of the dogs.

6. The frequency table shows the scores when a dice was rolled 20 times.

score	1	2	3	4	5	6
frequency	2	5	3	4	1	5

   Calculate the mean score.

7. (a) Copy the diagram.
   (b) Reflect the L shape in the x axis.
   (c) Reflect the L shape in the line $y = x$.

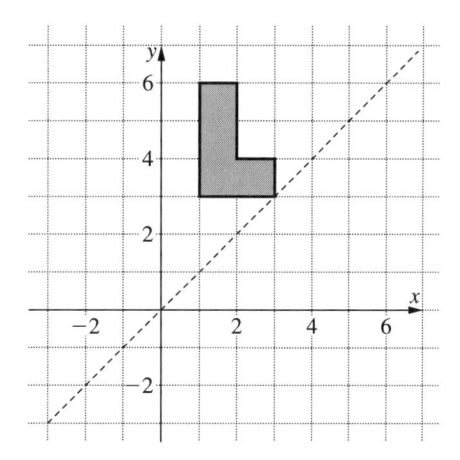

8. Work out in your head.
   (a) $57 + 19$
   (b) $68 - 29$
   (c) $47 + 23 + 18$
   (d) double 67
   (e) 24×50
   (f) 22×25
   (g) double 136
   (h) $74 + 29$

9. Draw axes with x and y from 0 to 6.
   Plot A(1, 4) B(1, 1) C(3, 1)
   Plot D(5, 4) E(5, 1) F(3, 1)
   Write down the equation of the mirror line which reflects △ABC onto △DEF.

10. Work out the following (remember 'BIDMAS')
    (a) $40 - 9 \times 2$ (b) $25 + 4^2$ (c) $(7-2)^2$
    (d) $4 \times (3 \times 3 - 1)$ (e) $15 - 12 \div 3$ (f) $(3^2 - 5)^2$

11. Use a calculator to work out the following. Give your answers correct to 1 decimal place or as a fraction.

    (a) $18 \cdot 3 - (1 \cdot 91 \times 2 \cdot 62)$ (b) $\dfrac{5 \cdot 23}{(9 \cdot 2 - 7 \cdot 63)}$ (c) $3\frac{2}{5} + \frac{1}{2}$

    (d) $\dfrac{8 \cdot 91}{1 \cdot 6} + \left(\dfrac{1 \cdot 54}{0 \cdot 97}\right)$ (e) $\left(\dfrac{1 \cdot 4 + 0 \cdot 761}{1 \cdot 76}\right)^2$ (f) $2\frac{1}{4} \div \frac{3}{4}$

12. The cost of Mrs West's shopping is given by the formula $C = n^2 - 3n + 50$, where n is the number of her children staying at home.
    Find C, when $n = 4$.

13. Find the value of these expressions when $n = 3$
    (a) $n + 5$ (b) $4n$ (c) n^2
    (d) $\dfrac{n+6}{n}$ (e) $\dfrac{5n}{n-2}$ (f) $n^2 + n$

14. Find the value of these expressions when $n = -2$
    (a) $n + 8$ (b) $3n$ (c) $2n + 4$
    (d) n^2 (e) $n - 10$ (f) $2(n+2)$

15. Work out $10^5 - [1357 + 8642]$

16. I am a 3 digit number. The product of my digits is 4. I am an odd number less than 200. What am I?

17. I am a 4 digit number. The product of my digits is 4 and the sum of my digits is 6. I am an even number less than 1200. What am I?

Review exercise 4

Crossnumbers

Make three copies of the pattern below and complete the puzzles using the clues given. To avoid confusion it is better not to write the small reference numbers 1, 2–18 on your patterns.

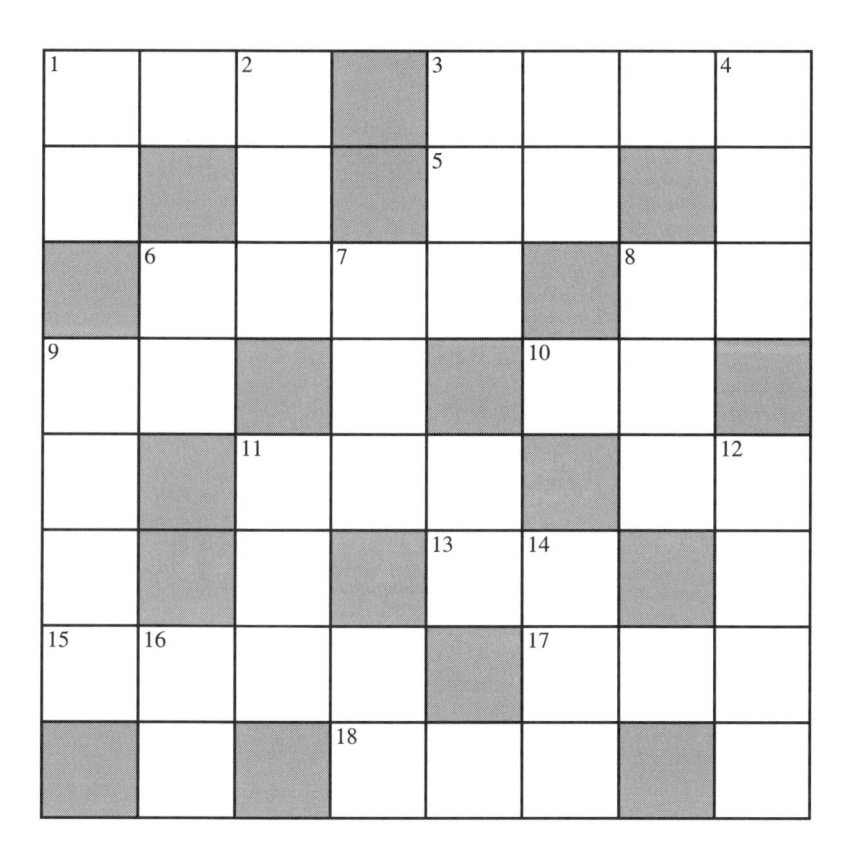

Part A [No calculators]

Across

1. $499 + 43$
3. 216×7
5. $504 \div 9$
6. $8214 - 3643$
8. Half of 192
9. 20% of 365
10. Prime number between 30 and 36
11. $213 + 62 + 9$
13. $406 \div 7$
15. $0 \cdot 7268 \times 10 \times 10 \times 10 \times 10$
17. $1000 - 731$
18. $2 \times 10^2 + 11$

Down

1. 1% of 5700
2. $600 - 365$
4. 6^3
7. $4488 \div 6$
8. $30^2 + 3 \times 6$
9. $10\,000 - 2003$
11. $4 \times 4 \times 4 \times 4$
12. $58 \cdot 93 \times (67 + 33)$
14. $1136 - 315$
16. $11^2 - 10^2$

In parts **B** and **C** a calculator may be used (where absolutely necessary!) Write any decimal points on the lines between squares.

Part B
Across

1. $9 \times 10 \times 11$
3. Ninety less than ten thousand
5. $\left(7\frac{1}{2}\right)^2$ to the nearest whole number
6. $140.52 \div 0.03$
8. Last two digits of 99^2
9. $3^2 + 4^2 + 5^2 + 6^2$
10. Angle between the hands of a clock at 2.00 pm
11. Eight pounds and eight pence
13. Next prime number after 89
15. 11% of 213
17. 3·1 m plus 43 cm, in cm
18. Area of a square of side 15 cm.

Down

1. $\dfrac{5 \times 6 \times 7 \times 8}{2} - 11 \times 68$
2. 26% as a decimal
4. 0.1^2
7. Next in the sequence $102\frac{1}{2}$, 205, 410,
8. $1 - 0.97$
9. 52% of £158·50
11. $0.0854 \div (7 - 6.99)$
12. $10^3 + 11^3$
14. $3 \times 5 \times 7^2$
16. Half of a third of 222

Part C
Across

1. double $97 - 5$ squared
3. 5·2 m written in mm
5. Total of the numbers on a dice
6. $0.1234 \div 0.01^2$
8. The value of $n^2 - 5n + 16$ when $n = 5$.
9. Inches in a yard
10. $3^4 + 56.78 \times 0$
11. Next in the sequence 1, 2, 6, 24, 120
13. One foot four inches, in inches
15. 234 m written in km
17. $\frac{1}{25}$ as a decimal
18. (Number of letters in 'ridiculous')^2

Down

1. $1\frac{4}{5}$ as a decimal
2. $\dfrac{14^2 + 488}{(0.9 - 0.15)}$
4. $0.066 \div 0.1$
7. Days in a year minus 3
8. Number of minutes between 1322 and 1512
9. Seconds in an hour
11. Double 225 plus treble 101
12. A quarter to midnight on the 24 h clock
14. $2^3 \times 3 \times 5^2$
16. $\left(5\frac{1}{3}\right)^2$ to the nearest whole number

Part 4

4.1 Rotation and combined transformations

Rotate the triangle through 90° anticlockwise about the point O.

The diagram on the right shows how tracing paper may be used.

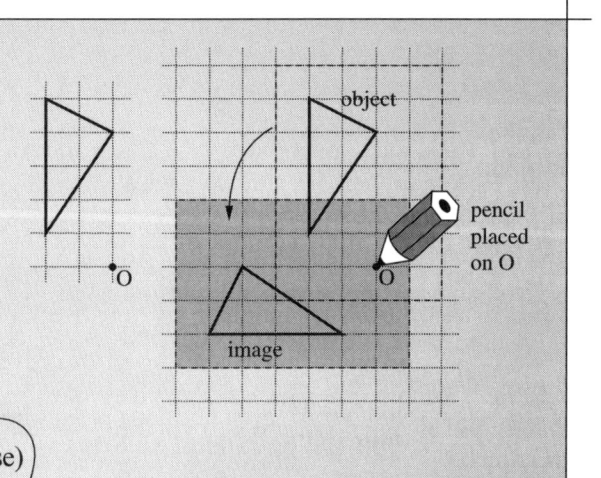

Notice that we need three things to describe fully a rotation:

(a) the angle,
(b) the direction, (clockwise or anticlockwise)
(c) the centre of rotation.

Exercise 1

In Questions **1** to **6** draw the object and its image under the rotation given. Take O as the centre of rotation in each case.

1. 90° clockwise

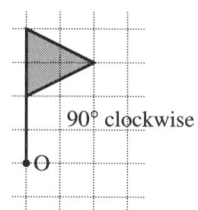

2. 90° anticlockwise

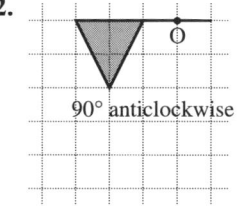

3. 180°

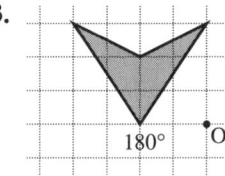

4. 90° clockwise

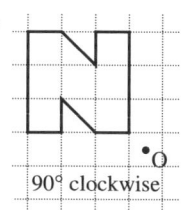

5. 90° anticlockwise

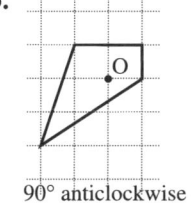

6. 45° anticlockwise

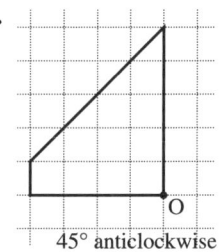

7. Copy the diagram shown, using axes from −6 to 6.
   (a) Rotate △1 90° clockwise about (0, 0) onto △A.
   (b) Rotate △2 180° about (0, 0) onto △B.
   (c) Rotate shape 3 90° anticlockwise about (2, 2) onto shape C.

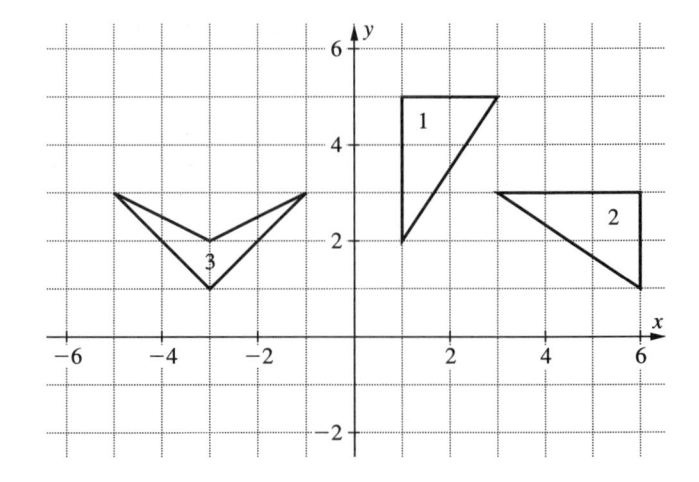

8. Copy the diagram shown.
   (a) Rotate shape 1 90° anticlockwise about (−3, −4), onto shape A.
   (b) Rotate △2 90° clockwise about (1, 0) onto △B.
   (c) Rotate shape 3 90° clockwise about (2, 1) onto shape C.
   (d) Rotate shape 3 180° about (−2, 3) onto shape D.

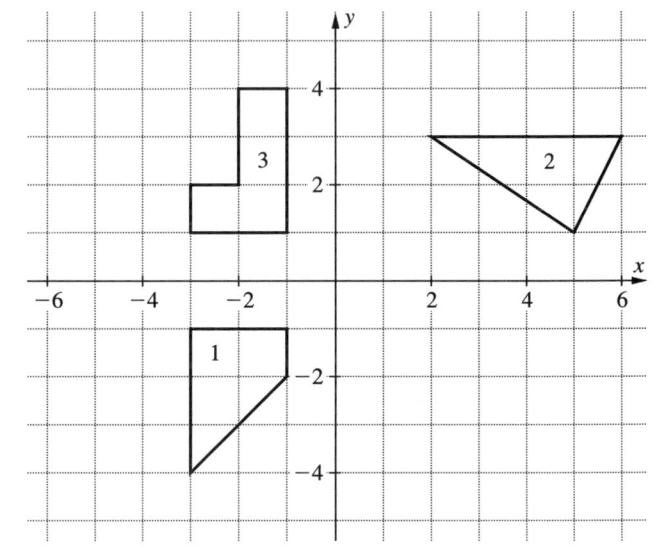

9. (a) Draw axes with values from −6 to 6 and draw △1 with vertices at (2, 6), (6, 6), (6, 4).
   (b) Rotate △1 90° clockwise about (2, 6) onto △2.
   (c) Rotate △2 180° about (2, 0) onto △3.
   (d) Rotate △3 90° clockwise about (1, 0) onto △4.
   (e) Rotate △4 90° anticlockwise about (−1, 4) onto △5.
   (f) If △5 is in the correct position you can now easily rotate △5 onto △1. Give the angle, direction and centre for this rotation.

10. (a) Draw axes with values from −6 to 6 and draw △1 with vertices at (−5, 2), (−5, 6), (−3, 5).
    (b) Rotate △1 90° clockwise about (−4, −2) onto △2.
    (c) Rotate △2 90° clockwise about (6, 0) onto △3.
    (d) Rotate △3 180° about (1, 1) onto △4.
    (e) Rotate △4 90° anticlockwise about (−5, 1) onto △5.
    (f) Describe fully the rotation which moves △5 onto △1.

Finding the centre of a rotation

Exercise 2

In Questions **1** to **4** copy each diagram. Draw the shaded shape on tracing paper. Place the tip of a pencil on different points until the shape can be rotated onto the other shape. Mark the centre of rotation with a dot.

1.

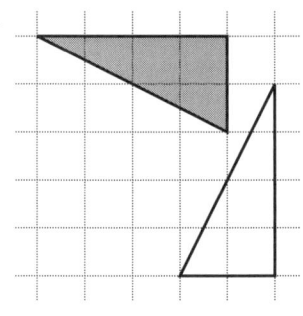

2.

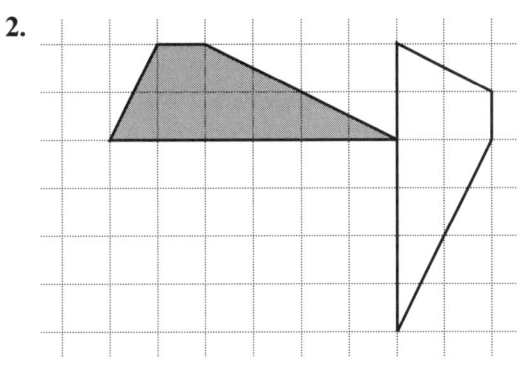

3.

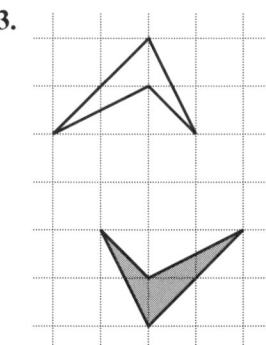

4.

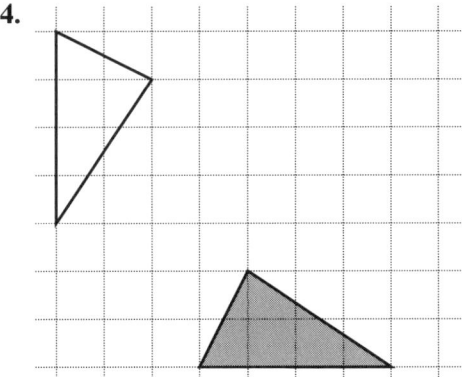

5. Find the coordinates of the centres of the following rotations:
   (a) △1 → △2
   (b) △1 → △3
   (c) △1 → △4
   (d) △3 → △5

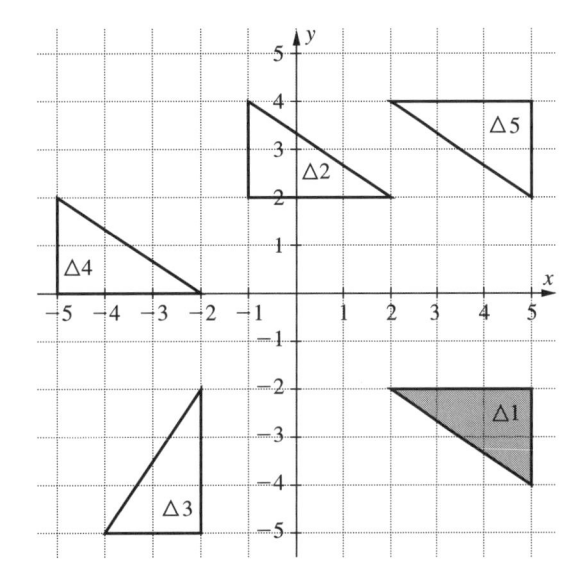

Combinations of two transformations

Reflection, rotation, translation and enlargement are all transformations. Sometimes we need a combination of transformations to move a shape where we want to.

Exercise 3

1. (a) Reflect shape A in line 1 onto shape B.
    (b) Reflect shape B in line 2 onto shape C.
    (c) What single transformation will move shape A onto shape C?

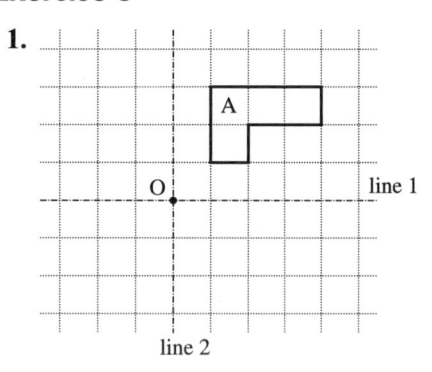

2. (a) Rotate △D 90° clockwise about (0, 0). Label the image △E.
    (b) Rotate △E 90° clockwise about (0, 0). Label the image △F.
    (c) What single transformation will move △D onto △F?

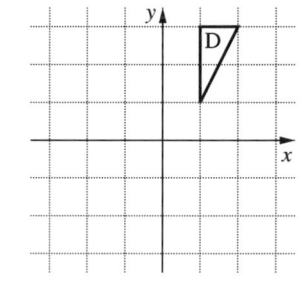

3. 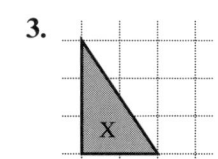 (a) Draw △X.
    (b) Translate △X 4 units right onto △Y.
    (c) Translate △Y 1 unit right and 2 units up onto △Z.
    (d) What single translation will move △X onto △Z?

4. Describe the transformations below. Mark any points and lines necessary to write the answers.
    (a) △A → △B in one move.
    (b) △B → △C in one move.
    (c) △D → △C in one move.
    (d) △A → △C in two moves.

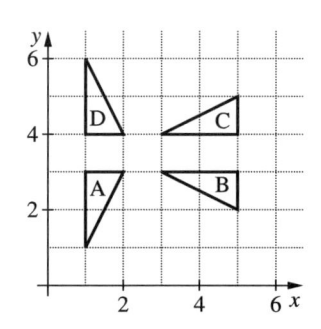

5. Describe fully the following transformations
   (a) △A → △B
   (b) △B → △C
   (c) △A → △D
   (d) △C → △E
   (e) △A → △C (in two transformations)
   (f) △A → △E (in two or three transformations).

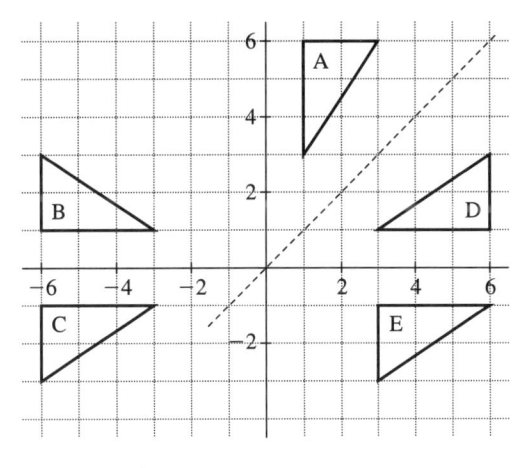

6. Make three copies of the diagram below, but leave out the dotted lines.

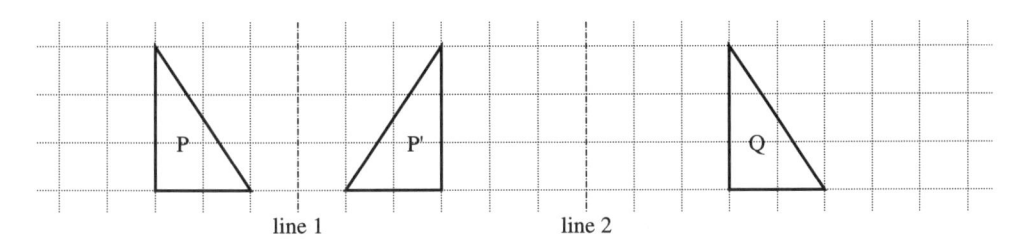

   Triangle P is reflected in line 1 onto triangle P'.
   Then triangle P' is reflected in line 2 onto triangle Q.
   (a) Show that P can be reflected onto Q using two different mirror lines.
       Do this three times.
   (b) What do you notice each time? (How far apart are your two lines?)
   (c) Do you obtain the same connection if one of the mirror lines is to the left of triangle P?

7. Show that △B can be transformed onto △A by a combination of a translation and a reflection. Describe the translation and the reflection.
   Find another way of doing this.

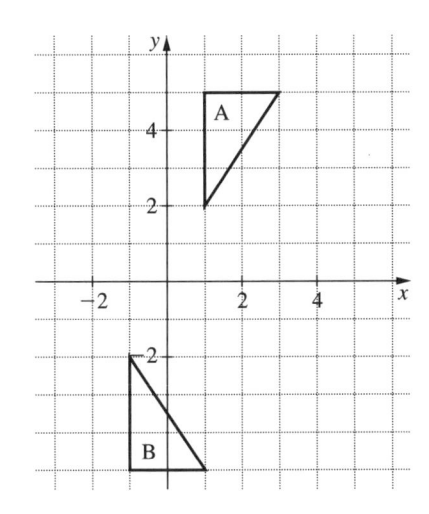

4.2 Real-life graphs

Exercise 1

1. The number of children inside a school is counted every ten minutes from 7.30 a.m. until 9.00 a.m., when the bell rings; the results are shown below.

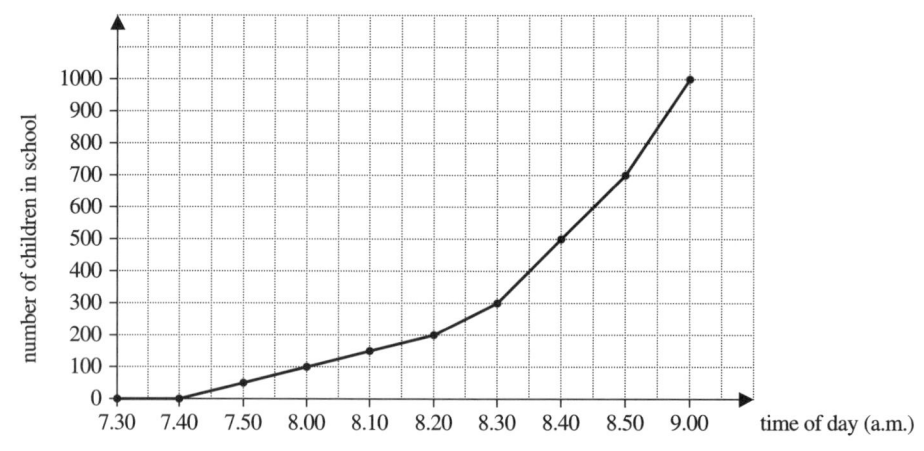

   (a) How many children were inside the school at
   (i) 8.00 a.m.?   (ii) 8.35 a.m.?
   (iii) 8.55 a.m.?
   (b) How many children arrived between 7.30 a.m. and 8.30 a.m.?
   (c) Estimate when the first children arrived.
   (d) How many children arrived during the last 10 minutes before the bell rang at 9.00 a.m.?
   (e) At what time were there 250 children in school?

2. This diagram shows the temperature and rainfall readings in one week.
   The rainfall is shown as the bar chart. The temperature is shown as the line graph.

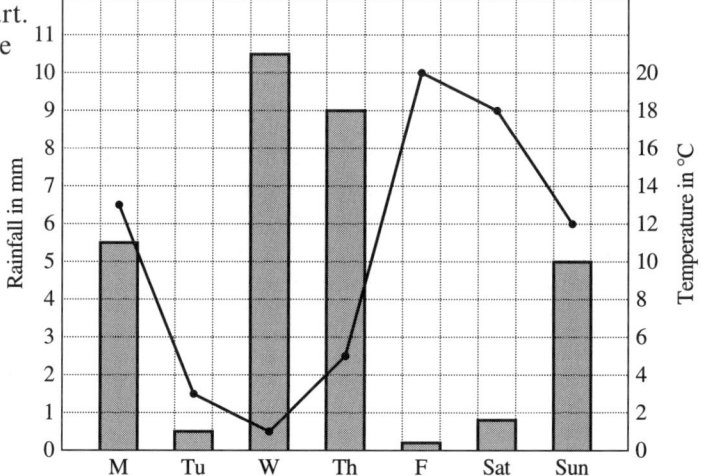

   (a) Use *both* graphs to describe the weather on Wednesday.
   (b) On which two days was the weather fairly wet and warm?
   (c) Compare the weather on Tuesday and Saturday.

3. A scientist records the height of a growing plant every day for 20 days. The results are shown below.

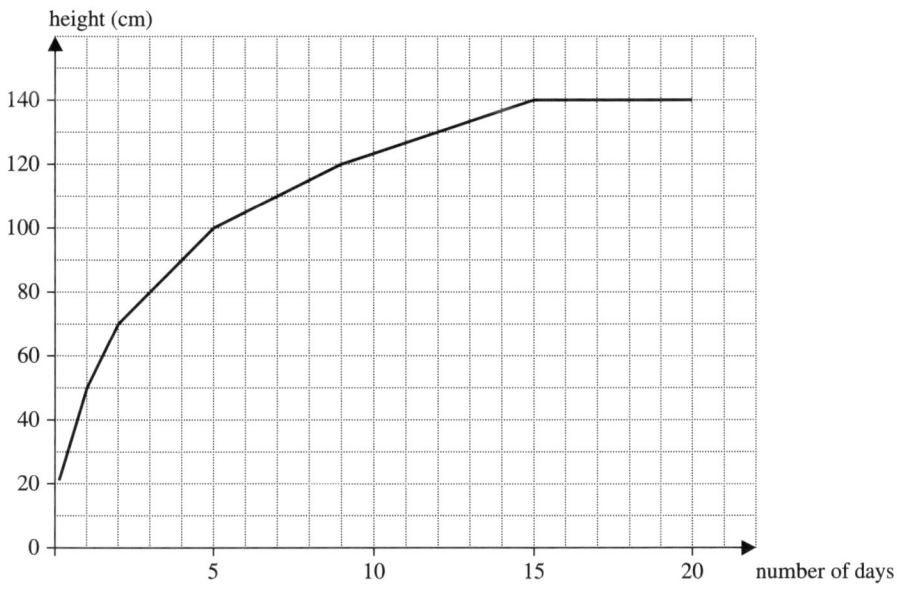

(a) What was the height of the plant after 5 days?
(b) After how many days was the height
 (i) 70 cm (ii) 105 cm?
(c) What was the greatest increase in height in one day?
(d) What was the full-grown height of the plant?

4. The graph shows the minimum distance between cars at different speeds in good or bad weather.
 (a) Think carefully and decide which line is for good weather and which line is for bad weather.
 (b) A car is travelling at 50 m.p.h in good weather. What is the minimum distance between cars?
 (c) In bad weather John is driving 60 metres behind another car. What is the maximum speed at which John should drive?

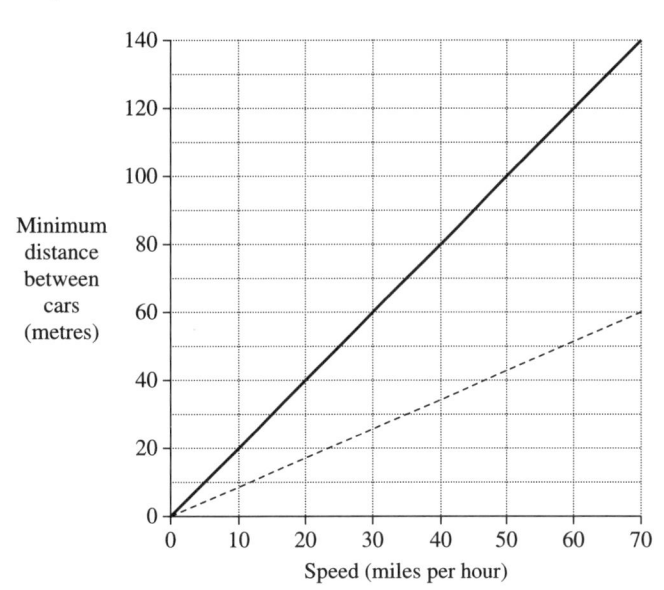

5. The number of people sitting down in a cinema was recorded every quarter of an hour; the results are shown below.

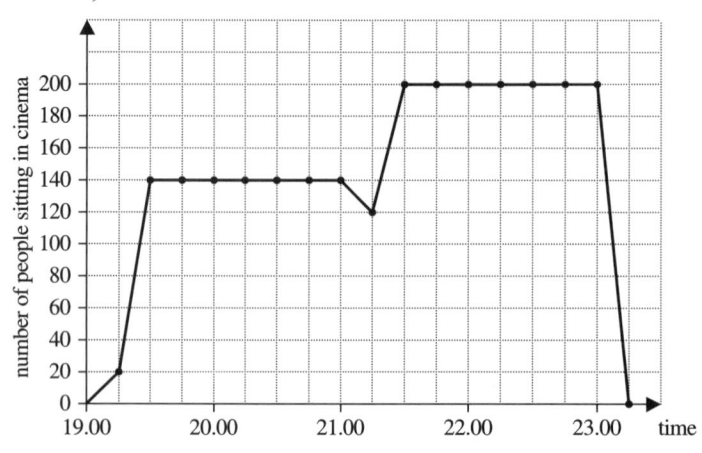

(a) How many people were sitting down at 20.00?
(b) How many people were sitting down at 21.15?
(c) When do you think the first film started?
(d) When do you think the first film ended?
(e) How long was the interval between the two films?
(f) Which film was more popular?

6. The petrol consumption of a car depends on the speed, as shown below.

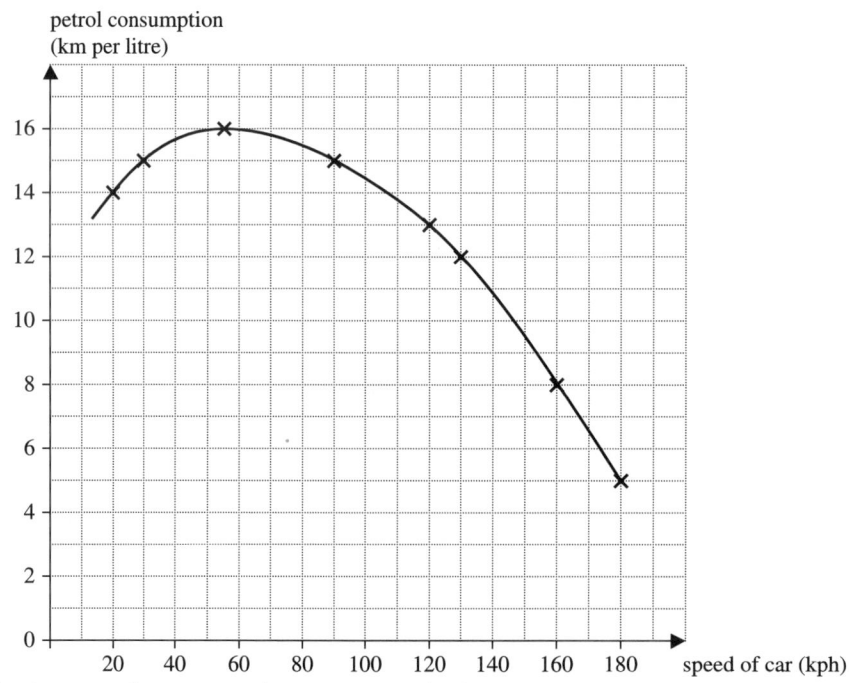

(a) What is the petrol consumption at a speed of
   (i) 30 km per hour   (ii) 100 km per hour   (iii) 180 km per hour?
(b) At what speed is the petrol consumption
   (i) 8 km per litre   (ii) 12 km per litre   (iii) 9 km per litre?
(c) At what speed should the car be driven in order to use the least amount of petrol?

7. Water is poured at a constant rate into each of the containers A, B and C.
The graphs X, Y and Z shows how the water level rises.
Decide which graphs fits each container. State your reasons.

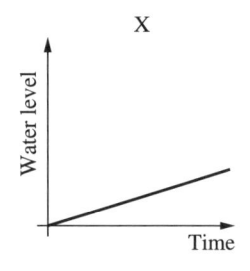

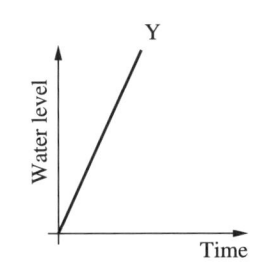

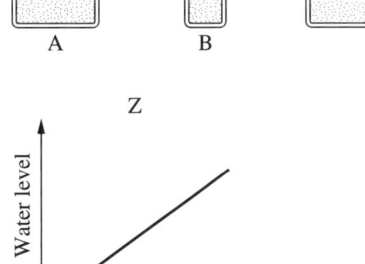

8. The graph shows the mass of crisps in a packet during the time after opening the packet.
   (a) Were all the crisps eaten?
   (b) What is the mass of a full packet of crisps?
   (c) Explain the shape of the graph. Why are some vertical lines on the graph longer than others?

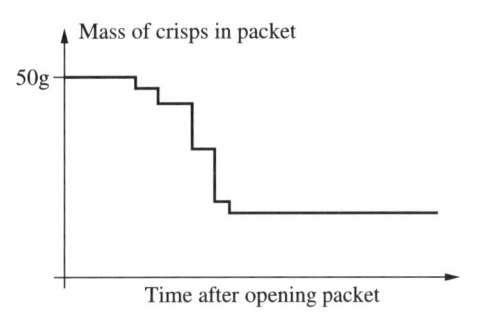

9. A packet of frozen fish is taken out of a freezer and left on a kitchen table for 4 hours. The fish is then heated in a frying pan. Sketch a graph to show the temperature of the fish after it is taken from the freezer.

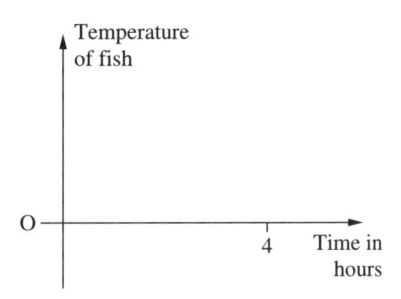

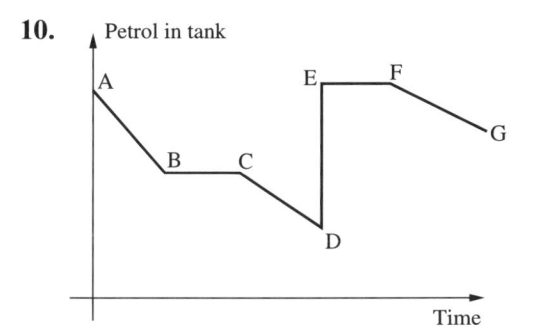

10. The graph shows the amount of petrol in the tank of a car.
Explain briefly what you think is happening in each section of the graph:
AB, BC, CD, DE, EF, FG.

Travel graphs

Exercise 2

1. The graph shows a car journey from A to B and back to A.
   (a) How far is it from A to B?
   (b) For how long does the car stop at B?
   (c) At what two times is the car half between A and B?
   (d) What is the speed of the car?
      (i) from A to B
      (ii) from B back to A?

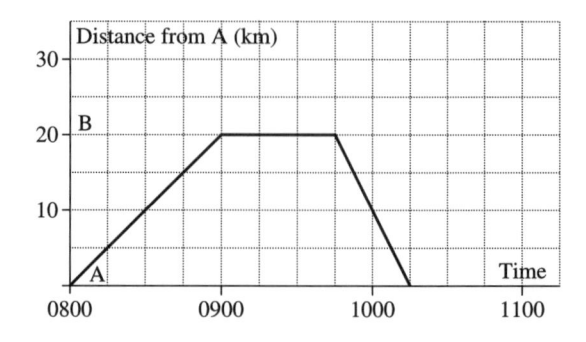

2. 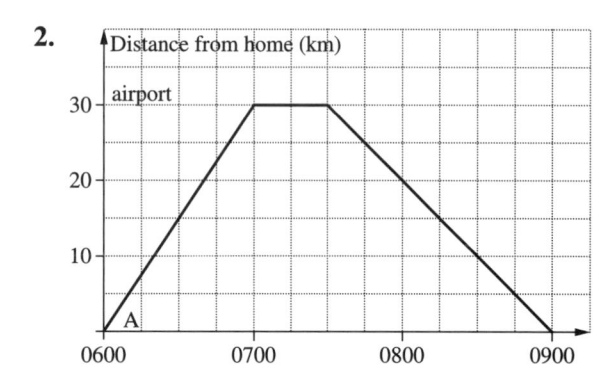 The graph shows Sue's journey between home and the airport.
   (a) When did she arrive at the airport?
   (b) When did she arrive home?
   (c) What happened between 0700 and 0730?
   (d) At what speed did she travel
      (i) from home to the airport
      (ii) from the airport back to her home?

3. The graph shows a return journey from A.
   (a) When is the car halfway between A and C on the outward journey?
   (b) Between what times does the car stop at B?
   (c) When is the car halfway between C and B on the return journey?
   (d) Find the speed of the car
      (i) From A to C
      (ii) From C back to B
      (iii) From B back to A.

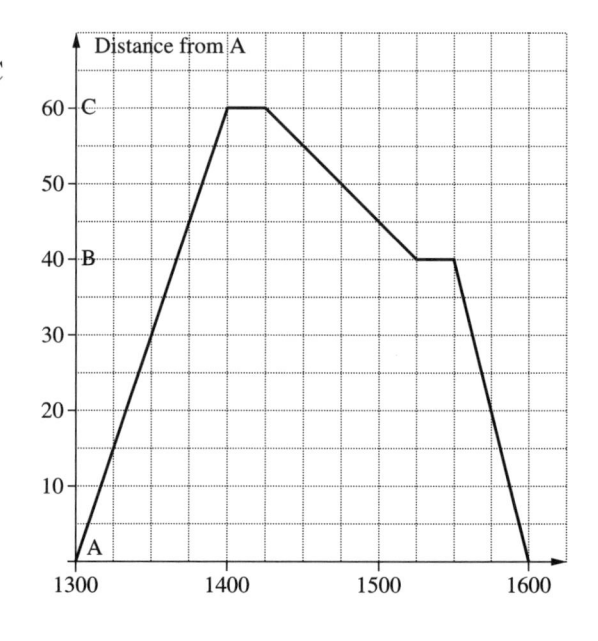

4. This graph shows a car journey from London to Stevenage and back.

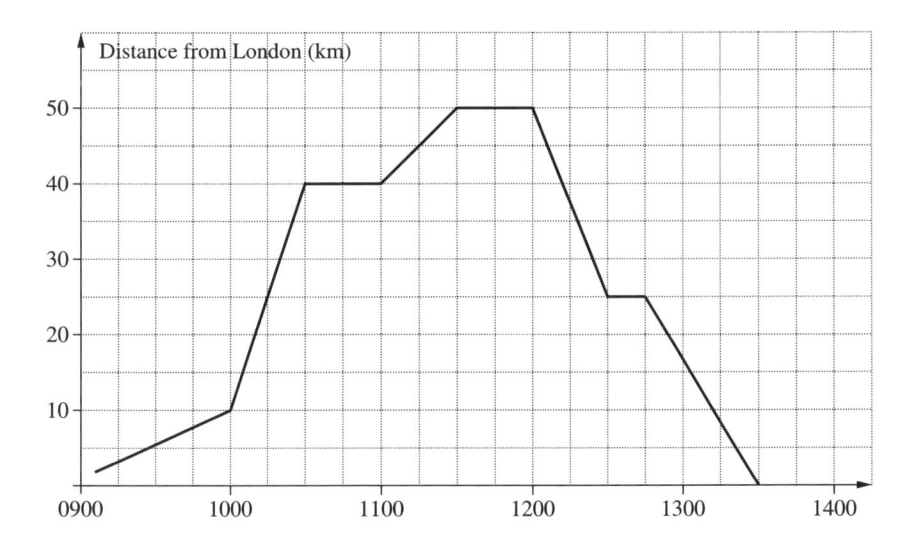

(a) For how long in the whole journey was the car at rest?
(b) At what time was the car half way to Stevenage on the outward journey?
(c) Between which two times was the car travelling at its highest speed?

In Questions 5 to 6 use the same scales as in question 4 above.

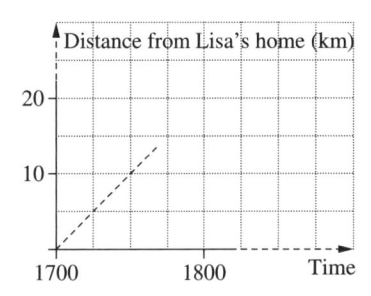

5. At 17 00 Lisa leaves her home and cycles at 20 km/h for 1 hour. She stops for $\frac{1}{4}$ hour and then continues her journey at a speed of 40 km/h for the next $\frac{1}{2}$ hour. She then stops for $\frac{3}{4}$ hour. Finally she returns home at a speed of 40 km/h.

   Draw a travel graph to show Lisa's journey.
   When did she arrive home?

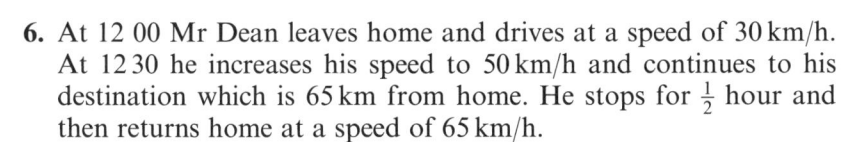

6. At 12 00 Mr Dean leaves home and drives at a speed of 30 km/h. At 12 30 he increases his speed to 50 km/h and continues to his destination which is 65 km from home. He stops for $\frac{1}{2}$ hour and then returns home at a speed of 65 km/h.

   Draw a graph to show Mr Dean's journey.
   Use the graph to find the time at which he arrives home.

4.3 Brackets and equations

The area of the whole rectangle shown can be found by multiplying its length by its width.
Area = $4(x + 2)$
Alternatively the area can be found by adding together the areas of the two smaller rectangles.
Area = $4x + 4 \times 2$

We see that $4(x + 2) = 4x + 4 \times 2$

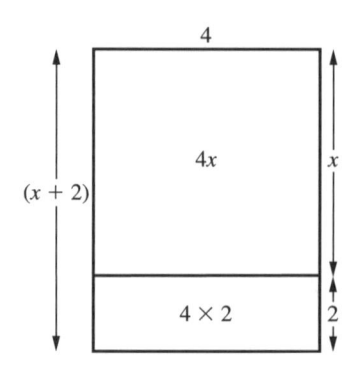

In general a number or symbol outside a pair of brackets multiplies each of the numbers or symbols inside the brackets.

$5(x + 2) = 5x + 10$ $3(x - 2) = 3x - 6$

$4(2x + 1) = 8x + 4$ $2(1 + 3x) = 2 + 6x$

$a(x + b) = ax + ab$ $n(a + b + c) = na + nb + nc$

Remove the brackets and simplify.

(a) $3(x + 2) + 2(x + 1)$
       $= 3x + 6 + 2x + 2$
       $= 5x + 8$

(b) $4(x + 1) + 2(2x + 3)$
       $= 4x + 4 + 4x + 6$
       $= 8x + 10$

Note the method: First remove the brackets.
                        Second add the x terms and the number terms separately.

(c) Find expressions for the area and the perimeter of the photo

    Area $= 7(x + 5)$
           $= 7x + 35$

    Perimeter $= x + 5 + x + 5 + 7 + 7$
                  $= 2x + 24$

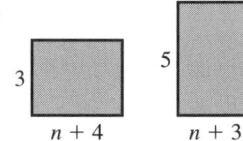

Exercise 1

In Questions **1** to **15** remove the brackets.

1. $3(x + 4)$
2. $5(x + 3)$
3. $4(x - 2)$
4. $6(x - 2)$
5. $2(2x + 1)$
6. $3(2x + 3)$
7. $4(3x + 1)$
8. $3(4x + 5)$
9. $9(2 - x)$
10. $2(4x - 5)$
11. $7(3x - 1)$
12. $10(2x + 5)$
13. $5(3x - 5)$
14. $2(3 - 2x)$
15. $3(x + y)$

In Questions **16** to **35** remove the brackets and simplify.

16. $2(x + 1) + 3(x + 3)$
17. $3(x + 4) + 2(x + 1)$
18. $4(x + 2) + 2(x + 2)$
19. $5(x + 1) + 3(x + 2)$
20. $2(4x + 3) + 4(3x + 4)$
21. $3(4x + 5) + 2(x + 5)$
22. $5(x + 1) + 3(x - 2)$
23. $6(2x + 1) + 3(1 + 2x)$
24. $4(3x + 1) + (2x - 1)$
25. $2(4 + x) + (5x - 2)$
26. $3(2x + 4) + 2(x + 1)$
27. $5(3 + 2x) + 10x$
28. $7(2x - 1) - 4x$
29. $4x + 5(2x + 1)$
30. $6x + 3(2x + 3)$
31. $9 + 3(3x - 1)$
32. $5(3x - 1) + 6(2x + 1)$
33. $8(1 + 2x) - 5$
34. $x + 6(3x + 2)$
35. $4(3x - 2) - 10x$

36. Find an expression for the total area of the three rectangles. Simplify your answer.

Rectangles: 3 by $n+4$; 5 by $n+3$; 2 by $n-1$.

37. (a) Write an expression for the area of the picture.
    (b) Write an expression for the perimeter of the picture.

Picture dimensions: $x + 3$ by 5.

Remove the brackets and simplify. Be careful with negative numbers.

(a) $3(n + 3) - 2(n + 1)$
$= 3n + 9 - 2n - 2$
$= n + 7$

(c) $3(a + b) - 2(a + 2b)$
$= 3a + 3b - 2a - 4b$
$= a - b$

(b) $2(a + 1) - (a - 2)$
            ↑
    [put a '1' here]
$= 2(a + 1) - 1(a - 2)$
$= 2a + 2 - a + 2$
$= a + 4$

(d) $5(a + b) - (2a + b)$
$= 5(a + b) - 1(2a + b)$
$= 5a + 5b - 2a - b$
$= 3a + 4b$

Exercise 2

Remove the brackets and simplify

1. $3(n + 2) + (n - 2)$
2. $4(n + 3) - 2(n + 1)$
3. $8(a + 1) - 3(a + 2)$
4. $7(a + 3) - 2(a - 1)$
5. $5(m + 2) - (m + 3)$
6. $6(m + 1) - (m - 2)$
7. $3(a + b) + 5(2a + b)$
8. $3(3a + b) - 2(a + b)$
9. $4(2a + b) - 2(a - b)$
10. $5(a + 3b) - (2a + b)$
11. $5(a - b) - 3(a - 2b)$
12. $4(2a + b) - (3a - b)$

Write in a more simple form.

13. $a^2 + a^2$
14. $2n^2 - n^2$
15. $m^3 + 2m^3$
16. $a^2 + 2a + a^2$
17. $n + 2n^2 + 5n$
18. $2a^2 - a - a^2$
19. $n \times n^2$
20. $n \times n \times n \times n$
21. $n^3 \div n$

22. In number walls each brick is made by adding the two bricks underneath it.

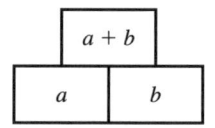

	$a + b$	
a		b

Draw the walls below and fill in the missing expressions.

(a)
	?	
$a + b$		$a + b$

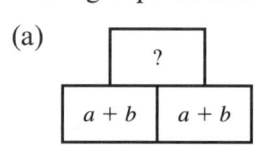

(b)
		?		
	?		?	
$m - n$		$m + n$		$2n$

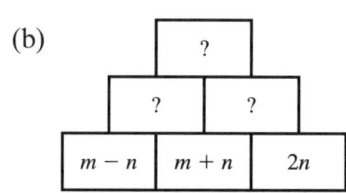

(c)
		?		
	?		?	
$a + 2b$		$a - b$		a

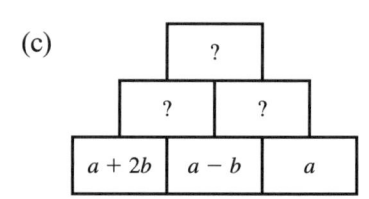

23. Draw the walls and fill in the missing expressions.

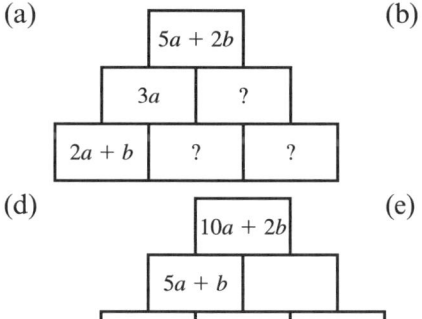

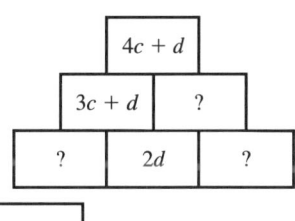

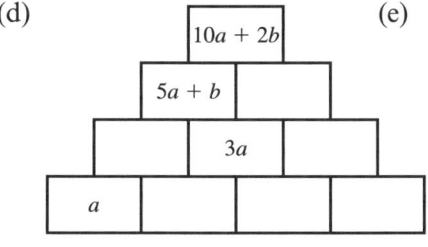

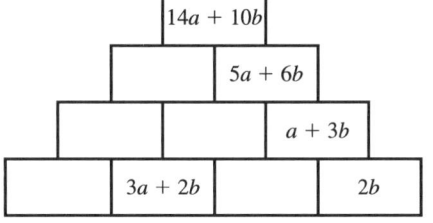

(a)
```
        | 5a + 2b |
     | 3a |   ?   |
  | 2a + b |  ?  |  ?  |
```

(b)
```
        | 2a + 4b |
     |  ?  |  a  |
  |  ?  |  ?  | a − b |
```

(c)
```
        | 4c + d |
     | 3c + d |  ?  |
  |  ?  |  2d  |  ?  |
```

(d)
```
         | 10a + 2b |
      | 5a + b |       |
   |       |   3a   |       |
|  a  |       |       |       |
```

(e)
```
            | 14a + 10b |
         |        | 5a + 6b |
      |        | a + 3b |        |
   |        | 3a + 2b |        | 2b |
```

Rules for solving equations

Equations are solved in the same way as we solve the weighing scale problems.

The main rule when solving equations is

> 'Do the same thing to both sides'

You may *add* the same thing to both sides.
You may *subtract* the same thing from both sides.
You may *multiply* both sides by the same thing.
You may *divide* both sides by the same thing.

Solve the equations. The operations circled are performed on both sides

(a) $n + 5 = 12$
  $(-5) \quad (-5)$
  $n = 7$

(b) $n - 7 = 11$
  $(+7) \quad (+7)$
  $n = 18$

(c) $2n + 3 = 15$
  $(-3) \quad (-3)$
  $2n = 12$
  $(\div 2) \quad (\div 2)$
  $n = 6$

(d) $3n - 5 = 16$
  $(+5) \quad (+5)$
  $3n = 21$
  $(\div 3) \quad (\div 3)$
  $n = 7$

Exercise 3

Solve the equations.

1. $n + 7 = 11$
2. $n + 3 = 15$
3. $n - 7 = 7$
4. $n - 5 = 25$
5. $6 + n = 100$
6. $8 + n = 28$
7. $11 = n + 2$
8. $7 = n - 52$
9. $0 = n - 3$
10. $6 + n = 6$
11. $n - 11 = 11$
12. $14 = 5 + n$

Questions **13** to **24** involve different operations.

13. $3a = 18$ **14.** $2a = 60$ **15.** $5a = 40$
16. $8 = 2a$ **17.** $6 = 2a$ **18.** $2a = 1$
19. $2a + 1 = 7$ **20.** $3a + 2 = 14$ **21.** $4a + 7 = 19$
22. $3a + 2 = 17$ **23.** $4a + 6 = 50$ **24.** $6a + 5 = 41$

Questions **25** to **36** are more difficult

25. $5x - 3 = 7$ **26.** $3x - 4 = 11$ **27.** $7x + 3 = 24$
28. $6x + 5 = 6$ **29.** $9x + 1 = 100$ **30.** $3x - 5 = 10$
31. $3 + 2x = 15$ **32.** $5 + 3x = 11$ **33.** $8 + 4x = 8$
34. $14 = 3x - 1$ **35.** $31 = 7x + 3$ **36.** $100 = 5x - 5$

Equations involving brackets

(a) $3(2x + 1) = 15$
$6x + 3 = 15$
    ⊖3   ⊖3
$6x = 12$
    ÷6   ÷6
$x = 2$

(b) $4(3x - 1) = 8$
$12x - 4 = 8$
    +4   +4
$12x = 12$
    ÷12   ÷12
$x = 1$

Notice that in both examples we began by *removing the brackets*.

Exercise 4

Solve the equations for x.

1. $2(x + 1) = 10$ **2.** $2(x + 3) = 12$ **3.** $3(x + 4) = 21$
4. $3(x - 2) = 12$ **5.** $3(2x + 1) = 9$ **6.** $4(x - 2) = 8$
7. $5(x + 1) = 5$ **8.** $2(3x - 1) = 10$ **9.** $2(3x + 2) = 10$
10. $2(x + 3) = 7$ **11.** $4(x + 1) = 5$ **12.** $6(x + 2) = 13$

Questions **13** to **24** involve different unknowns.

13. $5(a + 1) = 20$ **14.** $3(t - 1) = 18$ **15.** $4(b + 3) = 20$
16. $3(2y + 3) = 10$ **17.** $14 = 2(3a + 1)$ **18.** $16 = 4(n - 2)$
19. $18 = 2(2m + 3)$ **20.** $5(2x + 2) = 10$ **21.** $3(2n - 7) = 3$
22. $8(2 + x) = 24$ **23.** $10(3 + x) = 100$ **24.** $5(1 + 2x) = 20$

Using equations to solve problems

Mike is thinking of a number. He tells us that when he doubles it and adds 5, the answer is 12. What number is Mike thinking of?

Suppose that Mike is thinking of the number x.

He tells us that $\qquad 2x + 5 = 12$
Subtract 5 from both sides $\qquad 2x = 7$
Divide both sides by 2 $\qquad x = \frac{7}{2}$
$\qquad\qquad\qquad\qquad\qquad x = 3\frac{1}{2}$

So Mike is thinking of the number $3\frac{1}{2}$

Exercise 5

In each question I am thinking of a number. Use the information to form an equation and then solve it to find the number.

1. If we multiply the number by 3 and then add 1, the answer is 25.

2. If we multiply the number by 10 and then subtract 3, the answer is 57.

3. If we multiply the number by 5 and then add 8, the answer is 68.

4. If we multiply the number by 4 and then subtract 3, the answer is 13.

5. If we double the number and add 7, the answer is 10.

6. If we treble the number and subtract 7, the answer is 14.

7. If we double the number and subtract 20, the answer is 9.

In Question **8** to **13** form an equation with brackets

8. If we add 3 to the number and then double the result, the answer is 14.

9. If we subtract 5 from the number and then treble the result, the answer is 15.

10. If we add 7 to the number and then multiply the result by 3, the answer is 22.

11. If we subtract 4 from the number and then multiply the result by 5, the answer is 15.

12. If we double the number, add 3 and then multiply the result by 4, the answer is 16.

13. If we double the number, subtract 5 and then multiply the result by 7, the answer is 7.

Equations with the unknown on both sides

(a) $2n + 3 = n + 7$
$\quad\quad \ominus{-n} \ominus{-n}$
$\quad\quad n + 3 = 7$
$\quad\quad \ominus{-3} \ominus{-3}$
$\quad\quad n = 4$

(b) $5n - 3 = 2n + 9$
$\quad\quad \ominus{-2n} \ominus{-2n}$
$\quad\quad 3n - 3 = 9$
$\quad\quad \ominus{+3} \ominus{+3}$
$\quad\quad 3n = 12$
$\quad\quad n = 4$

Exercise 6

Solve the equations.

1. $5n = 3n + 10$
2. $7n = n + 12$
3. $3n = n + 2$
4. $4n = n + 30$
5. $4n = n + 15$
6. $12n = n + 66$
7. $13n = 7n + 24$
8. $10n = 3n + 21$
9. $5n = 8 + n$
10. $2n = 7 + n$
11. $4n + 3 = n + 9$
12. $7n + 1 = 6n + 8$
13. $3n + 7 = n + 15$
14. $6n - 1 = 3n + 8$
15. $5n - 4 = 2n + 5$
16. $1 + 3n = n + 2$
17. $4n - 11 = 2n + 11$
18. $1 + 5n = 3n + 13$
19. $6n = 3n + 24$
20. $5n - 4 = n$

Questions **21** to **30** involve brackets.

21. $3(x + 2) = 2(x + 5)$
22. $4(x + 1) = 3(x + 3)$
23. $2(x + 5) = x + 13$
24. $6x - 10 = 2(x + 7)$
25. $3(x - 1) = 2(x + 6)$
26. $5(x - 2) = 3(x + 2)$
27. $6(2x + 1) = 10x + 4$
28. $2(2x - 3) = 3(x + 7)$
29. $7(2x - 1) = 7$
30. $5(5x + 2) = 2(3x + 5)$

Problem solving

The length of a rectangle is three times its width. The perimeter is 40 cm. Find the width of the rectangle.

Let the width be x.
So the length is $3x$.
Form the equation:
$3x + x + 3x + x = 40$
$\quad\quad\quad\quad 8x = 40$
$\quad\quad\quad\quad\ \ x = 5$ 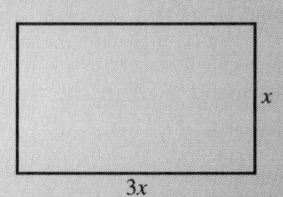
So the width is 5 cm. [Check $5 + 15 + 5 + 15 = 40$ ✓]

Exercise 7

1. The length of a rectangle is twice its width. The perimeter is 30 cm. Find the width.

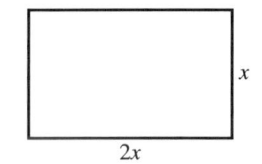

2. The length of a rectangle is three times its width. If the perimeter is 32 cm, find its width.
   [Hint: Let the width be x.]

3. The length of a rectangle is five times its width. If the perimeter is 60 cm, find its width.

4. Form equations to find x.

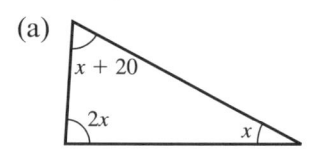

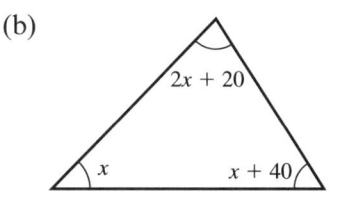

   (a) triangle with angles $x + 20$, $2x$, x

   (b) triangle with angles $2x + 20$, x, $x + 40$

In Questions **5** to **10** form an equation to find the unknown number.

5. If we multiply the number by 10 and then add 4, the answer is 9.

6. If we add 2 to the number and then double the result, the answer is 14.

7. If we multiply the number by 6 and subtract 1, the answer we get is the same as when we double the number and add 7.

8. If we treble the number, add 2 and then double the result, the answer is 6.

9. If we multiply the number by 7 and subtract 10, we get the same answer as when we add 2 to the number and then double the result.

10. If we double the number, add 3 and then multiply the result by 5, we get the same answer as when we double the number and then add 21.

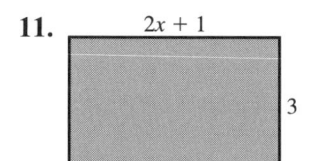

11. The rectangle has an area of 27 square units. Form an equation and solve it to find x. (rectangle with sides $2x + 1$ and 3)

12. In the triangle, BC is twice as long as AB.
AC is 9 cm long.
If the perimeter is 24 cm, form an equation and solve it to find x.

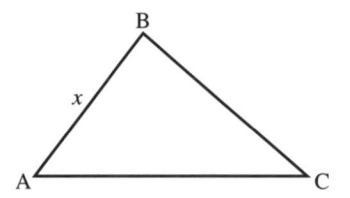

13. The total mass of three stones A, B and C is 60 kg. Stone B is twice as heavy as stone A. Stone C is 30 kg heavier than stone A. Find the mass of stone A. [Call it x kg.]

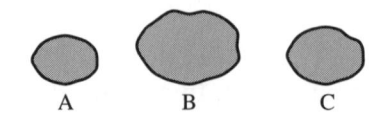

14. An equilateral triangle has sides of length $3x + 1$, $2x + 3$ and $2x + 3$. Find x.

15. The perimeter, P, of a rectangle is given by the formula $P = 2(a + b)$.
If $P = 19$ and $b = 7$, find the value of a.

16. The volume of a cuboid is given by the formula $V = \ell b h$.
If $V = 30$, $\ell = 2$ and $b = 6$, find the value of h.

17. In an arithmagon, the number in a square is the sum of the numbers in the two circles either side of it.

(a) Explain why the number in circle B is $20 - x$.
(b) Explain why the number in circle C is $15 - x$.
(c) Form an equation across the lowest side of the triangle.
Solve the equation to find x.

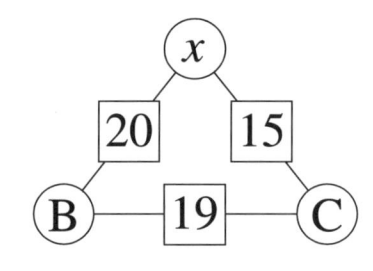

18. Use the method above to find x in these arithmagons.

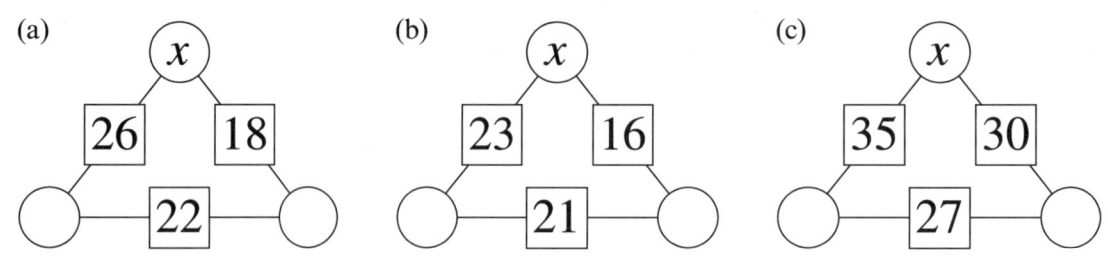

(a) 26, 18, 22

(b) 23, 16, 21

(c) 35, 30, 27

4.4 Handling data

Bar charts

Exercise 1

1. The bar chart shows the spectators attending various sporting fixtures.

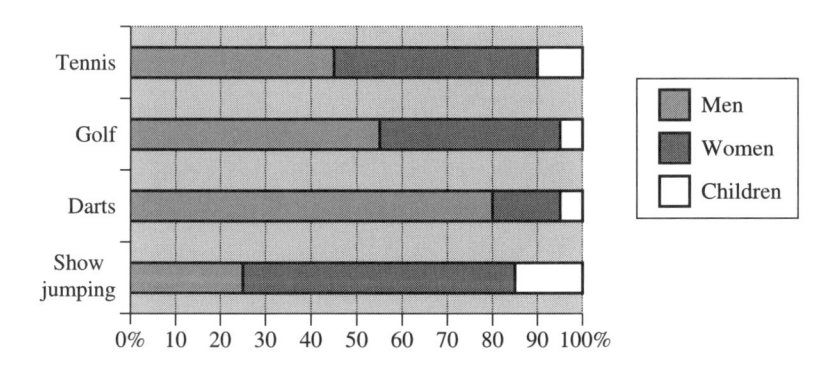

    (a) What percentage of the spectators at the golf were men?
    (b) What percentage of the spectators at the tennis were children?
    (c) What percentage of the spectators at the show jumping were women?
    (d) What percentage of the spectators at the darts were **not** men?

2. The bar chart shows age groups on three different holidays.

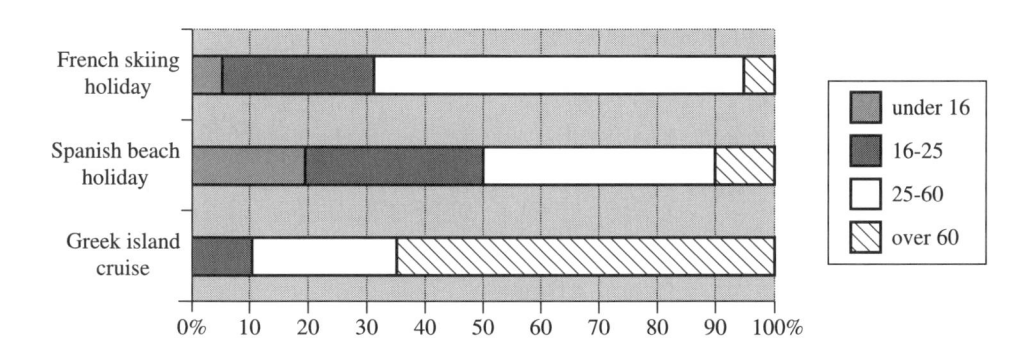

    (a) What percentage of holiday makers are:
        (i)   between 25 and 60 on the Spanish beach holiday,
        (ii) under 25 on the Greek island cruise,
        (iii) over 25 on the French skiing holiday?
    (b) Describe the main difference between the top and bottom charts. Why are they so different?

3. Here are two charts about the ages of drivers committing speeding offences.

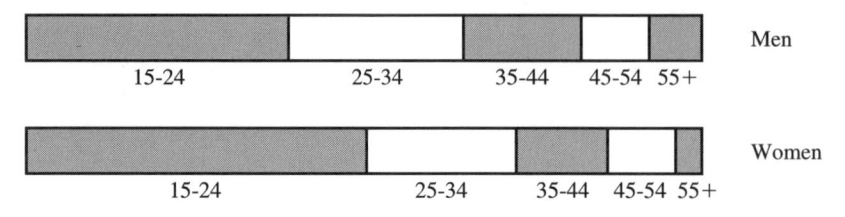

```
[███████  15-24  ] [  25-34  ] [███ 35-44 ███] [ 45-54 ] [██ 55+ ██]   Men

[████████  15-24  ████████] [   25-34   ] [██ 35-44 ██] [ 45-54 ] [█ 55+]   Women
```

(a) Write a sentence to describe the main features which these charts show for different age-groups.

(b) What is the main difference between the charts for men and women?

4. Look at the words used in this question (including the words on the chart). Make a tally chart for the number of letters in the words and then draw a bar chart to display the data.

Number of letters	Tally	Frequency
1	//	2
2		
3		
⋮		

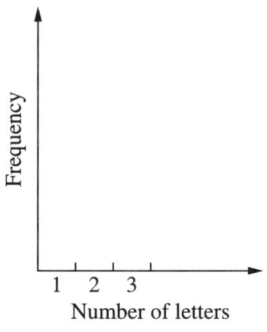

5. Here are the heights of the 21 members of a school swimming team

136·8, 146·2, 141·2, 147·2, 151·3, 145·0, 155·0,
149·9, 138·0, 146·8, 157·4, 143·1, 143·5, 147·2,
147·5, 158·6, 154·7, 144·6, 152·4, 144·0, 151·0.

(a) Put the heights into groups

class interval	frequency
135 ⩽ h < 140	
140 ⩽ h < 145	
145 ⩽ h < 150	

(b) Draw a frequency diagram

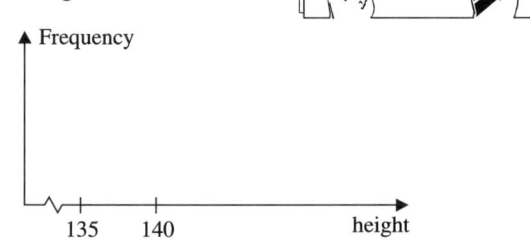

6. A group of 7 year-olds were each accompanied by one of their parents on a coach trip to a zoo. Each person on the coach was weighed in kg. Here are the weights:

21·1, 45·7, 22·3, 26·3, 50·1, 24·3, 44·2,
54·3, 53·2, 46·0, 51·0, 24·2, 56·4, 20·6,
25·5, 22·8, 52·0, 26·5, 41·8, 27·5, 29·7,
55·1, 30·7, 47·4, 23·5, 59·8, 49·3, 23·4,
21·7, 57·6, 22·6, 58·7, 28·6, 54·1.

(a) Put the weights into groups.

class interval	frequency
20 ≤ w < 25	
25 ≤ w < 30	
30 ≤ w < 35	
⋮	

(b) Draw a frequency diagram.
(c) Why is the shape of the frequency diagram different to the diagram you drew in Question 1?
(d) What shape of frequency diagram would you expect to obtain if you drew a diagram to show the heights of pupils in your class?

7. A drug company claims that its new nutrient pill helps people to improve their memory.
As an experiment two randomly selected groups of people were given the same memory test. Group A took the new pills for a month while group B took no pills. Here are the results of the tests: (A high score indicates a good memory).

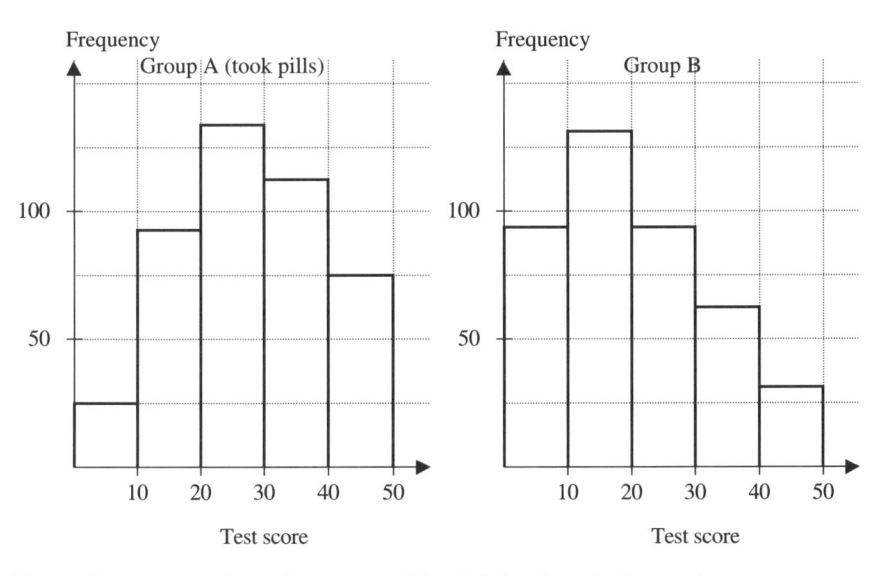

Does it appear that the new pills did in fact help to improve memory?

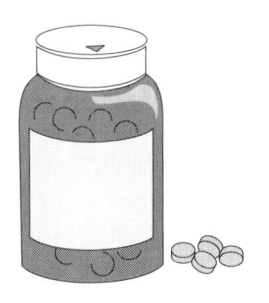

8. Here is an age distribution pyramid for the children at a Center Parcs resort.
   (a) How many girls were there aged 5–9?
   (b) How many children were there altogether in the 0–4 age range?
   (c) How many girls were at the resort?

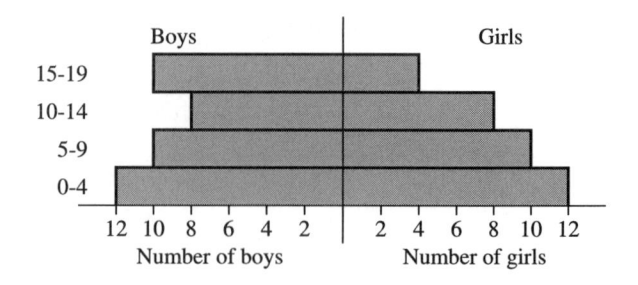

9. Here are age distribution pyramids for the U.K., Kenya and Saudi Arabia. The bars represent the percentage of the population in the age group shown.

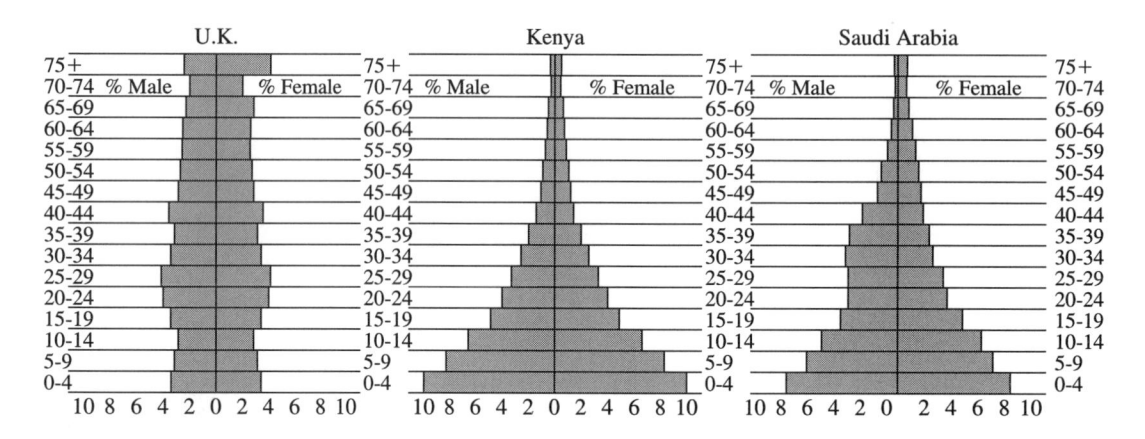

   (a) For the U.K. about what percentage of the population are *male aged 20–24*?
   (b) For Kenya about what percentage are *female aged 0–4*?
   (c) What percentage of the population are *female aged 75+*
       (i) for the U.K.?
       (ii) for Kenya?
   (d) Look carefully at the charts for the U.K. and Kenya. Write a sentence to describe the main differences in the age distribution for the two countries. Write a possible explanation for the differences you observed.
   (e) Look carefully at the charts for Kenya and Saudi Arabia. Do both countries have about half male and half female populations? Explain your answer using information in the charts.

10. Explain how each of the diagrams below is misleading in some way.

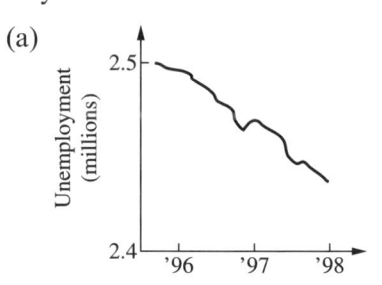

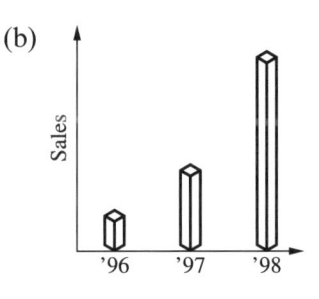

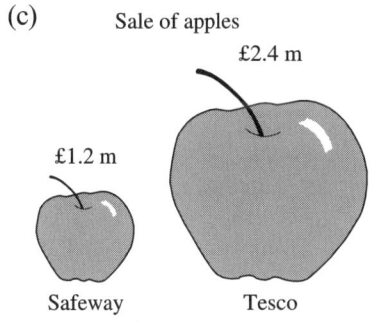

(a) [Graph: Unemployment (millions) from '96 to '98, y-axis 2.4 to 2.5]

(b) [Bar chart: Sales from '96 to '98]

(c) Sale of apples
£1.2 m Safeway, £2.4 m Tesco

Pie charts

You begin this section by calculating the angles in pie charts. Later you will learn how to draw pie charts using a computer.

> A farmer divides his land into three parts. He uses 5 acres for corn, 3 acres for carrots and 2 acres for pigs.
>
> (a) Add the three parts: $5 + 3 + 2 = 10$ acres
> (b) 10 acres = 360°
>   1 acre = $\frac{360}{10}$
>   = 36°
> (c) For corn, 5 acres = $5 \times 36° = 180°$
>   For carrots, 3 acres = $3 \times 36° = 108°$
>   For pigs, 2 acres = $2 \times 36° = 72°$

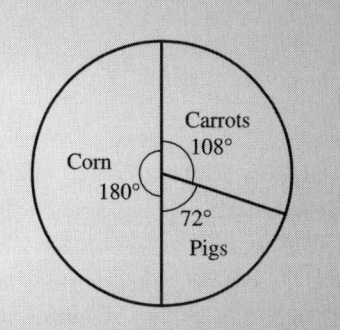

[Pie chart: Corn 180°, Carrots 108°, Pigs 72°]

Exercise 2

1. A 'Chewit' bar contains these four ingredients:

   Oats   6 g
   Barley 9 g
   Sugar   3 g
   Rye   18 g

   (a) Work out the total weight of the ingredients.
   (b) Work out the angle on a pie chart for 1 g of the ingredients [i.e. 360° ÷ (total weight)].
   (c) Work out the angle for each ingredient and draw a pie chart.

In Questions **2, 3, 4** work out the angle for each sector and draw a pie chart.

2. Number of programmes per night.

Programme	Frequency
News	2
Soap	5
Comedy	4
Drama	5
Film	2

3. Pupils' favourite sports.

Sport	Frequency
Rugby	5
Football	7
Tennis	4
Squash	2
Athletics	3
Swimming	3

4. Periods per subject.

Subject	Frequency
Maths	5
English	5
Science	6
Humanities	4
Arts	4
Others	16

5. At the 'Crooked Corkscrew' last Friday, 120 customers ordered meals.

    40 ordered beefburger
    20 ordered ham salad
    16 ordered curry
    25 ordered snake
    19 ordered snake with egg

Draw a pie chart to show this information.

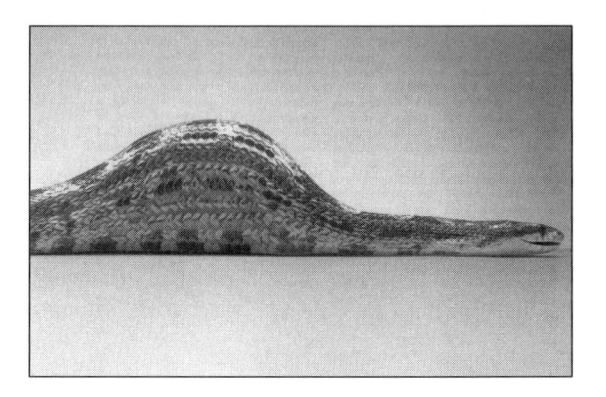

6. Eurostar did a survey of over a thousand passengers on one of their trains. Here are their nationalities:

    British 30%   French 20%
    German 15%   Dutch 35%

On a pie chart, the angle for British passengers is found by working out 30% of 360°. Find the angle on a pie chart representing

(a) French passengers   (b) Dutch passengers.

7.* The pie chart illustrates the sales of four brands of crisps.
    (a) What percentage of total sales does KP have?
    (b) If Walkers accounts for 35% of total sales, calculate the angles x and y.

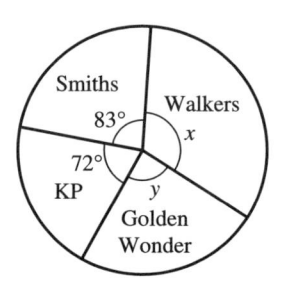

8.* In a survey 320 people on an aircraft and 800 people on a ferry were asked to state their nationality.

Aircraft 320 people

Ferry 800 people

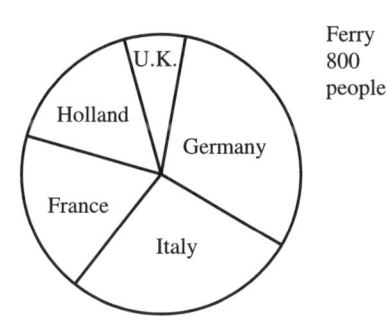

Jill looked at the charts and said 'There were about the same number of people from Italy on the aircraft and on the ferry'. Explain why Jill is wrong.

9.* Andrew and Martin intend to go snowboarding at Christmas, and cannot decide where to go. They have this information about two possible places.

Expected snow cover.

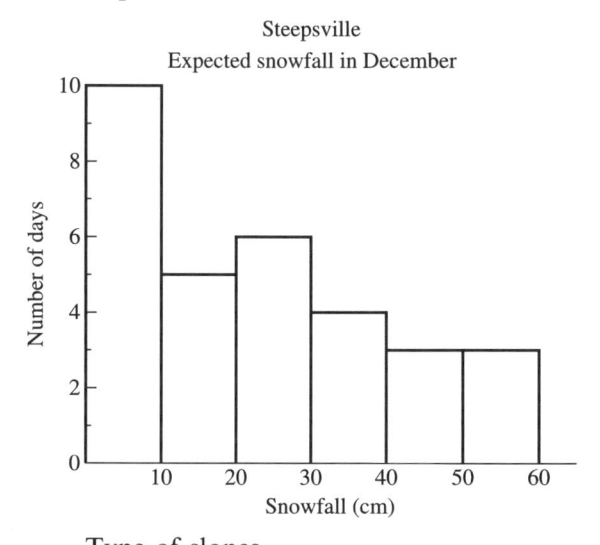

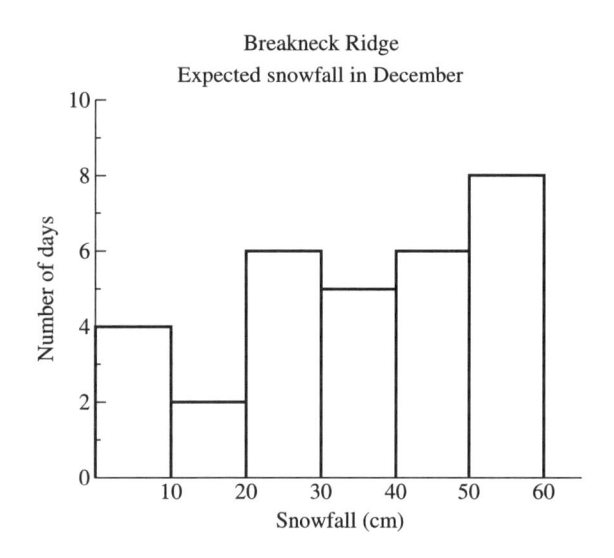

Steepsville
Expected snowfall in December

Breakneck Ridge
Expected snowfall in December

Type of slopes

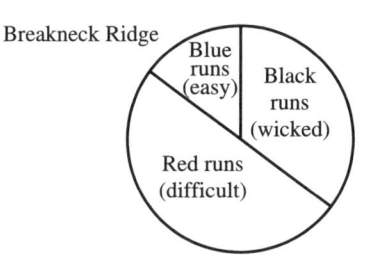

Steepsville

Breakneck Ridge

Decide where you think they should go. It doesn't matter where you decide, but you *must* say why, using the 2 types of diagram to help you explain.

Scatter graphs

Sometimes it is important to discover if there is a connection or relationship between two sets of data.
Examples

- Do tall people weigh more than short people?
- If you spend longer revising for a test, will you get a higher mark?
- Do tall parents have tall children?
- Do older people have higher pulse rates?

If there is a relationship, it will be easy to spot if your data is plotted on a scatter diagram – that is a graph in which one set of data is plotted on the horizontal axis and the other on the vertical axis

- Here is a scatter graph showing the test marks of some pupils in a maths test and a science test.
- We can see a connection: the pupils who got a high mark in science generally got a high mark in maths.

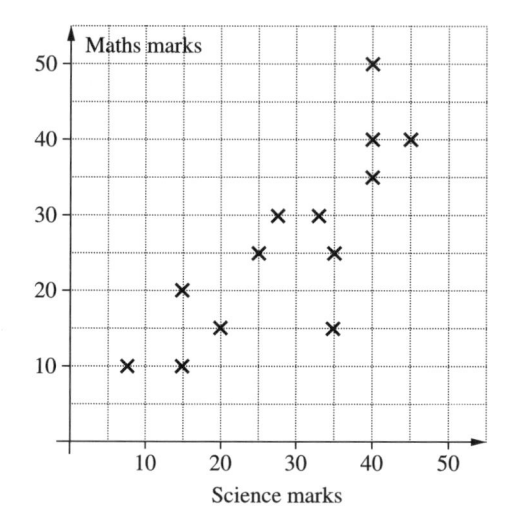

Exercise 3

1. Here are the heights and masses of 9 people. Draw the axes shown and complete the scatter graph.

Name	Mass (kg)	Height (cm)
Alice	45	115
Fred	60	160
Jack	65	155
John	55	125
Percy	75	160
Hugh	75	170
Mabel	65	140
Diana	85	180
Cyril	52	146

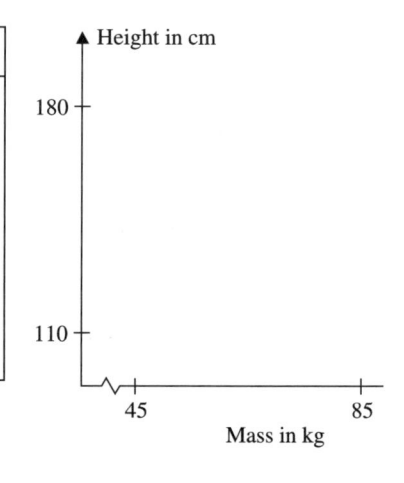

2. The scatter graph shows the number of hot drinks sold by a cafe and the outside temperature.
   (a) On how many days was it less than 12C?
   (b) How many hot drinks were sold when it was 35C?
   (c) On how many days were 40 or more hot drinks sold?
   (d) Fill the blank with either 'increases' or 'decreases': As temperature *increases* the number of drinks sold _____.

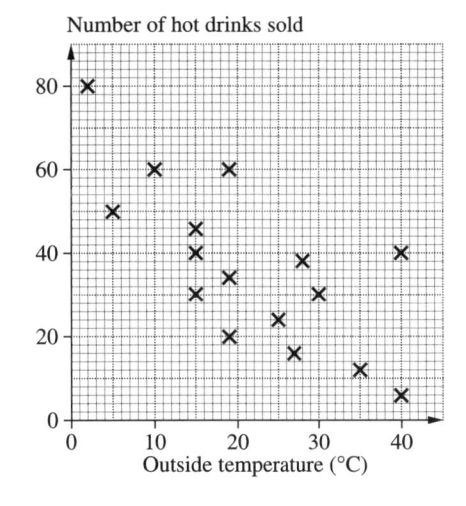

3. The graph shows the scores in a spelling test and the shoe sizes of 14 children.
   (a) How many take size 6 or less?
   (b) The pass mark is 4 or more. How many people failed?
   (c) Is there a connection between a person's shoe size and test score?

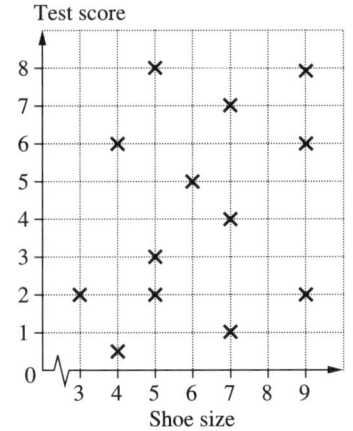

Two-way tables

Exercise 4

1.

JANUARY	Max. Temperature	Hours of sunshine	Rainfall in mm
Vancouver	42	2	8
Rio de Janeiro	84	7	2
London	45	2	2

The table gives the expected weather in January for Vancouver, Rio de Janeiro and London.
   (a) Which city expects the most rainfall?
   (b) Which city expects the most sunshine?
   (c) What is the expected maximum temperature in London?

2. Jane, John and Joan all work in a restaurant. The tips they receive one week are recorded below.

	Jane	John	Joan
Under £3	8	12	6
£3 to £5	17	14	20
Over £5	10	18	8

(a) How many tips between £3 and £5 did Joan receive?
(b) Who received the most tips this week?

3. The Table shows the age at which one hundred mothers had their first child in 1950 and 2000.

	1950	2000
under 18	16	12
18 to 24	44	23
25 to 30	27	35
Over 30	13	30

How many mothers had their first child
(a) between the ages of 18 and 24 in 2000?
(b) between the ages of 25 and 30 in 1950?
(c) Write a sentence about any differences you notice between 1950 and 2000.

4. International dialling codes.

From / To

	France	Germany	UK	USA
France	—	1949	1944	191
Germany	0033	—	0044	001
UK	0033	0049	—	001
USA	01133	01149	01144	—

What code would you need to dial
(a) from UK to Germany
(b) from France to the USA
(c) from the USA to UK?

5. How far is it from
   (a) Berlin to Helsinki
   (b) Amsterdam to Paris
   (c) What would be the total distance of the round trip from Berlin to Paris on to Rome and back to Berlin?

Road distances in km

Amsterdam				
665	Berlin			
1205	505	Helsinki		
487	1047	1605	Paris	
1653	1476	2041	1399	Rome

Pie charts and bar charts using a spreadsheet on a computer

Teacher's note: There is an introduction to using spreadsheets in section 5.7.

Example: Display the data about the activities in one day.

Enter the headings: Sleep in A1, School in B1 etc. [Use the *tab* key to move across the page.]

Enter the data: 8 in A2, 7 in B2 etc.

	A	B	C	D	E	F	G	H	I
1	Sleep	School	TV	Eating	Homework	Other			
2	8	7	1.5	1	1.5	5			
3									
4									
5									
6									
7									

Now highlight all the cells from A1 to F2. [Click on A1 and drag across to F2.]

Click on the (📊) Chart wizard on the tool bar.

Select 'pie' and then choose one of the examples displayed. Follow the on-screen prompts.

Alternatively, for a bar chart, select 'charts' after clicking on the chart wizard. Proceed as above.

You will be able to display your charts with various '3D' effects, possibly in colour. This approach is recommended when you are presenting data that you have collected as part of an investigation.

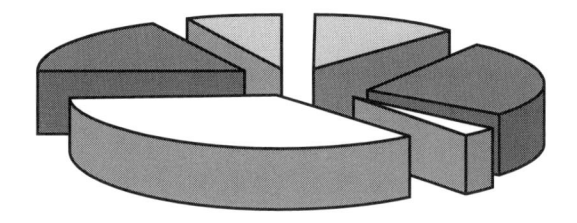

Scatter graphs on a computer

Example: Plot a scatter graph showing the marks of 10 students in Maths and Science.

Enter the headings: *Maths* in A1, *Science* in B1
Enter the data as shown.

Now highlight all the cells from A2 to B11.
[Click on A1 and drag across and down to B11.]

Click on the [icon] Chart wizard on the toolbar.

Select XY (Scatter) and select the picture which looks like a scatter graph.

Follow the on-screen prompts.

On 'Titles' enter: Chart title: Maths/Science results
                    Value (X) axis: Maths
                    Value (Y) axis: Science

	A	B
1	Maths	Science
2	23	30
3	45	41
4	73	67
5	35	74
6	67	77
7	44	50
8	32	41
9	66	55
10	84	70
11	36	32

Experiment with 'Axes', 'Gridlines', 'Legend' and 'Data Labels'.

Task 1 Enter the data on a spreadsheet and print a scatter graph.
What does each scatter graph show?

(a)

Height	Armspan
162	160
155	151
158	157
142	144
146	148
165	163
171	167
148	150
150	147

(b)

Temperature	Sales
23	7
18	14
7	23
20	9
4	30
12	19
15	15
18	15
10	20

4.5 Fractions, decimals, percentages

Changing fractions to decimals

(a) In Book 7i we changed fractions to decimals using known equivalents.

Eg. $\dfrac{3}{12} = \dfrac{1}{4} = 0\cdot 25 \qquad \dfrac{11}{20} = \dfrac{55}{100} = 0\cdot 55 \qquad \dfrac{12}{25} = \dfrac{48}{100} = 0\cdot 48$

(b) We can think of the fraction $\frac{3}{5}$ as $3 \div 5$. When we perform the division, we obtain the decimal which is equivalent to $\frac{3}{5}$.

$\begin{array}{r}0\cdot 6\\5\overline{)3\cdot {}^30}\end{array}$ $\qquad$ Answer: $\frac{3}{5} = 0\cdot 6$

(c) $\frac{5}{8}$ can be thought of as $5 \div 8$.

$\begin{array}{r}0\cdot 6\,2\,5\\8\overline{)5\cdot {}^50{}^20{}^40}\end{array}$ $\qquad$ Answer: $\frac{5}{8} = 0\cdot 625$

Exercise 1

Without using a calculator, change the following fractions to decimals. Afterwards use your calculator to check your answer.

1. $\frac{2}{5}$ 2. $\frac{1}{4}$ 3. $\frac{3}{8}$ 4. $\frac{1}{5}$ 5. $\frac{9}{10}$
6. $\frac{3}{4}$ 7. $\frac{3}{5}$ 8. $\frac{4}{8}$ 9. $\frac{3}{10}$ 10. $\frac{7}{8}$

Change these mixed numbers to decimals.

11. $1\frac{2}{5}$ 12. $4\frac{3}{4}$ 13. $3\frac{1}{2}$ 14. $1\frac{7}{8}$ 15. $5\frac{1}{100}$

Use a calculator, to convert the fractions to decimals. Write in order of size, smallest first.

16. $\frac{7}{8}$, $0\cdot 85$, $\frac{9}{10}$ $\qquad$ 17. $\frac{13}{20}$, $0\cdot 645$, $\frac{31}{50}$

18. $\frac{3}{4}$, $0\cdot 715$, $\frac{29}{40}$ $\qquad$ 19. $\frac{3}{16}$, $0\cdot 18$, $\frac{1}{5}$

20. What fraction of each shape is shaded?

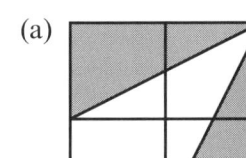

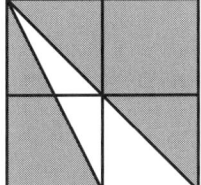

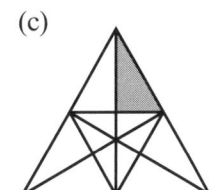

(a) (b) (c)

Recurring decimals

Some fractions give rise to decimals which repeat themselves forever. We call these recurring decimals, and use the notation below to save us from writing out the number until our ink runs out!

(a) 0·555...   We write 0·$\dot{5}$
(b) 0·434343...   We write 0·$\dot{4}\dot{3}$
(c) 0·5265265...   We write 0·$\dot{5}2\dot{6}$

(a) Change $\frac{1}{3}$ to a decimal

$$\begin{array}{r} 0{\cdot}\,3\;3\;3\;3\;3\ldots \\ 3\overline{)1{\cdot}{}^1 0^1 0^1 0 1 0^1 0\ldots} \end{array}$$

The calculation is never going to end.
We write $\frac{1}{3} = 0{\cdot}\dot{3}$. We say 'nought point three recurring'.

(b) Change $\frac{3}{11}$ to a decimal.

$$\begin{array}{r} 0{\cdot}\,2\;7\;2\;7\;2\;2\ldots \\ 11\overline{)3{\cdot}{}^3 0^8 0^3 0^8 0^3 0^8 0\ldots} \end{array}$$

This time a *pair* of figures recurs.

We write $\frac{3}{11} = 0{\cdot}\dot{2}\dot{7}$

(c) Change $\frac{1}{7}$ to a decimal.

$$\begin{array}{r} 0{\cdot}\,1\;4\;2\;8\;5\;7\;1\;42\ldots \\ 7\overline{)1{\cdot}{}^1 0^3 0^2 0^6 0^4 0^5 0^1 0^3 00\ldots} \end{array}$$

The sequence '142857' recurs.

We write $\frac{1}{7} = 0{\cdot}\dot{1}4285\dot{7}$

Exercise 2

Change the following fractions to decimals.

1. $\frac{2}{3}$ 2. $\frac{2}{9}$ 3. $\frac{7}{9}$ 4. $\frac{1}{6}$ 5. $\frac{2}{7}$
6. $\frac{3}{7}$ 7. $\frac{5}{6}$ 8. $\frac{6}{7}$ 9. $\frac{2}{11}$ 10. $\frac{5}{11}$

Changing decimals to fractions

- $0{\cdot}8 = \frac{8}{10} = \frac{4}{5}$ $0{\cdot}21 = \frac{21}{100}$

  $0{\cdot}35 = \frac{35}{100} = \frac{7}{20}$ $0{\cdot}08 = \frac{8}{100} = \frac{2}{25}$

  Simplify the answer if possible

Exercise 3

Change the following decimals to fractions in their most simple form.

1. 0·4   2. 0·7   3. 0·03   4. 0·05   5. 0·007
6. 0·006 7. 0·08   8. 0·12   9. 0·38   10. 0·015
11. 0·25 12. 0·45 13. 0·37 14. 0·025 15. 0·125

Changing to a percentage and vice versa

> To change a fraction or a decimal to a percentage, multiply by 100

(a) To change $\frac{2}{5}$ to a percentage, multiply by 100.
$\frac{2}{5} \times \frac{100}{1} = \frac{200}{5}$
$= 40\%$

(b) To change $\frac{1}{8}$ to a percentage, multiply by 100.
$\frac{1}{8} \times \frac{100}{1} = \frac{100}{8}$
$= 12\frac{1}{2}\%$

(c) To change $\frac{3}{7}$ to a percentage, multiply by 100.
$\frac{3}{7} \times \frac{100}{1} = \frac{300}{7}$
$= 42 \cdot 857 \ldots \%$
$= 43\%$, to the nearest whole number.

(d) To change 0·37 to a percentage, multiply by 100.
$0 \cdot 37 \times 100 = 37\%$

Exercise 4

Change these fractions to percentages.

1. $\frac{1}{2}$ 2. $\frac{3}{4}$ 3. $\frac{2}{5}$ 4. $\frac{7}{10}$ 5. $\frac{13}{20}$
6. $\frac{1}{8}$ 7. $\frac{5}{8}$ 8. $\frac{1}{4}$ 9. $\frac{7}{20}$ 10. $\frac{71}{100}$

11. Here are some examination results. Change them to percentages.
    (a) $\frac{14}{25}$ (b) $\frac{33}{40}$ (c) $\frac{42}{60}$ (d) $\frac{66}{120}$

12. Class 8P and class 8W were each set a maths test. The average mark for 8P was $\frac{25}{40}$ and the average mark for 8W was $\frac{15}{25}$. Which class had the higher average percentage result?

13. Change these decimals to percentages.
    (a) 0·32 (b) 0·14 (c) 0·03 (d) 0·815 (e) 1·4

14. Change these fractions to percentages, rounding to the nearest whole number.
    (a) $\frac{5}{6}$ (b) $\frac{7}{12}$ (c) $\frac{4}{9}$ (d) $\frac{6}{11}$ (e) $\frac{2}{3}$

15. The chart opposite shows the way that 40 people travel to work. What percentage travel
    (a) By car
    (b) By train
    (c) By bus
    (d) By some other method

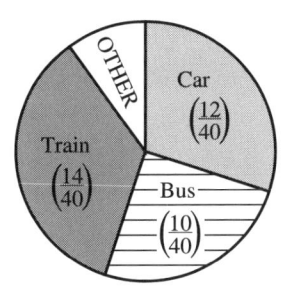

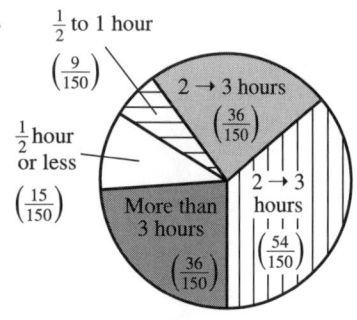

16. The chart opposite shows the T.V. viewing habits of 150 people in a survey. What percentage watch
(a) ½ hour or less
(b) more than 3 hours
(c) 2 → 3 hours.

17. The chart opposite shows the favourite foods of 80 people.
What percentage prefer
(a) Italian
(b) Asian
(c) French
(d) Anything but Chinese?

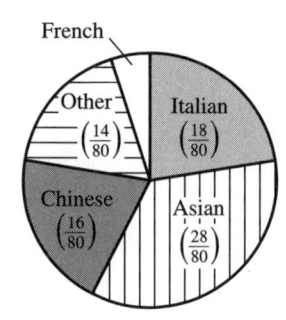

18. Change these percentages to decimals.
(a) 23%   (b) 37%   (c) 7%   (d) 1%
(e) 99%   (f) 5·5%   (g) 7·5%   (h) 0·5%

19. Change these percentages to fractions in their most simple form
(a) 30%   (b) 35%   (c) 90%   (d) 5%
(e) 12%   (f) 6%   (g) 0·1%   (h) 2·5%

20. Some fractions can be converted to decimals using equivalent fractions. For example: $\frac{1}{5} = \frac{2}{10} = 0·2$; $\frac{3}{20} = \frac{15}{100} = 0·15$. Use this method to change the following to decimals.
(a) $\frac{3}{5}$ (b) $\frac{7}{50}$ (c) $\frac{1}{25}$ (d) $\frac{7}{20}$

21. Copy and complete the table.

	fraction	decimal	percentage
(a)		0·3	
(b)			24%
(c)		0·01	
(d)	$\frac{3}{8}$		
(e)			3%

Exercise 5

1. The letters shown on the right are each given a number as either a fraction, a decimal or a percentage.
   In (a), (b), (c) below the numbers 1, 2, 3, ... give the positions of the letters in a sentence. So 1 is the first letter, 2 is the second letter and so on.
   Find the letter whose value is the same as the number given, and write it in the correct position.

A	24%	N	0.9
E	0.05	O	0.625
F	0.32	R	0.6
G	$\frac{3}{20}$	S	$\frac{7}{20}$
H	0.36	T	0.02
I	3%	U	$\frac{3}{25}$
L	0.49	V	0.1%
M	$\frac{3}{4}$	Y	99%

   For example in part (a) number 1 is $\frac{3}{5}$.
   Since $\frac{3}{5} = 0.6$, letter R goes in the first box.
   Find the sentence in each part.

   (a) 1 2 3 4 5 6 7 8 9 10 11 12

   | R | | | | | | | | | | | |

   1. $\frac{3}{5}$ 2. 0.24 3. 2% 4. 0.03 5. $\frac{5}{8}$ 6. 0.35
   7. $\frac{6}{25}$ 8. 60% 9. $\frac{1}{20}$ 10. 32% 11. 0.12 12. $\frac{9}{10}$

   (b) 1. 15% 2. $62\frac{1}{2}$% 3. 49% 4. $\frac{8}{25}$ 5. $\frac{3}{100}$ 6. 35%
   7. 0.75 8. 0.99 9. 0.15 10. 0.24 11. 75% 12. 5%

   (c) 1. $(0.6)^2$ 2. $0.2 + 0.04$ 3. $\frac{1}{2}$ of 0.98 4. 32% 5. $\frac{5}{8}$ 6. $\frac{8}{25}$
   7. $0.2 \div 10$ 8. 5% 9. 90% 10. $\frac{15}{500}$ 11. 50% of $\frac{7}{10}$ 12. $\frac{64}{200}$
   13. $3 \div 100$ 14. $\frac{1}{1000}$ 15. $(0.2)^2 + (0.1)^2$

2. Make up a sentence of your own using the letters given in Question 1. Write clues and try it out on a friend.

3. 24% of the grid below is shaded (Of the 100 squares on the grid exactly 24 are shaded).

   Draw a grid like this one and draw a number of your own choice. For example if you chose '16' make sure you shade in 16 out of the 100 squares. Try to make both figures the same size!

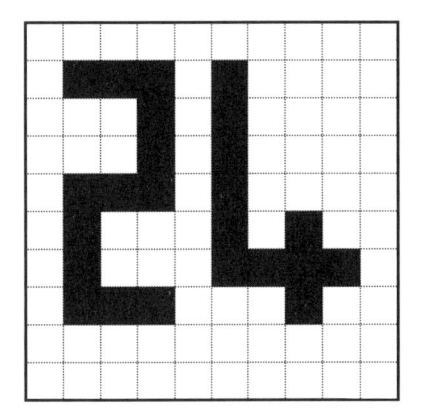

4.6 Solving problems 2

Exercise 1

1. One month after its birth a giraffe was 1·8 m tall. In the next two weeks it grew a further 35 cm. How tall was it then?

2. How many 10 mm pieces of wire can be cut from a wire of length 1 metre?

3. Every day Lucy spends 11 minutes combing her hair. How many hours and minutes is that in one week?

4. A grocer bought one thousand apples for £70. How much profit did he make if he sold them all at 12 p each?

5. A scorpion weighs 30 g and has enough poison to sting 50 people.
   (a) How much do 1000 scorpions weigh in kg?
   (b) How many scorpions are needed to sting 600 people?

6. The number in each square is the product of the two numbers in circles on either side of it. Copy and complete.

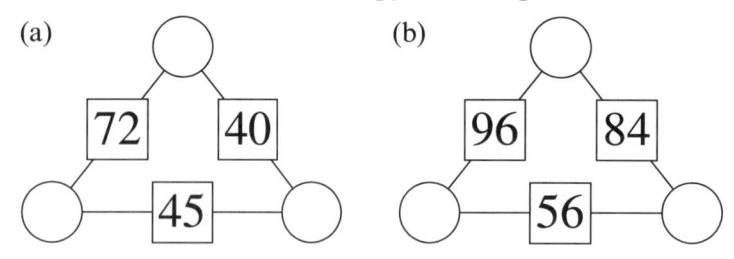

   (a) 72, 40, 45

   (b) 96, 84, 56

7. Find the cost of turfing a rectangular lawn 8 m by 10 m if the turf costs £1·50 per square metre.

8. Find the difference between 0·37 and 0·07.

9. A 2 kg bag of sugar is put into 50 g packets. How many packets are there?

10. A silk factory employs 200 000 worms to make one curtain measuring 4 m by 5 m. How many worms are needed for a curtain measuring 8 m by 10 m?

11. Jim's book has 240 pages. After one week he has read two fifths of the book. How many more pages are there left to read?

12. How many square pieces of glass measuring 50 cm by 50 cm can be cut from a large sheet measuring 4 m by 3 m?

13. The perimeter of a rectangle is 22 cm. Find the width of the rectangle if its length is 8 cm.

Exercise 2

1. A rodeo rider's prize was three hundred thousand dollars. How much was that in pounds, if £1 = $1·50?

2. How much is left from a wooden pole of length 3·2 m if a piece 65 cm long is cut off?

3. How many Kit-Kats at 30 p each can be bought for £5 and how much change will there be?

4. A salmon weighing 3 kg ate a small fish weighing 30 g. How much did it weigh after its meal?

5. A square field has an area of one hectare (1 hectare = 10 000 m^2). Find the perimeter of the field.

6. The slaves in a prison were paid 5 p a day. How much would a slave owner have to pay for 100 slaves for a year?

7. 200 roses were planted in rows of 8. How many rows were there?

8. Alvin put 56 litres of petrol in the tank of his car. How many litres were left after he used three quarters of it?

9. (a) Find two consecutive numbers which multiply together to give 210.
   (b) Find three consecutive numbers which multiply together to give 7980.

10. On January 1 a hippopotamus weighed 555 kg so she was put on a diet. By February 1 she had lost 8·5 kg. What was her new weight?

Exercise 3

1. How many 26p stamps can be bought for £10 and how much change will there be?

2. Which of the shapes below can be drawn without taking the pen from the paper and without going over any line twice?

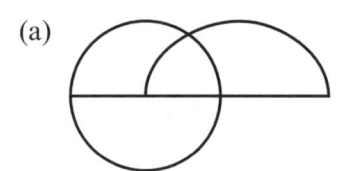

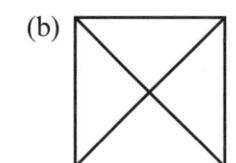

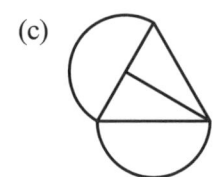

   (a)   (b)   (c)

3. At the Post Office, stamps are printed on large sheets 38 cm across by 60 cm down. How many stamps are there on each sheet?

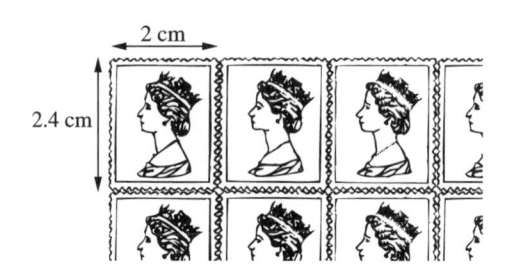

4. A suitcase is packed with 24 books and 85 magazines. The total weight of the suitcase and its contents is 8·85 kg. The empty suitcase weighs 880 g and each book weighs 70 g. Find the weight of each magazine.

5. Write down any fraction less than one.
   Add one to the numerator (top) and denominator (bottom).
   Is the new fraction larger or smaller than the original.

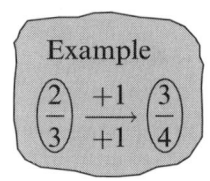

   Example
   $\frac{2}{3} \xrightarrow[+1]{+1} \frac{3}{4}$

6. I think of a number. If I add 5 and then multiply the result by 10 the answer is 82. What number was I thinking of?

7. A boat sails 2·4 km in 30 minutes. How long will it take to sail one km?

8. Show how the 3 by 8 rectangle can be cut into two identical pieces and joined together to make a 2 by 12 rectangle.

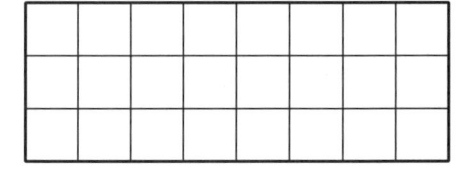

9. What is the smaller angle between the hands of a clock at
   (a) Four o'clock
   (b) (harder) Half past two?

10. Work out 33^2, 333^2 and 3333^2.
    Use your answers to predict the values of 33333^2 and 333333^2.

Exercise 4

1. A floor measuring 5 m by 3 m is to be covered with square tiles of side 10 cm. A packet of 20 tiles costs £6·95. How much will it cost to tile the floor?

2. An Audi kangaroo car travels 350 km on 125 litres of fuel. How much fuel is needed for a journey of 630 km?

3. In a restaurant six glasses of wine cost £7·50. How many glasses of wine could be bought for £22?

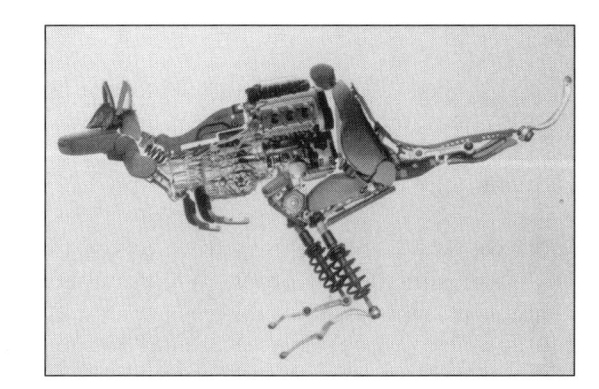

4. When a car journey starts, the mileometer reads 23 715 miles.
   After half an hour the mileometer reads 23 747 miles.
   What is the average speed of the car?

5. A shop keeper bought 30 books at £3·40 each and a number of C.D.'s costing £8·40 each. In all he spent £312. How many C.D.'s did he buy?

6. It costs 18p per minute to hire a tool. How much will it cost to hire the tool from 08.50 to 11.15?

7. Copy and complete this multiplication square.

×	4	6		
		18		24
			77	
5	20			
			99	72

8. A computer is advertised at £800 plus V.A.T. Work out the full price, including V.A.T. at $17\frac{1}{2}\%$.

9. The symbols $*, \nabla, \square, \bigcirc$ represent numbers.
   Use the clues in (a), (b) and (c) to answer part (d).
   (a) $* + \nabla = \square$ (b) $* = \nabla + \bigcirc$
   (c) $* + * + \nabla = \square + \bigcirc + \bigcirc$ (d) $\nabla =$ How many $\bigcirc$'s?

Exercise 5

1. In 2002 Ian was paid £368 per week and 18% of his pay was deducted for tax. What was his 'take home pay' in 2002?

2. A rectangular box, without a lid, is to be made from cardboard.
   Find the area of the cardboard for the box.

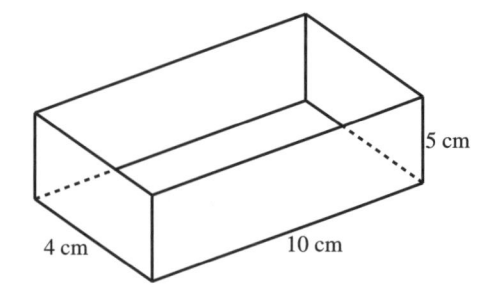

3. The numbers '7' and '3' multiply to give 21 and add up to 10. Find two numbers which:
   (a) multiply to give 48 and add up to 19.
   (b) multiply to give 180 and add up to 27.

4. The words for the numbers from eleven to twenty are written in a list in alphabetical order. What number will be third in the list?

5. The diagram shows a corner torn from a sheet of graph paper measuring 5 cm by 7 cm.
   Calculate the total length of all the lines drawn on the whole sheet of graph paper.

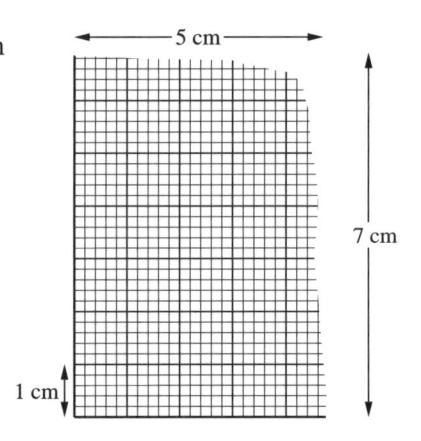

6. Sima has the same number of 10p and 50p coins. The total value is £9. How many of each coin does she have?

7. A supermarket has two special offers, one on Bran Flakes and one on Frosties. Work out the missing numbers.

   (a) **Bran Flakes**
   20% extra free
   ▮ g for the price of 375g

   (b) **Frosties**
   50% extra free
   ▮ g for the price of 320g

8. 'Muirfield' grass seed is sown at a rate of 40 grams per square metre and a 2 kg box of seed costs £5. Mrs James wishes to sow a square lawn and she has up to £40 to spend on seed. Find the side of the largest square lawn she can sow.

9. As part of an advertising campaign, the message 'Exercise is good for you' is taped individually right around 500 000 tennis balls, each of circumference 30 cm. Find the total cost of the tape for the campaign, given that a 40 m roll of tape costs 96 p.

10. In a code the 25 letters from A to Y are obtained from the square using a 2 digit grid reference similar to coordinates. So letter 'E' is 24 and 'U' is 52.
 The missing letter 'Z' has code 10.

[Second digit] 5	N	A	Y	M	D
4	R	E	S	X	I
3	J	T	L	B	P
2	V	C	O	F	U
1	K	W	G	Q	H
	1	2	3	4	5

[First digit]

Decode the following messages:

(a) 53, 54, 24
 22, 51, 25, 14, 23, 34
 25, 14, 24
 14, 32, 52, 15, 55

(b) 45, 35
 23, 24, 25, 22, 51, 24, 14
 54, 34
 22, 33, 24, 12, 24, 14

(c) 45, 35
 24, 44, 25, 45, 34
 25, 14, 24
 23, 32, 32
 24, 25, 34, 35

In part (d) each pair of brackets gives one letter.

(d) $(40 - 8)$, $(4^2 - 1)$, (8×3)
 $(3^2 + 4^2)$, $(75 \div 5)$, $(8 \times 7 - 1)$
 $(2 \times 2 \times 2 \times 2 \times 2)$, $(114 - 99)$, $(5^2 - 1)$
 (9×6), $(12 \times 3 - 2)$
 $(31 - 8)$, $(\frac{1}{2}$ of $42)$, $(160 \div 5)$

(e) Write your own message in code and ask a friend to decode it.

Part 5

5.1 Ratio and proportion

- We use ratio to compare parts of a whole.
  In a mixed class of 30 children, 13 are girls.
  Since there are 30 children altogether, there are 17 boys.
  The ratio girls : boys is 13 : 17

- Ratios can sometimes be written in a simpler form:
  The ratios 4 : 10 and 2 : 5 are the same.   [divide by 2]
  The ratios 10 : 20 : 25 and 2 : 4 : 5 are the same   [divide by 5]

Exercise 1

In Questions **1** to **4**, make sure that your answers are in their simplest form.

1. In a hall there are 36 chairs and 9 tables.
   Find the ratio of chairs to tables.

2. In a room there are 14 women and 12 men.
   Find the ratio of women to men.

3. In a mixed class of 20 children, 8 are boys
   Write down the ratio boys : girls.

4. In an office there are twice as many men as women.
   Write down the ratio men : women.

5. Write these ratios in a more simple form.
   (a) 9 : 6   (b) 15 : 25   (c) 10 : 40
   (d) 48 : 44   (e) 18 : 24   (f) 40 : 25

6. In a box, the ratio of rulers to pencils is 1 : 3. If there are 5 rulers, how many pencils are there?

7. In a classroom the ratio of girls to boys is 3 : 2.
   If there are 14 boys, how many girls are there?

8. In a greengrocer's shop, the ratio of apples to pears is 5 : 2. If there are 200 pears, how many apples are there?

9. A factory produces mainly cars but also the occasional washing machine! The ratio of cars to washing machines is 5 : 1. One day 400 cars were made. How many washing machines were produced?

10. Write these ratios in a more simple form.
    (a) $9:6:12$
    (b) $40:5:15$
    (c) $12:10:8$
    (d) $18:12:18$
    (e) $70:10:50$
    (f) $14:7:35$

11. In a box, the ratio of apples to peaches to bananas is $3:1:2$. If there are 24 apples, how many peaches are there and how many bananas are there?

12. On a Saturday the football results gave a ratio of home wins to away wins to draws of $6:2:1$. If there were 10 away wins, how many home wins were there and how many draws were there?

13. On a farm, the ratio of cows to sheep to pigs is $3:4:5$. If there are 35 pigs, how many sheep are there and how many cows are there?

14. Find the ratio (shaded area) : (unshaded area) for each diagram.
    (a)   (b)   (c)

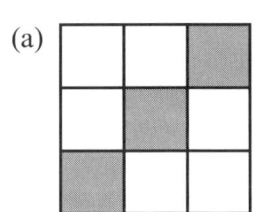

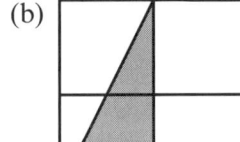

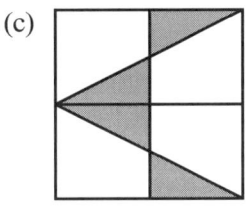

15. If $\frac{2}{5}$ of the children in a school are girls, what is the ratio of girls to boys?

Ratio and sharing

- Share 30 apples between Ken and Denise in the ratio $2:3$

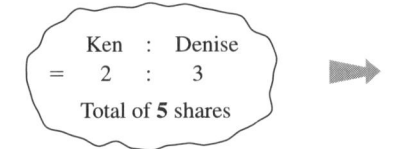

  Ken : Denise
  = 2 : 3
  Total of **5** shares

  Each share = $30 \div 5$
  = 6 apples
  So Ken's share is $2 \times 6 = 12$ apples
  Denise's share is $3 \times 6 = 18$ apples

  [Check: $12 + 18 = 30$ ✓]

- Share a prize of £63 between Ann, Ben and Carol in the ratio $2:3:4$.

  Ann : Ben : Carol
  = 2 : 3 : 4
  Total of **9** shares

  Each share = £63 $\div$ **9**
  = £7
  So Ann gets $2 \times 7 = £14$
  Ben gets $3 \times 7 = £21$
  Carol gets $4 \times 7 = £28$

  [Check: $14 + 21 + 28 = 63$ ✓]

Exercise 2

1. Alex and Debbie share a bag of 30 sweets in the ratio $3:2$. How many sweets does each person get?

2. A mother and her son share a prize of £60 in the ratio $3:1$. How much does each person receive?

3. Share each quantity in the ratio given.
   (a) 54 cm, $4:5$ (b) £99, $4:7$ (c) 132 km, $6:5$
   (d) £36, $2:3:4$ (e) 200 kg, $5:2:3$ (f) £2000, $1:9$

4. Three starving dogs share a meal weighing 660 g in the ratio $2:5:3$. Find the largest share.

5. Find the largest share in these problems
   (a) £64, ratio $3:5$
   (b) 90 kg, ratio $7:2$
   (c) 220 m, ratio $3:3:4$

6. Find the smallest share in these problems
   (a) £72, ratio $1:11$
   (b) 66 cm, ratio $2:1$
   (c) 35 litres, ratio $2:3:2$

7. Two squares are shown with their perimeters.
   (a) Write down the ratio of the lengths of their sides.
   (b) Work out the ratio of their areas.

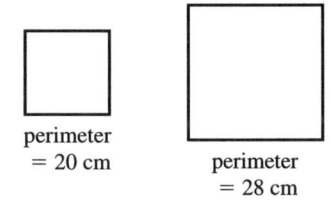

   perimeter = 20 cm   perimeter = 28 cm

8. Rod A is 40 cm long and rod B is 1·1 m long. Change 1·1 m into cm and then write down the ratio, length of rod A : length of rod B.

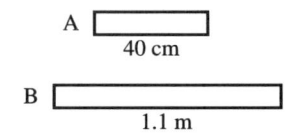

   A 40 cm
   B 1.1 m

In Questions **9** to **16** write the ratios in a more simple form.

9. 20 cm : 1 m
10. 20 mm : 5 cm
11. 400 g : 2 kg
12. 250 m : 1 km
13. 200 ml : 2 litres
14. 50 cm : 4 m
15. 0·5 m : 60 cm : 3 m
16. 300 g : 0·7 kg : 3 kg

17. The angles in a triangle are in the ratio $3:1:2$. Find the sizes of the three angles.

18. The angles in a quadrilateral are in the ratio $2:2:3:2$. Find the largest angle in the quadrilateral.

19. The sides of a rectangle are in the ratio $3:1$. The area of the rectangle is 48 cm². Find the sides of the rectangle.

Map scales

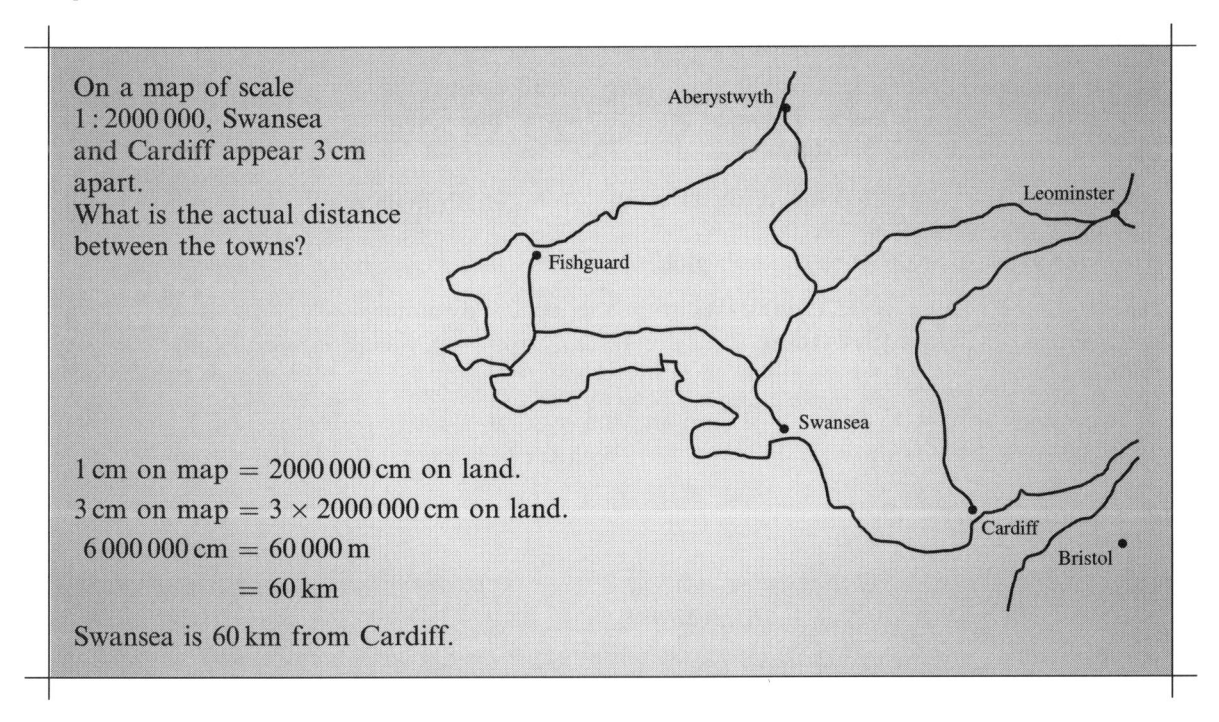

On a map of scale 1 : 2 000 000, Swansea and Cardiff appear 3 cm apart.
What is the actual distance between the towns?

1 cm on map = 2 000 000 cm on land.
3 cm on map = 3 × 2 000 000 cm on land.
6 000 000 cm = 60 000 m
            = 60 km
Swansea is 60 km from Cardiff.

Exercise 3

1. On a map whose scale is 1:1000, the distance between two houses is 3 cm. Find the actual distance between the two houses, giving your answer in metres.

2. The distance on a map between two points is 8 cm. Find the actual distance in metres between the two points, given that the scale of the map is 1:100.

3. The scale of a certain map is 1:10 000. What is the actual distance in metres between two churches which are 4 cm apart on the map?

4. On a map whose scale is 1:100 000, the distance between two villages is 7 cm. What is the actual distance in kilometres between the two villages?

5. The distance on a map between two towns is 9 cm. Find the actual distance in kilometres between the two towns, given that the scale of the map is 1:1 000 000.

6. Find the actual distance in metres between two towers which are 5 cm apart on a map whose scale is 1:10 000.

7. A river is 5 cm long on a map whose scale is 1:20 000.
Find the actual length of the river.

8. Andrew finds that the distance between two cities on a map whose scale is 1:1 000 000 is 12 cm. What is the actual distance in kilometres between the two cities?

9. If the distance between two places on a map is 10 cm, find the actual distance in kilometres between the two places, given that the scale of the map is 1:10 000.

10. Two places are separated by a distance of 20 cm on a map having a scale of 1:6000.
How far apart in reality are the two places?

11. The scale of a map is 1:200 000. What is the actual distance between two villages given that they are 8·5 cm apart on the map?

12. If two towns are 5·4 cm apart on a map and the scale of the map is 1:3 000 000, what is the actual distance between the two towns?

Direct proportion

If 10 calculators cost £89·50, find the cost of 7.

Find the cost of 1 calculator and then find the cost of 7.

10 calculators cost £89·50
1 calculator costs £89·50 ÷ 10 = £8·95
∴ 7 calculators cost £8·95 × 7 = £62·65

Exercise 4

1. If 5 hammers cost £20, find the cost of 7.

2. Magazines cost £16 for 8. Find the cost of 3 magazines.

3. Find the cost of 2 cakes if 7 cakes cost £10·50.

4. A machine fills 1000 bottles in 5 minutes. How many bottles will it fill in 2 minutes?

5. A train travels 100 km in 20 minutes. How long will it take to travel 50 km?

6. 11 discs cost £13·20. Find the cost of 4 discs.

7. There are 528 cars in a 3 mile traffic jam. About how many cars are there in an 8 mile jam?

8. If 7 cartons of milk hold 14 litres, find how much milk there is in 6 cartons.

9. A worker takes 8 minutes to make 2 circuit boards. How long would it take to make 7 circuit boards?

10. The total weight of 8 tiles is 1720 g. How much do 17 tiles weigh?

11. A machine can fill 3000 bottles in 15 minutes. How many bottles will it fill in 2 minutes?

12. A witch travels 40 km in 120 minutes. How long will she take to travel 55 km at the same speed?

13. If 4 grapefruit can be bought for £2·96, how many can be bought for £8·14?

14. £15 can be exchanged for 126 francs. How many francs can be exchanged for £37·50?

15. Usually it takes 10 hours for 4 men to build a wall. How many men are needed to build a wall twice as big in 10 hours?

16. A car travels 280 km on 35 litres of petrol. How much petrol is needed for a journey of 440 km?

5.2 Enlargement

- The original picture here has been enlarged by a scale factor of 2

  2 cm
  3.4 cm
  4 cm
  6.8 cm

  Notice that both the height *and* the width have been doubled.

- For an enlargement the original and the enlargement must be exactly the same shape. All angles in both shapes are preserved.

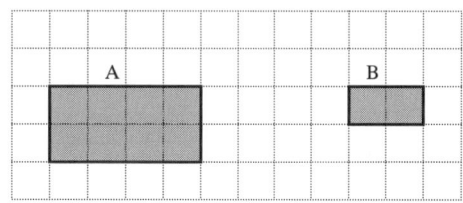

-
  A   B

  Length of A = 2 × length of B
  Width of A = 2 × width of B
  ∴ A *is* an enlargement of B

Exercise 1

Look at each pair of diagrams and decide whether or not one diagram is an enlargement of the other. For each question write the scale factor of the enlargement or write 'not an enlargement'.

1. 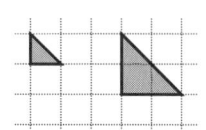
2. 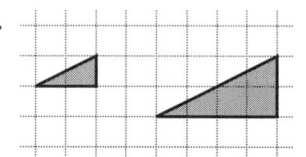
3. 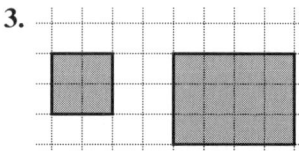
4. 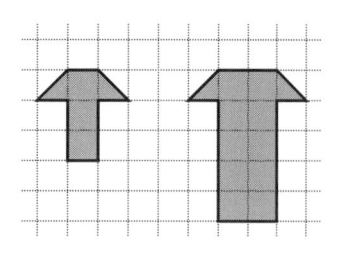
5. 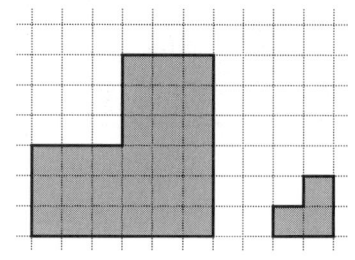
6.

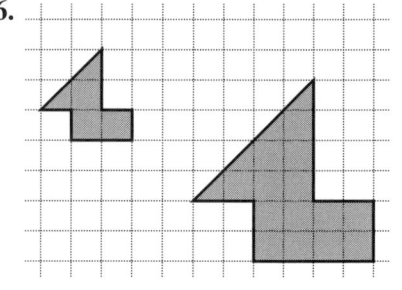

Exercise 2

Enlarge the following shapes by the scale factor given. Make sure you leave room on your page for the enlargement!

1. ×2

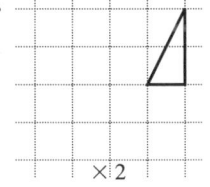

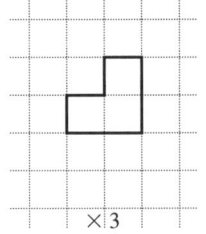

2. ×3

3. ×2

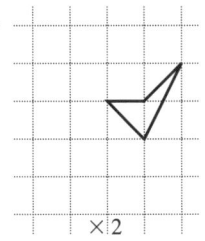

4. ×2

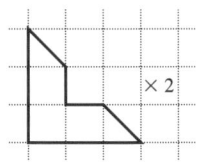

5. ×3

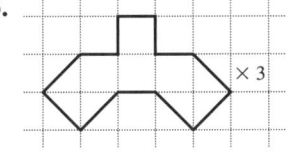

6. ×3

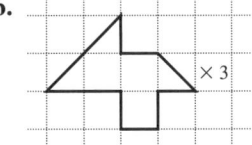

7. Here are some letters of the alphabet.
   (a) Enlarge them by a scale factor of 2.
   (b) Draw your own initials and enlarge them by a scale factor of 2.

   A B C D E

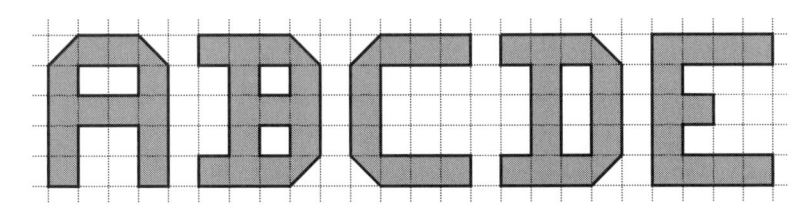

8. This picture is to be enlarged to fit the frame. Find the height of the frame.

   60 mm
   40 mm

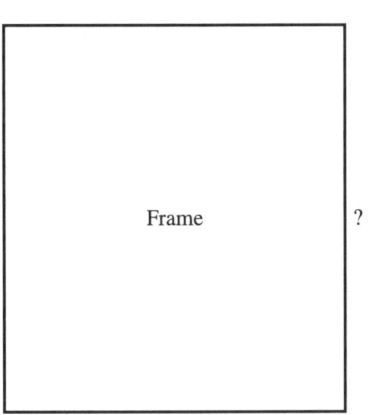

   Frame
   ?
   80 mm

9. A photograph measuring 5 cm by 3·5 cm is enlarged so that it fits exactly into a frame measuring 20 cm by x cm. Calculate the value of x.

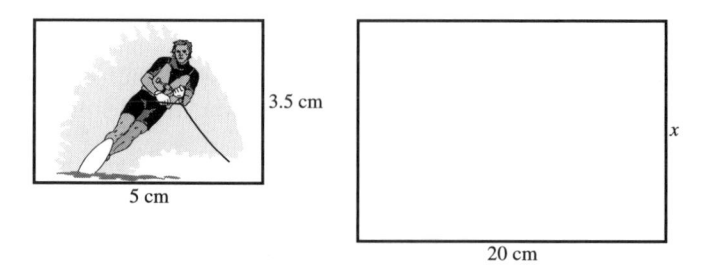

10. A photograph measuring 6 cm by 4 cm is reduced to fit frame A and another copy of the photograph is enlarged to fit frame B.

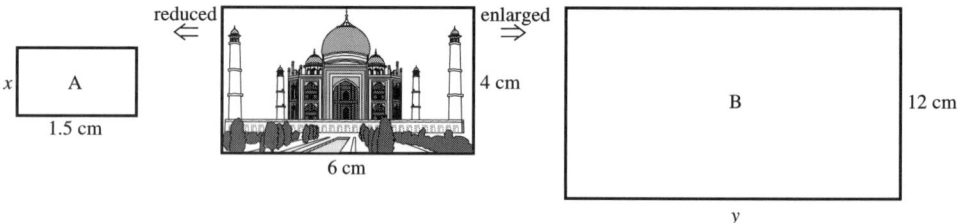

Calculate the value of x and the value of y.

Centre of enlargement

A mathematical enlargement always has a *centre of enlargement* as well as a scale factor. The centre of enlargement is found by drawing lines through corresponding points on the object and image and finding where they intersect. For greater accuracy it is better to count squares between points because it is difficult to draw construction lines accurately over a long distance.

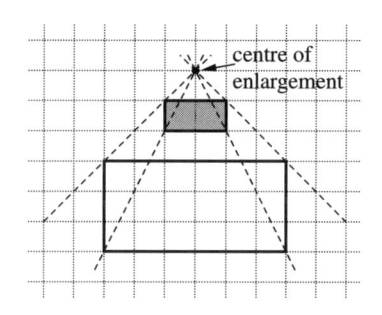

In the second diagram, A'B'C' is an enlargement of ABC with scale factor 2 and centre O.
Observe that $OA' = 2 \times OA$
$OB' = 2 \times OB$
$OC' = 2 \times OC$

Always measure distances from the centre of enlargement.

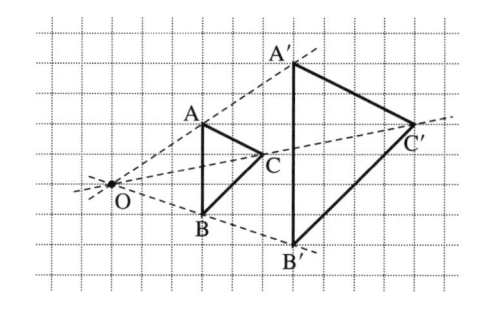

Exercise 3

Draw the shapes and then draw lines through corresponding points to find the centre of enlargement. Don't draw the shapes too near the edge of the page!

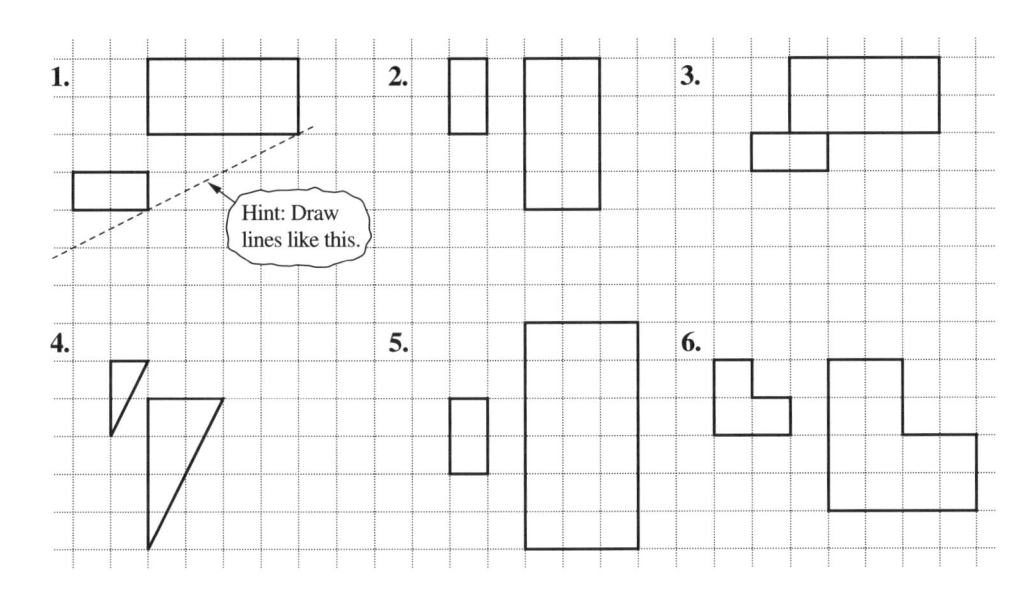

1.

Hint: Draw lines like this.

2.

3.

4.

5.

6.

To fully describe an enlargement we need two things: the scale factor and the centre of enlargement.

(a) Draw an enlargement of △1 with scale factor 3 and centre O.

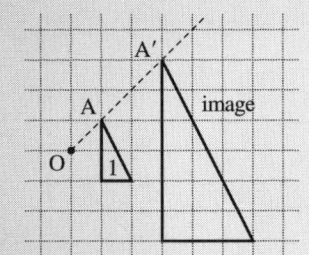

Notice that $OA' = 3 \times OA$.

(b) Draw an enlargement of shape P with scale factor 2 and centre O.

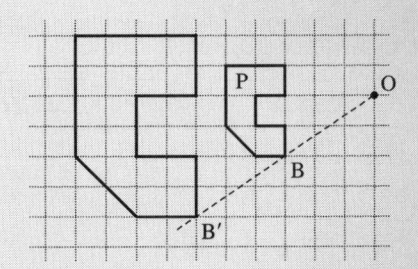

Notice that $OB' = 2 \times OB$.

In both diagrams, just one point on the image has been found by using a construction line or by counting squares. When one point is known the rest of the diagram can easily be drawn, since the size and shape of the image is known.

Exercise 4

In questions **1** to **6** copy the diagram and then draw an enlargement using the scale factor and centre of enlargement given.
Leave room for enlargement!

1. scale factor 2

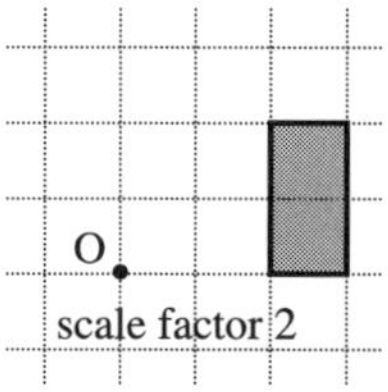

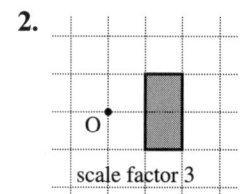

2. scale factor 3

3. scale factor 2

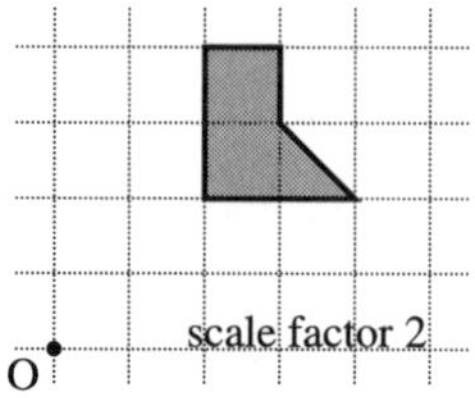

4. scale factor 2

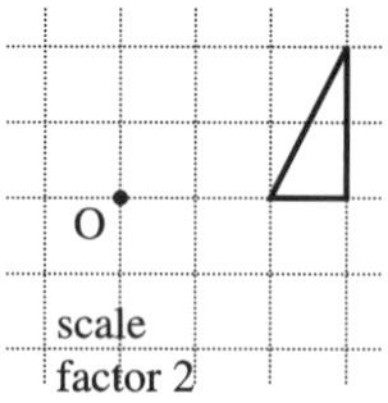

5. scale factor 3

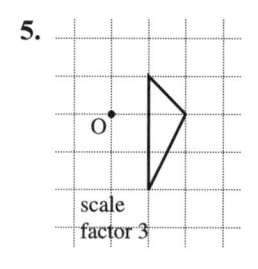

6. scale factor 2

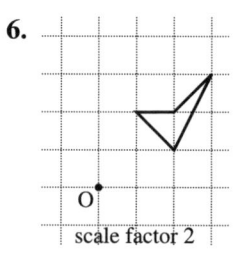

7. Copy the diagram
Draw an enlargement of the triangle with scale factor 2 and centre of enlargement (0, 0).

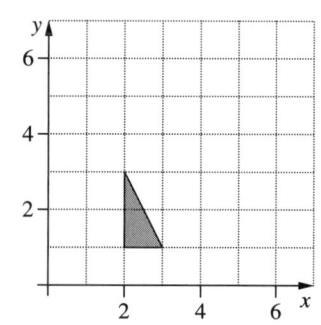

8. For (a), (b) and (c) draw a grid similar to the one in Question 7.
Draw an enlargement of each shape.

Shape	Centre of enlargement	Scale factor
(a) (1, 1) (2, 1) (2, 2) (1, 2)	(0, 0)	3
(b) (2, 1) (4, 2) (2, 2)	(0, 0)	2
(c) (4, 5) (6, 5) (6, 6) (4, 6)	(8, 8)	2

5.3 Sequences, the *n*th term

(a) For the sequence 4, 8, 12, 16, 20,... the rule is 'add 4'.

Here is the *mapping diagram* for the sequence.

Term number (*n*)	Term
1 ⟶	4
2 ⟶	8
3 ⟶	12
4 ⟶	16
⋮	⋮
10 ⟶	40
⋮	⋮
n ⟶	4*n*

The terms are found by multiplying the term number by 4.
So the 10th number is 40, the 20th term is 80.

A *general* term in the sequence is the *n*th term, where *n* stands for any number.
The *n*th term of this sequence is 4*n*.

(b) Here is a more difficult sequence: 4, 7, 10, 13,...

The rule is 'add 3' so, in the mapping diagram, we have written a column for 3 times the term number [i.e. 3*n*].

Term number (*n*)	3*n*	Term
1 ⟶	3 ⟶	4
2 ⟶	6 ⟶	7
3 ⟶	9 ⟶	10
4 ⟶	12 ⟶	13

We see that each term is 1 more than 3*n*.
So, the 10th term is $(3 \times 10) + 1 = 31$
the 15th term is $(3 \times 15) + 1 = 46$
the *n*th term is $(3 \times n) + 1 = 3n + 1$

(c) Look at these two mapping diagrams. Decide what the missing numbers would be.

Term number (*n*)	2*n*	Term
1 ⟶	2	3
2 ⟶	4	5
3 ⟶	6	7
4 ⟶	8	9
⋮	⋮	⋮
10 ⟶	□ ⟶	□
⋮		
n ⟶	2*n* ⟶	□

Term number (*n*)	5*n*	Term
1 ⟶	5 ⟶	7
2 ⟶	10 ⟶	12
3 ⟶	15 ⟶	17
4 ⟶	20 ⟶	22
⋮	⋮	⋮
20 ⟶	□ ⟶	□
⋮	⋮	⋮
n ⟶	□ ⟶	□

Exercise 1

1. Copy and complete these mapping diagrams.

(a)
Term number (n)	Term
1	→ 6
2	→ 12
3	→ 18
4	→ 24
⋮	⋮
12	→ ☐
⋮	⋮
n	→ ☐

(b)
Term number (n)	Term
1	→ 8
2	→ 16
3	→ 24
4	→ 32
⋮	⋮
8	→ ☐
⋮	⋮
n	→ ☐

(c)
Term number (n)	Term
1	→ 10
2	→ 20
3	→ 30
⋮	⋮
15	→ ☐
⋮	⋮
n	→ ☐

2. Copy and complete these mapping diagrams. Notice that an extra column has been written.

(a)
Term number (n)	$4n$	Term
1	→ 4	→ 5
2	→ 8	→ 9
3	→ 12	→ 13
4	→ 16	→ 17
⋮	⋮	⋮
20	→ ☐	→ ☐
⋮	⋮	⋮
n	→ ☐	→ ☐

(b)
Term number (n)	$5n$	Term
1	→ 5	→ 4
2	→ 10	→ 9
3	→ 15	→ 14
4	→ 20	→ 19
⋮	⋮	⋮
12	→ ☐	→ ☐
⋮	⋮	⋮
n	→ ☐	→ ☐

3. Write down each sequence and select the correct expression for the nth term from the list given.

(a) 3, 6, 9, 12, ...
(b) 5, 10, 15, 20, ...
(c) $1^2, 2^2, 3^2, 4^2, ...$
(d) 7, 14, 21, 28, ...
(e) 2, 3, 4, 5, 6, ...
(f) $1^3, 2^3, 3^3, 4^3, ...$
(g) 1, 3, 5, 7, 9, ...

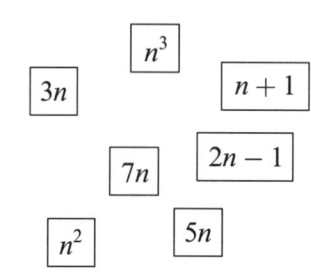

$3n$ n^3 $n+1$ $7n$ $2n-1$ n^2 $5n$

4. Here you are given the nth term. Copy and complete the diagrams.

(a)
Term number (n)	$7n$	Term
1 →	7 →	8
2 →	☐ →	☐
3 →	☐ →	☐
4 →	☐ →	☐
⋮	⋮	⋮
n →	$7n$ →	$7n+1$

(b)
Term number (n)	$3n$	Term
1 →	3 →	1
2 →	☐ →	☐
3 →	☐ →	☐
4 →	☐ →	☐
⋮	⋮	⋮
n →	$3n$ →	$3n-2$

(c)
Term number (n)	$5n$	Term
1 →	5 →	☐
2 →	☐ →	☐
3 →	☐ →	☐
8 →	☐ →	☐
⋮		
n →	$5n$ →	$5n+1$

(d)
Term number (n)	$10n$	Term
1 →	☐ →	☐
2 →	☐ →	☐
5 →	☐ →	☐
10 →	☐ →	☐
⋮	⋮	⋮
n →	$10n$ →	$10n+1$

- It is convenient to use the notation: T(1) for the first term,
  T(2) for the second term,
  T(3) for the third term and so on.

  The nth term of a sequence is written as T(n).

- The nth term of a sequence is $3n + 1$.
  So we have T(n) = $3n + 1$.

The first term, T(1) = $3 \times 1 + 1 = 4$
The second term, T(2) = $3 \times 2 + 1 = 7$
The seventh term, T(7) = $3 \times 7 + 1 = 22$

Remember:
For the first term, put $n = 1$
For the second term, put $n = 2$.

Exercise 2

1. For the sequence 3, 5, 7, 9, 11, 13, ... write down
   (a) T(1)   (b) T(2)   (c) T(5)

   Remember:
   T(1) means 'the first term'
   T(2) means 'the second term'
   ... and so on.

2. For the sequence 2, 4, 6, 8, 10, ... write down
   (a) T(1)   (b) T(4)   (c) T(6)

3. The *n*th term of a sequence is T(*n*) and T(*n*) = 2*n* + 1.
   Copy and complete the following
   (a) T(1) = 2 × 1 + 1 = ☐
   (b) T(2) = 2 × ☐ + 1 = ☐
   (c) T(3) = 2 × ☐ + 1 = ☐
   (d) T(10) = 2 × ☐ + 1 = ☐

4. The *n*th term of a sequence in T(*n*) and T(*n*) = 4*n*.
   Find (a) T(1)   (b) T(2)   (c) T(20)

5. For a sequence, T(*n*) = 5*n* + 1.
   Find (a) T(1)   (b) T(3)   (c) T(10)

6. For a sequence, T(*n*) = 20 − *n*.
   Find (a) T(2)   (b) T(5)   (c) T(11)

7. The *n*th term of a sequence is 3*n* − 1.
   Find (a) T(1)   (b) T(100)

8. Write the first five terms of the sequence whose *n*th term, T(*n*) = 2*n* + 3.

9. Write the first five terms of the sequence where T(*n*) is:
   (a) *n* + 2   (b) 5*n*   (c) 10*n* − 1
   (d) *n* − 2   (e) $\frac{1}{n}$ (f) n^2

Finding the *n*th term

- In an *arithmetic* sequence the difference between successive terms is always the same number.
  Here are some arithmetic sequences:
      5, 7, 9, 11, 13,
      12, 32, 52, 72, 92,
      20, 17, 14, 11, 8,
- The expression for the *n*th term of an arithmetic sequence is always of the form *an* + *b*

  The *difference* between successive terms is equal to the number *a*.
  The number *b* can be found by looking at the terms.

Find the nth term of the sequence 5, 7, 9, 11, 13, ...

This is an arithmetic sequence, so the nth term is of the form $an + b$.
The difference between terms is 2, so $a = 2$.

Put the sequence in a table and write a column for $2n$.

We can see that the term is always 3 more than $2n$, so $b = 3$.

The nth term is $2n + 3$.

n	$2n$	term
1	2	5
2	4	7
3	6	9
4	8	11

Exercise 3

1. Look at the sequence 5, 9, 13, 17, ...

   The difference between terms is 4.
   Copy the table, which has a column for $4n$.
   Copy and complete: 'The nth term of the sequence is $4n + \square$.'

n	$4n$	term
1	4	5
2	8	9
3	12	13
4	16	17

2. Look at the sequence and the table underneath. Find the nth term in each case.

   (a) Sequence 7, 10, 13, 16, ...

n	$3n$	term
1	3	7
2	6	10
3	9	13
4	12	16

   nth term = $\square$

   (b) Sequence 4, 9, 14, 19, ...

n	$5n$	term
1	5	4
2	10	9
3	15	14
4	20	19

   nth term = $\square$

3. In the sequence 6, 10, 14, 18, ... the difference between terms is 4. Copy and complete the table and write an expression for the nth term of the sequence.

n	$\square$	term
1	$\square$	6
2	$\square$	10
3	$\square$	14
4	$\square$	18

4. Look at the sequence 5, 8, 11, 14, ...
   Write down the difference between terms.
   Make a table like the one in Question 3 and use it to find an expression for the nth term.

5. Write down each sequence in a table and then find the nth term.
   (a) 8, 10, 12, 14, 16, ...
   (b) 3, 7, 11, 15, ...
   (c) 8, 13, 18, 23, ...

6. Make a table for each sequence and write the nth term.
   (a) 11, 19, 27, 35, ...
   (b) $2\frac{1}{2}, 4\frac{1}{2}, 6\frac{1}{2}, 8\frac{1}{2}, \ldots$
   (c) $-7, -4, -1, 2, 5, \ldots$

7. Here is a sequence of shapes made from sticks

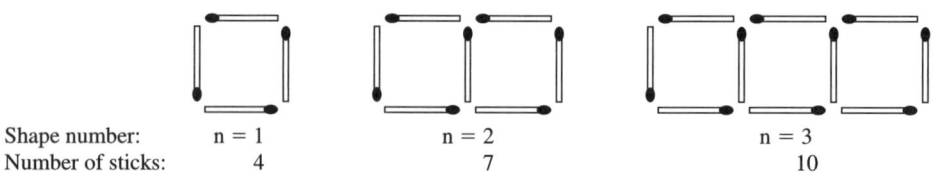

Shape number:	n = 1	n = 2	n = 3
Number of sticks:	4	7	10

   The number of sticks makes the sequence 4, 7, 10, 13, ...
   Make a table for the sequence and find the nth term.

In Questions 8 to 13 you are given a sequence of shapes made from sticks or dots. For each question make a table and find the nth term of the sequence.

8. Here is a sequence of triangles made from dots. Draw the next diagram in the sequence. How many dots are there in the nth term?

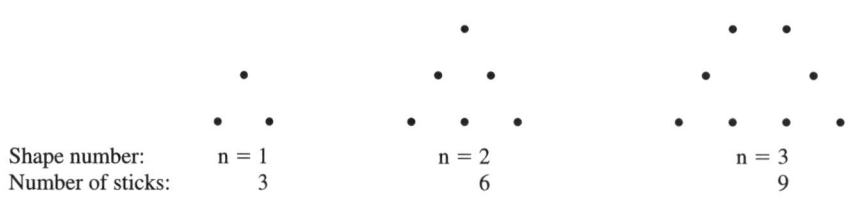

Shape number:	n = 1	n = 2	n = 3
Number of sticks:	3	6	9

9. Here is a sequence of 'steps' made from sticks.
   Draw the next diagram in the sequence and make a table. How many sticks are there in the nth term?

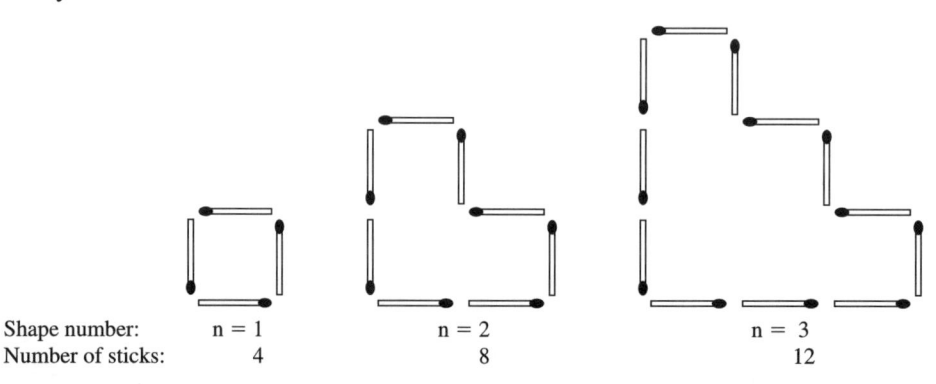

Shape number:	n = 1	n = 2	n = 3
Number of sticks:	4	8	12

10. Louise makes a pattern of triangles from sticks.

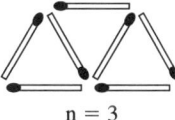

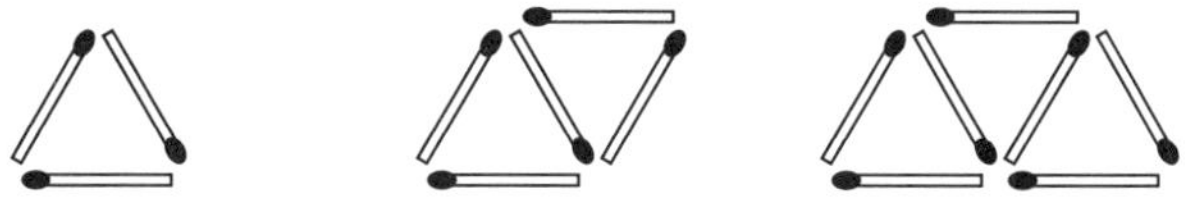

Shape number:	n = 1	n = 2	n = 3
Number of sticks:	3	5	7

(a) Draw shape number 4 and shape number 5 and make a table. How many sticks are there in the nth term?

11. Here is a sequence of houses made from sticks

Shape number:	n = 1	n = 2	n = 3
Number of sticks:	5	9	13

Draw shape number 4 and make a table. How many sticks are there in the nth term?

12. Paul makes a pattern of squares from dots.

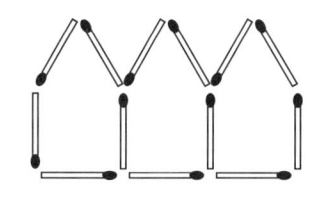

Shape number:	n = 1	n = 2	n = 3
Number of sticks:	4	6	8

Draw shape number 4 and shape number 5 and make a table. How many dots are there in the nth term?

13. Here is another sequence made from dots.

Shape number:	n = 1	n = 2	n = 3
Number of dots:	6	10	☐

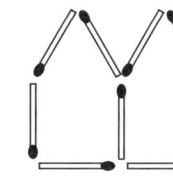

Draw shape numbers 4 and 5 and make a table. How many dots are there in the nth term?

5.4 Drawing graphs

- The points P, Q, R and S have coordinates (4, 4), (4, 3), (4, 2) and (4, 1) and they all lie on a straight line. Since the x-coordinate of all the points is 4, we say the *equation* of the line is $x = 4$.

- The points A, B, C and D have coordinates (1, 3), (2, 3), (3, 3) and (4, 3) and they all lie on a straight line. Since the y-coordinate of all the points is 3, we say the *equation* of the line is $y = 3$.

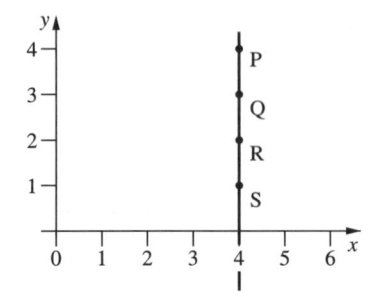

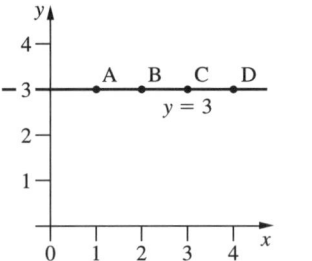

- The sloping line passes through the following points: (1, 1), (2, 2), (3, 3), (4, 4), (5, 5).

  For each point, the y-coordinate is equal to the x-coordinate.
  The equation of the line is $y = x$ (or $x = y$).

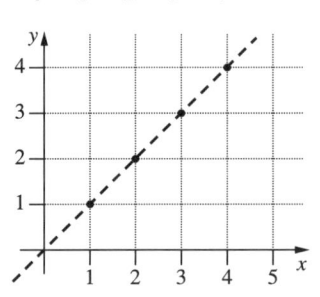

Exercise 1

1. Copy the graph and then write down the coordinates for each point.
   A (2, 1) H (,)
   B (,)   I (,)
   C (,)   J (,)
   D (,)   K (,)
   E (,)   L (,)
   F (,)   M (,)
   G (,)   N (,)

2. L lies on the line $x = 10$.
   Which other letter lies on $x = 10$?

3. Which letter lies on $x = 6$?
4. Which letters lie on $x = 4$?
5. G lies on the line $y = 8$.
   Which letter lies on $y = 10$?
6. Which letters lie on $y = 2$?
7. Which letters lie on $y = 5$?

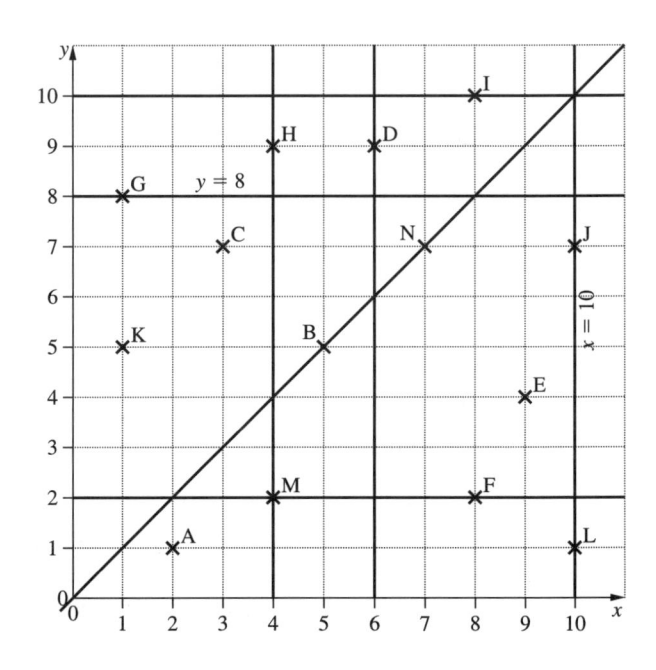

8. Which letters lie on $y = 7$?

9. Which letter lies on $x = 9$?

10. The x coordinate of B is the same as the y coordinate. We say that B lies on the line $y = x$ (or $x = y$).
    Which other letter lies on $y = x$?

11. Point M lies on $x = 4$ *and* $y = 2$. What point lies on $x = 8$ and $y = 2$?

12. What point lies on $x = 2$ and $y = 1$?

13. What point lies on $x = 10$ and $y = 7$?

Negative coordinates

Exercise 2

1. Copy the diagram and then write down the coordinates for each point.
    A(2, 4)
    B(5, 2)
    C(−2, 5)
    ⋮
    N(5, −3)

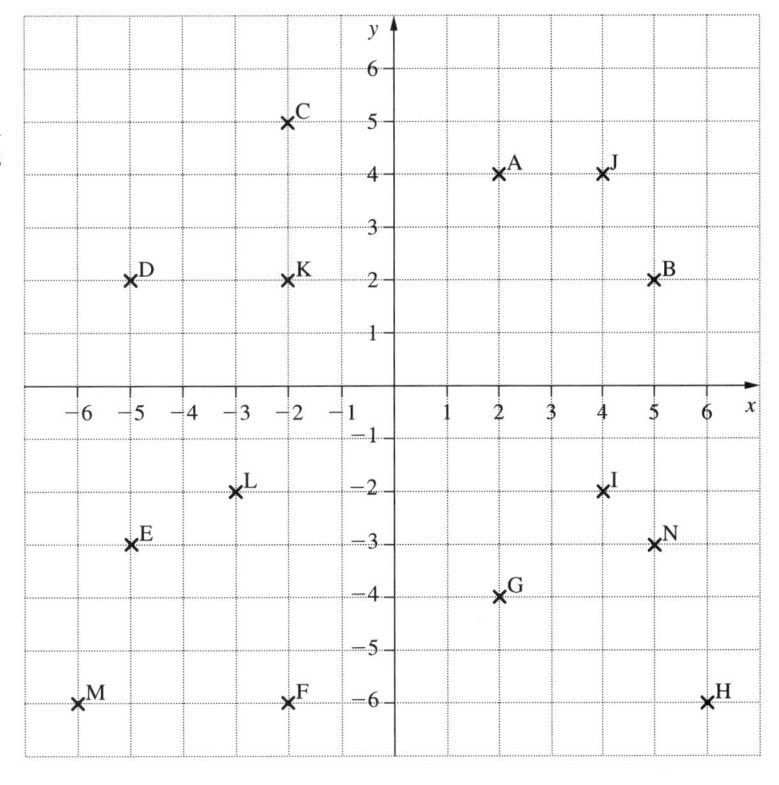

2. Point A lies on the line $x = 2$. Which other letter lies on $x = 2$?

3. Point N lies on the line $y = -3$. Which other letter lies on $y = -3$?

4. Which letters lie on the line $x = -5$?

5. Which letter lies on the line $y = 5$?

6. Which letters lie on the line $y = x$?

7. Write down the coordinates of the mid-point of the following line segments
    (a) AG   (b) AJ   (c) CK   (d) KF   (e) GH   (f) KA

8. Point H lies on the line $y = -x$. Which other letter lies on $y = -x$?

9. On a graph plot the points P(6, 6), Q(0, 4), R(2, −2). Write down the coordinates of the mid-point of
   (a) PQ   (b) PR   (c) QR

In Questions **10** and **11** there is a line of dots A and a line of crosses B.

Write down the equations of the lines in each question.

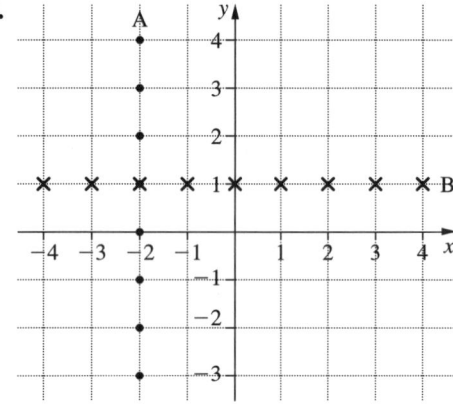

10.

11.

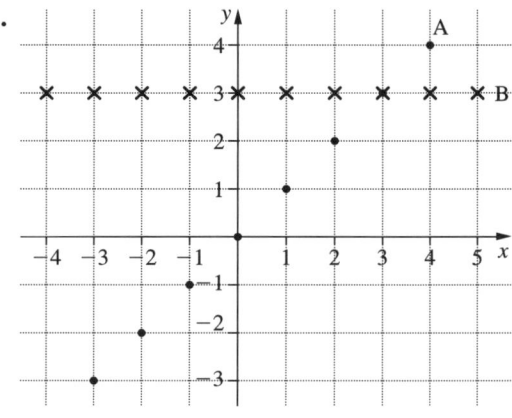

Drawing graphs: order of operations

- We have seen that when a calculation [like $5 + 7 \times 3$] is performed, the order of operations follows 'BIDMAS'.

   Brackets
   Indices
   Divide
   Multiply
   Add
   Subtract

   The same rules apply for the expressions involved in graphs.

- Consider the graph $y = 3x - 1$. Two operations are performed: 'multiply by 3', 'subtract 1'.

   Multiply is done before subtract and a *flow chart* can be drawn

   $$x \rightarrow \boxed{\times 3} \rightarrow \boxed{-1} \rightarrow y$$

   So when $x = 2$, $y = 2 \times 3 - 1 = 5$. On the graph plot (2, 5)
   when $x = 4$, $y = 4 \times 3 - 1 = 11$. On the graph plot (4, 11)
   when $x = 7$, $y = 7 \times 3 - 1 = 20$. On the graph plot (7, 20)

- Consider the graph $y = 2(x + 1)$. The operation in brackets is done first.
  The flow chart is:

  $$x \to \boxed{+1} \to \boxed{\times 2} \to y$$

  When $x = 2$, $y = (2 + 1) \times 2 = 6$. Plot (2, 6)
  $x = 3$, $y = (3 + 1) \times 2 = 8$. Plot (3, 8)
  $x = 5$, $y = (5 + 1) \times 2 = 12$. Plot (5, 12)

Using the flow diagram, complete the table below.
Hence draw the graph of $y = 2x + 4$ for x from 0 to 5

x	0	1	2	3	4	5
y	4	6	8	10	12	14
coordinates	(0, 4)	(1, 6)	(2, 8)	(3, 10)	(4, 12)	(5, 14)

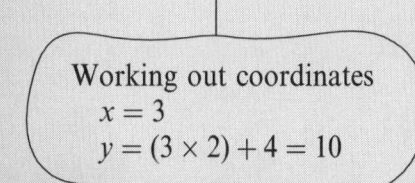

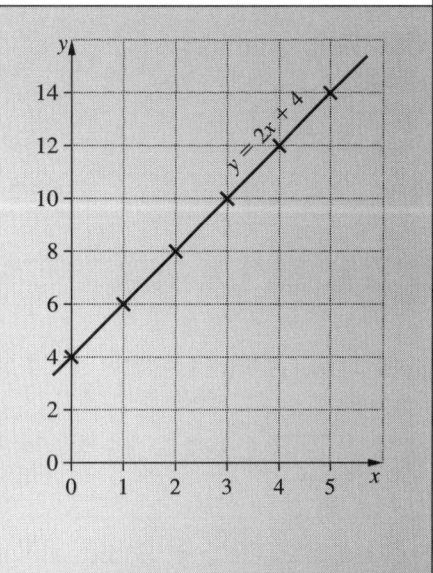

Working out coordinates
$x = 3$
$y = (3 \times 2) + 4 = 10$

Important points:
(a) Start both axes at 0 and take care with scales around 0
(b) Label the axes 'x' and 'y'.
(c) Label the graph with its equation.

Exercise 3

For each question, copy and complete the table using the flow diagram. Then draw the graph using the scales given.

1. $y = 2x + 1$ for x: 0 to 6 $\quad \begin{pmatrix} x\colon 1\,\text{cm} = 1\,\text{unit} \\ y\colon 1\,\text{cm} = 1\,\text{unit} \end{pmatrix}$

$$x \to \boxed{\times 2} \to \boxed{+1} \to y$$

x	0	1	2	3	4	5	6
y					9		
coordinates					(4, 9)		

2. $y = x + 4$ for x: 0 to 7 $\begin{pmatrix} x: 1\,\text{cm} = 1\,\text{unit} \\ y: 1\,\text{cm} = 1\,\text{unit} \end{pmatrix}$

$x \rightarrow \boxed{+4} \rightarrow y$

x	0	1	2	3	4	5	6	7
y			6					
coordinates			(2, 6)					

3. $y = 3x$ for x: 0 to 5 $\begin{pmatrix} x: 1\,\text{cm} = 1\,\text{unit} \\ y: 1\,\text{cm} = 2\,\text{units} \end{pmatrix}$

$x \rightarrow \boxed{\times 3} \rightarrow y$

x	0	1	2	3	4	5
y		3				
coordinates		(1, 3)				

4. $y = \dfrac{x}{2}$ for x: 0 to 7 $\begin{pmatrix} x: 1\,\text{cm} = 1\,\text{unit} \\ y: 2\,\text{cm} = 1\,\text{unit} \end{pmatrix}$

$x \rightarrow \boxed{\div 2} \rightarrow y$

x	0	1	2	3	4	5	6	7
y						$2\frac{1}{2}$		
coordinates						$(5, 2\frac{1}{2})$		

5. $y = 6 - x$ for x: 0 to 6 $\begin{pmatrix} x: 1\,\text{cm} = 1\,\text{unit} \\ y: 1\,\text{cm} = 1\,\text{unit} \end{pmatrix}$

$x \rightarrow \boxed{\text{subtract from 6}} \rightarrow y$ $\begin{pmatrix} \text{Set up your} \\ \text{own table} \end{pmatrix}$

6. $y = 12 - 2x$ for x: 0 to 6 $\begin{pmatrix} x: 1\,\text{cm} = 1\,\text{unit} \\ y: 1\,\text{cm} = 1\,\text{unit} \end{pmatrix}$

$x \rightarrow \boxed{\times 2} \rightarrow \boxed{\text{subtract from 12}} \rightarrow y$

7. $y = 3(x + 1)$ for x: 0 to 5 $\begin{pmatrix} x: 1\,\text{cm} = 1\,\text{unit} \\ y: 1\,\text{cm} = 2\,\text{units} \end{pmatrix}$

$x \rightarrow \boxed{+1} \rightarrow \boxed{\times 3} \rightarrow y$

8. $y = 3(6 - x)$ for x: 0 to 6
$\begin{pmatrix} x\text{: 1 cm} = 1 \text{ unit} \\ y\text{: 1 cm} = 2 \text{ units} \end{pmatrix}$

$x \rightarrow \boxed{\text{subtract from 6}} \rightarrow \boxed{\times 3} \rightarrow y$

9. $y = 2x + 4$ for x: 0 to 8
$\begin{pmatrix} x\text{: 1 cm} = 1 \text{ unit} \\ y\text{: 1 cm} = 2 \text{ units} \end{pmatrix}$

$x \rightarrow \boxed{\times 2} \rightarrow \boxed{+ 4} \rightarrow y$

10. $y = \frac{1}{2}x + 3$ for x: 0 to 8
$\begin{pmatrix} x\text{: 1 cm} = 1 \text{ unit} \\ y\text{: 2 cm} = 1 \text{ unit} \end{pmatrix}$

11. $y = 20 - 3x$ for x: 0 to 6
$\begin{pmatrix} x\text{: 1 cm} = 1 \text{ unit} \\ y\text{: 1 cm} = 2 \text{ units} \end{pmatrix}$

12. $y = 4x + 1$ for x: 0 to 6
$\begin{pmatrix} x\text{: 1 cm} = 1 \text{ unit} \\ y\text{: 1 cm} = 2 \text{ units} \end{pmatrix}$

13. $y = 26 - 4x$ for x: 0 to 6
$\begin{pmatrix} x\text{: 1 cm} = 1 \text{ unit} \\ y\text{: 1 cm} = 2 \text{ units} \end{pmatrix}$

Exercise 4

Use a graphical calculator or a graph plotter on a computer.

1. Draw the graphs of $y = x + 5$, $y = x + 3$, $y = x - 1$, $y = x - 4$
Write down what you notice. [Look at the point where the lines cut the y axis.]

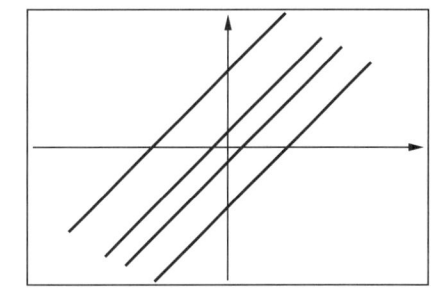

2. Draw the graphs of $y = 2x + 1$, $y = 2x - 3$, $y = 2x + 5$.
Write down what you notice.

3. Draw the graphs of $y = 3x$, $y = 3x - 5$, $y = 3x + 6$
What do you notice?

4. (a) Where do you expect $y = 4x + 7$ to cut the y axis?
(b) Where do you expect $y = 4x - 3$ to cut the y axis?

5. Write down the equation of any line parallel to $y = 6x + 3$.

6. Draw the graphs of $y = x^2$, $y = 12 \div x$, $y = x^2 - 5$.

7. State which of the following represent straight line graphs
$y = 3x + 2$ $y = 10 \div x$ $y = 5x - 1$ $y = x^3$

Relating x and y

- The sloping line passes through the following points:
  (1, 1), (2, 2), (3, 3), (4, 4), (5, 5).

  For each point, the y-coordinate is equal to the x-coordinate.

  The equation of the line is $y = x$ (or $x = y$).

- This line passes through:
  (0, 2), (1, 3), (2, 4), (3, 5), (4, 6).

  For each point the y-coordinate is two more than the x-coordinate. The equation of the line is $y = x + 2$.

  We could also say that the x coordinate is always one less than the y coordinate. The equation of the line could then be written as $x = y - 2$.
  [Most mathematicians use the equation beginning '$y =$'].

- This line slopes the other way and passes through:
  (0, 4), (1, 3), (2, 2), (3, 1), (4, 0).

  The sum of the x coordinate and the y coordinate is always 4. The equation of the line is $x + y = 4$.

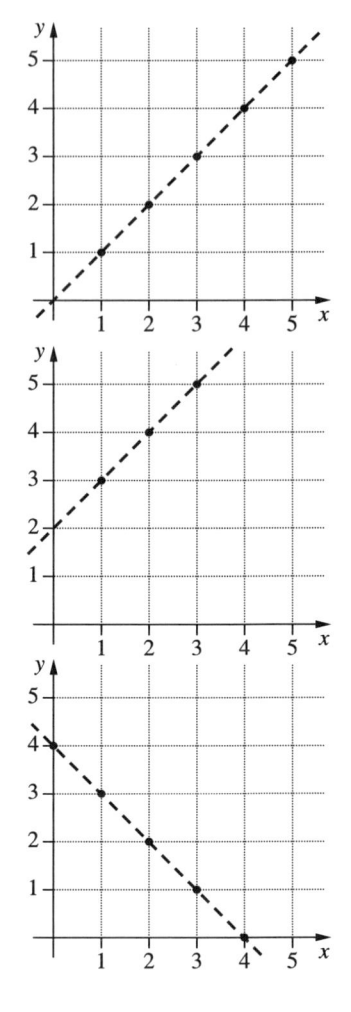

Exercise 5

For each question write down the coordinates of the points marked.
Find the equation of the line through the points.

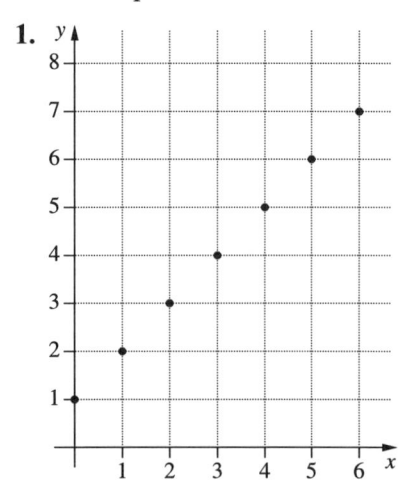

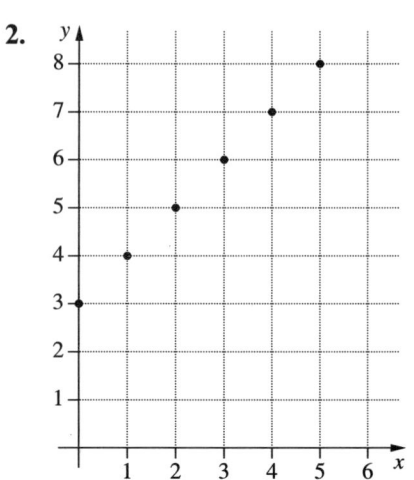

1.

2.

189

3.

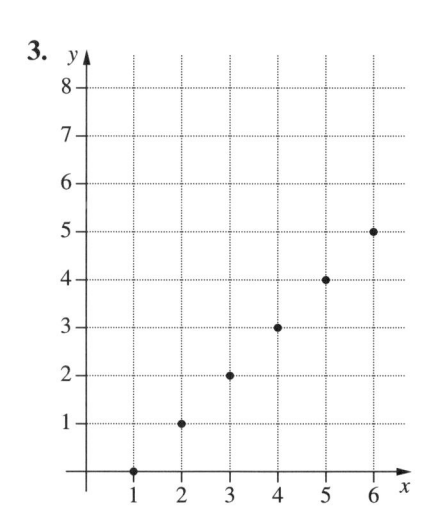

4.

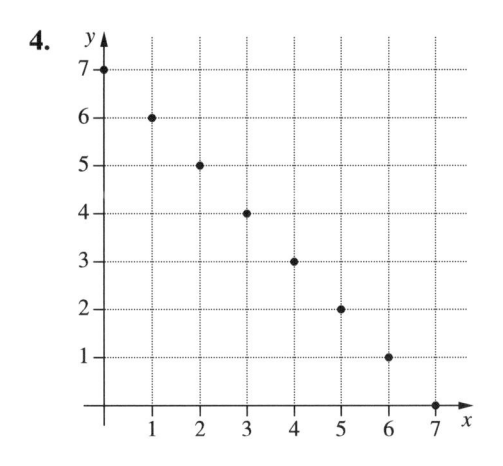

5.

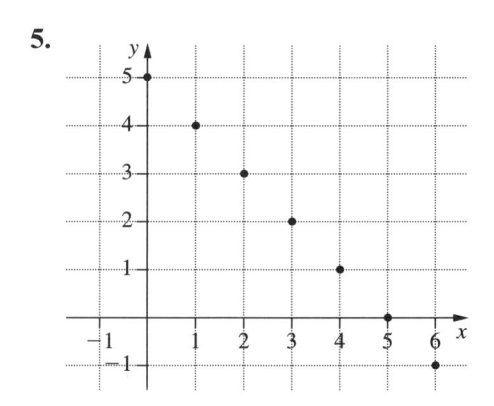

6.

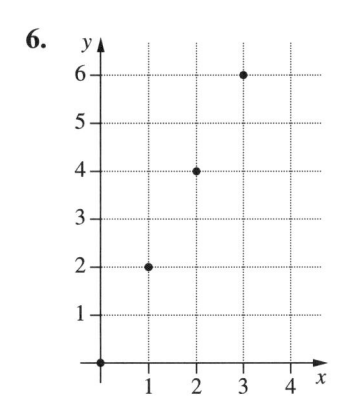

In Questions **7** and **8** there is a line of dots A and a line of crosses B.
Find the equation of each line.

7.

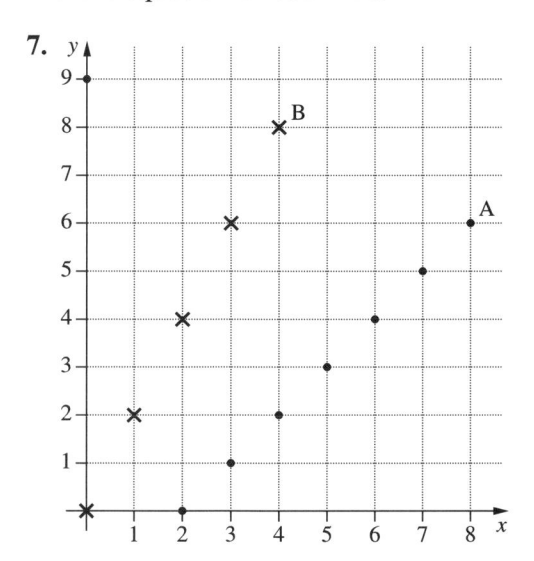

8.

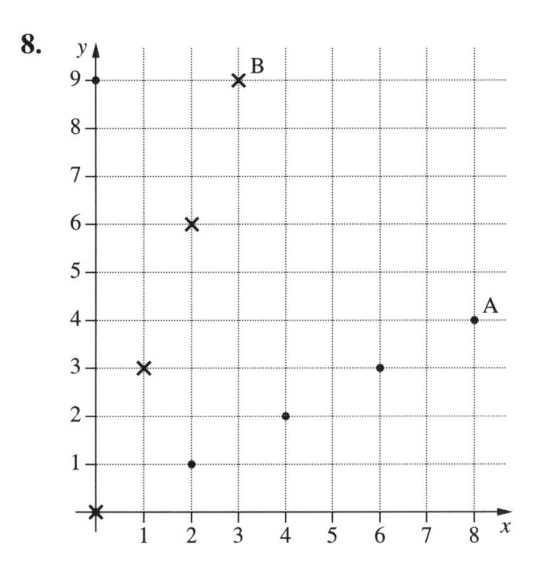

In Questions **9** to **20** you are given the coordinates of several points on a line. Find the equation of each line.

9.

x	1	2	3	4	5	6
y	4	5	6	7	8	9

10.

x	1	2	3	4	5	6
y	6	7	8	9	10	11

11.

x	1	3	5	7
y	8	10	12	14

12.

x	2	4	6	8
y	0	2	4	6

13.

x	10	12	14	16
y	4	6	8	10

14.

x	1	2	3	4	5
y	2	4	6	8	10

15.

x	2	4	5	6
y	6	12	15	18

16.

x	8	7	6	5	4	3
y	0	1	2	3	4	5

17.

x	5	4	3	2	1	0
y	0	1	2	3	4	5

18.

x	1	2	3	4	5
y	3	5	7	9	11

19.

x	1	2	3	4	5
y	5	7	9	11	13

20.

x	1	2	3	4
y	7	10	13	16

21. Find the equation of the line through (a) A and B
(b) B and C
(c) C and A

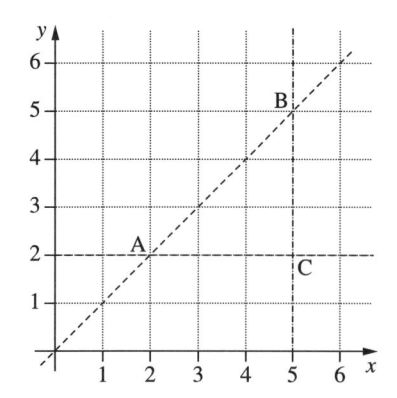

22. Find the equation of the line through (a) D and E
(b) E and F
(c) D and F

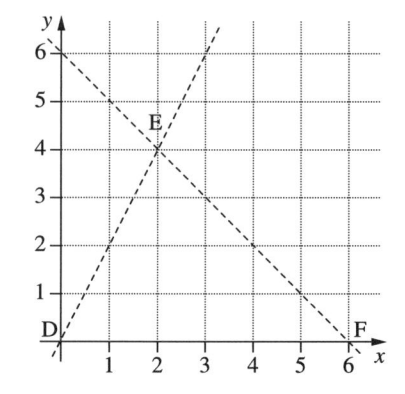

Using graphs

Exercise 6

1. A car hire firm charges an initial fee plus a charge depending on the number of miles driven, as shown.

    (a) Find the total cost for driving 140 miles.
    (b) Find the total cost for driving 600 miles.
    (c) Find how many miles I can drive for a cost of £45.

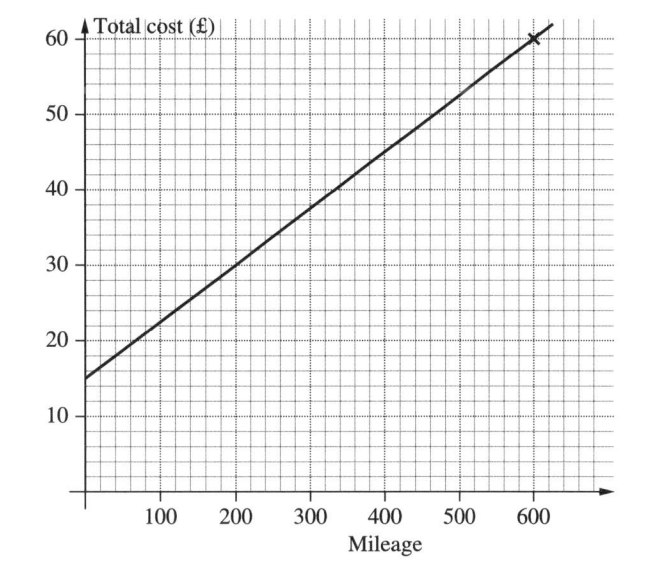

2. A teacher has marked a test out of 80 and wishes to convert the marks into percentages. Draw axes as shown and draw a straight line through the points (0, 0) and (80, 100).
    (a) Use your graph to convert
        (i) 63 marks into a percentage
        (ii) 24 marks into a percentage
    (b) The pass mark was 60%. How many marks out of 80 were needed for a pass?

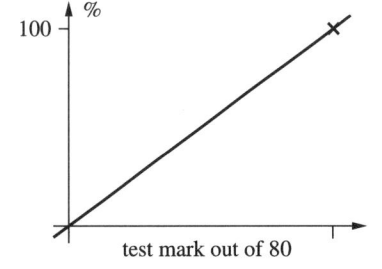

3. The graph converts pounds into French francs.
    (a) convert into francs
        (i) £2   (ii) £3·50
    (b) convert into pounds
        (i) 20F   (ii) 12F.
    (c) A Mars bar costs 75p. Find the equivalent price in France.
    (d) A few years ago, the exchange rate was about 10 francs to the pound. Is it cheaper or more expensive nowadays as a British tourist in France?

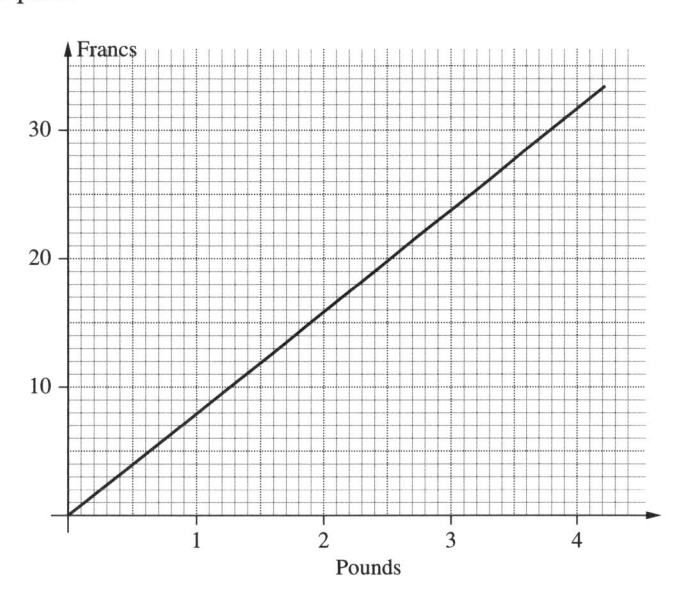

4. (a) Draw axes, as shown, with a scale of 1 cm to 5°. Two equivalent temperatures are 32°F = 0°C and 86°F = 30°C.
   (b) Draw a line through the points above and use your graph to convert:
      (i) 20°C into °F
      (ii) −10°C into °F
      (iii) 50°F into °C
   (c) The normal body temperature of a healthy person is 98°F. Susie's temperature is 39°C. Should she stay at home today, or go to school as usual?

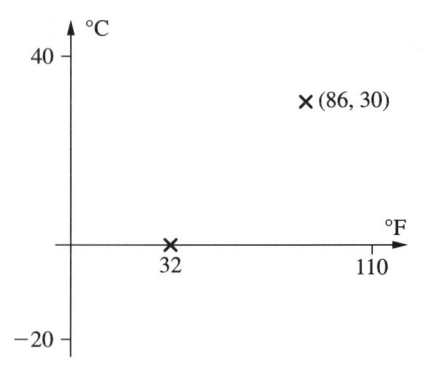

5. In the U.K., petrol consumption for cars is usually quoted in 'miles per gallon'. In other countries the metric equivalent is 'km per litre'.
   (a) Convert 20 m.p.g. into km per litre.
   (b) Convert 5 km per litre into m.p.g.
   (c) A car travels 9 km on one litre of petrol. Convert this consumption into miles per gallon. Work out how many gallons of petrol the car will use, if it is driven a distance of 100 miles.

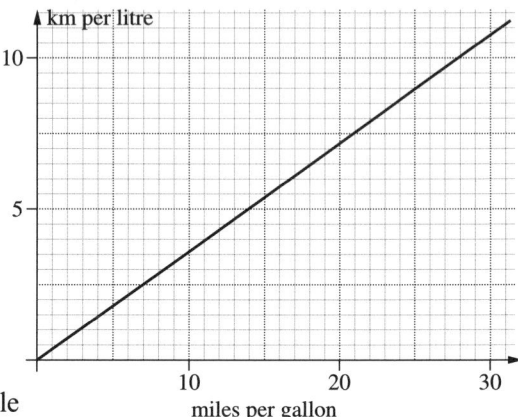

6. Selmin and Katie make different charges for people wanting pages typed professionally.

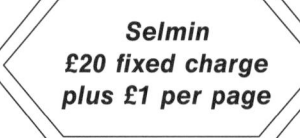

   Selmin
   £20 fixed charge plus £1 per page

   Katie
   £1·50 per page

   (a) How much would Selmin charge to type 30 pages?
   (b) How much would Katie charge to type 10 pages?
   (c) Draw axes for the number of pages typed and the total cost, using the scales given.
   (d) On the same diagram, draw a graph for each typist to show their charges for up to 60 pages.
   (e) Use your graphs to decide for what number of pages Selmin is the cheaper typist to choose.

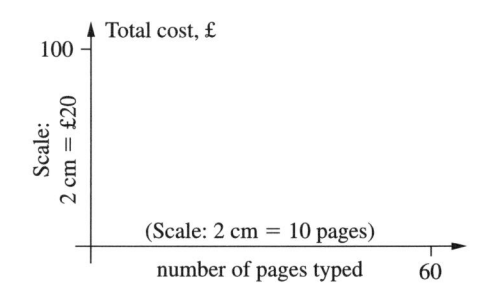

5.5 Congruent shapes, tessellation

Congruent shapes are exactly the same in shape and size. Shapes are congruent if one shape can be fitted exactly over the other.

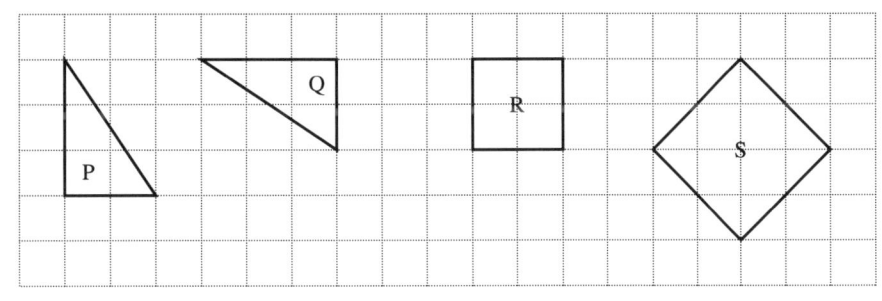

P and Q are congruent   R and S are not congruent

Exercise 1

1. Decide which shapes are congruent pairs. [You can use tracing paper]

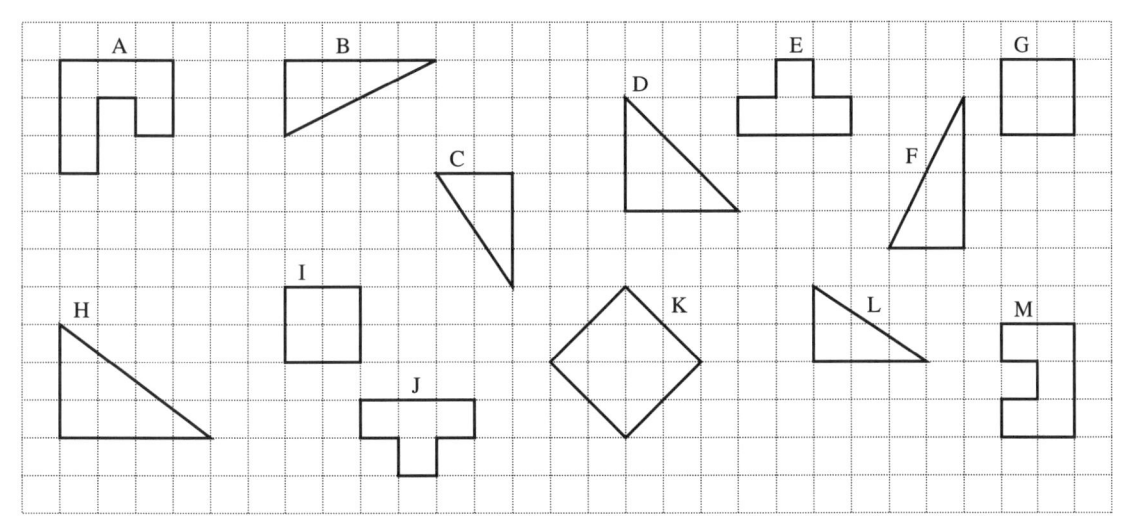

2. Copy the diagram and colour in congruent shapes with the same colour.

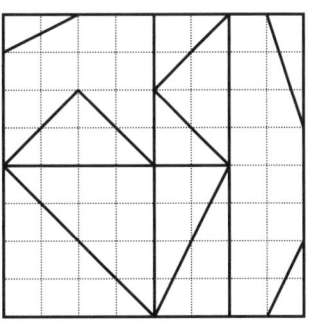

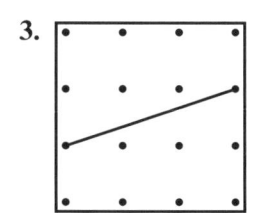

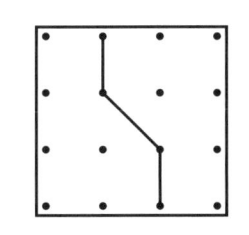

3. The 4 × 4 grids are divided into two congruent shapes. Do this in as many different ways as possible.

4. Two congruent right angled triangles are joined together along equal sides
   (a) How many shapes are possible?
   (b) How many shapes are possible if the congruent triangles are scalene ... or equilateral?

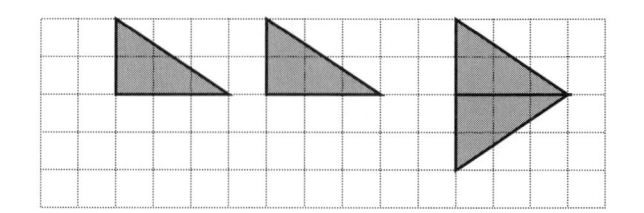

5. You are told that triangles DBC and CFA are congruent. Copy and complete:
   (a) side AF = side ☐
   (b) side CF = side ☐
   (c) angle CFA = angle ☐
   (d) angle ☐ = angle CDB.

Tessellation

- in tessellation we study the different ways we can regularly tile any flat surface, no matter how large. The examples below show tessellation using quadrilaterals:

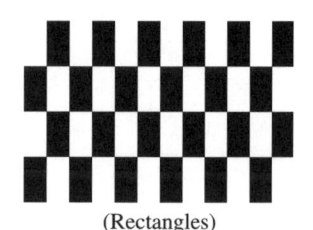

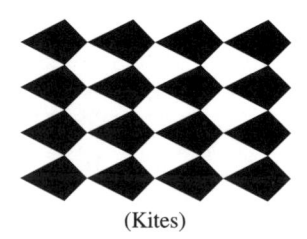

   (Rectangles)   (Kites)

- Draw *any* quadrilateral on card and make a tessellation.

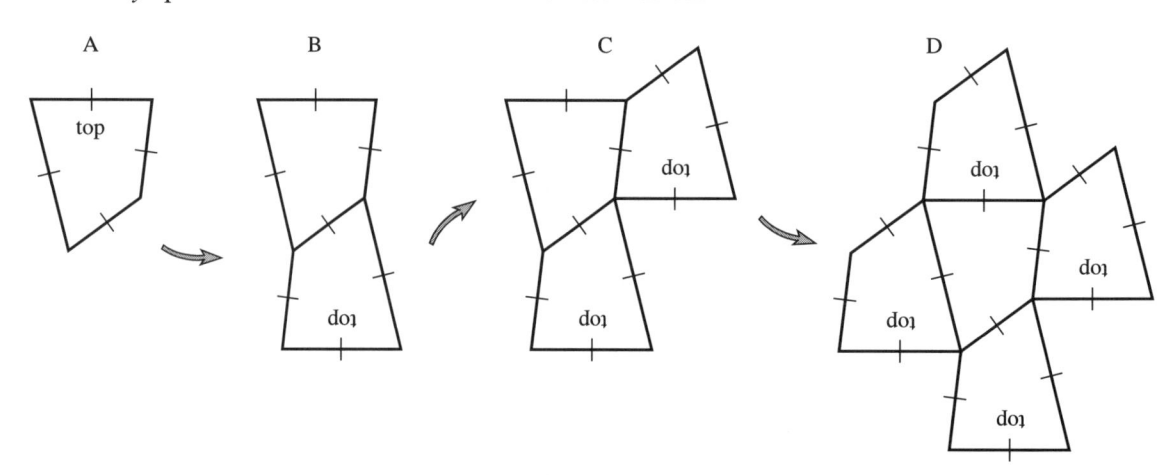

Interesting tessellations may be formed using sets of different shapes, provided the lengths of their sides are compatible

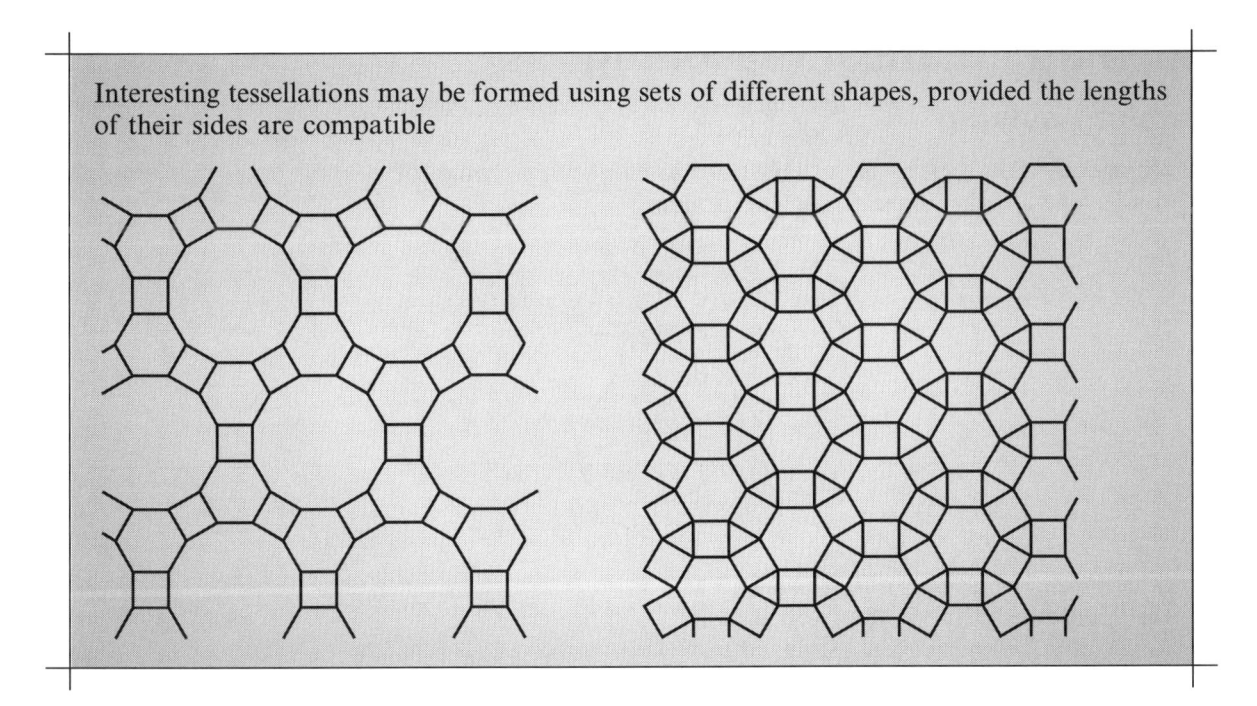

Exercise 2

1. Draw and cut out a template on card for each of the shapes below:
   (You can trace the shapes below to save time. All their sides are compatible).

   Octagon   Hexagon   Dodecagon

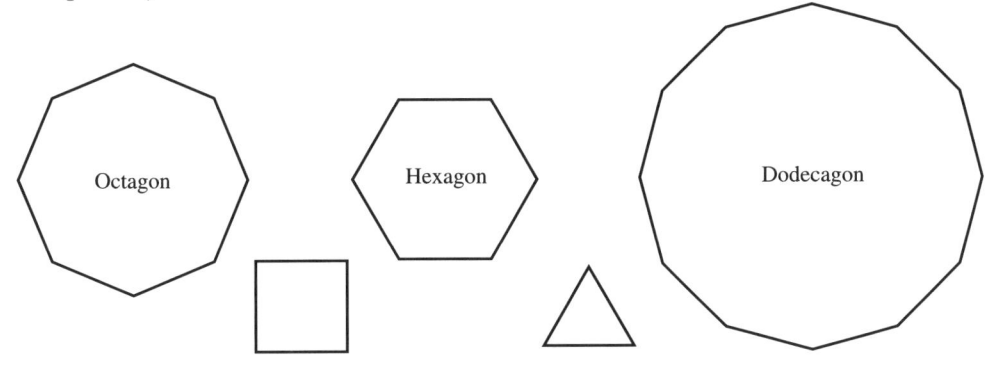

2. Either (i) draw a tessellation on plain paper or (ii) draw a tessellation directly onto tracing paper, using:
   (a) only hexagons
   (b) only octagons and squares
   (c) only dodecagons and equilateral triangles.
   (d) only hexagons, squares and equilateral triangles.
   (e) only dodecagons, hexagons and squares.
   (f) only squares and equilateral triangles.

3. For each tessellation in **2**, colour the pattern in an interesting way.

5.6 Mathematical reasoning

Problem solving

1. Villages A, B, C, D, E, F, G, H, I are joined by a network of roads. The lengths of the roads are in miles.

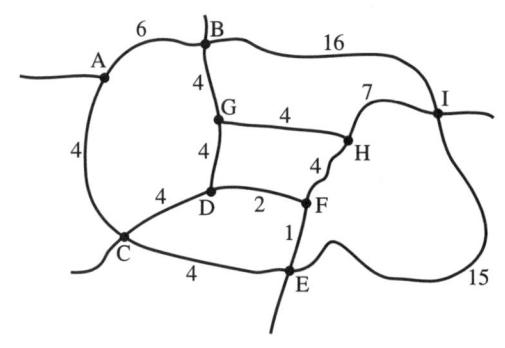

   (a) Find the shortest route from A to I.
   (b) Find the shortest route from B to E.
   (c) A family on a sight-seeing tour wish to visit all of the villages as they go from A to I. Find the shortest route passing through all the villages.

2. This network shows the roads joining towns A, B, ... L.
   (a) Find the shortest route from B to K.
   (b) Find the shortest route from G to L.
   (c) Find the shortest route for a waste disposal lorry which has to visit every town as it travels from A to L.

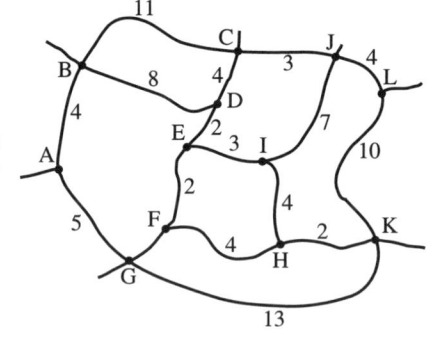

3. Four travellers W, X, Y, Z have to make a journey, for which 4 tickets are available: by plane; by train; by car; by boat.

   W prefers to go by plane or car
   X prefers to go by boat
   Y prefers to go by train or boat
   Z prefers to go by train, car or boat.

   Work out who should take each ticket so that everyone is happy with their method of transport.

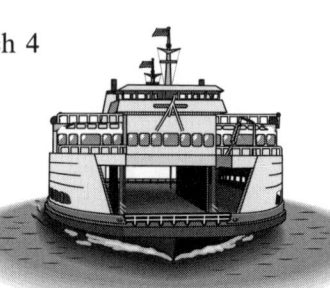

4. A class is electing five girls as captains of the following teams; swimming; gymnastics; netball; athletics; tennis.
It is clearly best if the girl elected is good at the sport for which she is to be captain.

Vera is good at swimming and gymnastics.
Wilma is good at gymnastics, netball and tennis.
Xenia is good at swimming and athletics.
Yasmin is good at netball.
Zara is good at netball and athletics.

Work out the five games captains.

5. Six actors A, B, C, D, E, F are trying to decide who should play the six parts in a play. The parts are:
the hero (H); the princess (P); the villain (V); the reporter (R); the tree (T); the nurse (N).

A would like to be the princess or the reporter.
B would like to be the hero or the villain
C would like to be the hero or the nurse
D would like to be the villain or the tree
E would like to be the nurse or the tree
F would like to be the villain, the reporter or the tree.

Work out who should play each part.
Find two different solutions.

Puzzles

1. The totals for the rows and columns are given. Find the values of the letters.

(a)
W	Y	X	Z	24
Y	Y	Y	Y	36
Z	Y	X	X	26
X	Z	Y	W	24
24	30	32	24	

(b)
E	D	E	C	E	45
A	B	D	C	E	41
E	C	E	C	E	41
D	A	C	C	A	33
E	E	D	C	C	43
42	41	47	35	38	

(c) Find P, Q, R, S and find the letter hidden by an ink blot.

S	Q	R	S	42
Q	Q	Q	Q	36
Q	Q	■	S	44
S	Q	P	R	41
44	36	41	42	

(d) This one is more difficult

A	B	B	A	38
A	A	B	B	38
A	B	A	B	38
B	B	A	B	49
27	49	38	49	

2. Here is a 5 × 5 square cut into 8 smaller squares.
   (a) Cut up a 7 × 7 square into 9 smaller squares.
   (b) Cut up a 9 × 9 square into 10 smaller squares but you can use only one 3 × 3 square.

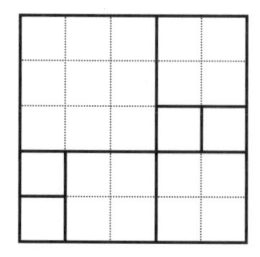

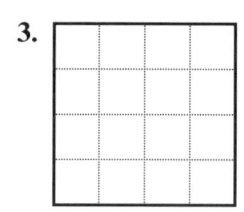

3. Fill up the square with the numbers 1, 2, 3, 4 so that each number appears only once in every row and column.
   [You can have the same numbers in any diagonals.]

4. Fill up the square with the numbers 1, 2, 3, 4 so that each number appears only once in every row, column and *main* diagonal.
   The main diagonals are marked: AC and BD. [You can repeat a number on a 'short' diagonal, as shown.]

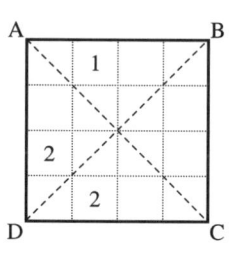

5. More difficult
   Fill up the square with the numbers 1, 2, 3, 4, 5 so that each number appears only once in every row, column and *any* diagonal.

   Note that you are not allowed to write the same digit twice on *any* diagonal.
   The solution on the right is not allowed because there are two 2's on the diagonal marked with a broken line.

6. Three friends are trying to weigh themselves but the weighing machine only works for weights over 90 kg and they all weigh less than that. They decide to go on the machine two at a time.
   John and Steve together weigh 119 kg.
   John and Mark together weigh 115 kg.
   Steve and Mark together weigh 107 kg.
   How much does John weigh?

Cross numbers without clues

Here are cross number puzzles with a difference. There are no clues, only answers, and you have to find where the answers go.

(a) Copy out the cross number pattern.
(b) Fit all the given numbers into the correct spaces. Work logically and tick off the numbers from lists as you write them in the squares.

1.

2 digits	*3 digits*	*4 digits*	*5 digits*
23	146	2708	25404
26	235	2715	25814
42	245		37586
57	337		
59	539		
87	695		

2.

2 digits	*3 digits*	*4 digits*	*5 digits*
18	244	2163	36918
21	247	4133	46514
31	248	4213	54374
33	332	4215	54704
47	333	4283	87234
63	334	4317	
64	608	4394	
77			

3.

2 digits	*3 digits*	*4 digits*	*5 digits*	*7 digits*
36	145	2286	16145	4235824
52	185	5235	66145	
56	245	5248	66152	
63	246	5249	66272	
65	374	5452	91671	
77	437	6241		
90	646			
	896			

4.

2 digits	3 digits	4 digits	5 digits
14	123	1325	14251
22	231	1478	29163
26	341	1687	29613
43	439	1976	29872
65	531	2523	34182
70	670	4798	54875
81		5601	63712
82		5611	67358
		5621	82146
		6109	84359
		8171	97273

6 digits	7 digits
145026	9354234
740136	
983514	

5. This one is more difficult.

2 digits	3 digits	4 digits	5 digits
15	137	2513	29666
19	206	3048	31873
21	276	3214	40657
22	546	3244	43104
28	592	3437	43158
31	783	3514	54732
77		3517	60783
90		3544	62114
		4122	80751
		4127	82614
		6934	93654

6 digits	7 digits
235785	9733764
235815	
452705	

Break the codes

1. The symbols γ, ↑, !, ⊖, ⊥ each stand for one of the digits 1, 2, 3, 5 or 9 but not in that order. Use the clues below to work out what number each symbol stands for.

   (a) ↑ × ↑ = ⊥
   (b) ⊖ × ↑ = ↑
   (c) ⊖ + ⊖ = γ
   (d) γ + ↑ = !

2. The ten symbols below each stand for one of the digits 0, 1, 2, 3, 4, 5, 6, 7, 8 or 9 but not in that order.

   ♂ W □ ⊙ ↑ ∗ ⊠ △ ① ⊠

   Use the clues below to work out what number each symbol stands for.

   (a) ♂ + ♂ + ♂ + ♂ + ♂ = W
   (b) W + ⊠ = W
   (c) W + ♂ = ⊙
   (d) ① + ① + ① + ① = ↑
   (e) ∗ × ∗ = ⊠
   (f) ⊙ − ① = △
   (g) ∗ + △ = □

3. The ten symbols used in part 2 are used again but with different values.

   (a) ⊠ × ⊙ = ⊙
   (b) ⊠ + ⊠ + ⊠ = ∗
   (c) ∗ − ⊠ = △
   (d) △ × △ × △ = ⊙
   (e) ⊙ − ⊠ = ↑
   (f) ∗ + W = ∗
   (g) ⊙ ÷ △ = ①
   (h) ∗ + △ = □
   (i) ↑ − ⊠ = ⊠
   (j) ♂ − △ = ↑

4. These clues are more difficult to work out.

   (a) □ + ↑ = □
   (b) ♂ × □ = ♂
   (c) ⊠ × ⊠ × ⊠ = ♂
   (d) ♂ − ⊠ = ①
   (e) ① − ⊠ = △
   (f) ① − □ = ⊠
   (g) ⊠ + ⊠ = ⊙
   (h) W × W = ∗

5.7 Using a spreadsheet on a computer

This section is written for use with Microsoft Excel. Other spreadsheet programs work in a similar way.

Select Microsoft Excel from the desk top.

A spreadsheet appears on your screen as a grid with rows numbered 1, 2, 3, 4,...... and the columns lettered A, B, C, D, ...
The result should be a window like the one below.

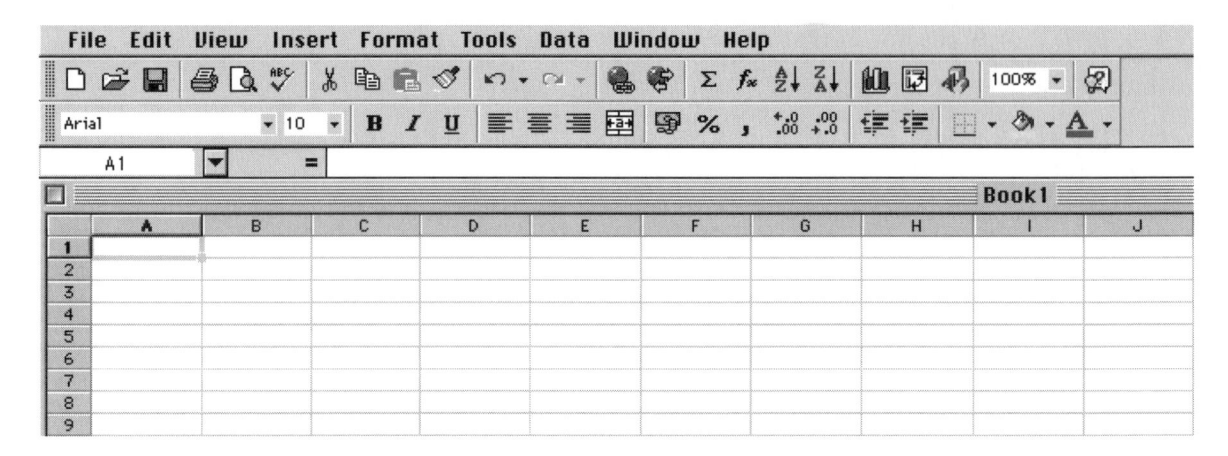

Cell The spaces on the spreadsheet are called cells. Individual cells are referred to as A1, B3, F9, like grid references. Cells may contain *labels*, *values* or *formulas*. The current cell has a black boarder.

Label Any words, headings or messages used to help the layout and organisation of the spreadsheet.

Value A number placed in a cell. It may be used as input to a calculation.

Tasks 1, 2 and 3 are written for you to become familiar with how the main functions of a spreadsheet program work. Afterwards there are sections on different topics where spreadsheets can be used.

Task 1. To generate the whole numbers from 1 to 10 in column A.

(a) In cell A1 type '1' and press *Return*. This will automatically take you to the cell below. (NOTE that you must use the *Return* button and not the arrow keys to move down the column.)

(b) In cell A2 type the formula ' = A1 + 1' and press *Return*. [NOTE that the = sign is needed before any formula.]

(c) We now want to copy the formula in A2 down column A as far as A10. Click on A2 again and put the arrow in the bottom right corner of cell A2 (a + sign will appear) and drag down to A10.

Task 2. To generate the odd numbers in column B.

(a) In B1 type '1' (press *Return*).

(b) In B2 type the formula ' = B1 + 2' (press *Return*).

(c) Click in B2 and copy the formula down column B as far as B10.

Task 3. To generate the first 15 square numbers.

(a) As before generate the numbers from 1 to 15 in cells A1 to A15.

(b) In B1 put the formula ' = A1 ∗ A1' and press *Return*.

(c) Click in B1 and copy the formula down as far as B15.

Part 6

6.1 Probability

Probability is a measure of how likely an event is to occur.
A probability can be shown on a scale from 0 to 1.

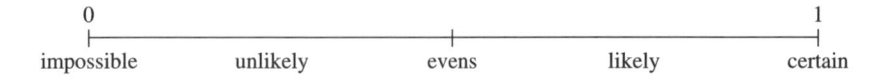

```
0                                                    1
|──────────┼──────────┼──────────┼──────────|
impossible  unlikely    evens       likely    certain
```

Exercise 1

1. Say which word below best describes the events

    'impossible, unlikely, evens, likely, certain.'

   (a) It will snow tomorrow.
   (b) You will make a spelling mistake in your next lesson.
   (c) Your mother will ask you to tidy your room tomorrow.
   (d) You will blink in the next minute.
   (e) Your calculator will work out $55 + 55$ correctly.
   (f) You will roll an even number on a dice.
   (g) A dog will wag its tail when food is coming.

2. Think of an event with an evens chance of happening.

3. Give an example of an event with a probability of zero.

4. Sally tossed a fair coin six times and got a 'head' six times. What is the chance of tossing a 'tail' on her next go?

5. Suppose England play Luxembourg in the next football World Cup. What word would best describe England's chance of winning?

6. Think of an event with a probability of about 0·1.

7. Sarah says 'when you have to roll a double to get out of jail at Monopoly, you never do.' Explain why you agree or disagree with Sarah.

8. There are ten balls in a bag. Tina takes a ball from the bag, notes its colour and then returns the ball to the bag. She does this 20 times. Here are the results.

Blue	6
Green	10
Red	4

(a) What is the smallest number of blue balls there could be in the bag?
(b) Tina says 'There cannot be any white balls in the bag because there are no whites in my table.' Explain why Tina is wrong.

Events occurring or not occurring

- If the probability of an event occurring is p, then the probability of it not occurring is $1 - p$.
- Ten identical discs numbered 1, 2, 3, 4, 5, 6, 7, 8, 9, 10 are put into a bag. One disc is selected at random.

In this example there are 10 possible equally likely outcomes of a trial.

(a) The probability of selecting a '2' $= \frac{1}{10}$

This may be written p(selecting a '2') $= \frac{1}{10}$

(b) p (not selecting a 2) $= 1 - \frac{1}{10}$
$= \frac{9}{10}$

(c) p (selecting a number greater than 7) $= \frac{3}{10}$

(d) p (not selecting a number greater than 7) $= 1 - \frac{3}{10} = \frac{7}{10}$

Exercise 2

1. One card is picked at random from a pack of 52.
   Find the probability that it is
   (a) a diamond   (b) not a diamond
   (c) the King of hearts   (d) not the King of hearts

2. Ten discs numbered 1, 1, 2, 2, 4, 5, 6, 7, 8, 8 are placed in a bag.
   One disc is selected at random. Find the probability that it is
   (a) an even number   (b) not an even number
   (c) a six   (d) not a six

3. Mo puts these numbered balls in a bag.
   (a) He shakes the bag and takes one ball without looking. What is the probability of getting a '2'?
   (b) Mo wants to put more balls in the bag so that the chance of getting a '4' is *twice* the chance of getting a '3'. What balls could he put in the bag?

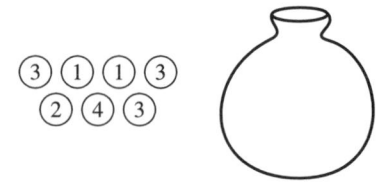

4. A dice has its faces numbered 2, 3, 3, 3, 4, 7.
   Find the probability of rolling
   (a) a '7'
   (b) an even number.

5. One card is selected at random from the nine cards shown.

   Find the probability of selecting
   (a) the ace of diamonds   (b) a king
   (c) an ace   (d) a red card

6. If Mala throws a 3 or a 5 on her next throw when playing 'Snakes and Ladders' she will slide down a snake on the board. What is the probability that she will avoid a snake on her next throw?

7. The 26 letters of the alphabet are written on discs. The five discs with vowels are put in bag A and the other discs are put in bag B.
   Find the probability of selecting
   (a) an 'o' from bag A
   (b) a 'z' from bag B
   (c) a 'w' from bag A

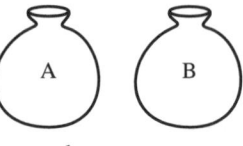

8. A shopkeeper is keen to sell his stock of left-handed scissors. He has read that 9% of the population is left-handed. What is the probability that the next person to enter his shop is right-handed?

9. A field contains 10 cows, 5 horses and 1 lion. The lion is thought to be tame and half of the cows are mad. One animal is chosen at random.
   Find the probability that the animal:
   (a) is mad
   (b) enjoys eating grass
   (c) might eat you.

10. Nicole has 3 kings and 1 ace. She shuffles the cards and takes one without looking.

    Nicole asks two of her friends about the probability of getting an ace

    Angie says:
    'It is $\frac{1}{3}$ because there are 3 kings and 1 ace.'

    Syline says
    'It is $\frac{1}{4}$ because there are 4 cards and only 1 ace.'

    Which of her friends is right?

11. A bag contains the balls shown. One ball is taken out at random. Find the probability that it is
    (a) red   (b) not red   (c) blue
    One more red ball and one more blue ball are added to the bag.
    (d) Find the new probability of selecting a red ball from the bag.

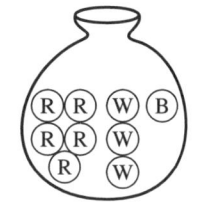

    R = red
    W = white
    B = blue

12. A fair dice is rolled 480 times. How many times would you expect to roll:
    (a) a 'two'
    (b) an odd number?

13. A spinner, with 12 equal sectors, is spun 600 times. How often would you expect to spin:
    (a) a shaded sector
    (b) an even number
    (c) a vowel
    (d) a prime number?
    [a prime number is divisible only by itself and by one]

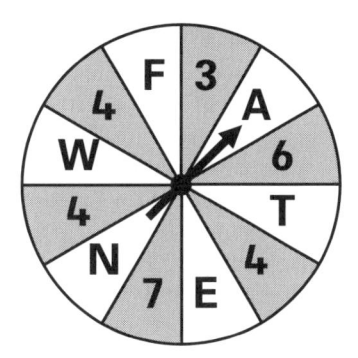

14. A coin is biased so that the probability of tossing a 'head' is 0·58.
    (a) How many 'heads' would you expect when the coin is tossed 200 times?
    (b) How many 'tails' would you expect when the coin is tossed 1000 times?

Exercise 3 (More difficult)

1. Each of the 11 letters of the word 'CALCULATION' was written on a small card. One card was selected at random.
Find the probability that the letter drawn was
   (a) a 'T'
   (b) an 'A'

2. A box contains 12 balls: 3 red, 2 yellow, 4 green and 3 white.
   (a) Find the probability of selecting
      (i) a red ball
      (ii) a yellow ball
   (b) The 3 white balls are replaced by 3 yellow balls. Find the probability of selecting
      (i) a red ball
      (ii) a yellow ball.

3. A pack of cards is split into two piles. Pile P contains all the picture cards and aces and pile O contains all the other cards.
   (a) Find the probability of selecting
      (i) the Jack of hearts from pile P
      (ii) a seven from pile O
   (b) All the diamonds are now removed from both piles. Find the probability of selecting
      (i) the King of clubs from pile P
      (ii) a red card from pile O.

4. (a) Steve has taken a number of cards at random from a pack. The probability of picking a red card from Steve's cards is $\frac{3}{5}$.
   What is the probability of picking a black card?
   (b) How many cards of each colour *could* there be in Steve's cards?
   (c) Write down another possibility for the number of cards of each colour that are in Steve's cards.

5. One person is selected at random from the crowd of 14 750 watching a tennis match at Wimbledon. What is the probability that the person chosen will have his or her birthday that year on a Sunday?

6. One ball is selected at random from a bag containing x red balls and y white balls. What is the probability of selecting a red ball?

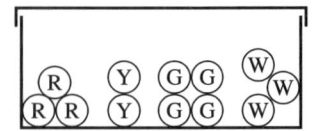

7. Helen played a game of cards with Michelle. The cards were dealt so that both players received two cards. Helen's cards were a seven and a four. Michelle's first card was a 10.

   Find the probability that Michelle's second card was
   (a) a picture card [a King, Queen or Jack]
   (b) a seven.

8. A dice has its six faces marked
   0p, 0p, 0p, 0p, 5p, 20p.
   In a game at a school fair players pay 5p to roll the dice and they win the amount shown on the dice. 
   During the afternoon the game is played 540 times.
   (a) How much money would be paid by the people playing the game?
   (b) How many times would you expect the dice to show '20p'?
   (c) How many times would you expect the dice to show '5p'?
   (d) How much profit or loss would you expect the stall to make?

9. At another stall at the fair players pay 20p to spin the pointer on the board shown. Players win the amount shown by the pointer.

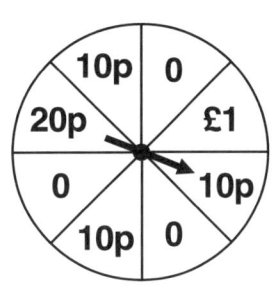

   The game is played 800 times.

   Work out the expected profit or loss on this game.

Listing possible outcomes: two events

- When a 10p coin and a 20p coin are tossed together there are four possible outcomes. So, for example, the probability of tossing two tails = $\frac{1}{4}$.

10p	20p
head	head
head	tail
tail	head
tail	tail

- Suppose a red dice and a blue dice are rolled together. This time there are *many* possible outcomes. With the red dice first the outcomes can be listed systematically:
  (1, 1) (1, 2) (1, 3) (1, 4) (1, 5) (1, 6)
  (2, 1) (2, 2) (2, 3) (2, 4) (2, 5) (2, 6)
  (3, 1) (3, 2) ,   ,   ,   ,
    ,   ,   ,   ,   ,   ,
    ,   ,   ,   ,   ,   ,
    ,   ,   ,   ,   (6, 5) (6, 6)

  There are 36 equally likely outcomes

- A neat way of listing the outcomes is on a grid.

  This is called a sample space

  The point marked . shows a four on the red dice and a five on the blue dice.

  The probability of rolling a four on the red dice and a five on the blue dice is $\frac{1}{36}$.

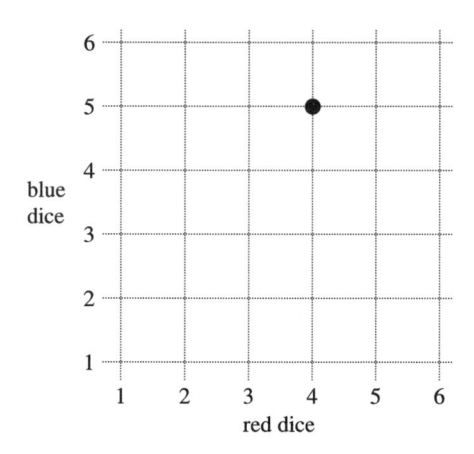

Exercise 4

1. Roll a pair of dice many times and in a tally chart record the frequency of obtaining the totals from 2 to 12.

Total	Frequency
2	
3	
⋮	
12	

2. (a) Work out the expected probability of getting a total of 5 when two dice are rolled together.
   Compare your answer with the experimental probability of getting a total of 5 obtained in the experiment in Question **1**.
   (b) Work out the expected probability of other totals and compare them with the experimental results.

3. A red dice is thrown first and then a blue dice is thrown.
   (a) Find the probability that the score on the blue dice is the same as the score on the red dice.
   (b) Find the probability that the score on the blue dice is one more than the score on the red dice.

4. A bag contains a 1p coin, a 10p coin and a 20p coin. Two coins are selected at random.
   (a) List all the possible combinations of two coins which can be selected from the bag.
   (b) Find the probability that the total value of the two coins selected is
      (i) 11p
      (ii) 30p

5. The four cards shown are shuffled and placed face down on a table.

   Two cards are selected at random.
   (a) List all the possible pairs of cards which could be selected.
   (b) Find the probability that the total of the two cards is
      (i) 5
      (ii) 9

Experimental probability

$$\text{Experimental probability} = \frac{\text{Number of trials in which event occurs}}{\text{Total number of trials made}}$$

Exercise 5

Carry out experiments to work out the experimental probability of some of the following events.

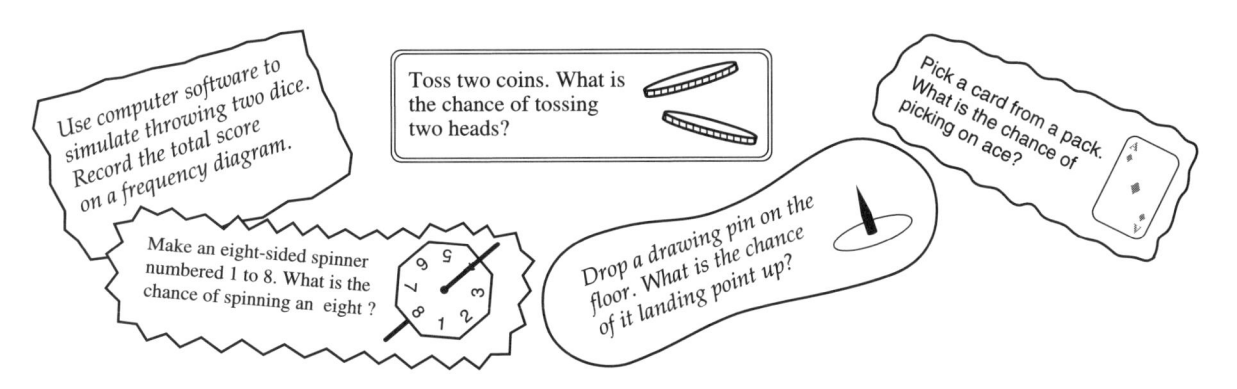

Use computer software to simulate throwing two dice. Record the total score on a frequency diagram.

Toss two coins. What is the chance of tossing two heads?

Pick a card from a pack. What is the chance of picking on ace?

Make an eight-sided spinner numbered 1 to 8. What is the chance of spinning an eight?

Drop a drawing pin on the floor. What is the chance of it landing point up?

Exercise 6

1. A bag contained coloured balls. Rajiv randomly selects a ball and then replaces it. Here are the results.

Colour	White	Green	Blue
Frequency	10	31	19

   Estimate the probability that on his next draw he will select
   (a) a white ball   (b) a green ball.

2. Dimpna and Jenny both did the 'dropping a drawing pin' experiment. Here are their results.

   Dimpna

Trials	20
'Point up'	10

   Jenny

Trials	150
'Point up'	61

   Another drawing pin is dropped.
   (a) For Dimpna, what is the probability of getting 'point up'?
   (b) For Jenny, what is the probability of getting 'point up'?
   (c) Whose result is likely to be more reliable? Why?

3. Sean collected the results of 40 Liverpool home games. Estimate the probability that in their next home game:

Won	18
Lost	10
Drawn	12

   (a) they will win
   (b) they will lose.

   For Liverpool's next 40 games, the results were:

Won	23
Lost	11
Drawn	6

   Using all 80 results, estimate the probability of

   (c) winning their next game.
   (d) drawing their next game.

   Would you expect these probabilities to be more accurate than those based on the first 40 matches? Why?

4. Roll a fair dice 60 times. How many 'ones' would you expect to roll?
   Compare your experimental result with the theoretical one.

   Suppose you do the experiment again (i.e. roll the dice another 60 times.)
   Would you expect to get the same result?

6.2 Percentages

(a) Work out 16% of £15.

16% of £15

$= \frac{16}{100} \times \frac{15}{1}$

$= £2{\cdot}40$

(b) Work out 14% of £260.
(Quick way)
14% = 0·14 as a decimal

So 14% of £260 = 0·14 × 260

$= £36{\cdot}40$

(c) Work out, to the nearest penny:
8% of £11·99

$= \frac{8}{100} \times \frac{11 \cdot 99}{1}$

$= 0 \cdot 9592$

$= £0{\cdot}96$, to the nearest penny

(d) Work out, to the nearest penny:
(Quick way)
21% of £6·92

$= 0 \cdot 21 \times 6 \cdot 92$

$= 1 \cdot 4532$

$= £1{\cdot}45$, to the nearest penny

Exercise 1

Work out.

1. 12% of £600
2. 6% of £250
3. 81% of £9
4. 8% of £450
5. 7% of £440
6. 43% of £185
7. 5% of £22
8. 4% of £660
9. 8% of £2555
10. 85% of £400
11. 6·5% of £200
12. 7% of £6
13. 29% of £2000
14. 4·5% of £400
15. 17% of £175

16. The number of children having school dinners is 640. When chips are not on the menu the number goes down by 5%. How many fewer children have school dinners?

17. In a restaurant a service charge of 10% is added to the price of a meal. What is the service charge on a meal costing £28·50?

In Questions **18** to **32** give the answer correct to the nearest penny.

18. 13% of £2·13
19. 27% of £5·85
20. 15·1% of £7·87
21. 11% of £6·27
22. 13% of £6·17
23. 16% of £0·87
24. 37% of £5·20
25. 15% of £11·23
26. 4% of £0·65
27. 6·2% of £8·55
28. 31% of £35·04
29. 78% of £3·17
30. 8·9% of £17·10
31. 6·8% of £16·10
32. 23% of £18·05

33. At a garage 140 cars were given a safety test and 65% of the cars passed the test.
    (a) How many passed the test?
    (b) How many failed the test?

34. Of the 980 children at a school 45% cycle to school, 15% go by bus and the rest walk.
    (a) How many cycle to school?
    (b) How many walk to school?

35. A lottery prize of £65 000 is divided between Steve, Pete and Phil so that Steve receives 22%, Pete receives 32% and Phil the rest. How much money does Phil receive?

Percentage increase or decrease

At the end of the year the price of a car is increased from £9640 by 4%. What is the new price?

4% of £9640

$= \frac{4}{100} \times \frac{9640}{1}$

$= £385 \cdot 60$

∴ New price of car $= £9640 + £385 \cdot 60$
$= £10025 \cdot 60$

Exercise 2

1. The price of a painting was £6400 but it is increased by 6%. What is the new price?

2. In a closing-down sale, a shop reduces all its prices by 20%. Find the sale price of a jacket which previously cost £60.

3. The petrol consumption of a car is 35 miles per gallon. After a service the car does 6% more miles per gallon. What is the new consumption?

4. A dog normally weighs 28 kg. After being put on a diet for three months its weight is reduced by 35%. How much does it weigh now?

5. The length of a new washing line is 21 m. After being used it stretches by 3%. Find the new length.

6. A shop increases all its prices by 4%. What are the new prices of the items below?

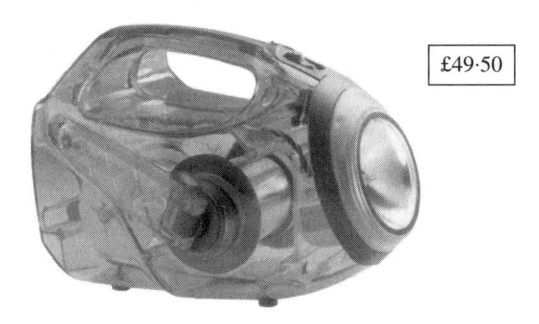

£15

£49·50

7. A marathon runner weighs 55 kg at the start of a race. During the race his weight is reduced by 4%. How much does he weigh at the end of the race?

8. A hen weighs 2·7 kg. After laying an egg her weight is reduced by 1%. How much does she weigh now?

9. A mouse weighs 630 g. While escaping from a cat it loses its tail and its weight is reduced by 4%. How much does it weigh now?

10. A holiday costs £620. After a 12% increase the new price is 112% of £620. The 'quick' way to work this out is as follows:

$$\begin{aligned} \text{New price} &= 112\% \text{ of } £620 \\ &= 1{\cdot}12 \times 620 \\ &= £694{\cdot}40 \end{aligned}$$

Use this quick method to find the new price of a boat costing £560, when the price is increased by 8%.

11. Copy and complete:
(a) To increase £400 by 6%, work out $1{\cdot}\boxed{}\boxed{} \times 400$.

(b) To reduce £720 by 15%, work out $0{\cdot}85 \times \boxed{}$.

12. Increase a price of £80 by 4%
13. Increase a price of £250 by 4%
14. Increase a price of £400 by 8%
15. Increase a price of £16 by 1%
16. Reduce a price of £3000 by 7%
17. Increase a price of £90 by 23%
18. Increase a price of £85 by 20%
19. Reduce a price of £8000 by 2·5%
20. Increase a price of £6500 by 2%
21. Reduce a price of £23 by 5·7%

22. A price of £650 is increased by 11% and then, a week later, it is increased by a further 8%. Find the final price.

6.3 Statistical problems

In general problems that can be answered by statistical methods are complicated! At the start you need to think carefully about questions which may be related.

It is helpful to go through the following procedure.

- **A** Discuss the problem. Identify related questions
- **B** Decide which data to collect
- **C** Decide how to collect the data
- **D** Present the data.

A Discuss the problem. Here is an example.

> '*Do parents watch more TV than their children?*'

What counts as 'active TV watching'?
Does it count if you are just in the room?
If you conduct a survey, how can you make sure the data is accurate?
Can people remember accurately what they watched 24 hours ago?
Are people going to answer honestly?
Suppose one or both parents arrive home late every day. How would this affect the survey?
What about watching videos?

B Which data to collect.

For different problems you might obtain data from:
- a questionnaire or survey of a sample of people.
- secondary sources like newspapers, reference books, websites or historical records.

You should realise that data which you collect might be time consuming. On the other hand, you can decide exactly what questions to ask and to whom you ask them.

Realise also that a small sample may not accurately represent a large group.

Is a sample of 10 enough to represent a year group of 180?
Perhaps you should join with others to make a group effort.

C How to collect the data.

- You need to design a data collection sheet or questionnaire like those below.

data collection sheet

Name	Height (cm)	Distance to school	Transport to school	Hours of T.V.	Favourite day
Emma					
Lynne					
Bjorn					
Lars					
Narishta					
David					

Questionnaire

- Your name:
- Height (cm)
- Distance to school (nearest mile)
- How do you get to school?
- Hours of T.V. watched each week (estimate)
- Favourite day of the week at school
-

- For continuous data (like heights) you could use a frequency table. You might also use a two-way table.

height	frequency
151–160	11
161–170	8
171–180	5

D Present the data.

- Remember 'A picture paints a thousand words.' Use bar charts, pie charts, scatter graphs ......

Suppose you get 20 different answers to the question: 'What is your favourite T.V. program?'
A bar chart with a bar for each program will look very dull! You could try putting the programs into groups like 'comedy', 'soaps', 'sports', 'drama' etc. The choice is yours.

- Write a short report, interpreting results and write a clear *conclusion* to say what you found.

Collecting your own data

- For many people the most interesting data is the data *they* decide to find because it is what interests *them*. Below are some suggestions for the sort of problem you could attempt.

1. Are you more accurate at throwing with your writing hand than with your other hand?

   Class activity: Each person throws a screwed-up ball of paper into a rubbish bin from a fixed distance. Throw five with each hand and collect results for the whole class.

On target	Writing hand	Other hand
0		
1		
2		
3		
4		
5		

2. Are absences from school equally likely on any day of the week?
   Are Mondays and Fridays more frequent than other days for absences?
   Are days when PE is taught more often chosen?
   Do year 11 pupils take more days off school than year 7 pupils?

   Where could information be obtained to answer these questions?

3. 'More babies are born in the spring than at any other time of year.'
   What exactly do we mean by 'the spring'?

   Investigate your year group to see if this is a true statement for your generation.

4. Test the following theory:
   'To find a child's potential height take the mean height of the parents, then add 8 cm for a boy and subtract 8 cm for a girl.'
   What would be a suitable age group on which to test this theory? Collect data and draw two separate scatter graphs. Plot the mean height of parents on the horizontal axis and height of son or daughter on the vertical axis.

6.4 3-D Objects

A drawing of a solid is a 2-D representation of a 3-D object. Below are two pictures of the same object.

(a) On squared paper.   (b) On isometric dot paper.

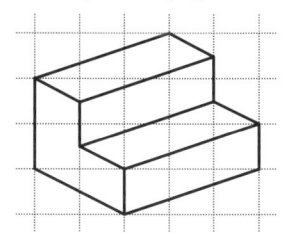

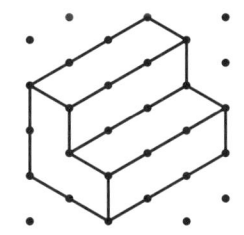

The dimensions of the object cannot be taken from the first picture but they can be taken from the second. Isometric paper can be used either as dots (as above) or as a grid of equilateral triangles. Either way, the paper must be the right way round (as shown here).

N.B. Most of the questions in this section are easier, and more fun to do, when you have an ample supply of 'unifix' or 'multilink' cubes.

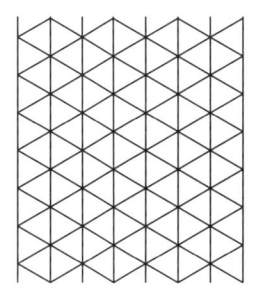

Exercise 1

1. On isometric paper make a copy of each object below. Underneath each drawing state the number of 'multilink' cubes needed to make the object. (Make sure you have the isometric paper the right way round!)

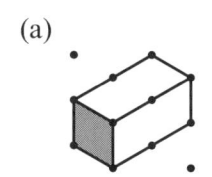

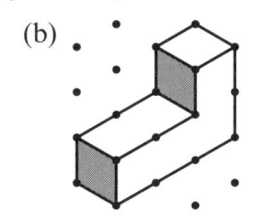

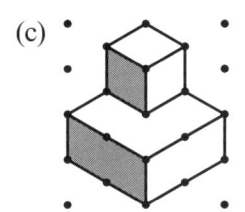

   (a)   (b)   (c)

2. Using four cubes, you can make several different shapes. A and B are different shapes but C is the same as A.

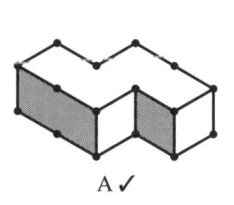

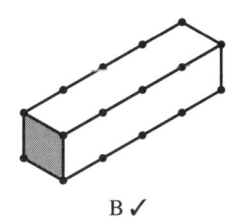

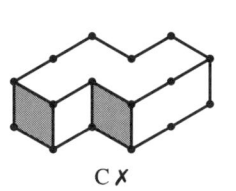

   A ✓   B ✓   C ✗

   Make as many different shapes as possible, using four cubes, and draw them all (including shapes A and B above) on isometric paper.

3. Make the object shown using cubes.
Now draw the object *from a different view*.

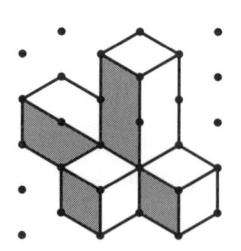

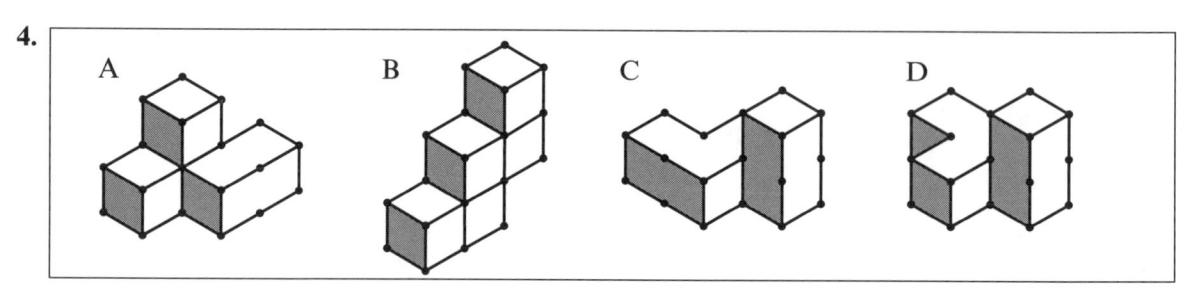

4.

A   B   C   D

Build your own 3-D models of shapes A, B, C and D above. If possible use a different colour for each one.

Decide which of the shapes below are the same as shape A.
Repeat for shapes B, C and D.
Which shape is neither A, B, C nor D?

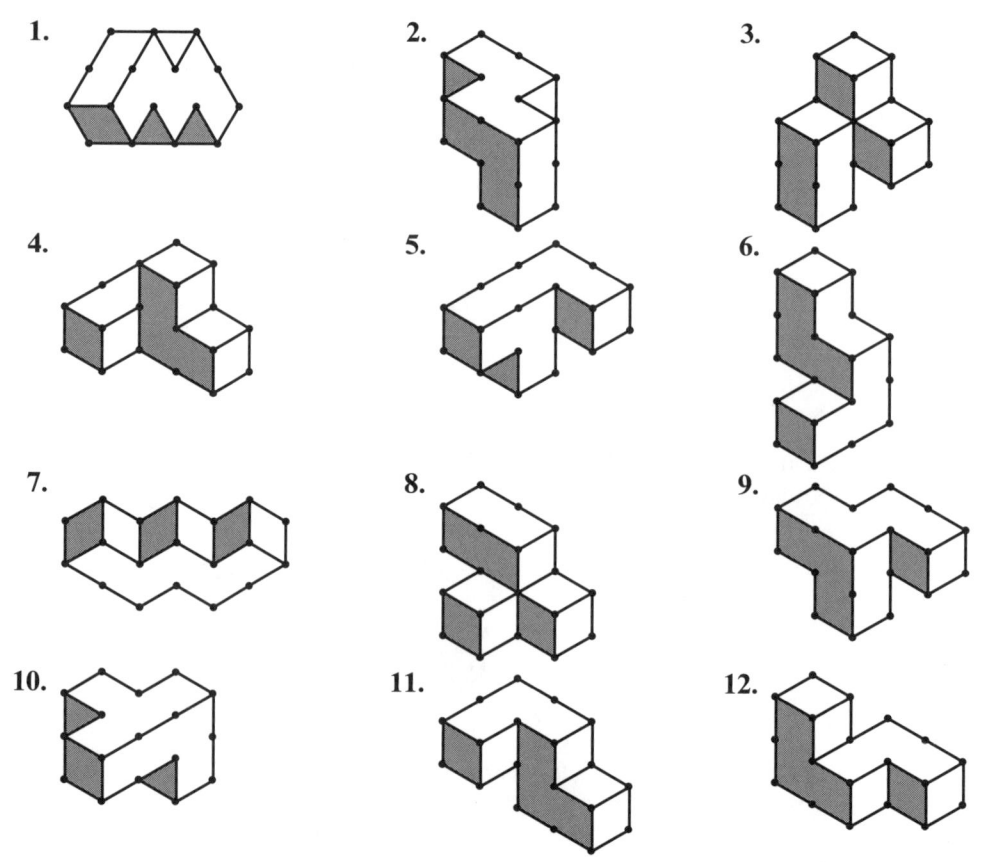

1.   2.   3.

4.   5.   6.

7.   8.   9.

10.   11.   12.

5. You need 18 cubes.

Make the two shapes below. Arrange them to make a $3 \times 3 \times 2$ cuboid by adding a third shape, which you have to find.
Draw the third shape on isometric paper.

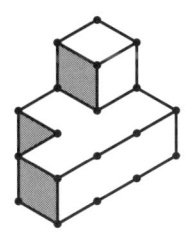

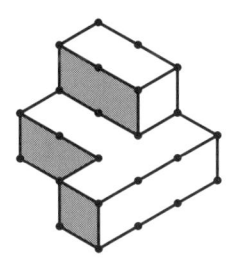

6. You need 27 small cubes for this question.

Make the four shapes below and arrange them into a $3 \times 3 \times 3$ cube by adding a fifth shape, which you have to find. Draw the fifth shape on isometric paper. (The number next to each shape indicates the number of small cubes in that shape).

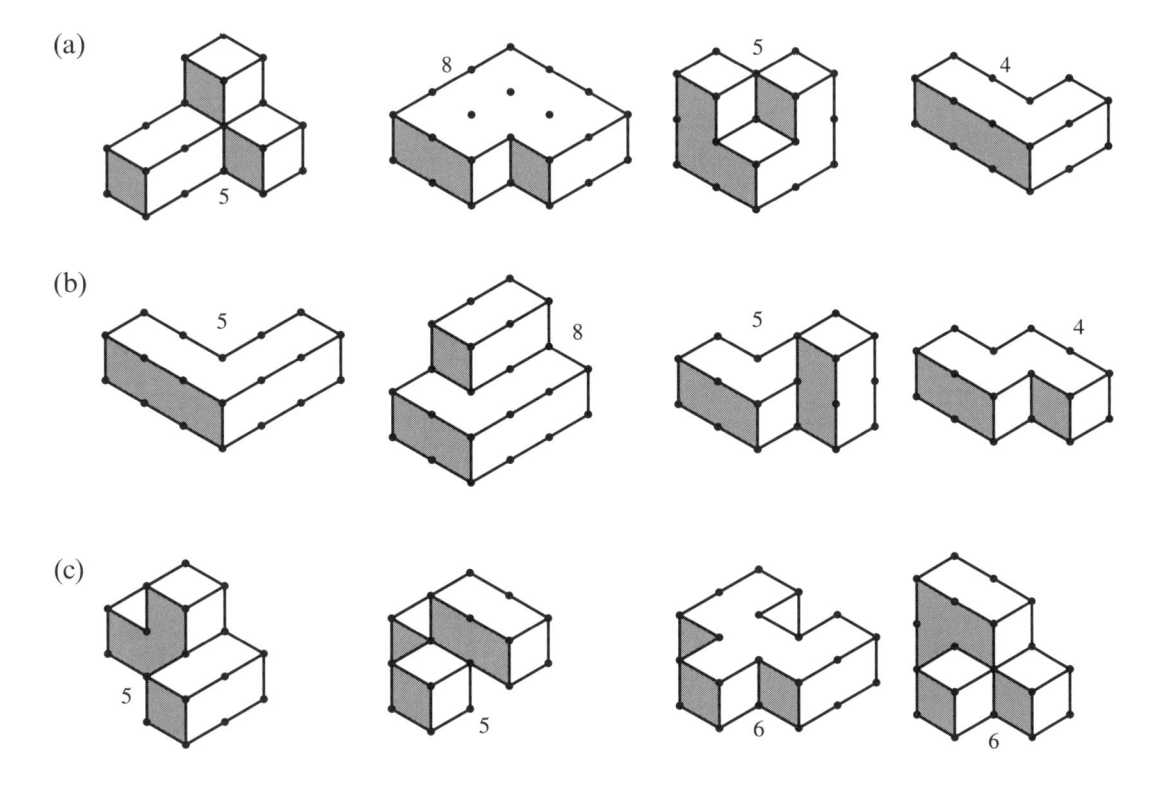

(a)

(b)

(c)

Three views of a shape

Here is a 3-D object made from centimetre cubes.
We can draw 3 views of the object on squared paper.

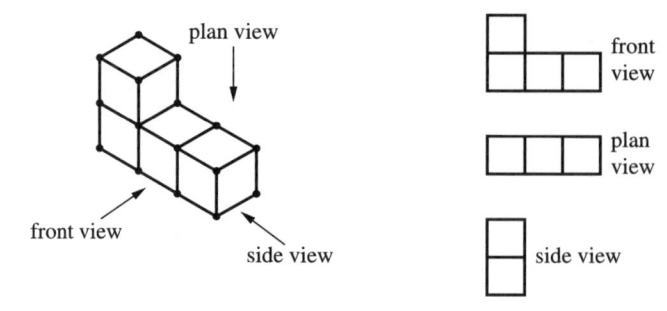

Exercise 2

In Questions **1** to **6** draw the plan view, the front view and the side view of the object

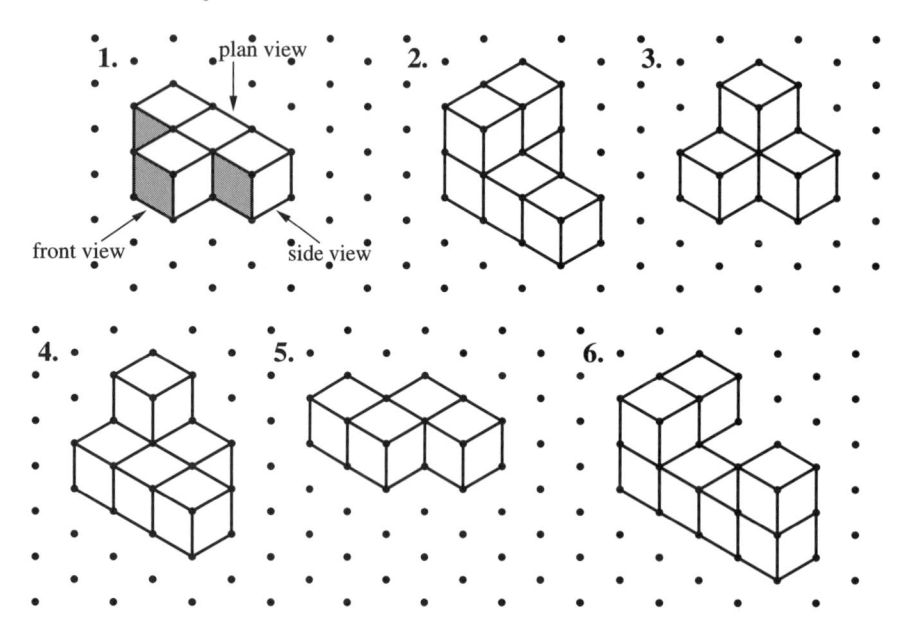

In Questions **7** to **10** you are given three views of a shape. Use the information to make the shape using centimetre cubes.

6.5 Bearings and scale drawing

Bearings are used by navigators on ships and aircraft and by people travelling in open country.
Bearings are measured from north in a *clockwise* direction. A bearing is always given as a three-figure number.

A bearing of 090° is due east. If you are going south-west, you are on a bearing 225°.

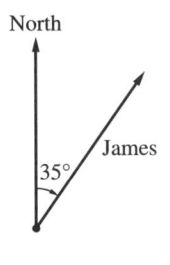

James is walking on a bearing of 035°.

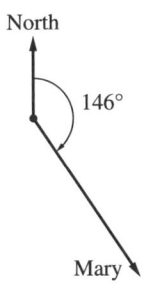

Mary is walking on a bearing of 146°

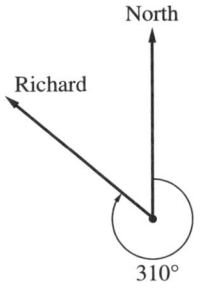

Richard is walking on a bearing of 310°

Exercise 1

1. Ten children on a treasure hunt start in the middle of a field and begin walking in the directions shown on the right. On what bearing is each child walking?

2. Ten pigeons are released and they fly in the directions shown below. On what bearing is each pigeon flying?

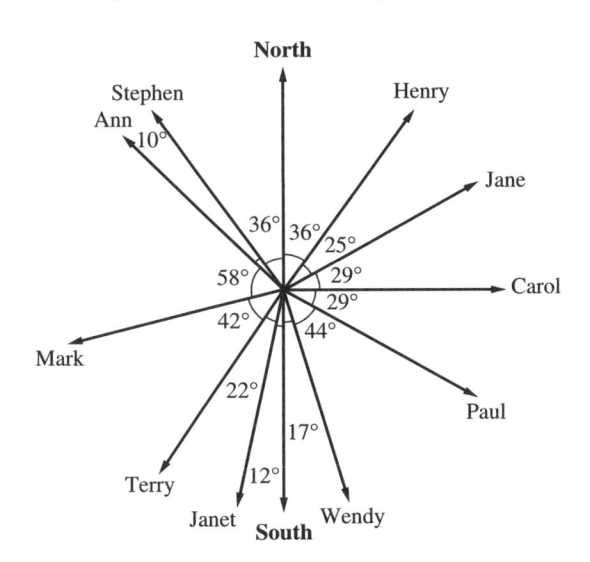

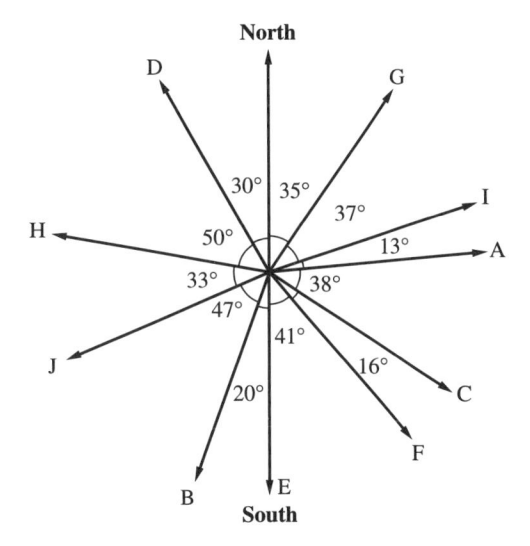

3. Measure the bearing on which each person is moving.

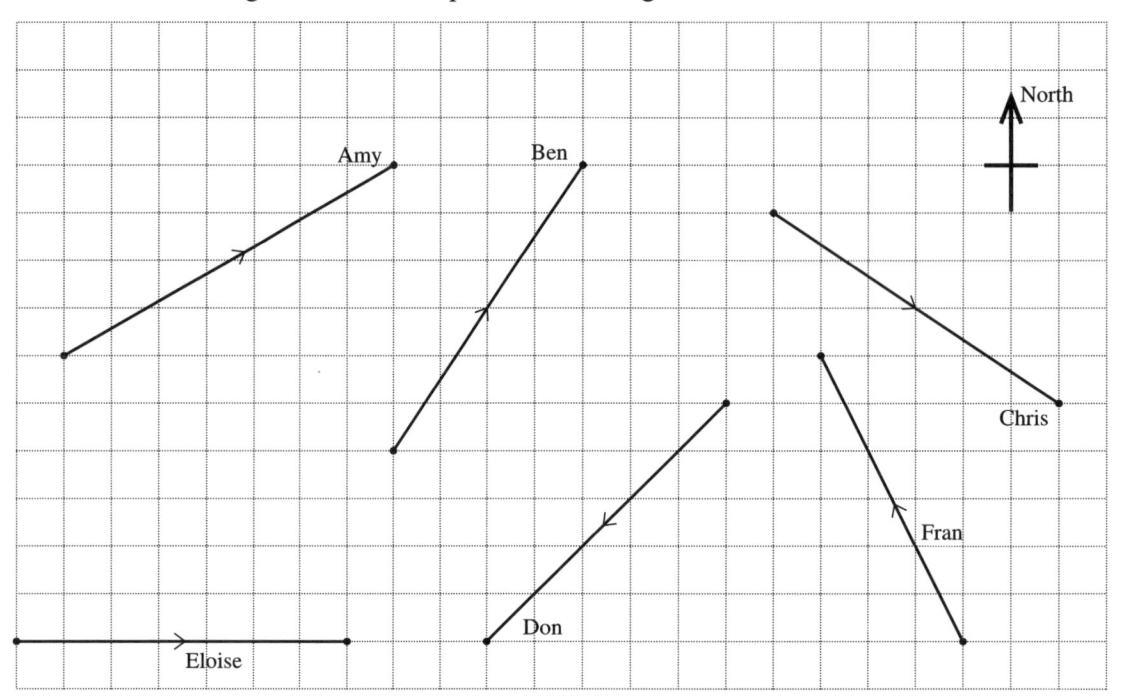

4. Measure the bearing of these journeys.
   (a) A to B   (b) B to C   (c) A to C   (d) A to D   (e) C to D

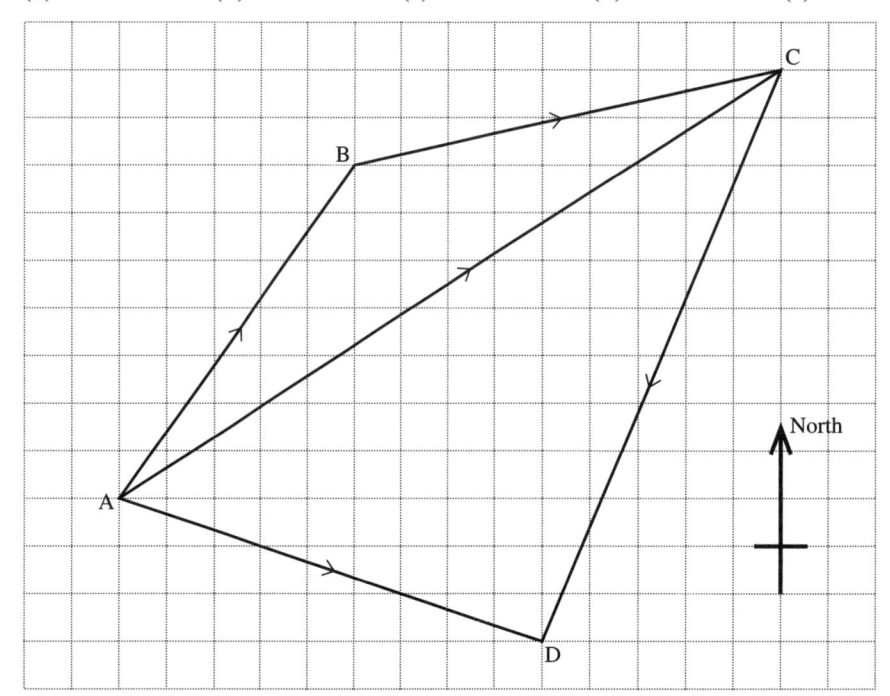

5. Draw lines on the following bearings.
   (a) 040°   (b) 075°   (c) 120°   (d) 200°   (e) 300°

6. The map shows several features on and around an island. Axes are drawn to identify positions. [eg The coordinates of the cave are (9, 3).]

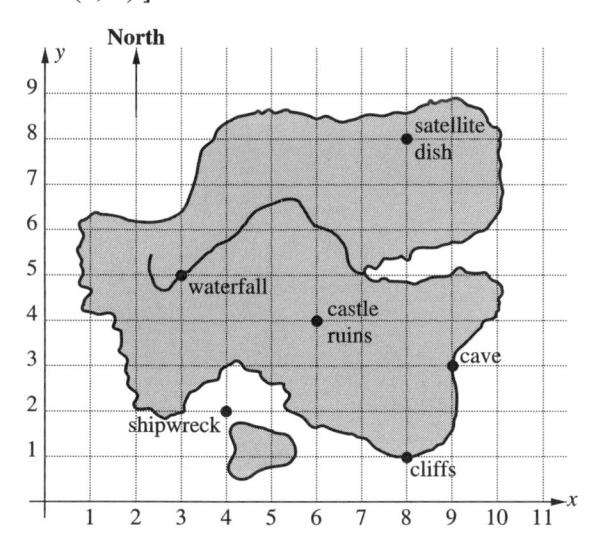

Four commandos, Piers, Quintin, Razak and Smudger, are in hiding on the island. Find the coordinates of the commandos, using the following information.
(a) The castle ruins are due south of Piers and the waterfall is due west of him.
(b) From Quintin, the bearing of the satellite dish is 045° and the shipwreck is due south of him.
(c) From Razak, the bearing of the waterfall is 315° and the bearing of the castle ruins is 045°.
(d) From Smudger, the bearing of the cave is 135° and the bearing of the waterfall is 225°.
(e) The leader of the commandos is hiding somewhere due north of the shipwreck in a hollow tree. From this tree, the castle ruins and the cliffs are both on the same bearing. Find the coordinates of this hollow tree.

7. For each diagram, write down the bearing of C from D.

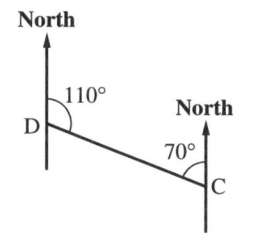

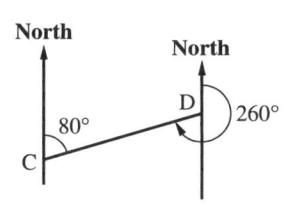

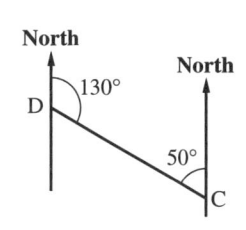

Scale drawing

Many problems involving lengths can be solved using a scale drawing. With questions about compass directions it is helpful to begin by drawing a small sketch to get an idea of where the lines will go. Choose as large a scale as possible for greater accuracy.

A ship sails 7 km north-east and then a further 10 km due south. How far is the ship from its starting point?

We will use a scale of 1 cm to 1 km.
(a) Mark a starting point S and draw a line at 45° to the lines on the page.
(b) Mark a point A, 7 cm from S.
(c) Draw a line vertically through A and mark a point F, 10 cm from A
(d) Measure the distance SF.
   Answer: The ship is 7·1 km from its starting point.
   (An answer between 7·0 km and 7·2 km would be acceptable.)

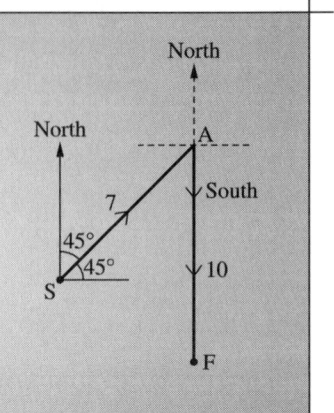

Exercise 2

In Questions **1** to **7** use a scale of 1 cm to represent 1 km.

1. A ship sails 7 km due east and then a further 5 km due south. Find the distance of the ship from its starting point.

2. A ship sails 10 km due west and then a further 4 km south-east. Find the distance of the ship from its starting point.

3. A ship sails 8 km due north and then a further 7 km on a bearing 080°.
   How far is the ship now from its starting point?

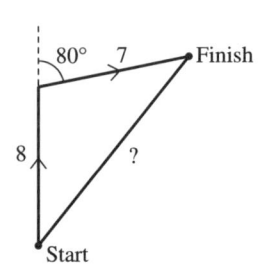

4. A ship sails 6 km on a bearing of 120° and then a further 4 km due south. How far is the ship from its starting point?

5. A ship sails 7 km on a bearing of 075° and then a further 5 km on a bearing of 130°. How far is the ship from its starting point?

6. A bird leaves its nest and flies around its territory in three stages.

   (a) Make a scale drawing to show the journey.
   (b) How far does the bird have to fly to return to its nest?

	Direction	Distance
1st stage	west	5 km
2nd stage	south-east	6 km
3rd stage	east	12 km

7. The diagram shows parts P and Q where P is 10 km west of Q. An aircraft carrier A is 9 km north-east of P. An enemy submarine S is 4 km north-west of Q. The torpedoes on the submarine have a range of 4 km. Is the aircraft carrier in range of the torpedoes?

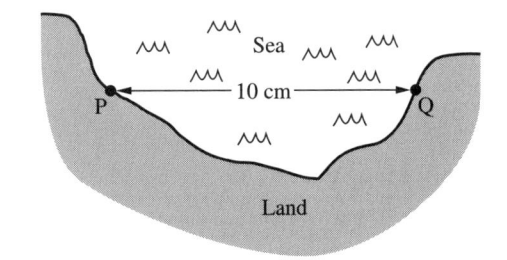

8. Captain Campbell has buried his greatest treasure somewhere in the field shown.
   Here is a section of his secret directions to the treasure:

   Make a scale drawing of the field and shade the region where you think the treasure lies. Use a scale of 1 cm to 100 m.

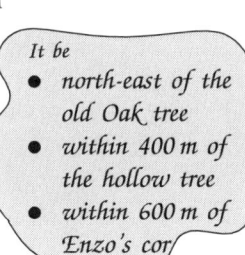

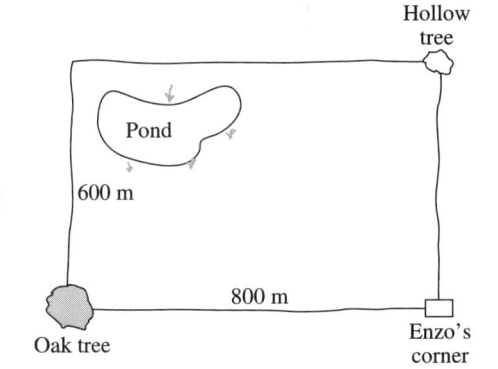

   It be
   - *north-east of the old Oak tree*
   - *within 400 m of the hollow tree*
   - *within 600 m of Enzo's cor*

9. Here is a sketch of a company logo which is to be painted full size on the side of a ship.
   The designer needs to know the total height of the logo. Make a scale drawing of the logo with a scale of 1 cm to 1 m and find the height of the logo.

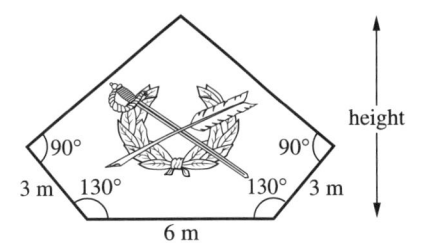

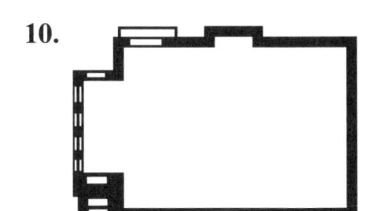

10. Make a scale drawing of a room in your house. Design a layout for the furniture you would like to have in the room.

6.6 Volume

- Volume is a measure of how much physical space an object takes up.

Blocks A and B are each made from eight cubes, measuring 1 cm × 1 cm × 1 cm. They each have a volume of 8 cubic cm, which is written 8 cm³.

Rectangular blocks like these are called *cuboids*. A cube, like block B, is a special kind of cuboid.

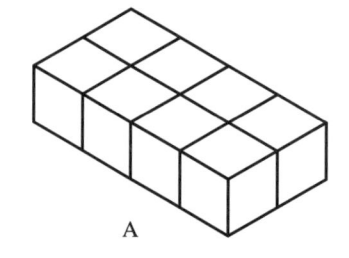

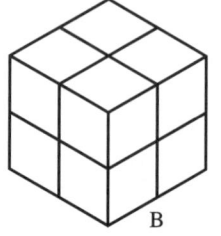

- The volume of a cuboid is given by the formula,

Volume = (length) × (width) × (height)

(a) Find the volume of the cuboid

Volume = 2 × 6·5 × 1
       = 13 cm²

(b) Find the volume of the cuboid

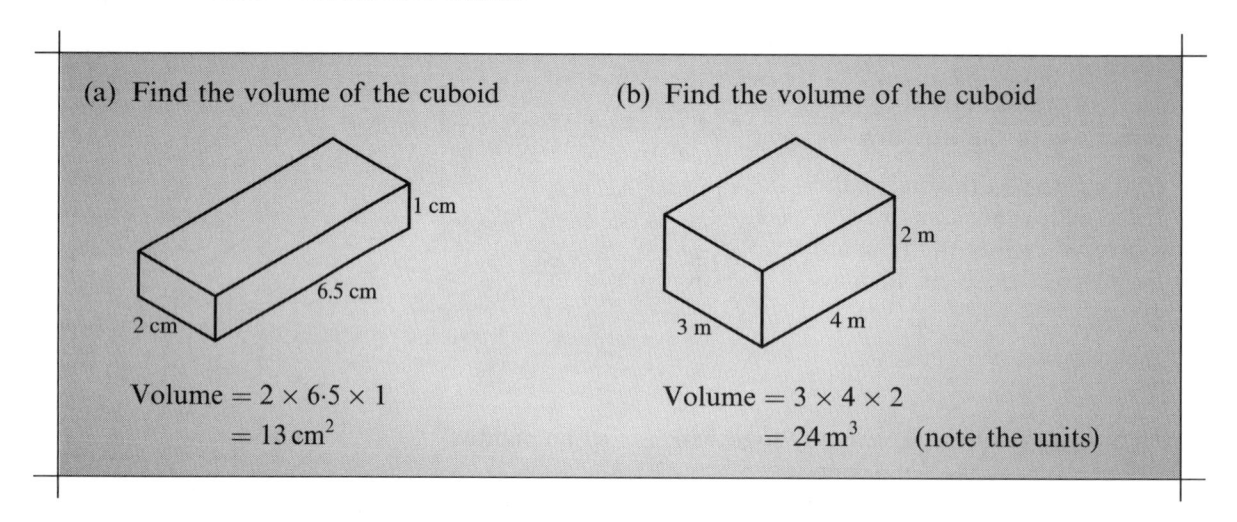

Volume = 3 × 4 × 2
       = 24 m³   (note the units)

Exercise 1

In Questions **1** to **9** work out the volume of each cuboid. Give your answer in the correct units

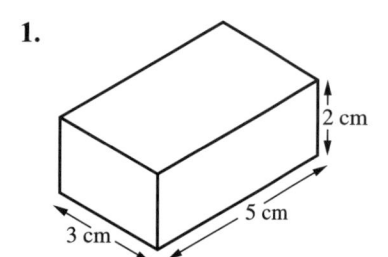

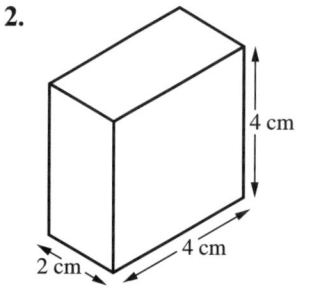

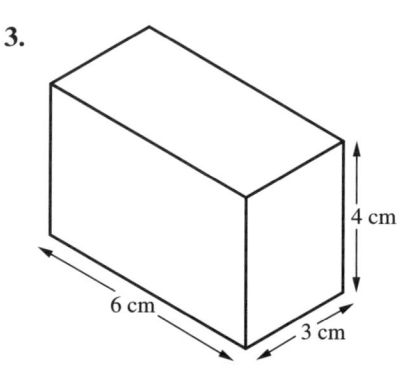

1. 3 cm, 5 cm, 2 cm

2. 2 cm, 4 cm, 4 cm

3. 6 cm, 3 cm, 4 cm

4. [cuboid: 2 cm by 4 cm by 6 cm]

5. [cuboid: 6 cm by 3 cm by 3 cm]

6. [cuboid: 2 mm by 3 mm by 2.5 mm]

In Questions **7** to **12** write down the volume of the object. All the objects are made from centimetre cubes.

7.

8.

9.

10.

11.

12.

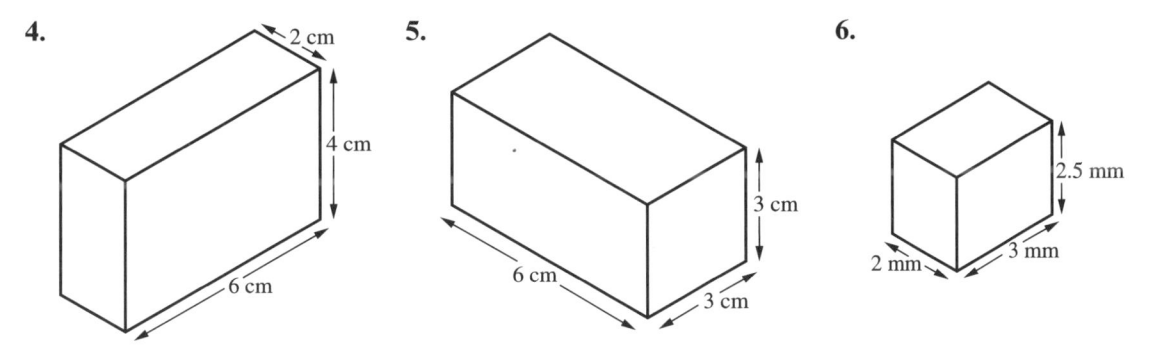

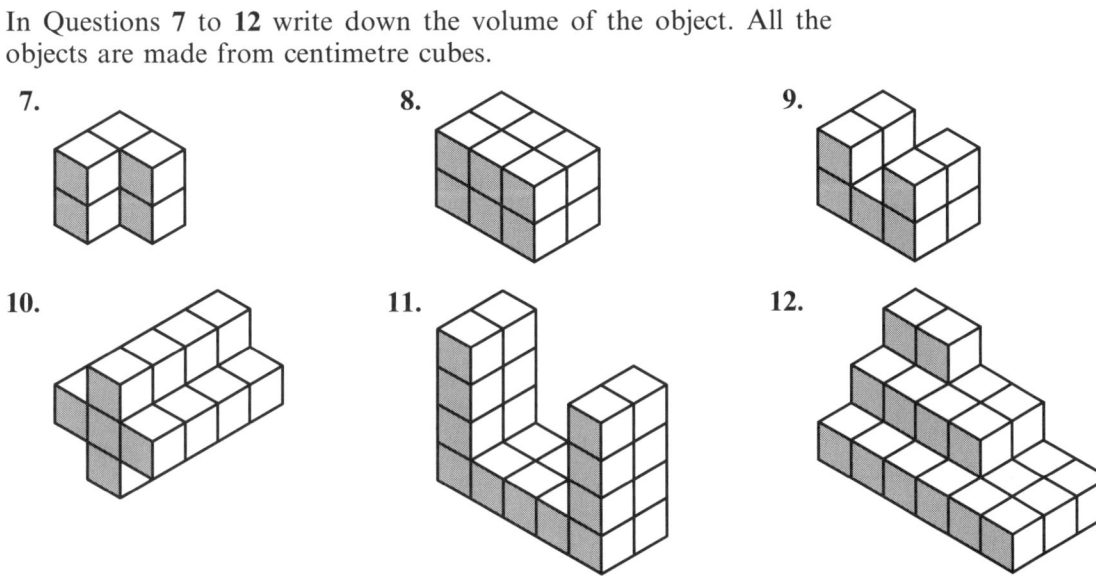

13. (a) Draw a sketch of 4 m by 4 m by 2 m cuboid.
   (b) Calculate the volume of the cuboid.
   (c) Calculate the total surface area of the cuboid.

14. Calculate the volume of each girder by splitting them into cuboids. All lengths are in cm.

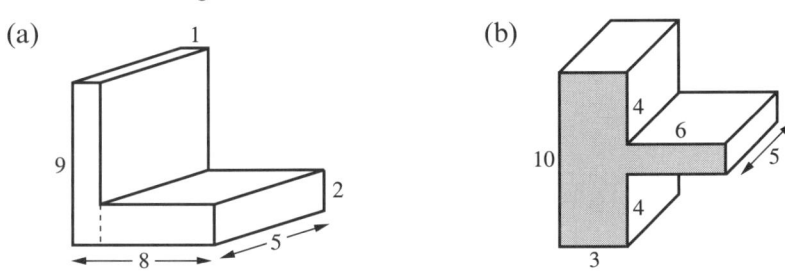

(a) [L-shaped girder: 1, 9, 8, 5, 2]

(b) [T-shaped girder: 10, 4, 6, 5, 4, 3]

Exercise 2

1. How many times can the small box be filled from the large container which is full of grass seed?

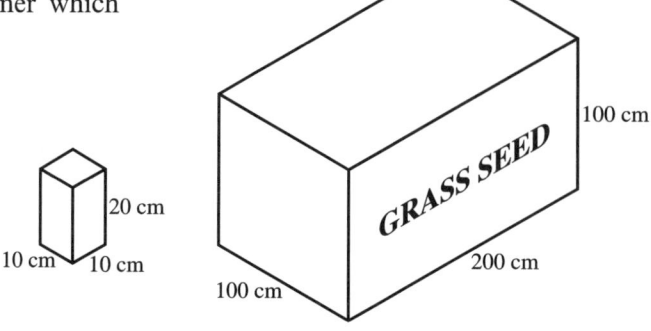

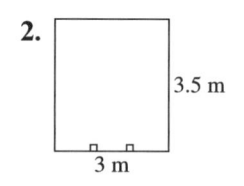

2. A mine shaft 400 m long is dug with the cross-section shown. Calculate the volume of earth which must be removed to make way for the shaft.

3. The diagram shows an empty swimming pool. Water is pumped into the pool at a rate of $2\,m^3$ per minute. How long will it take to fill the pool?

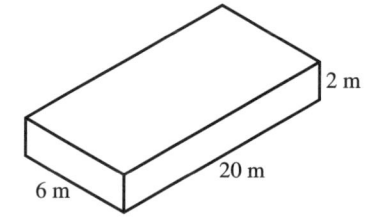

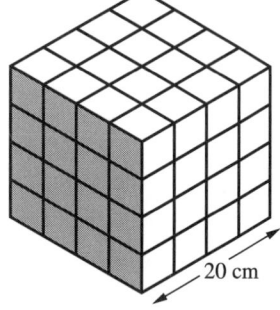

4. The large cube is cut into lots of identical small cubes as shown. Calculate the volume of each small cube.

5. The shapes below are nets for closed boxes. Work out the volume of the box in each case, giving your answer in cubic cm.

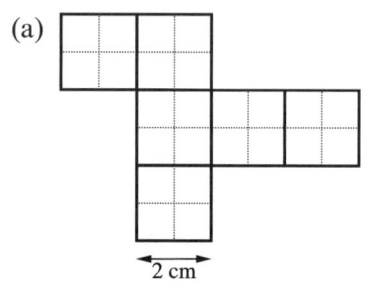

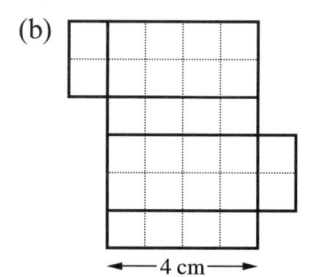

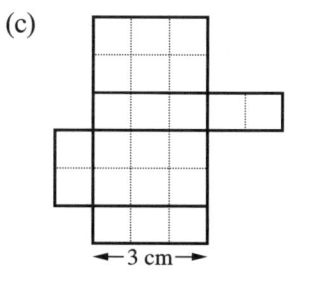

   (a) 2 cm
   (b) 4 cm
   (c) 3 cm

6. In a storm 2 cm of rain fell in 1 hour. Calculate the volume of water, in cm³, which fell on the roof of the garage shown. (Hint: Think about the units!)

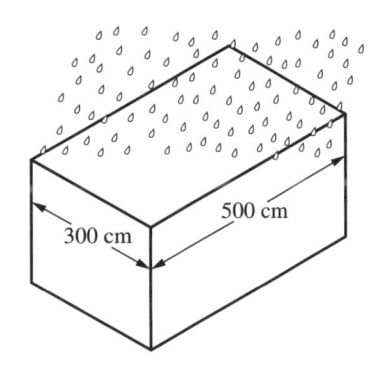

500 cm
300 cm

7. The inside of a spaceship orbiting the earth is a cuboid measuring 200 cm by 300 cm by 200 cm. Unfortunately air is leaking from the spaceship at a rate of 1000 cm³/sec. How long will it take for all the air to leak out?

8. Find the length x.

(a) 4 cm, x, 7 cm; volume = 70 cm³

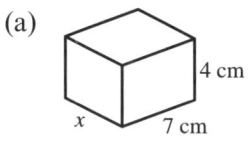

(b) 5 cm, 8 cm, x; volume = 120 cm³

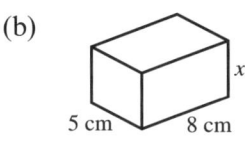

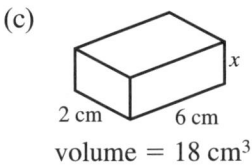

(c) 2 cm, 6 cm, x; volume = 18 cm³

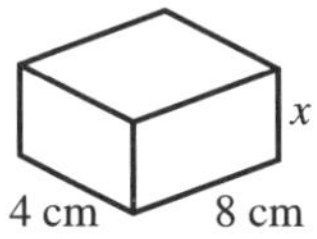

(d) 4 cm, 8 cm, x; volume = 32 cm³

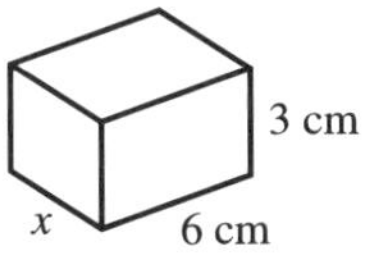

(e) x, 6 cm, 3 cm; volume = 27 cm³

(f) x, x, 4 cm; volume = 100 cm³

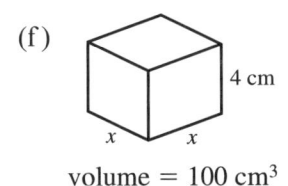

9. The diagram shows an object of volume 7 cm³. Use isometric paper to draw the following objects:
   (a) a cuboid with volume 45 cm³
   (b) a T-shaped object with volume 15 cm³
   (c) an L-shaped object with volume 20 cm³
   (d) any object with a volume of 23 cm³.

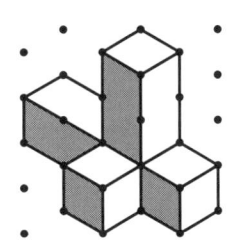

10. Sketch a cuboid a cm by b cm by c cm.
    (a) Write an expression for the volume of the cuboid.
    (b) Write an expression for the total surface area of the cuboid.

Cube problem: an investigation

- The diagrams below show 5 different sized cubes formed by unit cubes.

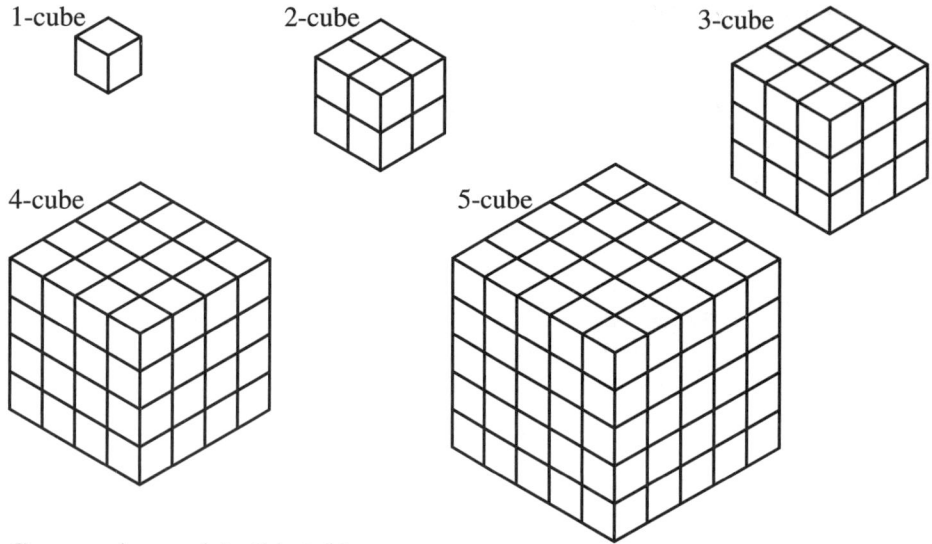

  1-cube   2-cube   3-cube

  4-cube   5-cube

- Copy and complete this table

Object	1-cube	2-cube	3-cube	4-cube	5-cube	6-cube	7-cube	8-cube
Number of cubes	1	8						

- The outside of each cube is now painted red.
  All of the unit cubes which form a 2-cube would have 3 of their 6 faces painted red.
  On larger sized cubes some unit cubes will have 3 faces painted red, some will have 2 painted red, some will have only 1 painted red, and some will stay completely unpainted.
- Copy out and complete the table below showing the number of unit cubes with 3, 2, 1 or 0 faces painted red.

Object	Number of unit cubes	Number of red faces			
		3	2	1	0
2-cube	8	8 cubes	0	0	0
3-cube					
4-cube					
5-cube					

- Use your table to help you predict the number of unit cubes with 3, 2, 1, 0 face coloured red for a 6-cube and for a 7-cube.
  How many unit cubes will have 1 red face for a 10-cube?
  How many unit cubes will have no red faces for a 20-cube?

6.7 Mathematical games

Round the class: a game for the whole class

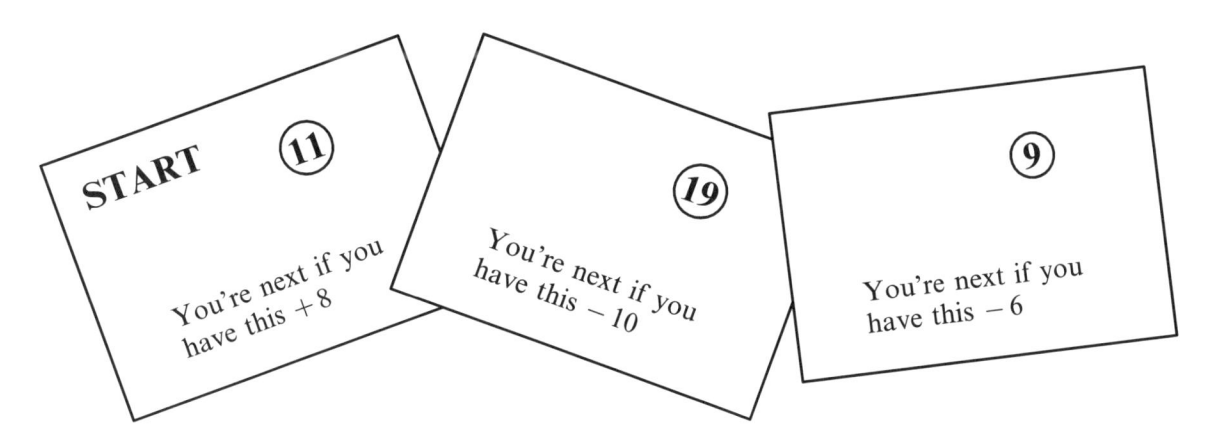

(Card 1) START **11** — You're next if you have this + 8

(Card 2) **19** — You're next if you have this − 10

(Card 3) **9** — You're next if you have this − 6

- Fifty cards like those above are handed out around the class.

- One person has a START card. He/she reads the number in the ring at the top of the card (11) and then reads the statement 'You're next if you have this +8'.

- Someone in the class will have the card shown in the middle. That person says '19' and then reads 'You're next if you have this −10'.

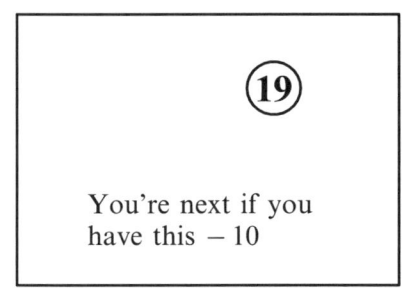

(Card) **19** — You're next if you have this − 10

- This process continues around the room until card 50 with the word 'END' is reached. The object of the game is to complete the 50 cards as quickly as possible.

- The class can be split into two teams. Each team completes the 50 cards against the stopwatch and the winner is the team with the quicker time.

- Teacher's note: The cards appear in the Answer Book from which they can be photocopied preferably on card and cut up. A master sheet is also printed for the teacher to keep track of what is going on.

Find the hidden treasure

This is a game for two players: one player hides the treasure and the other player tries to find it.

(a) Player A draws a grid with x and y from -6 to 6. He puts the treasure at any point with whole number coordinates. Say $(4, -2)$.

(b) Player B draws his own grid and makes his first guess. Say $(1, 1)$.

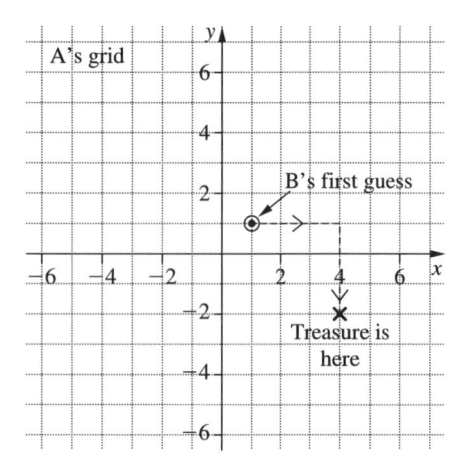

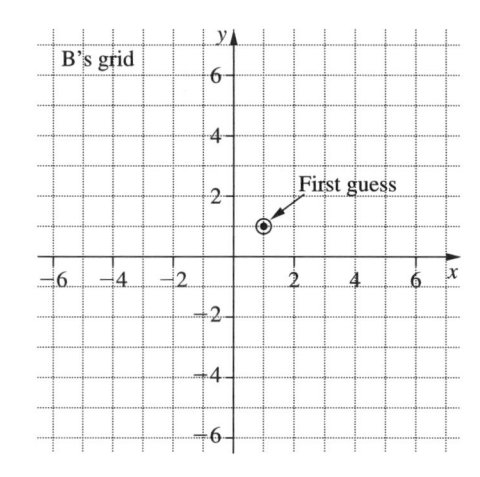

(c) Player A tells player B how far away he is by adding the *horizontal* and *vertical* distances from his guess to the treasure. So the point $(1, 1)$ is a distance 6 away.
(d) Player B has another guess and player A gives the distance from the new point to the treasure.
(e) Play continues until player B finds the treasure.
(f) Roles are then reversed so that B hides a new treasure and A tries to find it in as few goes as possible.

- After several games you may realise that you can improve your chances by using a 'mathematical strategy'.

Random numbers

You need a calculator with a random number key.
Everyone presses the random key on their calculator.

[It may be SHIFT RAN # .] Ignore the decimal point.

The person who gets nearest to the number which the teacher gets wins that round. It's as simple as that!

Fraction, Decimal or Percentage pairs

This is a game for 2, 3 or 4 players using the Fraction, Decimal and Percentage cards.

How to play:

- Shuffle the cards, place them face down in a 6 rows by 4 columns pattern.
- Decide who will go first.
- Each turn requires a player to turn over a pair of cards.
- If the pair are equivalent such as 0·5 and 50% the player keeps the pair. If not turn the cards face down again.
- Try to remember which cards are where!
- If you find a pair you get another go, the player with the most pairs when no cards are left is the winner.
- You can increase the degree of difficulty in the game by including more fraction, decimal and percentage equivalents.
- Teacher's note. The cards may be photocopied from the answer book. Some teachers prefer to have the cards made by the pupils as a preparation.

Printing a book

When a book is made giant sheets of paper containing several pages of the book are printed. These large sheets are then folded to make either 16 or 32 page 'signatures'. The signatures are then bound together to make the whole book and then the edges of the pages are trimmed.

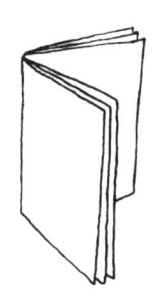

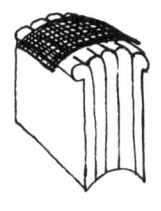

The printed pages are spread all over the large sheet and are upside down in many cases.

Take a sheet of A3 paper (twice the size of A4, 'normal' school paper) and fold it to make a 16 page signature. Work out where pages 1 to 16 would be and also which way up they should be printed.

Now either make drawings, stick in pictures or write a short story on *both* sides of your A3 sheet and number the pages. Finally fold and cut your booklet and fix the pages together with staples.

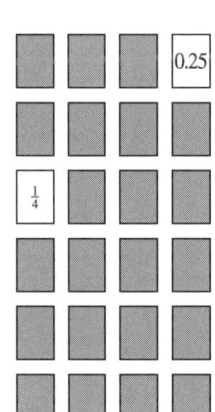

236

Distorted grids

- Below the word 'Hi' is shown on an ordinary grid and also on a distorted grid.

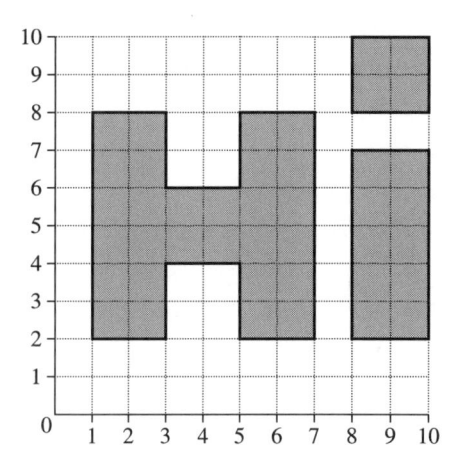

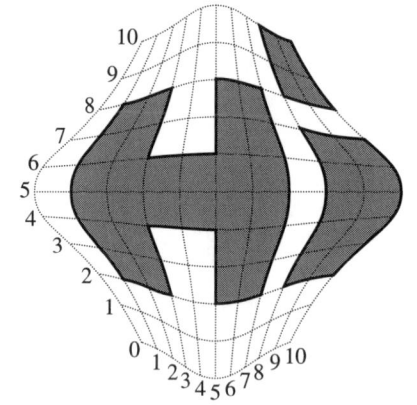

- You can achieve some interesting results by drawing shapes on the grids on the next two pages.

  Ask your teacher for a photo-copy of the grids.

- Begin by drawing some or all of theses shapes.

  (a) (1, 1) (1, 5) (3, 5) (3, 3) (5, 3) (5, 9) (7, 9) (7, 1) (1, 1).

  (b) (1, 5) (1, 7) (5, 7) (5, 9) (7, 9) (7, 7) (9, 7) (9, 5) (7, 5) (7, 1) (5, 1) (5, 5) (1, 5).

  (c) (2, 4) (2, 9) (3, 9) (3, 5) (5, 5) (5, 6) (6, 6) (6, 5) (8, 5) (8, 4) (6, 4) (6, 2) (5, 2) (5, 4) (2, 4).

  (d) (4, 1) (8, 5) (8, 6) (7, 7) (5, 7) (4, 6) (3, 7) (4, 6) (3, 7) (4, 8) (7, 8) (9, 6) (9, 5) (6, 2) (9, 2) (9, 1) (4, 1).

- Now draw any shape of your own design. It could be the first letter of your names ... or a bird ... or a box. It's up to you. Colour in your designs.

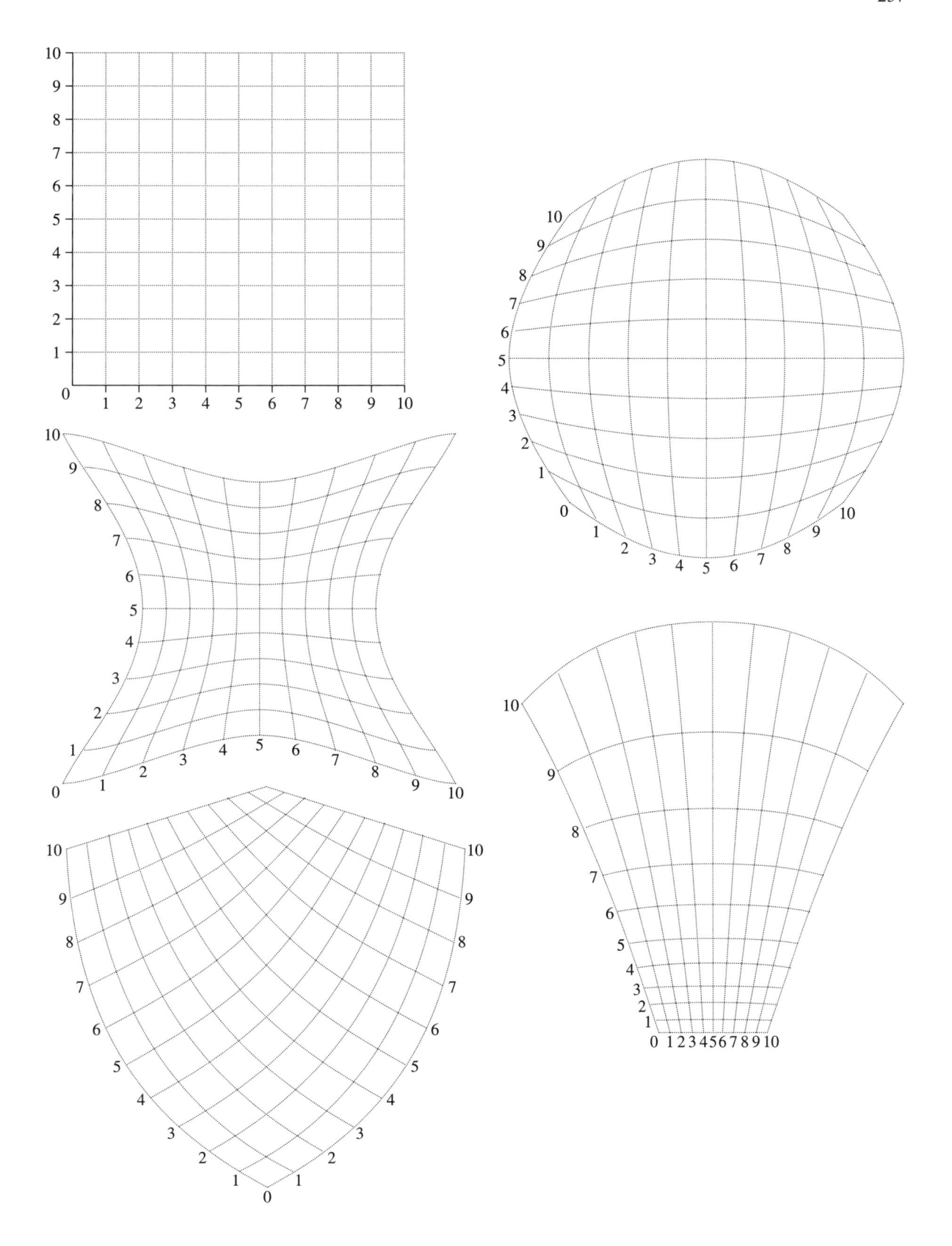

237

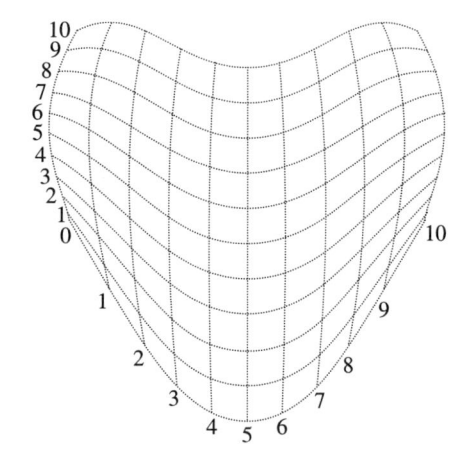

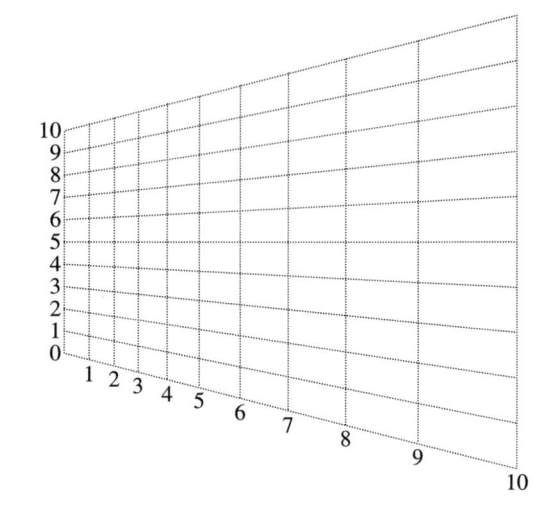

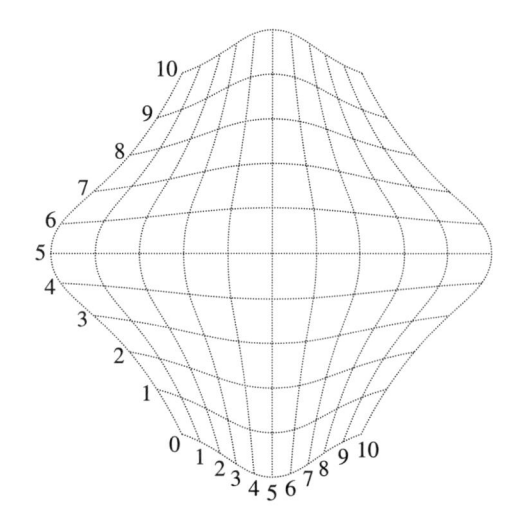

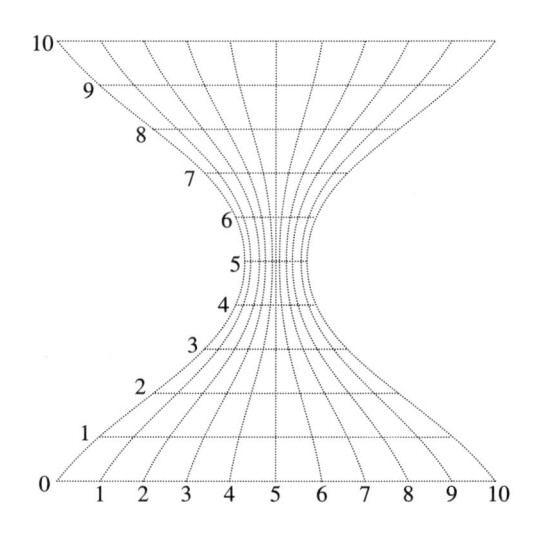

238

Part 7

7.1 Check-up

Numeracy check-up

Do not use a calculator.

A Whole numbers
1. $27 + 118$
2. $71 + 91 + 11$
3. $472 - 29$
4. 17×6
5. $348 \div 3$
6. $196 \div 7$
7. 214×5
8. $2174 - 326$

B Decimals
1. $3 \cdot 2 + 11 \cdot 9$
2. $5 \cdot 6 + 13$
3. $9 - 3 \cdot 3$
4. $23 \times 0 \cdot 3$
5. $213 \times 0 \cdot 5$
6. $13 \cdot 2 \div 5$
7. $0 \cdot 7 \times 0 \cdot 3$
8. $8 \cdot 6 \div 0 \cdot 2$

C Fractions
1. $\frac{2}{3}$ of 36
2. $\frac{4}{5}$ of 60
3. $\frac{1}{2} \times \frac{3}{5}$
4. $\frac{3}{4} \times \frac{3}{4}$
5. $\frac{3}{4} - \frac{1}{2}$
6. $\frac{5}{6} - \frac{1}{3}$
7. $\frac{5}{8} + \frac{1}{4}$
8. $1\frac{2}{3} \times \frac{2}{5}$

D Percentages
1. 20% of £30
2. 8% of £50
3. Increase £300 by 5%
4. Decrease £40 by 10%
5. 15% of 40 kg
6. Write $\frac{9}{20}$ as a percentage

E Negative numbers
1. $-7 + 10$
2. $-2 - 6$
3. $(-3) \times 4$
4. $3 - (-3)$
5. $(-4) \times (-5)$
6. $-5 + 5$
7. $12 \div (-2)$
8. $8 - 11$

F Estimation. Estimate the answer.
1. $98 \cdot 3 \times 2 \cdot 04$
2. $0 \cdot 987 \times 21 \cdot 45$
3. $9815 \times 31 \cdot 4$
4. $5913 \div 29 \cdot 1$

G Miscellaneous
1. How many of these statements are true?
   $0 \cdot 3 = 30\%$; $\quad \frac{3}{4} = 0 \cdot 75$; $\quad 0 \cdot 1 \times 0 \cdot 2 = 0 \cdot 2$; $\quad 17 \div 0 \cdot 5 = 34$
2. 8 boys are 25% of the children in a class.
   How many children are there altogether in the class?

3. Which of the decimals is equal to $\frac{33}{100}$?
   A 3·3   **B** 10·33   **C** 0·33   **D** 0·033

4. Which of these decimals is equal to $\frac{727}{1000}$?
   A 7·27   **B** 0·727   **C** 1·727   **D** 72·7

5. Which of these percentages is equivalent to 0·7?
   A 0·7%   **B** 7%   **C** 70%   **D** 0·07%

6. Find the missing numbers so that the answer is always 36.
   (a) 99 − ☐
   (b) $\frac{1}{3}$ of ☐
   (c) 21 + ☐
   (d) 180 ÷ ☐
   = 36

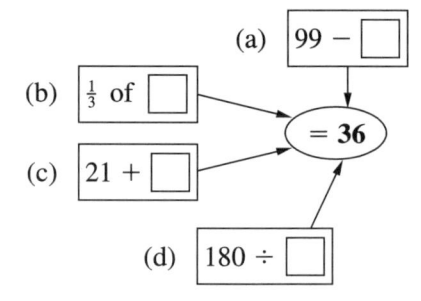

Operator squares

Each empty square contains either a number or a mathematical symbol (+, −, ×, ÷). Copy each square and fill in the missing details.

1.
	×	5	→	40
+		−		
	×	2	→	
↓		↓		
19	×		→	

2.
8	×	20	→	
÷		÷		
	×	5	→	
↓		↓		
4	×		→	

3.
	×	5	→	105
−		×		
9	×	6	→	
↓		↓		
	×		→	

4.
	+	5	→	6.2
×		+		
10		2.4	→	24
↓		↓		
	−		→	4.6

5.
2	×	60	→	
+		÷		
10	÷		→	2
↓		↓		
	×		→	

6.
18	×	6	→	
÷		÷		
9	×	12	→	
↓		↓		
	×		→	

7.

	×	5	→	120
÷		×		
	−	8	→	0
↓		↓		
	×		→	

8.

6	−	10	→	120
5	÷	4	→	
↓		↓		
30	−		→	−10

9.

	×	(−4)	→	−12
÷		+		
	−		→	
↓		↓		
−1	+	−3	→	

The last three are more difficult.

10.

$\frac{1}{2}$		$\frac{1}{4}$	→	$\frac{3}{4}$
+		×		
$\frac{1}{4}$	+		→	$2\frac{1}{4}$
↓		↓		
	−		→	

11.

			→	$\frac{3}{8}$
×		+		
8	÷		→	16
↓		↓		
5	−		→	$4\frac{1}{4}$

12.

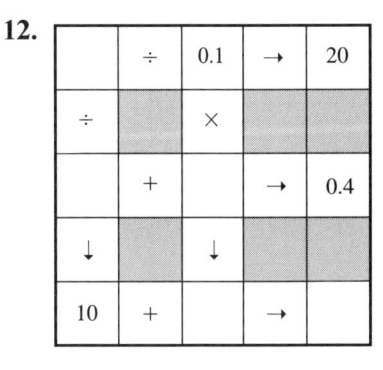

	÷	0.1	→	20
÷		×		
	+		→	0.4
↓		↓		
10	+		→	

Scale reading

Work out the value indicated by the arrow.

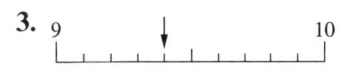

1. 4 ↓ 5

2. 0 ↓ 1

3. 9 ↓ 10

4. 40 ↓ 50

5. 40 ↓ 50

6. 0 ↓ 1

7. 3 ↓ 4

8. 0 ↓ 20

9. 22 ↓ 23

10. 0 ↓ 1

11. 7 ↓ 8

12. 50 ↓ 55

13. 5 ↓ 10

14. 2 ↓ 3

15. 20 ↓ 30

16. 100 ↓ 200

17. 1 ↓ 2

18. 160 ↓ 210

19. 15 ↓ 15.5

20. 0 ↓ 1

21. 5 ↓ 6

7.2 Review exercises

Review Exercise 1: Number and Algebra

1. Work out:
   (a) 5^2
   (b) 2^3
   (c) $3 + 4 \times 2$
   (d) $7(8 - 5)$

2. Work out:
   (a) $(-3) + (-4)$
   (b) $(+2) \times (-3)$
   (c) $(-4)^2$
   (d) $24 \div (-8)$

3. Two shops usually sell compact discs at the same price. Today there is a sale at both shops. Each shop has a different offer on compact discs.

   Dharat's discs
   $\frac{1}{4}$ off
   all C.D.s

   Stefan's sounds
   30% off
   all C.D.s

   Which shop is more expensive for compact discs?

4. Write down the unit of measurement which fits the following sentences:
   (a) Telephone boxes are about 2·5 ____ tall
   (b) An adult man weighs between 60 and 90 ____.
   (c) Arnold Schwarzenegger is just over 6 ____ tall
   (d) A compact disc, without its case, weighs around 30 ____.
   (e) From Cambridge to York is about 150 ____.
   (f) The average school text book is $1\frac{1}{2}$ ____ thick.

5. Write down the reading from each scale
   (a) 0 to 1 grams
   (b) 20 cm to 30 cm
   (c) 2 to 3 kg

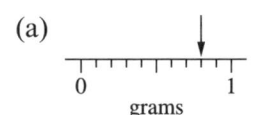

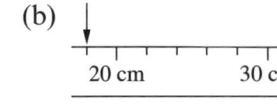

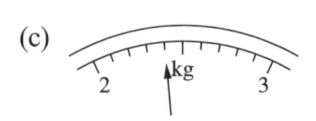

6. Solve the following equations:
   (a) $2x + 3 = 35$
   (b) $8x - 1 = 3$
   (c) $5 + 7x = 7$
   (d) $4(x + 1) = 20$
   (e) $3(x - 2) = 15$
   (f) $7(x + 5) = 49$

7. *Estimate* the following (do NOT use a calculator). Show your working.
   (a) 10% of £24·95
   (b) 20% of £494
   (c) 75% of £398·75
   (d) 33% of £239·99
   (e) 2% of 40 105 kg
   (f) 9·7% of £68 400.

8. In number walls each brick is made by adding the two bricks underneath it.

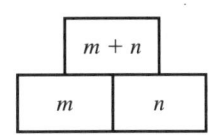

   Fill in the missing expressions on these walls

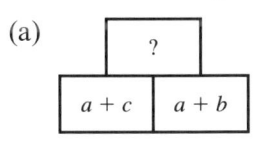

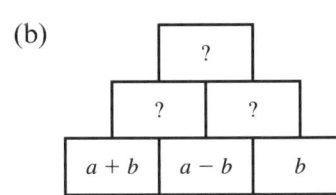

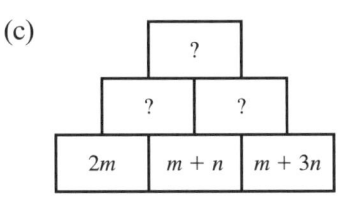

   (a) Top: ?; Bottom: $a+c$, $a+b$

   (b) Top: ?; Middle: ?, ?; Bottom: $a+b$, $a-b$, b

   (c) Top: ?; Middle: ?, ?; Bottom: $2m$, $m+n$, $m+3n$

9. Here are some cards.

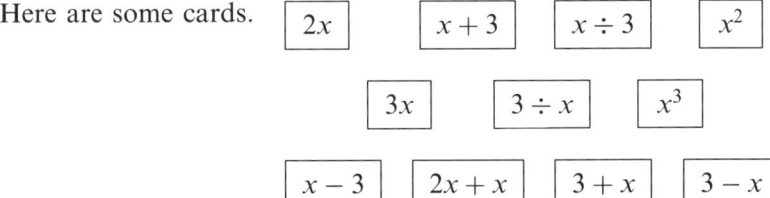

   $2x$ $x+3$ $x \div 3$ x^2

   $3x$ $3 \div x$ x^3

   $x-3$ $2x+x$ $3+x$ $3-x$

   (a) Which card will always be the same as $x \times x$?

   (b) Which cards will always be the same as $x+x+x$?

   (c) Which card will always be the same as $\dfrac{x}{3}$?

   (d) Draw a new card which will always be the same as $x+3x$.

10. Look at these number cards: 5 -2 0 7 -6 3 2 -4

    (a) Fill in the missing number: $-2 + \boxed{?} = 5$

    (b) Which card will give the *highest* possible answer here: $-2 \times \boxed{}$?

    (c) Which card will give the *lowest* possible answer here: $-4 - \boxed{}$?

    (d) Which card will give the *highest* possible answer here: $3 - \boxed{}$?

11. Steve and Tom each have 30 sweets.
    (a) Steve eats $\tfrac{2}{5}$ of his sweets. How many does he eat?
    (b) Tom eats 5 of his sweets. What *fraction* of his sweets does he eat?

12. Susie makes a pattern of rectangles from sticks.

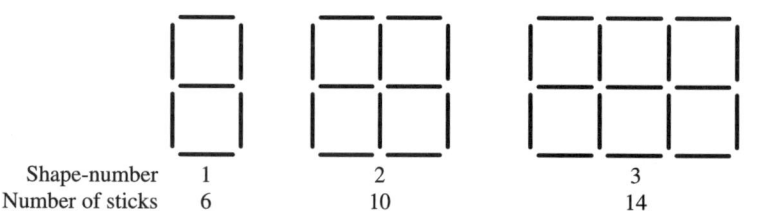

Shape-number	1	2	3
Number of sticks	6	10	14

Susie's rule is 'The number of sticks is four times the shape-number and then add 2.'

(a) Work out the number of sticks in shape-number 8.
(b) One of the shapes needs 50 sticks. What is its shape-number?
(c) Write a formula, without words, to work out the number of sticks for any shape-number. Use S for the number of sticks and N for the shape-number. Write '$S = \ldots\ldots$'.

13. Anna has n marbles in a bag.

(a) She takes 3 marbles from the bag. Write an expression for the number of marbles now in the bag.
(b) Steve has four bags, each containing n marbles. Write an expression for the number of marbles there are altogether in the four bags.
(c) In a game Steve wins 10 more marbles. Write an expression for the number of marbles which he has now.

Review Exercise 2: Shape and Space

1. Work out the area of the shapes shown below. All lengths are in cm.

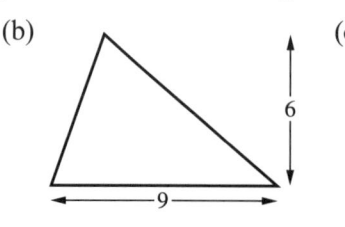

(a) rectangle 5 by 6
(b) triangle, height 6, base 9
(c) trapezium, parallel sides 5 and 4, width 4

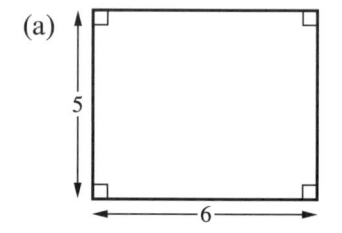

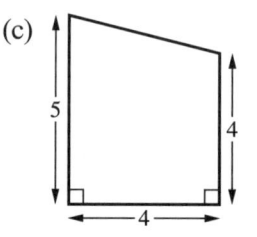

2. The diagram shows the lengths of six pieces of fencing. Amos chooses three pieces, and finds that he cannot form a triangular sheep pen with them.

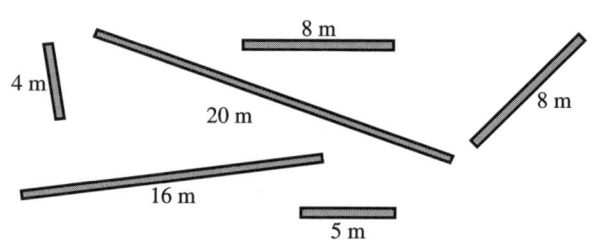

Lengths: 4 m, 8 m, 20 m, 8 m, 16 m, 5 m

(a) Write down the lengths of the pieces Amos could have chosen.
(b) Explain why these pieces would not form a triangle.

3. Draw an accurate full size copy of each triangle and find the length x and the angle y.

(a)

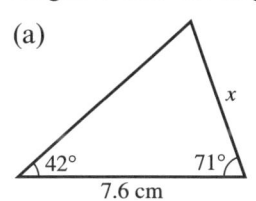

(b)

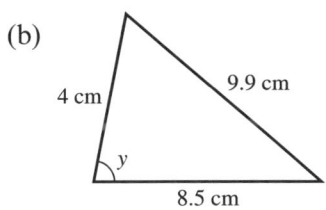

4. Copy each diagram and reflect the shaded squares in the broken lines.

(a)

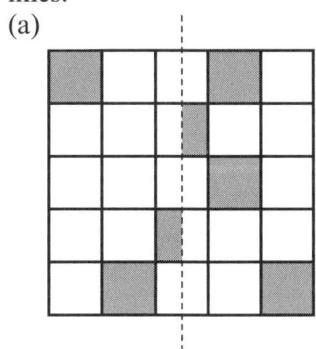

(b)

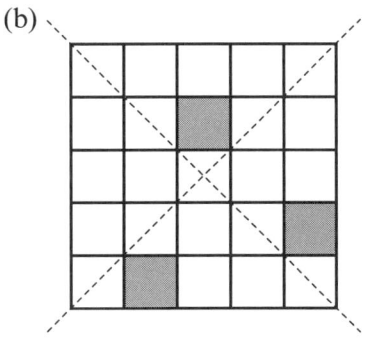

5. Find the angles marked with letters

(a)

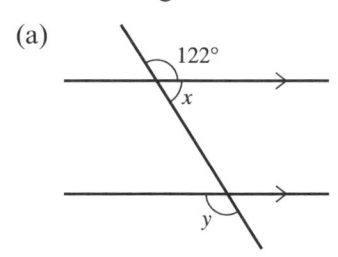

(b)

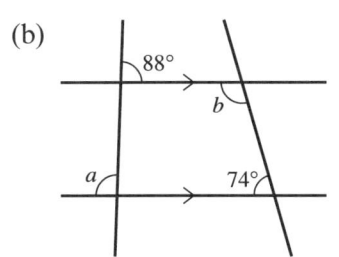

(c)

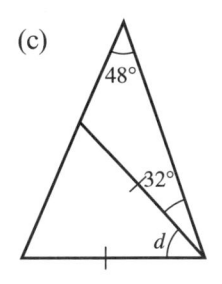

6. Draw this shape, on squared paper, as viewed from
(a) A
(b) B
(c) C
(d) D

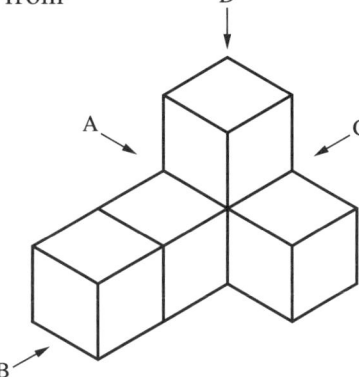

7. Copy each shape and then enlarge it using the centre of enlargement and the scale factor shown.

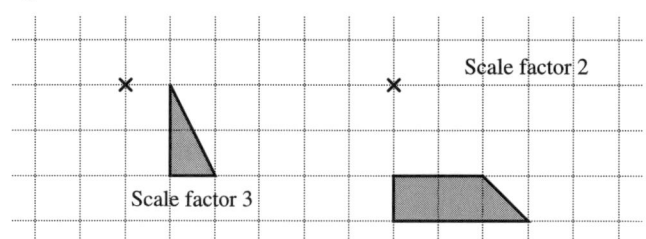

Scale factor 3

Scale factor 2

8. The sketch shows a cardboard box with a lid hinged at the top. Draw an accurate, full size net for the box.

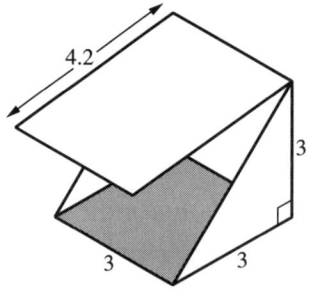

All lengths are in cm.

9. Copy the diagram.
   Describe fully the following transformations:
   (a) △1 → △3
   (b) △1 → △5
   (c) △3 → △2
   (d) △3 → △4

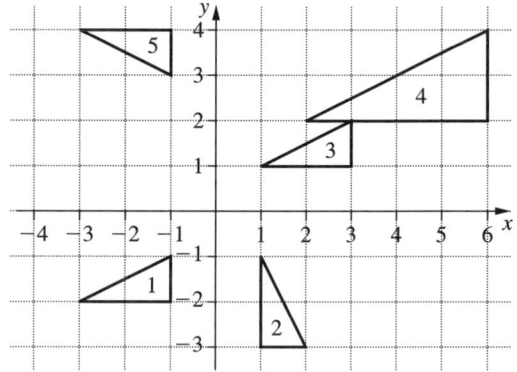

10. Follow the instructions below to produce the outline of an egg.
    (a) Draw line AB 10 cm long and mark the centre of the line.
    (b) Draw a semi-circle of radius 5 cm below AB.
    (c) Mark point C, 5 cm above the mid-point of AB.
    (d) Draw lines AC and BC and extend them.
    (e) Draw arc AD with radius 10 cm and centre B.
    (f) Draw arc BE with radius 10 cm and centre A.
    (g) Draw arc DE with radius CE and centre C.

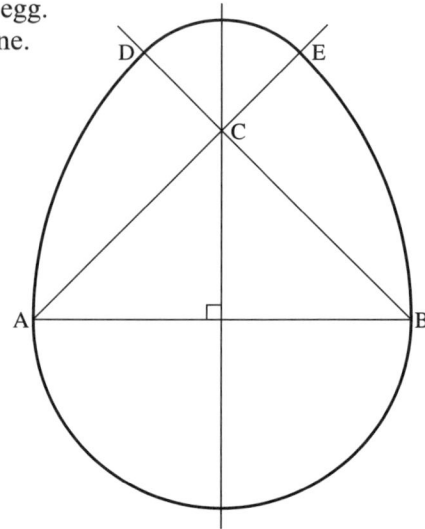

Review Exercise 3: Handling data

1. The scatter graphs show the sales of ice cream, soup and sandwiches on different days. Describe the connection, if any, between the sales of each product and the temperature.

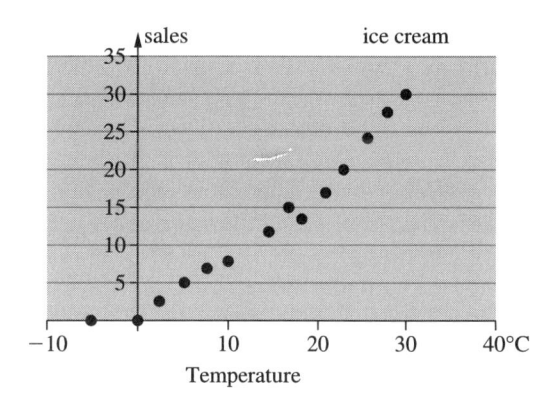

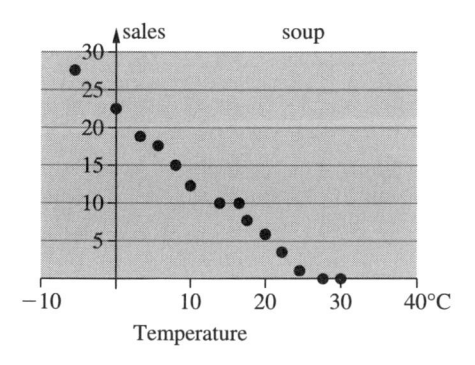

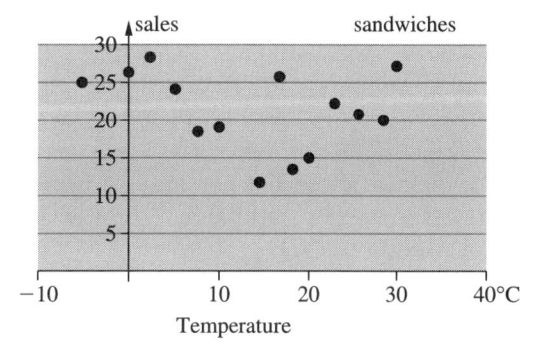

2. The marks of 24 children in a test are shown.

32	15	43	20	47	55	63	51
47	22	49	58	37	12	68	26
35	38	31	19	26	52	49	19

(a) Draw a stem and leaf diagram. The first three entries are shown.
(b) What is the range of the marks?
(c) What is the median mark?

Stem	Leaf
1	5
2	
3	2
4	3
5	
6	

Key
1 | 5 means 15

3. The pie chart shows the division of the world's energy resources.
   (a) The petroleum sector has an angle of 120°. What percentage of the whole chart does this represent?
   (b) Estimate the percentage represented by
      (i) coal
      (ii) nuclear.

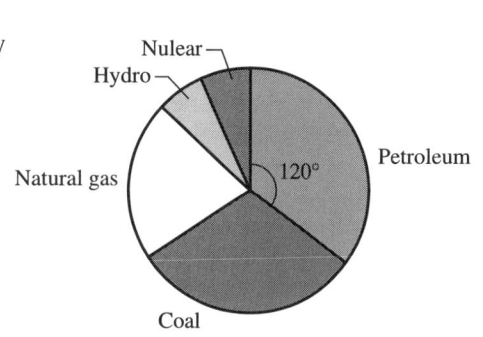

4. 100 raffle tickets are numbered 1 to 100. The winning ticket is chosen at random.
   (a) My lucky number is 77. What is the probability that I will win?
   (b) Steve bought tickets numbered 1, 2, 3, 4, 5.
       Assam bought tickets numbered 10, 20, 30, 40, 50.
       Who is more likely to win?
   (c) Geri bought several tickets and has a 25% chance of winning.
       How many tickets did she buy?
   (d) 7 people lost their tickets. What is the probability that nobody will win?

5. Sumita has 3 different spinners
   She spins each spinner 100 times.

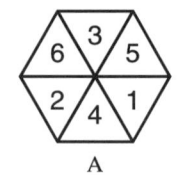

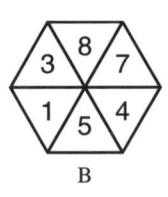

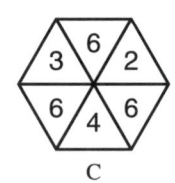

   (a) Draw a number line and draw arrows labelled A, B and C to show your estimate of how many times each spinner will land on a six.

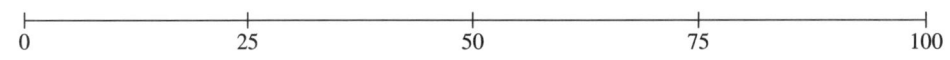

   ```
   +————+————+————+————+
   0    25   50   75   100
   ```

   (b) Explain how you worked out your estimate for spinner C.

6. A box contains six coloured blocks. One block is selected at random and then returned to the box. The procedure is repeated until 50 selections have been made. Here are the results:

   B Y B Y B Y B Y B G   B = Blue
   B Y B G B B B B Y G   G = Green
   B Y B G B Y Y B Y Y   Y = Yellow
   B B B G B B Y B B Y
   B Y G B Y B Y B G B

   (a) Construct a tally and frequency table
   (b) How many of each colour do you think there are in the box? Justify your answer.

7. There were ten people in a triangle. The mean age of the people was 21 and the range of their ages was 4. Write each statement below and then write next to it whether it is *True, Possible* or *False*.
   (a) The youngest person was 19 years old.
   (b) Every person was 21 years old.
   (c) All the people were at least 20 years old.

8.
| 6 | 3 | 7 | 4 |

The cards above show the scores awarded by four judges in a diving contest.
(a) Find the mean score.
(b) Find the median score.
(c) Write down the range of scores.

9. The number of occupants in the 33 houses in a street is as follows:

2	4	3	4	1	4	2	4	1	5	2
3	0	5	3	4	3	6	7	3	3	6
4	1	4	2	0	1	4	3	2	5	0

(a) Draw a frequency table to show this data.
(b) What is the modal number of occupants in these houses?

number of occupants	frequency
0	
1	
2	

10. Karen is going to play a game called 'Lucky Dip.' There are three bags labelled A, B and C. Each bag contains red or white balls. You win if you draw out a red ball from a bag.

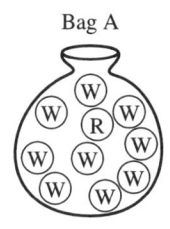

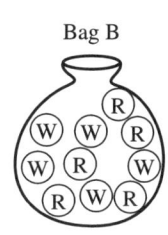

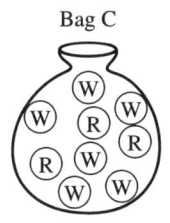

Bag A   Bag B   Bag C

Ⓡ = Red
Ⓦ = White

(a) Write down the probability of winning from bag A, from bag B, and from bag C.
(b) What is the probability of *not* winning from bag A?

11. A dice was thrown 20 times. Here are the results.

Score on dice	1	2	3	4	5	6
Number of throws	3	1	5	5	2	4

Copy and complete: mean score $= \dfrac{(1 \times 3) + (2 \times 1) + (3 \times 5) + \ldots}{20}$

$= \boxed{}$

Practice Test A

The marks for each question are shown in brackets.

1. Write 'fifty thousand and six' in figures (1)

2. Work out:
   (a) $257 + 369$ (b) $743 - 428$
   (c) 892×6 (d) $2464 \div 7$ (4)

3. 265 people attended a recent concert by "The Hairy Scarebellies". What is 265 to the nearest hundred? (1)

4. Write down the temperature which is:
   (a) $3°$ warmer than $-7°C$
   (b) $8°$ colder than $2°C$ (2)

5. In a survey on washing powder 180 people were asked to state which Brand they preferred. 45 chose Brand A. If 30 people chose Brand B and 105 chose Brand C, calculate the angles x and y. (2)

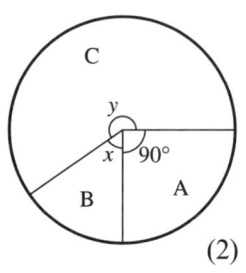

6. Look at these numbers: 25, 14, 8, 7, 40.
   From this list write down:
   (a) a prime number
   (b) a square number
   (c) a cube number (3)

7. In a survey, 26% of people ate toast every morning. What percentage of people did not? (1)

8. Write these numbers in the form required:
   (a) $\frac{7}{10}$ as a decimal
   (b) $\frac{5}{100}$ as a decimal
   (c) 6 out of 20 as a percentage
   (d) 40% as a fraction in its simplest form (4)

9. How many quarters are there in $2\frac{1}{2}$? (1)

10. Work out
    (a) $\frac{3}{5}$ of £60   (b) $\frac{6}{7}$ of $91 (2)

11. A young bodybuilder weighs 70 kg in September. His weight increases by 5%. Find
    (a) 5% of 70 kg   (b) His new weight (2)

12. (a) Copy the diagram onto squared paper.
    (b) Mark the centre of the rotation which rotates A onto B.
    (c) Describe *fully* the rotation.

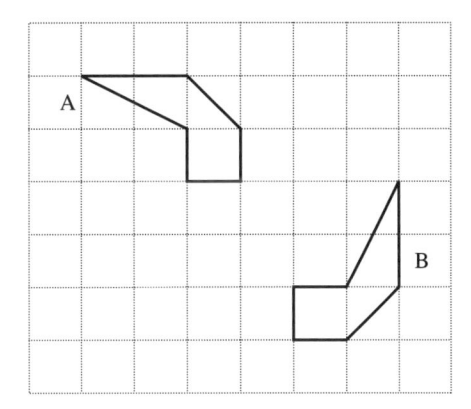

(2)

13. Rewrite these expressions using algebra:
    (a) add four to m
    (b) subtract p from six
    (c) triple t then take away two

(3)

14. Write down the coordinates of:
    (a) P
    (b) S
    (c) Q, if PQRS is a parallelogram.
    (d) the mid point of the line PS.

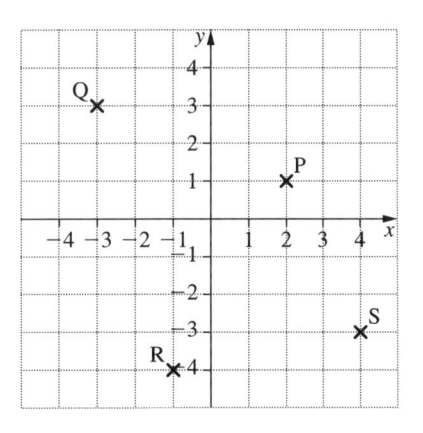

(4)

15. Write down the next two terms in these sequences:
    (a) 2, 5, 8, 11, ..., ...
    (b) 16, 12, 8, 4, ..., ...
    (c) 2, 4, 7, 11, ..., ...
    (d) 1, 3, 7, 15, 31, ..., ...

(4)

16. Find the weight x by removing weights from both pans. All weights are in kg.
    (a)
    (b)
    (c)
    (d)

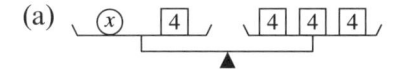

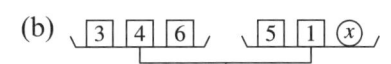

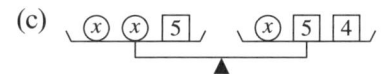

(4)

Practice Test B

1. Find the missing numbers
   (a) $200 \times 6 = \boxed{}$
   (b) $\boxed{} \times 7 = 210$
   (c) $300 \times \boxed{} = 6000$
   (d) $7 \times \boxed{} + 5 = 40$
   (e) $8 \times \boxed{} + 6 = 30$
   (f) $9 \times \boxed{} - 3 = 42$ (6)

2. A survey of 400 people reveals that 28% of people like 'Minty Fresh' toothpaste. Work out the number of people who liked 'Minty Fresh.' (2)

3. The spinner shows that the winning letter is D. Write down the winning letter after these spins (always starting from the position shown):
   (a) clockwise 90°
   (b) anticlockwise 180°
   (c) clockwise 150°
   (d) anticlockwise 60° (4)

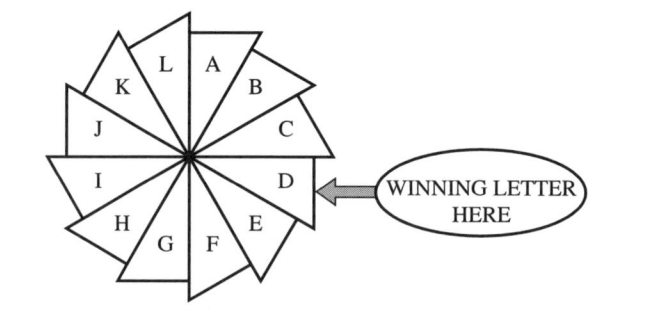

4. Write down the value of ? in each of these statements:
   (a) $? \times 5 = 15$
   (b) $6 \times ? = 24$
   (c) $35 \div ? = 7$
   (d) $? \div 8 = 6$
   (e) $(? \times 4) - 8 = 12$
   (f) $(72 \div ?) + 3 = 11$ (6)

5. A bucket weighs 1·2 kg when it is empty, and 6·6 kg when it is full of water. What will it weigh when it is half full? (2)

6. Solve these equations:
   (a) $4x + 3 = 15$
   (b) $2x - 5 = 19$
   (c) $5(x + 4) = 40$ (3)

7. Photograph B is an enlargement of photograph A. Calculate
   (a) the scale factor of the enlargement.
   (b) the height of photograph B. (2)

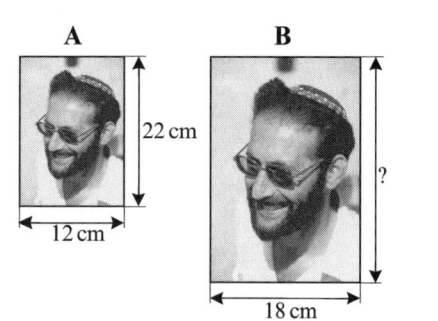

8. A worm weights 24 g. After providing lunch for a starling, the weight of the worm is decreased by 8%. By how much does the weight of the worm decrease? (1)

9. The model is made from matchboxes.

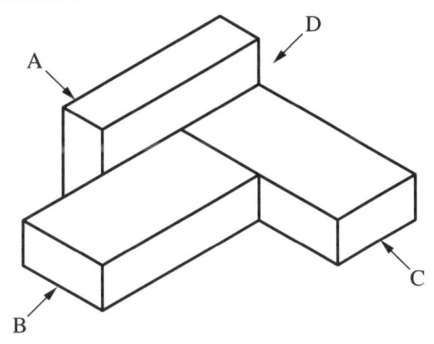

From which direction (A, B, C, or D) are these views taken?

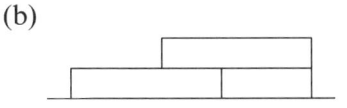

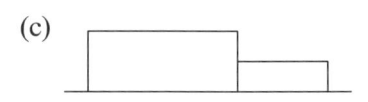

(a)   (b)

(c)   (d)

(4)

10. The diagrams show a letter 'T' and a letter 'L'. On isometric paper draw the two letters the right way up.

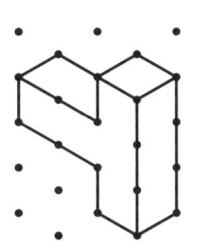

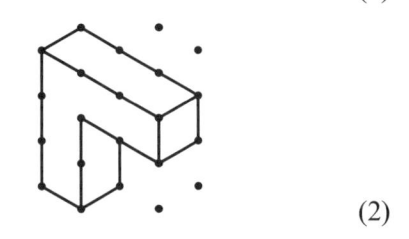

(2)

11. In a survey the children at a school were asked to state their favourite sport in the Olympics.
  (a) Estimate what fraction of the children chose gymnastics.
  (b) There are 120 children in the school. Estimate the number of children who chose athletics.
  (c) 15% of the children chose swimming. How many children was that?

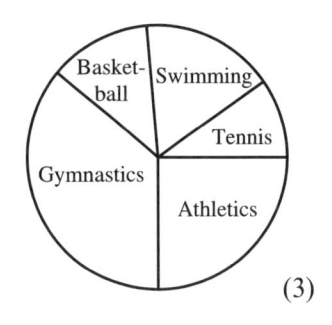

(3)

12. Draw the graph of $y = 2x + 3$ for values of x from 0 to 4.

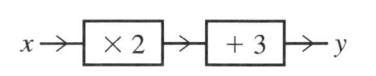

$x \to \boxed{\times 2} \to \boxed{+ 3} \to y$

x	0	1	2	3	4
y					

(4)

13. Here is a rough sketch of a sector of a circle.
    Make an accurate, full size drawing of this sector and measure the straight line distance from A to B.

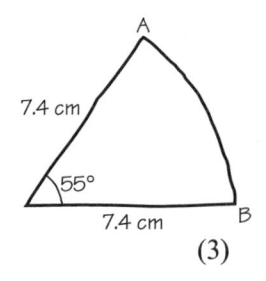

    (3)

14. Look at the diagram.
    (a) What fraction is shaded?
    (b) What percentage is *un*shaded?
    (c) Draw a similar diagram, with 10 blank squares, and then shade in $\frac{3}{5}$ of the diagram.

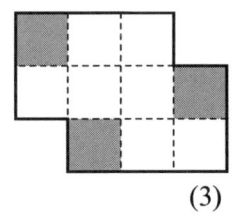

    (3)

15. Find the angles marked with letters. (Diagrams are not drawn to scale)

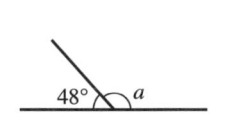

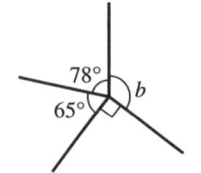

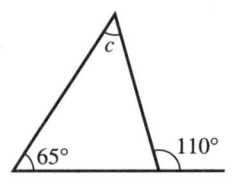

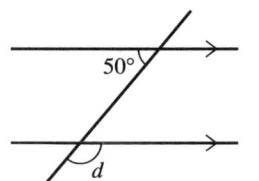

    (4)

16. These nets form cubical dice. Opposite faces of a dice always add up to 7. Write down the value of a, b, c, d, e, and f so that opposite faces add up to 7.

    (6)

17. Work out the areas of A, B, C,..., I in the shapes below. The dots are 1 cm apart.

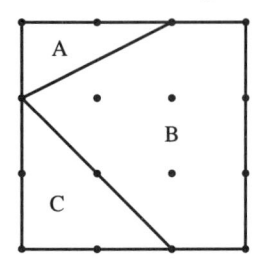

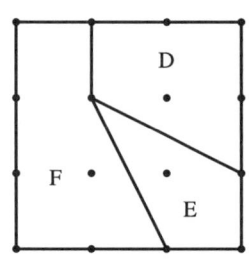

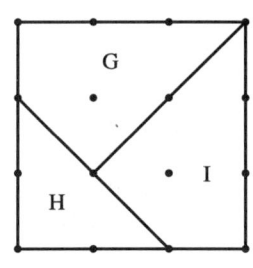

    (9)

Questions **18** to **25** are multiple choice. One mark for each question.

Use the diagram below for questions **18** to **21**

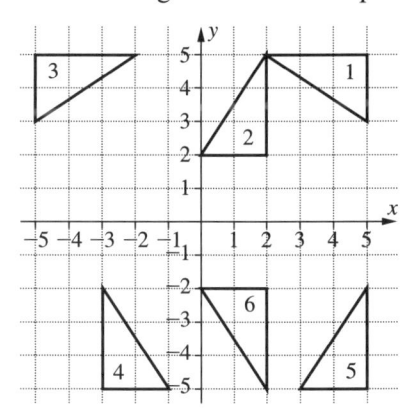

18. The image of △3, after reflection in the *y axis*, is
  - **A** △1
  - **B** △2
  - **C** △4
  - **D** △5

19. △4 is the image of △5 after reflection in the line:
  - **A** $x = 2$
  - **B** $x = 1$
  - **C** $y = 1$
  - **D** $y = 2$

20. The centre of the rotation which moves △1 onto △5 is
  - **A** (2, 5)
  - **B** (−5, 0)
  - **C** (0, 0)
  - **D** none of the above

21. The image of △2 after rotation through 180° about the point (0, 0) is
  - **A** △4
  - **B** △1
  - **C** △6
  - **D** none of the above

22. Which is the odd one out
  - **A** 20%
  - **B** 0·2
  - **C** $\frac{2}{100}$
  - **D** $\frac{1}{5}$

23. Find the area of triangle OAB in square units
  - **A** 7
  - **B** 8
  - **C** 9
  - **D** 10

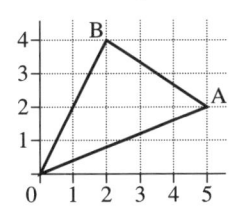

24. Which of the following statements are true?
  1. 1% of $10 = 0·1$
  2. $12 \div 5 = 2·4$
  3. $7 \div 8 = 0·875$
  - **A** 1 and 2
  - **B** 1 and 3
  - **C** 2 and 3
  - **D** 1, 2 and 3

25. On a map of scale 1:20 000 a road is 2 cm long. How long is the actual road?
  - **A** 40 000 km
  - **B** 10 000 km
  - **C** 400 km
  - **D** 4 km

INDEX

Algebra, rules of	44, 107
Angles	50
Approximating	37
Area	20
Arithmetic without a calculator	72
Averages	79
Bar charts	141
Bearings	223
Brackets	132
Calculator	95
Centre of rotation	121
Checking answers	37
Collecting terms	44
Congruent shapes	193
Construction	59
Coordinates	182
Crossnumbers	119, 199
Data collection	141, 216
Data in groups	141
Decimals	72, 153
Decimal places	37
Division by a fraction	14
Enlargement	170
Equations	135
Equivalent fractions	8
Estimation	37
Expressions	44, 107
Factors	33
Flow diagram	7
Formulas	107
Fractions, decimals, percentages	153
Fractions	8, 153
Games	43, 233
Geometrical reasoning	50
Graphs	126, 182
Hidden words	77
Indices	15
Investigations	18, 19, 232
Isometric drawing	219
Line graphs	126
Locus	56
Logic problems	199, 201
Map scales	167
Mathematical reasoning	196
Measures	61
Mental arithmetic	84
Metric and Imperial units	62
Mid book review	113
Mixed problems	61, 158, 196
Multiples	33
Negative numbers	26, 98
NNS Guide	front
nth term of sequence	175
Operator squares	240
Order of operations	94
Parallelogram	23
Parallel lines	52
Percentages	213, 153
Pie charts	145
Powers	15
Practice tests	250
Prime numbers	33
Probability	204
Problem solving	61, 158, 196
Properties of numbers	33
Proportion	164
Puzzles	197, 201
Range	79
Ratio	164
Real-life graphs	126
Recurring decimals	154
Reflection	101
Review exercises	242
Rotation	121
Rounding	37
Scale drawing	223
Scatter graphs	148
Sequences	1, 175
Spreadsheet on a computer	202
Square roots	17
Straight line graphs	182
Substitution	107
Statistical problems	216
Stem and leaf	83
Tessellation	193
Three dimensional objects	219
Transformations	121
Trapezium	23
Travel graphs	130
Volume	228